Weakness of Will and Practi

Among the many practical failures that threaten us, weakness of will or akrasia is often considered to be a paradigm of irrationality. The eleven new essays in this collection, written by an excellent international team including both well-established and younger philosophers, give a rich overview of the current debate over weakness of will and practical irrationality more generally.

Issues covered include classical questions such as the distinction between weakness and compulsion, the connection between evaluative judgement and motivation, the role of emotions in akrasia, rational agency, and the existence of the will. They also include new topics, such as group akrasia, strength of will, the nature of correct choice, the structure of decision theory, the temporality of prudential reasons, and emotional rationality. Because these questions cut across philosophy of mind and ethics, the collection will be essential reading for scholars, postgraduates, and upper-level undergraduates in both these fields.

Sarah Stroud is Associate Professor of Philosophy at McGill University.

Christine Tappolet is Canada Research Chair in Ethics and Meta-ethics and Associate Professor of Philosophy at Université de Montréal.

Contributors

Ronald de Sousa, Joseph Heath, Richard Holton, Duncan MacIntosh, Philip Pettit, Michael Smith, Sarah Stroud, Christine Tappolet, Sergio Tenenbaum, Gary Watson, Ralph Wedgwood.

Weakness of Will and Practical Irrationality

EDITED BY

Sarah Stroud and Christine Tappolet

CLARENDON PRESS · OXFORD

OXFORD
UNIVERSITY PRESS

Great Clarendon Street, Oxford OX2 6DP

Oxford University Press is a department of the University of Oxford.
It furthers the University's objective of excellence in research, scholarship,
and education by publishing worldwide in

Oxford New York

Auckland Bangkok Buenos Aires Cape Town Chennai
Dar es Salaam Delhi Hong Kong Istanbul Karachi Kolkata
Kuala Lumpur Madrid Melbourne Mexico City Mumbai Nairobi
SÐo Paulo Shanghai Taipei Tokyo Toronto

Oxford is a registered trade mark of Oxford University Press
in the UK and in certain other countries

Published in the United States
by Oxford University Press Inc., New York

© the several contributors 2003

The moral rights of the author have been asserted

Database right Oxford University Press (maker)

First published 2003
First published in paperback 2007

All rights reserved. No part of this publication may be reproduced,
stored in a retrieval system, or transmitted, in any form or by any means,
without the prior permission in writing of Oxford University Press,
or as expressly permitted by law, or under terms agreed with the appropriate
reprographics rights organization. Enquiries concerning reproduction
outside the scope of the above should be sent to the Rights Department,
Oxford University Press, at the address above

You must not circulate this book in any other binding or cover
and you must impose this same condition on any acquirer

British Library Cataloguing in Publication Data

Data available

Library of Congress Cataloging in Publication Data

Data available

Typeset by SPI Publisher Services, Pondicherry, India.
Printed in Great Britain
by Biddles Ltd., King's Lynn, Norfolk

ISBN 978–0–19–925736–2 (Hbk.)   978–0–19–923595–7 (Pbk.)

1 3 5 7 9 10 8 6 4 2

ACKNOWLEDGEMENTS

This volume grew out of a conference, Weakness of Will and Varieties of Practical Irrationality, which we organized together with Fabienne Pironet, and which was held at the Université de Montréal in May 2001. (All the present chapters save Richard Holton's are descendants of papers given there.) A conference grant from the Social Sciences and Humanities Research Council of Canada (SSHRC), and additional financial support from the Université de Montréal, made that gathering possible, and also funded the invaluable work of our research assistant, Gerry Beaulieu, on this volume. We would also like to thank Alex Sager for his work on the index. Our own work on this volume was supported by research grants from FCAR (Fonds pour la formation de chercheurs et l'aide Á la recherche) and SSHRC, which we gratefully acknowledge. Finally, we wish to thank our editor at Oxford University Press, Peter Momtchiloff, and the anonymous referees whose comments helped to improve both the individual contributions and the volume as a whole.

CONTENTS

Notes on the Contributors	ix
Introduction SARAH STROUD AND CHRISTINE TAPPOLET	1
1. Rational Capacities, or: How to Distinguish Recklessness, Weakness, and Compulsion MICHAEL SMITH	17
2. How is Strength of Will Possible? RICHARD HOLTON	39
3. Akrasia, Collective and Individual PHILIP PETTIT	68
4. Emotions and the Intelligibility of Akratic Action CHRISTINE TAPPOLET	97
5. Weakness of Will and Practical Judgement SARAH STROUD	121
6. *Accidie*, Evaluation, and Motivation SERGIO TENENBAUM	147
7. The Work of the Will GARY WATSON	172
8. Choosing Rationally and Choosing Correctly RALPH WEDGWOOD	201

viii / **Contents**

9. Prudence and the Temporal Structure of Practical Reasons 230
   DUNCAN MACINTOSH

10. Practical Irrationality and the Structure of
    Decision Theory 251
    JOSEPH HEATH

11. Paradoxical Emotion: On *Sui Generis* Emotional
    Irrationality 274
    RONALD DE SOUSA

    References 298

    Index 313

NOTES ON THE CONTRIBUTORS

RONALD DE SOUSA is Professor Emeritus at the University of Toronto. He is particularly interested in the ambiguous relations between emotions and rationality. His most recent book is *Why Think? Evolution and the Rational Mind* (2007: Oxford University Press) and he is currently working on a book on *Emotional Truth*. He now thinks weakness of will a pseudo problem.

JOSEPH HEATH is Associate Professor in the Department of Philosophy at the University of Toronto. He is the author of *Communicative Action and Rational Choice* (2001: MIT Press), *The Efficient Society* (2001: Penguin), and, with Andrew Potter, *The Rebel Sell* (2004: Harper Collins Canada).

RICHARD HOLTON is Professor of Philosophy at MIT. He is currently working on a book on the will.

DUNCAN MACINTOSH is Associate Professor of Philosophy at Dalhousie University. Most recently his interest has been relating rationality to morality and personal identity.

PHILIP PETTIT teaches political theory and philosophy at Princeton University, where he is Laurance S. Rockefeller University Professor of Politics and Human Values. He is the author of a number of books, including most recently a selection of his single-authored papers, *Rules, Reasons, and Norms* (2002: Oxford University Press), a selection of papers co-authored with Frank Jackson and Michael Smith, *Mind, Morality, and Explanation* (2004: Oxford University Press), a book co-authored with Geoffrey Brennan, *The Economy of Esteem* (2004: Oxford University Press), and *Made with Words: Hobbes on Language, Mind and Politics* (2007: Princeton).

MICHAEL SMITH is Professor of Philosophy at Princeton University. He is the author of *The Moral Problem* (1994: Blackwell) and *Ethics and the A Priori: Selected Essays on Moral Psychology and Meta-Ethics* (2004: Cambridge University Press), and the co-author, with Frank Jackson and Philip Pettit, of *Mind, Morality, and*

x / **Notes on the Contributors**

Explanation: Selected Collaborations (2004: Oxford University Press). His research focuses on problems at the intersection of moral philosophy and philosophical psychology.

SARAH STROUD is Associate Professor of Philosophy at McGill University. She has published articles on a variety of topics in moral philosophy and is currently working on partiality in moral psychology and moral theory.

CHRISTINE TAPPOLET is Canada Research Chair in Ethics and Meta-Ethics and Associate Professor in the Philosophy Department at the Université de Montréal. She has written several articles in meta-ethics, moral psychology, and the philosophy of emotions, and is the author of *Émotions et valeurs* (2000: Presses Universitaires de France) and, with Ruwen Ogien, of *Les concepts de l'éthique* (2008: La Découverte). She has also edited a number of volumes, including, with Luc Faucher, a collection of articles entitled *The Modularity of Emotions* (*Canadian Journal of Philosophy*, supp. vol. 32).

SERGIO TENENBAUM is Associate Professor of Philosophy at the University of Toronto. He is the author of *Appearances of the Good* (2007: Cambridge University Press) and several articles in ethics, particularly on practical reason, and on Kant.

GARY WATSON is Professor of Philosophy at the University of California at Riverside. He works primarily in moral and political philosophy, and in the theory of agency. He is the author of *Agency and Answerability* (2004: Clarendon Press, Oxford).

RALPH WEDGWOOD is a Professor of Philosophy at the University of Oxford and a Fellow of Merton College, Oxford. He is the author of *The Nature of Normativity* (2007: Oxford University Press) and of several articles on meta-ethics, epistemology, and practical reason. He is currently planning a second book that will give a unified presentation of his ideas about rationality (including both rational belief and rational choice).

Introduction

Sarah Stroud and Christine Tappolet

Imagine someone who often can't make up her mind what to do—she just keeps endlessly deliberating. Once she has decided what to do, though, she frequently ends up changing her mind, whether out of mere caprice or because she gives in to temptation. At other times, she is obstinate to the point of persisting with plans even when she has good reason to revise them. At yet other times she tends to procrastinate, leaving for later what she judges or even knows she should do now. Moreover, she often fails to do things that she believes prudence requires doing, given the desires she foresees having. Or she simply fails to do what she judges would be best and just chooses to do an inferior course of action instead. Sometimes she feels utterly depressed and is paralysed by a total lack of motivation. Things can get so bad with her that she is not even able to do what she would like to do: she just finds herself compulsively doing things she judges to be bad.

This character suffers from a number of practical failures—indecision, irresoluteness, caprice, weakness of will, obstinacy, procrastination, imprudence, akrasia, *accidie*, and compulsion—many of which have been considered to be forms of practical irrationality. One important philosophical task arising out of these all-too-common phenomena is the challenge of better understanding them, and, if possible, systematizing these different categories, which have been handed down to us by common-sense morality and psychology as well as philosophical tradition. What do these different phenomena involve, and what do they imply for our accounts of action, deliberation, and, more generally, practical rationality? What can we conclude from the nature of

2 / Sarah Stroud and Christine Tappolet

these phenomena about the principles that govern practical reasoning, rational choice, and rational action?

One sort of practical failure which has been considered paradigmatic has been called alternatively 'weakness of will', 'incontinence', or 'akrasia'. Philosophical discussions have focused not so much on weakness of will as a character trait than on the sort of action that manifests it: roughly, intentional action contrary to one's better judgement, that is, contrary to the judgement that another course of action would be better. The philosophical debate about weakness of will starts from the question whether it is even *possible* freely and intentionally to act against one's better judgement, or whether on the other hand Socrates was right when he claimed that no one willingly does wrong (Plato, *Protagoras* 352a ff.).

I

Donald Davidson's seminal paper 'How is Weakness of the Will Possible?' (1970*a*) is often taken to be the starting point of the contemporary debate on weakness of will. However, it is useful first to look at R. M. Hare's discussion of weakness of will (Hare 1952), for Davidson's account is in part a reaction to Hare's denial that weakness of will is, strictly speaking, possible. Hare denies the possibility of weakness of will because he defends prescriptivism, which maintains that moral judgements like 'I ought to do *x*' entail imperatives. Hare believes that in order to guide our choices and actions, moral judgements like 'I ought to do *x*' have to be construed in such a way that to assent to such a judgement is to assent to an imperative. In full-blown cases of moral judgement, if I judge that I ought to do *x*, I address to myself the imperative 'do *x*'. And this means that if I am free to do *x*, I will do *x*.

This view amounts to a very strong version of the 'internalist' idea that there is an internal relation between moral or more generally practical judgements, on the one hand, and motivation and action, on the other. Given his commitment to strong internalism, Hare has to deny that it is possible to make a full-blown moral judgement that one ought to do *x* while failing to act accordingly. He claims, rather, that what actually happens in cases of supposed weakness of will is either (*a*) that the agent does not really judge that he ought to do *x*—he fails to realize that the general claim that one ought to do certain things applies to him, for instance, or he merely judges that convention requires such actions—or (*b*) that the agent is not free: he is in fact physically or psychologically unable to do *x* (see Hare 1952, ch. 11; 1963, ch. 5; 1992: 1305–6).

Davidson, by contrast, wishes to deny that either (*a*) or (*b*) need follow. Not just with respect to moral judgements, but more generally practical judgements—as he shows, weakness of will is not only a matter of acting contrary to a moral judgement—Davidson aims to vindicate the common-sense idea that weakness of will as free and intentional action contrary to a full-blown practical judgement is possible. However, his account is closer to Hare than one might first think, for though he rejects prescriptivism as well as Hare's own version of internalism, he nonetheless remains faithful to the internalist idea. In particular, Davidson tries to show that weakness of will is compatible with the idea that intentional action is done in the light of what the agent judges to be good or simply better, a claim he suggests is self-evident. His aim is specifically to make weakness of will compatible with the following two principles:

(P1) If an agent wants to do *x* more than he wants to do *y* and he believes himself free to do either *x* or *y*, then he will intentionally do *x* if he does either *x* or *y* intentionally.

(P2) If an agent judges that it would be better to do *x* than to do *y*, then he wants to do *x* more than he wants to do *y*. (Davidson 1970*a*: 23)

Taken together, these two principles entail that if an agent judges that one course of action is better than another, and she judges herself to be free to do either one, then she will intentionally perform the first action if she does either one. Thus these two principles *appear* to be inconsistent with the possibility of free intentional actions contrary to one's better judgement. The problem is that both these principles, and the claim that weakness of will is possible, seem difficult to deny.

Davidson's solution to this puzzle lies in distinguishing different kinds of evaluative judgement. In particular, he distinguishes judgements as to what is better—which he calls 'unconditional' evaluative judgements, or 'evaluative judgements sans phrase'—from judgements as to what is better *all things considered*, which he considers to be merely prima facie evaluative judgements. The difference between them is that the latter type of judgement, unlike the former, is *relational*. An all-things-considered better judgement, unlike an unconditional better judgement, does not involve a commitment to the superiority of the option in question. Such relational judgements do not tell us what is better *simpliciter*, but what is better in light of some reason *r*; they

4 / Sarah Stroud and Christine Tappolet

are thus rather like a judgement to the effect that a particular piece (or body) of evidence favours a particular hypothesis. Davidson proposes (1970a: 38) that the logical form of such relational evaluative judgements involves a 'prima facie' operator which governs the entire judgement (and thus does not permit the evaluative conclusion to be 'detached'). Such judgements, he holds, are of the general form pf (x is better than y, r), where 'r' refers to the reason why x is judged better. An all-things-considered judgement is simply a relational judgement about what is better in light of all the reasons the agent considers relevant; it remains conditional in form.

With this distinction in hand, Davidson defines weakness of will as action contrary to an all-things-considered evaluative judgement, not to a judgement as to what is better *sans phrase*. His definition of akratic action is as follows:

(D) In doing x an agent acts incontinently if and only if: (a) the agent does x intentionally; (b) the agent believes there is an alternative action y open to him; and (c) the agent judges that, all things considered, it would be better to do y than to do x. (Davidson 1970a: 22)

Given that principles P1 and P2 postulate a relation between *unconditional* better judgement and intentional action, not between *all-things-considered* better judgement and intentional action, weakness of will turns out to be compatible with those principles. If the akratic agent had reached an *unconditional* judgement in favour of doing y, she would have done y rather than the akratic x. But she never did. She judged only that y was better all things considered.[1] The problem with such an agent is that she did not conclude that the action she considered to be better all things considered was also better *sans phrase*. As Davidson underlines, this is not a logical blunder: her judgements are not contradictory. But it is nonetheless a failure of rationality. The akratic agent violates what Davidson calls the 'principle of continence', that is, the rational requirement to 'perform the action judged best on the basis of all available relevant reasons' (Davidson 1970a: 41).

This argument secures only the possibility of intentional action contrary to a *relational* evaluative judgement—not intentional action contrary to an *unconditional* better judgement. Is that enough? It is now quite generally

---

[1] Indeed, given his conception of intentional action as action performed in light of one's unconditional evaluative judgement, it seems Davidson not only has to deny that it is possible to act against one's unconditional better judgement but, in addition, has to suppose that the akratic agent makes an unconditional evaluative judgement in favour of the akratic option. This latter implication emerges with greater clarity from Davidson 1978.

acknowledged that it is not. As Robert Audi (1979) and Michael Bratman (1979) argue, it certainly seems possible freely and intentionally to act in one way while judging that another course of action would be better *sans phrase*, or while thinking that it would be best to refrain. Accordingly, the debate since Davidson has focused on so-called 'strict akratic action' (Mele 1987) or 'last-ditch akrasia' (Pears 1982), namely free and intentional action performed contrary to a judgement held at the time of action that another course of action open to the agent would be better (period), or that there is sufficient reason against performing this action at this time.[2]

While the debate after Davidson has departed from his analysis on the important point just mentioned, it has tended to follow him in two other equally important respects. Most contemporary philosophers writing on weakness of will agree with Davidson that akratic action is not only possible, but actual; indeed, that it is quite a common feature of our lives. This means our philosophical theories ought to leave room for the possibility of weakness of will. However, most philosophers have also agreed with Davidson that akratic action, while possible, is *irrational*. They have thus sought to make room for akrasia, but *only as a species of practical irrationality*. These two general points of consensus have shaped the contemporary literature on weakness of will. However, each has also been subject to powerful challenges.

Gary Watson's influential paper 'Skepticism about Weakness of Will' (Watson 1977) threatens the first of these points of consensus. As Watson emphasizes, an important question that is pertinent to whether strict akratic action is possible is whether action contrary to one's better judgement can be free. For if it cannot, there is no clear difference between akrasia and compulsion, that is, cases in which an agent is motivated by a desire or emotion he is unable to resist. Watson asks what could explain a putatively weak agent's failure to resist a rebellious desire; he argues that what seem to be the only two possible explanations have both to be rejected. His failure cannot be explained in terms of what he chooses to do, since choice must follow better judgement. Nor can it be explained by a culpably insufficient effort to resist. Given that the action is supposedly free, we have to assume that the agent was able to control himself; thus the question of why he didn't make the requisite effort

---

[2] It is accepted that there are other places where, to borrow a useful phrase from Amélie Rorty (1980*b*), the *akratic break* can take place, such as when an agent fails to commit himself to the general value judgements from which he draws his practical conclusion. However, strict akratic action is the phenomenon that has attracted the most philosophical attention in the post-Davidson era.

6 / Sarah Stroud and Christine Tappolet

immediately presents itself. According to Watson, the answer cannot be that he misjudged the amount of effort required: that would be a different fault from akrasia. Watson claims that we are entitled to conclude that the agent was unable to resist, in which case his action was unfree. As Michael Smith's chapter in the present volume attests, however, this conclusion is controversial.[3]

The second point of consensus, namely that akrasia is necessarily a failure of rationality, has also come under attack in recent years.[4] The charge has come that this belief reflects an erroneous conception of what it is to act rationally. These objectors agree that *most* action against one's better judgement is irrational. But as Robert Audi asks (Audi 1990), what if the desires which ground the agent's better judgement are highly irrational, or fail to represent his overall desires, interests, or ideals? In certain cases, it is plausible to suppose that if the agent had thought long enough, he would have come to a different practical conclusion.

Alison McIntyre (1990) also presses this point. Following Bernard Williams (1980), she claims that a consideration constitutes an internal reason for an agent if, as a result of deliberation, she would come to see it as a reason for her. Given this, an agent can be wrong about her own internal reasons.[5] Thus her better judgement might not reflect the reasons she really has, and the akratic action may in fact be the one which she has better reason to perform. McIntyre argues that an akratic action is not irrational if it is motivated by considerations that the agent would have taken to be sufficient reasons for performing that action had she properly deliberated. In such cases, the agent's sensitivity to the reasons she has outstrips her intellectual ability to see that certain considerations are reasons for her to act in a particular way. Under those circumstances, following one's better judgement might well be a mark of obstinacy rather than the rational thing to do.

As the foregoing discussion shows, akrasia has proved to be a fertile ground for reflection on our broader conceptions of intentional action and practical rationality. Indeed this can be considered one of the principal strands of the contemporary philosophical literature on akrasia and other putative

---

[3] In fact, the majority view continues to be that strict akratic actions can be distinguished from compulsion. For discussion of this issue, see Kennett 2001, ch. 6; Pugmire 1982; Mele 1987, 2002; Buss 1997; Tenenbaum 1999; and Wallace 1999a.

[4] See, in addition to the papers discussed in the text, Arpaly 2000 and Ogien 2002.

[5] Of course, it is even easier to imagine that an agent could be wrong about her reasons on an 'external' construal of reasons. See Williams 1980 for the distinction between internal and external reasons.

instances of practical irrationality: exploration of the implications of these phenomena for the nature of practical reason and rationality.[6] One such issue which has been prominent in the literature concerns the implications of strict akratic action for the relation between evaluative judgements, on the one hand, and motivation and action, on the other. Debate has centred in particular on whether *internalism* should be completely abandoned or whether a weaker form of internalism compatible with the existence of akrasia can be developed. The difficulty, if one opts for the rejection of internalism (that is, for externalism), is that one seems forced to say that the relation between practical judgement and motivation is no different from that between the judgement that something is square, for instance, and motivation. That is why those who accept the possibility of strict akratic action have tended to place their hopes in the second option.[7]

Michael Smith, for instance, has argued (Smith 1994) for a weak form of moral internalism according to which an agent who judges that some course of action is right is motivated to act accordingly unless she is practically irrational (that is, unless she suffers from weakness of will or other forms of practical unreason). It is easy to generalize such a weak internalism from moral to practical judgements: the claim would be that an agent who judges that a course of action is best will be motivated to act in accordance with her judgement unless she suffers from practical unreason. Another way of formulating such a weak internalism would be to specify what a rational agent would do given her practical judgement. Thus one could claim with T. M. Scanlon that a rational agent who judges that there is compelling reason to perform a certain action normally forms the intention to do that action, her judgement then serving as sufficient explanation of both the intention and the action which is intended (Scanlon 1998: 33–4). On this view, failing to form an intention to do something while nonetheless taking oneself to have sufficient reason to do it constitutes one important form of irrationality.

We have been sketching one of the principal strands in the recent literature concerning weakness of will and other varieties of practical irrationality, namely that concerned with their implications for general conceptions of

---

[6] Of the chapters in the present volume, those by Stroud, Tenenbaum, Watson, Wedgwood, MacIntosh, and de Sousa can be viewed as contributions to this broad line of inquiry having to do with general conceptions of practical rationality. Many of these look anew at practical reason through the lens of putative examples of irrationality.

[7] Velleman (1992) is an exception, for he argues that intentional action need not be directed at outcomes regarded as good. See also Stocker 1979 for the claim that one can desire something one considers to be bad.

practical reason. A second general line of inquiry which has grown out of consideration of those same phenomena is of quite a different sort. It concerns the *explanation* of these phenomena, or the challenge of offering a plausible account of what is going on in cases of akrasia, *accidie*, or failure to act on one's resolutions (for instance). It is generally acknowledged that akrasia specifically, and practical irrationality generally, involves a coming apart of the motivational force of the agent's wants from his assessment of the objects of those wants. The course of action the agent judges to be better or more desirable turns out not to be the one he most desires (see Mele 1987, ch. 1; Pettit and Smith 1993). The question is how this gap arises.

One influential answer to this question, proposed by the later Davidson (1982), appeals to mind-partitioning. According to Davidson, action against one's better judgement involves mental causes that fail to be reasons for the mental items they cause. He claims that in order to understand how this can be so, we need to suppose that the mental cause in question is part of a semi-autonomous structure of the mind, whose boundaries are defined by the breakdown of reason-relations. However, a variety of other explanations of the gap between better judgement and motivation have been proposed that do not appeal to mind-partitioning. One such explanation, due to Ronald de Sousa, appeals to emotions (de Sousa 1987: 199–201). According to de Sousa, an emotion is responsible for the fact that a reason which the agent considers insufficient gets acted upon. He argues that emotions are perfectly tailored for this role, given their impact on attention.

More generally, the importance of attentional phenomena in the explanation of akrasia has often been noted (Bratman 1979: 156, 168; A. Rorty 1980*b*; Peacocke 1985; Mele 1987, ch. 6). There are, however, still other possible explanatory strategies, such as the proximity explanation, the habitual explanation, and the social explanation (A. Rorty 1980*b*; Mele 1987, ch. 6). As Amélie Rorty points out (A. Rorty 1980*b*), these strategies need not exclude each other; indeed, they often supplement each other. Alfred Mele draws on empirical studies to suggest that many strict akratic actions can be explained in terms of the perceived proximity of the rewards promised by the incontinent action, the agent's motivational level, his failure at self-control, and his attentional condition (Mele 1987: 92).

While this second, broadly explanatory, line of inquiry is in the first instance more focused on the putatively irrational phenomena themselves, it too has broader ramifications, in so far as it raises issues about the explanation of action in general.[8] For instance, the question of what mental entities one has to postulate in order fully to explain someone's action is obviously pertinent not just in the context of providing an account of akrasia and other types of irrational action, but also for the project of understanding rational action. Common sense speaks readily, in this domain, of intentions, decisions, choices, preferences, and emotions, in addition to beliefs and desires, the two kinds of state that contemporary philosophers have typically taken to be primordial for explaining action. The philosophical issues which such common-sense appeals raise are, first, whether these purported mental entities survive theoretical scrutiny as states which are distinct from beliefs and desires, and, if so, what role they play in action and particularly in irrational action. The same kinds of questions apply to putative mental *faculties* such as 'the will'. Until recently—and quite ironically when one thinks of the expression 'weakness of will'—it was generally thought that there was no need, and indeed no room, in our psychology for the will.[9] That assumption has now become controversial.

However these issues concerning particular mental states and faculties are resolved, it is surely only in tandem with a detailed picture of the workings of the mind that we can begin to formulate the norms of practical rationality that apply to it. An understanding of the nuts and bolts of akrasia and other putative forms of practical irrationality ought therefore to make possible a richer understanding of human action and the norms that govern it.[10]

II

We turn now to the chapters that make up the present volume. In his 'Rational Capacities, or: How to Distinguish Recklessness, Weakness, and Compulsion', Michael Smith responds to the challenge powerfully expressed in Watson 1977 (and noted above): the need to make out a distinction between weak-willed and compelled action. As Smith notes, such a distinction seems to be required in order to legitimize our holding weak-willed but not compelled agents responsible for their actions. Smith offers such an account

[8] Of the chapters in the present volume, those by Smith, Holton, Pettit, Tappolet, Tenenbaum, and Heath contribute to this broad explanatory project, either specifically with regard to (putatively) irrational actions, or with regard to action in general.

[9] As Gary Watson notes in his contribution to this volume, O'Shaughnessy was going against the then grain in writing his 1980 book *The Will*.

[10] Our thanks to Daniel Laurier for commenting on a draft of this first part of the Introduction.

10 / Sarah Stroud and Christine Tappolet

in terms of *rational capacities*. He defines each of the categories of the reckless, the weak-willed, and the compelled in terms of the agent's having, or lacking, a pertinent rational capacity. In cases of compulsion, for instance, the compelled agent lacks the rational capacity to bring her desires into line with her belief about what she ought to do, whereas in cases of weakness of will she has that capacity, although she does not exercise it. Smith then seeks to explicate rational capacities themselves via a possible-worlds analysis. He proposes that an agent has a rational capacity just in case, abstracting away from all properties except relevant aspects of her brain, she is situated in the context of a whole raft of nearby possible worlds in which she *does* form the correct belief or desire. His analysis explicitly holds of both belief and desire: for Smith, *both* can and ought to be the products of rational capacities.

Richard Holton's chapter, 'How is Strength of Will Possible?', also emphasizes, in a rather different way, the importance of a particular capacity: the capacity for strength of will, or success in persisting with one's resolutions. Holton understands weakness of will as the unreasonable abandonment of resolutions in the face of strong contrary inclinations. (He thus distinguishes weakness of will from akrasia.) At least sometimes, however, we are able to muster the opposite of weakness of will—strength of will—and stand firm in our resolutions. How is this possible? On a classical Humean approach to the explanation of action, an agent's action is determined solely by her beliefs and desires. Holton argues that this makes it difficult to account for strength of will. He proposes that we expand the conceptual repertoire used in the explanation of action by appealing to the operation of a distinct *faculty of will-power*. Our active deployment of this faculty, Holton argues, causally explains our ability to stick to our resolutions in the face of contrary inclinations. Holton adduces evidence from common sense and from psychology to elaborate on the existence and nature of this faculty. He argues that this faculty works much like a muscle: exerting it takes effort, it tires in the short term, but sustained exercise makes it stronger over the long term. Because reconsideration of resolutions is all too likely to result in revision, we exercise our will-power by refusing to reconsider our resolutions. Holton closes by making a case for the rationality of refusing to reconsider resolutions.

Philip Pettit's 'Akrasia, Collective and Individual' takes up the question of whether a *group* could properly be said to exhibit akrasia. Pettit understands akrasia as failing, even under intuitively favourable conditions, to act in the way required by one's intentional states; he concludes that certain kinds of groups can indeed manifest akrasia in this sense. Furthermore, he suggests, such cases of collective akrasia offer important lessons for our conception of individual akrasia. The chapter begins by considering different kinds of groups and collectives, concluding that only *self-unifying cooperatives* are agents in a sufficiently robust sense to admit of akrasia. Pettit then argues that even groups concerned for their own rational unity will be subject to what he calls 'discursive dilemmas'. These arise when—with respect to a set of rationally connected issues—the votes of each individual member of a group are consistent, but these sets of votes nonetheless result in an inconsistent set of majority decisions. In such cases, the group may have trouble 'getting its act together': individuals may be loath to set aside their own votes in order to arrive at a consistent set of group decisions. But then we have collective akrasia: a failure, on the part of the group, to live up to its own standards of rationally integrated agency. Pettit describes several strategies for achieving self-control in the group context, and extends his analysis to the individual case: the different 'voices' within a person can also fail, akratically, to get their act together.

Christine Tappolet's chapter, 'Emotions and the Intelligibility of Akratic Action', takes up a somewhat neglected question in the contemporary literature on akrasia, namely the role of emotions in akratic action. Tappolet rejects the tendency to see emotions only as (non-rational) *causes* of akratic actions; she is concerned to cast them in a more positive light. Proposing that emotions be viewed as perceptions of value, she argues that as such they have the capacity not just to cause but even to render intelligible actions which are contrary to one's better judgement. She holds that non-conceptual perception of a value can make one's action intelligible even when it is opposed by one's all-things-considered judgement, and indeed even when that perception is in fact erroneous. Sometimes, on the other hand, an akratic action prompted by an emotion can be *more rational* than following one's evaluative judgement, for it may be the judgement and not the perception which is in error. By contrast, Tappolet argues, akratic actions in which no emotion is involved (cases of 'cool' akrasia) are genuinely puzzling and of dubious intelligibility. In cases of emotional akrasia we can at least point to the emotion—a product of a subsystem which is independent of the agent's higher-order cognitive faculties—in order to make sense of the agent's action. But in cases of cool akrasia no such appeal is possible: we have available only states of the same *kind* as the overall judgement contrary to which the agent acts, and which have been judged to be insufficient. Tappolet concludes that it is not clear whether there really is such a thing as cool akratic action.

12 / Sarah Stroud and Christine Tappolet

Some (but not all) *internalists* about judgement, motivation, and action would welcome this last suggestion. For—as we noted earlier—the existence of akrasia seems to make trouble for various internalist claims. The next three chapters take up this issue: all seek to rehabilitate one or another internalist approach to such matters, even in the face of weakness of will and other 'recalcitrant' phenomena. Sarah Stroud, in 'Weakness of Will and Practical Judgement', considers whether the existence of weak-willed actions puts paid to the idea that we make genuinely practical judgements. A practical judgement, she says, is one which enjoys an internal, necessary relation to subsequent action or intention, and which can serve as a sufficient explanation of such action or intention. She contrasts the idea that deliberation characteristically issues in practical judgements with what she calls a 'Humean externalist' view of practical reasoning, according to which our deliberative conclusions are merely motivationally inert judgements which must be combined with an appropriate independent desire if they are to do any work. First Stroud argues that, contrary to appearances, the possibility of akratic actions does *not* favour the Humean externalist conception over the practical-judgement view. If the latter is properly interpreted—as a constitutive norm of rational agency—then it is not threatened by the existence of akrasia. She goes on to argue that in fact the Humean externalist view is committed to a highly questionable thesis concerning weakness of will, namely that *global* akrasia is a coherent possibility. She thus suggests that a fuller examination of the implications of weakness of will actually points in favour of the practical-judgement model.

Like Stroud, Sergio Tenenbaum, in '*Accidie*, Evaluation, and Motivation', is concerned with the implications for the nature of practical reason of an anomalous phenomenon. He focuses on *accidie*, a type of apathetic or depressed state in which the unfortunate agent seems to suffer from 'loss of will': he is completely unmotivated to pursue things which he nonetheless sincerely judges to be of value. Tenenbaum aims specifically to account for *accidie* within the framework of what he calls a 'scholastic' view of practical reason, according to which to desire something is to conceive it to be good. Desires, Tenenbaum proposes, are 'appearances of the good' from particular evaluative perspectives. But not all such appearances will be incorporated into one's overall reflective conception of the good. For instance, one may take an evaluative perspective to be *conditioned*: an evaluative perspective is *conditioned* by X if what appears to be good from that perspective can only be correctly judged to *be* good, and hence worth pursuing, if X obtains. Kant, for instance, thought that one's happiness cannot be considered good or worthy of pursuit unless one is virtuous. Tenenbaum uses this idea of conditioning to explain the accidic agent's malady in scholastic terms. He proposes that the accidic agent believes that *all* evaluative perspectives are subject to a condition which (he believes) does not obtain. Hence such an agent can truly be said to retain some appreciation of the value of the things he no longer finds worth pursuing.

Gary Watson's 'The Work of the Will' defends yet another type of internalism. Watson begins with the idea that *deciding* or *making up one's mind* is a primary locus of human agency. Understanding the *will* in these terms, Watson seeks to clarify the scope of its work. First, he asks whether the will has real work to do only on 'externalist' conceptions of agency: those which deny any necessary connection between the will and the good or the choiceworthy. Can internalist theories of agency support the idea of a power to make up one's mind which is distinct from normative assessment? Or do such theories simply—and wrongly—equate the will with practical judgement? Watson argues that they do not. The will can serve an executive function even on views that are not premissed on the need to make room for counter-normative agency. Secondly, Watson considers whether we ought to say that the will, and hence agency, exist not only in the practical domain, but also in the cognitive sphere. After all, we make up our minds what to believe as well as what to do. Watson argues that like 'deciding to', 'deciding that' should indeed be classified as an active phenomenon, and hence as a mode of agency. Watson in fact sees the answers to his two questions as linked. The natural line of thought supporting externalism about practical decision is at odds with the idea of doxastic activity; thus a negative verdict on the former paves the way for acceptance of the latter.

Ralph Wedgwood's chapter, 'Choosing Rationally and Choosing Correctly', is also concerned with choice and the rationality thereof. More specifically, it distinguishes, as the title suggests, between two standards for the assessment of choices. Wedgwood links the idea of choosing *rationally* to an 'internal', and that of choosing *correctly* to an 'external', 'should'. This distinction turns on whether what you 'should' do depends only on your overall state of mind, or on what your options are really like—in particular, on whether any of them really are *good things to do*. Wedgwood argues that choosing *correctly* is the basic notion, in the sense that truths about which choices are rational are explained by truths concerning which choices are correct, rather than the other way around. Internal requirements on *rational* choice are thus derived from the ultimate practical 'aim' of arriving at *correct* choices. In order to defend this 'recognitional' view of practical reason against the 'constructivist' who sees the internal, procedural requirements on rational choice as fundamental, Wedgwood distinguishes between substantive and formal versions of the recognitional view: the former, but not the latter, offer a determinate specification of what it is for something to be a good thing to do. Wedgwood argues that the objections which constructivists have raised against the recognitional view in fact apply only to substantive versions thereof. Furthermore, he urges, objections of the very same kind can be pressed against the constructivist view itself. Wedgwood ends by elaborating on his favoured 'formal' interpretation of the recognitional view.

Duncan MacIntosh's chapter, 'Prudence and the Temporal Structure of Practical Reasons', explores an approach to rationality which was one of Wedgwood's targets: a broadly Humean, present-aim conception thereof (see e.g. Williams 1980). MacIntosh's exploration in this chapter is situated in the context of the problem of prudence. MacIntosh argues—contra, for example, Thomas Nagel (1970)—that there is no rational requirement of prudence: that it is not rationally obligatory to act in light of one's foreseen future desires as well as one's current desires. Now one might worry that if there is no rational duty of prudence—if I need not take account now of my future desires—I might be rational in acting now so as to thwart desires which I foresee having tomorrow. The acts of a rational agent could thus be absurdly incoherent over time. MacIntosh seeks to rebut this worry by showing how a Humean, present-aim approach to rationality itself generates rational constraints on the evolution of desires and hence of reasons. In fact, MacIntosh seeks to generalize the point by arguing that whatever reasons are, your future reasons need not function as reasons for you now—and that there is nothing incoherent about this. MacIntosh's ultimate aim is to establish the true temporal structure of reasons, whatever they may be. One upshot of his arguments, however, is that we ought to remove from the category of practical irrationality a phenomenon which has often been taken to be one of the leading examples thereof: imprudence.

Joseph Heath's chapter also urges that some paradigm examples of practical irrationality may have been wrongly classified as such. This conclusion emerges out of an overall strategy which Heath shares with Richard Holton: broadly speaking, to expand the repertoire of psychological states, faculties, and intentional phenomena in terms of which we explain action. Heath argues, in 'Practical Irrationality and the Structure of Decision Theory', that our understanding and modelling of actions would be enhanced by accounting for them not just in terms of beliefs and desires as these are construed in standard decision theory, but also in terms of further factors which have not typically been incorporated into decision-theoretic explanations. Heath claims that if we do not help ourselves to these additional resources, we are liable wrongly to classify certain actions as practically irrational. He focuses on two examples: the apparently counter-preferential behaviour which many agents exhibit in a variety of games in experimental game theory, and the widespread phenomenon of yielding to temptation. Heath seeks to demonstrate that relative to an expanded set of intentional phenomena, including—crucially—deontic preferences over actions and hyperbolic temporal discount rates, the case for considering such actions as instances of practical irrationality simply vanishes. Thus, Heath suggests that the charge of practical irrationality may often just be an artefact of an unduly impoverished theory. A decision theory which incorporates more structure, Heath proposes, will better meet a standard of expressive adequacy. It will also yield a cleaner division of labour between the theory of practical rationality strictly construed, and assessments of the rationality of an agent's intentional states.

Ronald de Sousa's aims in 'Paradoxical Emotion: On *Sui Generis* Emotional Irrationality' are in a certain respect the opposite of Heath's and MacIntosh's. Whereas their arguments, if successful, would *contract* the scope of what can properly be called irrational, de Sousa's arguments, if successful, would have the effect of *broadening* the domain of application of the charge of irrationality. For de Sousa proposes in his chapter that there is a hitherto unrecognized *sui generis* framework of specifically *emotional* rationality. Attitudes and emotions can be rationally assessed within this new framework, which (de Sousa argues) cannot be reduced to either of the main existing templates for rationality, the strategic and the epistemic. However, the domain of emotional rationality, like the strategic and epistemic forms thereof, contains its own antinomies or paradoxes. De Sousa catalogues a number of emotions or attitudes which present a paradoxical aspect, in that there are good reasons both to consider them rational and to condemn them as irrational, with neither view clearly more persuasive than the other. These questionable attitudes typically have a temporal dimension: they include 'dessert last' and other principles for the temporal ordering of pleasures, and varying attitudes towards death. De Sousa highlights the exposed and seemingly arbitrary status of such assessments of emotional rationality and urges a strongly naturalistic approach to the resolution of these antinomies. On this approach, the emotions we actually have serve as the final court of appeal, both for the assessment of other emotions and for the resolution of conflicts between strategic and epistemic rationality.

1

Rational Capacities, or: How to Distinguish Recklessness, Weakness, and Compulsion

Michael Smith

In 'Skepticism about Weakness of Will' Gary Watson invites us to consider the distinction between recklessness, weakness, and compulsion.

Suppose that a particular woman intentionally takes a drink. To provide an evaluative context, suppose she ought not to have another because she will then be unfit to fulfill some of her obligations. Preanalytically, most of us would insist on the possibility and significance of the following three descriptions of the case. (1) the reckless or self-indulgent case; (2) the weak case; and (3) the compulsive case. In (1), the woman knows what she is doing but accepts the consequences. Her choice is to get drunk or risk getting drunk. She acts in accordance with her judgement. In (2) the woman knowingly takes the drink contrary to her (conscious) better judgement;

An earlier version of this chapter was read at the conference Weakness of Will and Varieties of Practical Irrationality organized by Fabienne Pironet, Sarah Stroud, and Christine Tappolet, at the Université de Montréal, May 2001. Subsequent versions were presented at the Australian National University, Keio University, the Ethics Group in North Carolina, the University of North Carolina at Chapel Hill, Oriel College, Oxford, Stanford University, and the University of St Andrews. I would like to thank all those who participated in these seminars. Special thanks are due to the editors, to two anonymous readers for Oxford University Press, and to Gerald Beaulieu, Michael Bratman, Bill Brewer, Sarah Broadie, Richard Holton, Lloyd Humberstone, Thomas Hurka, Philip Pettit, Geoffrey Sayre-McCord, Laura Schroeter, John Skorupski, Timothy Williamson, and the students and faculty who attended the graduate seminar on philosophy of action I gave at the University of Arizona in 2001.

18 / Michael Smith

the explanation for this lack of self-control is that she is weak-willed. In (3), she knowingly takes the drink contrary to her better judgement, but she is the victim of a compulsive (irresistible) desire to drink.

(Watson 1977: 324)

These three different ways of filling out the case are in turn important, Watson tells us, because they purport to legitimize the very different moral reactions that we have to the three cases.

We blame the woman who is reckless or self-indulgent, and what we blame her for is having the wrong belief about what she should do in the circumstances of action that she faces. She believes that the value associated with having another drink makes it worthwhile for her to risk being unable to fulfil some of her obligations, whereas we disagree. Though Watson doesn't say this, it is thus important that we blame her just to the extent that she could have believed otherwise than that she should have another drink in the light of that evidence. It would be totally inappropriate if she lacked the capacity to evaluate such evidence, or if, though she possessed that capacity, her belief were the product of (say) self-hatred which she could neither acknowledge nor get rid of. When we blame the woman who is weak, by contrast, we blame her not for her belief—she has the belief that she should have, after all—but rather for her failure to act on that belief. Blaming her is appropriate to the extent that she could instead have exercised self-control and desired otherwise. It would be totally inappropriate if she were unable to exercise self-control. This is why we don't blame the woman who is compelled. Given that she has the belief that she should have, she succeeds to the extent that she can. Being compelled, she could not have exercised self-control and desired otherwise, and so blame for that is inappropriate.

The important point on which I wish to focus in what follows is the point that has just emerged. In giving our accounts of the nature of recklessness, weakness, and compulsion, and the way in which each of these in turn legitimizes our different moral reactions, we have had to assume the truth of various 'could' claims. We suppose that the reckless woman *could* have had the right belief about what she should do, the belief that she shouldn't have another drink; we suppose that the weak woman *could* have acted in accordance with her belief that she shouldn't have another drink; and we suppose that the compulsive woman *could not* have acted in accordance with her belief that she shouldn't have another drink. But what do these various 'could' claims mean? This question turns out to be exceedingly difficult to answer.

My suggestion will be that the 'could' claims that we assume to be true (or false) when we describe someone as reckless, or weak, or compelled, all mean much the same thing. Specifically, they all signify the presence (or absence) of a rational capacity which we take to explain the relevant behaviour. The difficult task is to say what, precisely, makes it the case that someone has (or lacks) such a rational capacity.

To anticipate, the account I go on to offer of rational capacities is in much the same ballpark as earlier accounts (see, for example, Wolf 1990; Wallace 1994; Kennett and Smith 1994, 1996; Pettit and Smith 1996; Smith 1997*b*; and Fischer and Ravizza 1998). The novelty of the present account lies in part in the explicit suggestion that the 'could' required for responsibility in such cases can be elucidated in terms of the possibility of exercising such a rational capacity. Here there is a striking contrast with, say, Wallace's account (Wallace 1994) of the capacity for reflective self-control, and Fischer and Ravizza's account (Fischer and Ravizza 1998) of reasons responsiveness. For, under the influence of Harry Frankfurt (1969), these theorists have denied that the relevant notion of 'could' can be elucidated in such terms (see Watson 2001 for an expression of scepticism about this). The novelty also lies in part in the fact that I explicitly connect the difficulty involved in giving such an elucidation of the notion of 'could' with the issue in metaphysics about finkish dispositions (Martin 1994; Lewis 1997).

The chapter divides into two main sections. In the first I focus on the case of recklessness. In this section I give an account of what it means to say that someone has the capacity to have beliefs other than those she has, and how her failure to exercise that capacity might explain her having the beliefs she has. In the second section the focus shifts to the cases of weakness and compulsion. In this section I give an account of what it means to say that someone has the capacity to have desires other than those she has, and how her failure to exercise that capacity, if she has it, or her lack of that capacity, if she lacks it, might explain her having the desires that she has.

Rational Capacities and Belief

Let's begin by considering a purely cognitive case. Let's suppose that John is in the middle of a complicated philosophical argument with someone when she asks him a crucial question to which he doesn't have an answer. Let's assume that there is an answer, one which supports the line of argument that John

20 / Michael Smith

has been defending. He thinks the question through carefully, but he doesn't think of the answer at the time. However, later on that night he comes to realize what the answer to the question is. As with Watson's example of the woman who takes a drink, it seems that we can fill out this story in various different ways. Let me focus on just two for the moment.

In the first, what John does when he gets home is read some papers about the topic he had been discussing. Perhaps he hasn't read these papers before, but he has good reason to believe that they will address the question he was asked by his interlocutor. While reading through these papers he learns what the answer to the question he was asked is. The answer is complicated, but he comes to appreciate it by reading the article. He has the 'Oh, I see!' experience. He feels relief that what he was saying was defensible, albeit, as he now admits, that he wasn't able to see how it was to be defended at the time.

When we fill out the story in this way it seems that, in one perfectly ordinary sense of 'could', we do not suppose that John could have thought of the answer to the question he was asked at the time he was asked. Rather we admit that making moves in philosophical discussions requires that you have a relevant base of knowledge to begin with, and, by hypothesis, we acknowledge that John did not have the relevant base of knowledge at the time at which he was asked the question. He was simply ignorant.

Now consider a second way of filling out the story. Suppose that John doesn't need to read any further material in order to figure what the answer to the question is. The answer occurs to him while he is driving home, or while he is cooking dinner, or during an ad break when he is watching TV, or while he is taking a shower. Moreover, when it occurs to him he is overwhelmed not by the 'Oh, I see!' experience, but rather by the 'Oh dear! Of course!' experience. He doesn't feel relieved, but rather embarrassed at his failure to think of the answer on the spot. Perhaps it is an argumentative move similar to one that he has made elsewhere, or perhaps it is just, as we might say, 'so obvious'.

When we fill out the story in this way it seems that, again in one perfectly ordinary sense of 'could', we almost certainly would suppose that John could have thought of the relevant response when he was having his conversation, and that this is crucial in explaining the way he feels about himself. Embarrassment is the right reaction because he let himself down. He could have thought of the right response, the response he should have thought of, but he didn't. He just blanked.

In order to distinguish between these two ways of filling out the story let's call the first the story of Ignorant John and the second the story of Blanking

John. Indeed, for ease of exposition in what follows let's imagine that there were in fact duplicate conversations going on in different places, one between an interlocutor and Ignorant John and the other between an interlocutor and Blanking John. The question on which I wish to focus is what exactly it means to say, in this perfectly ordinary sense of 'could', that Blanking John could have thought of the right answer to the question at the time, whereas Ignorant John could not. Plainly it is to make a modal claim, but what modal claim?

A first suggestion is in the spirit of the usual elucidation of the 'could' at issue in the free-will debate (van Inwagen 1983). To say that Blanking John could have thought of the right answer to the question at the time is to say that there is a possible world which is identical in history and laws to the actual world in which he fails to think of the right answer to the question, but in which he instead thinks of the right answer to the question. The trouble with this first suggestion, however, is that, at least for the purposes of the present argument, we should suppose that there is no such possible world.

The problem is that if causal determinism is true in the actual world, a possibility that it seems best not to rule out for present purposes, then the history of the actual world up to the point at which Blanking John failed to think of the right answer to the question he was asked, plus a statement of the causal laws that hold in the actual world, entails that Blanking John fails to think of the right answer to the question he was asked. There is therefore no possible world identical in history and laws in which Blanking John thinks of the right answer. If this is right, then, in yet another perfectly ordinary sense of the word 'could', it follows that Blanking John could no more have thought of the right answer than Ignorant John.

Libertarians might object to the suggestion that, for present purposes, we should not rule out the possibility that causal determinism is true. They might insist that the falsity of causal determinism is precisely what is required for the truth of the various 'could' claims in which we are interested. But even if they were right about this—which, for the record, it seems to me they are not—I would see no need to take a stand on this issue just yet. For if the libertarians were right then we would expect that to emerge in what follows. It would emerge because we would be unable to give any alternative compatibilist account of what the various 'could' claims mean. I therefore propose to put the libertarians' objection to one side for the time being.

So far we have seen one thing that we cannot mean when we say that Blanking John could have thought of the right answer at the time. Is there

22 / **Michael Smith**

something else that we might mean instead? A familiar weakening of the constraints on possible worlds that we deem to be alternatives to the actual world, a weakening suggested by the literature on counterfactual reasoning, suggests that there is. According to the weakening I have in mind, to say that there is a possible world in which Blanking John thinks of the right answer to the question he was asked at the time is simply to say that there is a possible world which is similar to the actual world in terms of history and laws—similar but not identical, of course—but which contains a small difference, the smallest difference which allows Blanking John to think of the right answer to the question he was asked at the time. This would be a 'divergence miracle', in Lewis's terms (Lewis 1979, 1981). The suggestion is thus that Blanking John could have thought of the right answer to the question he was asked at the time because there is such a possible world.

The trouble with this suggestion, however, is that it doesn't allow us to divide the cases in the right way. There is, after all, a possible world which is similar in terms of history and laws to the actual world in which Ignorant John thinks of the right answer to the question at the time as well. This sense of 'could' is thus very weak indeed. It is therefore not a sense of 'could' which is going to help us explain why Blanking John could, whereas Ignorant John could not, have thought of the right answer to the question at the time at which he was asked.

Perhaps, though, we are on the right track. Perhaps we should say that Blanking John could, whereas Ignorant John could not, have thought of the right response at the time because the possible world in which Ignorant John thinks of the right response is much more dissimilar to the way the world actually is than is the possible world in which Blanking John thinks of the right response. The idea behind this suggestion is that the problem with the earlier proposal is that it fails to discriminate between possible worlds that are, as we might say, only remote possibilities—that is, the possible worlds that are very dissimilar to the actual world in terms of history and laws—and those possible worlds that are real live possibilities—that is, the possible worlds that are very similar indeed to the actual world in terms of history and laws.

Though an improvement, however, it seems to me that this account of what makes it true that Blanking John could have thought of the right response, whereas Ignorant John could not, cannot be right either. It cannot be right because it leaves various inappropriate hostages to empirical fortune. For all we know, the actual world is such that the possible world in which Blanking John thinks of the correct answer to the question is far less similar to the actual world in terms of history and laws than is the possible world in which Ignorant John thinks of the correct answer to the question.

An initial case that shows why this is so is a variation on an example of Harry Frankfurt's (Frankfurt 1969). Let's suppose that there is an evil scientist, Black, who wants Blanking John not to think of the right answer to the question that he was asked at the time. As it happens, Blanking John would have blanked of his own accord, but Black pre-emptively stops him having that thought. (Note that this is the relevant difference between this case and Frankfurt's original example.) Black is, however, totally indifferent to whether or not Ignorant John thinks of the right answer to the question that he was asked at the time.

With these assumptions in place it seems to me quite plausible to suppose that the possible world in which Ignorant John thinks of the correct answer to the question at the time it is asked is much more similar to the actual world than is the possible world in which Blanking John thinks of the correct response. It is quite plausible because we may have to imagine many more changes to the way things actually are in order to imagine Blanking John thinking of the correct response than we have to imagine in order to imagine Ignorant John thinking of the correct response. We have to imagine away not just whatever it is that made Blanking John blank, but Black and all of his devilish plans as well, whereas we only have to imagine away Ignorant John's ignorance.

What has gone wrong? At this point it seems to me important to remember that we are trying to figure out what makes it true that Blanking John could have thought of the answer to the question at the time in the sense of having a capacity to do so, albeit a capacity that he didn't exercise at that time. The problem, in these terms, is that the proposal we are currently considering doesn't zero in on what makes it true that Blanking John has that capacity. Instead it zeroes in on, if anything, what makes it true that the entire possible world that Blanking John inhabits—a possible world that, in our variation on the Frankfurt example, includes Black with all of his devilish plans—has the capacity to manifest the thought of the correct answer to the question in Blanking John at the time at which he was asked the question. And what it tells us, unsurprisingly given Black's devilish plans, is that it doesn't. What we thus need to do is to zero in in a more fine-grained way on Blanking John and his capacities.

Some might be doubtful that this is the proper diagnosis of what has gone wrong. In order to see that it is, it might be helpful to consider an analogous

24 / **Michael Smith**

case, a case of what has come to be called a 'finkish' disposition (Martin 1994; Lewis 1997). Mark Johnston describes a shy but powerfully intuitive chameleon (Johnston 1993). This is a chameleon that is green but which, when it intuits that it is about to be put into a viewing condition, instantaneously blushes bright red. Does the shy but powerfully intuitive chameleon lack the disposition that greenness is, that is, the disposition to look green in standard viewing conditions, when it is put into a viewing condition? (The point of asking the question about this analogous case is, I hope, plain, but in case it isn't let me make the point of analogy explicit. The question is whether the chameleon's being shy and intuitive falsifies the claim that it has the disposition to look green in standard viewing conditions, and this, I am suggesting, is analogous to asking whether the presence of Black, with all of his devilish plans, falsifies the claim that Blanking John has the capacity to think of the correct answer to the question at the time it was asked.)

The answer, Johnston suggests, is that the mere fact that the chameleon is shy but powerfully intuitive does nothing to make it lack the disposition that greenness is, that is, the disposition to look green in standard viewing conditions. It simply reminds us how much care we need to take in assessing whether or not an object has such a disposition. We need to take such care because dispositions to look a certain way in standard viewing conditions are constituted dispositions. That is to say, there are intrinsic properties that objects with such dispositions possess, properties of their surfaces, which cause the manifestation of the disposition they have to look a certain way in standard viewing conditions. But since these are constituted dispositions, and since what they are constituted by are properties of their surfaces, it follows that the effects of these constituting properties can be 'masked', or 'mimicked', as Johnston puts it, by other properties that the object possesses or by properties possessed by other objects in the object's environment.

Johnston's suggestion is thus that, when we assess whether or not objects have such constituted dispositions, we must abstract away from all but the relevant intrinsic properties of the object itself: in this case, all but the properties of the surface of the chameleon that constitute its disposition to look certain ways. The reason we can say that the shy but powerfully intuitive chameleon has the disposition to look green in standard viewing conditions, notwithstanding the fact that it is shy and intuitive, is thus (roughly speaking) that in the nearby possible worlds in which it doesn't have intrinsic properties that underwrite its being shy and intuitive as regards the presence of a viewer, but retains the intrinsic properties of its surface, it does indeed look green when viewed.

Let's now return to the case of Blanking John and apply the lesson we have just learned. What we have been trying to figure out is what makes it true that Blanking John could have answered the question at the time, in the sense of having the capacity to think of the correct answer to the question he was asked at the time at which it was asked, whereas Ignorant John couldn't, in the sense of lacking that capacity. The proposal we have been considering is that Blanking John has this capacity, and Ignorant John lacks it, because the possible world in which Ignorant John thinks of the right response is much more dissimilar to the way the actual world is than is the possible world in which Blanking John thinks of the right response. The objection to this proposal, recall, is that it leaves an inappropriate hostage to empirical fortune. If, as a matter of empirical fact, Black has set things up so as to guarantee that Blanking John will fail to think of the correct answer to the question, but is indifferent to whether or not Ignorant John thinks of the correct response, then the possible world in which Blanking John thinks of the correct response may be far more dissimilar to the actual world than is the possible world in which Ignorant John thinks of the correct response to the question. However, the discussion of the shy but intuitive chameleon suggests a principled response to this objection.

Note, to begin, that the reason the objection gets going in the first place is that Blanking John's capacity to think of the correct answer to the question when asked is a constituted capacity. That is to say, there is some intrinsic feature possessed by those who have this sort of capacity and it is their possession of this intrinsic feature that causes the thought of the answer to the philosophical question in appropriate circumstances. The capacity is presumably constituted by whatever it is that underwrites psychological states in general, which, for the sake of argument, we can assume to be some state of the brain. The reason the objection gets going in the first place is thus, in Johnston's terms, that the effects of this intrinsic property can be masked and mimicked by other causal factors, in this case, by Black with his devilish plans.

Accordingly, in testing whether or not Blanking John has the capacity to think of the correct answer to the question at the time, we should narrow the possible worlds in which we consider whether he thinks of the correct response when asked in a way analogous to the way in which Johnston suggests that we should narrow the possible worlds in which to test for the presence of the disposition to look green in standard viewing conditions. The revised suggestion is thus that Blanking John could, whereas Ignorant John could not, have thought of the right response at the time he was asked because he differs from Ignorant John in the following respect. Abstracting away from all those properties that could have an effect on what either of them thinks except the relevant properties of Blanking John's and Ignorant John's brains, the possible world in which Ignorant John thinks of the right response is much more dissimilar to the way the actual world is than is the possible world in which Blanking John thinks of the right response.

Now, though a vast improvement on the previous suggestion, it seems to me that this suggestion is still deeply flawed. The problem is that it still fails to capture the fact that we are trying to find out what makes it true that Blanking John could have thought of the correct answer to the question when asked in the sense of having a capacity to answer that question. In order to see that that is so it suffices to note that the current suggestion still leaves an inappropriate hostage to empirical fortune. It would, after all, seem to be at least possible that, even after abstracting away from the presence of Black with his devilish plans, Ignorant John's brain only needs to be different in a tiny way—perhaps only one neuron needs to fire instead of failing to fire—for the thought of the right response to the question that he was asked to occur to him, whereas a larger change in Blanking John's brain is required for the thought of the right response to the question he was asked to occur to him.

Indeed, this suggests a further variation on the story we have been considering thus far. In this variation, the answer occurs to John while he is driving home, or while he is cooking dinner, or during an ad break when he is watching TV, or while he is taking a shower—so far this is like the story of Blanking John—but when it occurs to him he is overwhelmed not by the 'Oh dear! Of course!' experience, or by the 'Oh, I see!' experience, but rather by the 'Why on earth did that occur to me!' experience. He doesn't feel relieved, and nor does he feel embarrassed at his failure to think of the answer on the spot. He has no qualms admitting that he could not have thought of the answer on the spot. Rather he feels utter amazement that the right answer should have popped into his head as it did. In this variation on the case it seems that we do not think of John as having manifested a capacity to answer the question he was asked at all, notwithstanding the fact that his thinking of the correct answer entails that he could have. Rather we think of him as having had a completely fluky flash.

Recklessness, Weakness, and Compulsion / 27

What has gone wrong this time? Let's call this the case of Fluky John. What this case shows—and, for that matter, what the case of Ignorant John we just imagined shows as well (the case in which only a tiny change in his brain state is required for him to think of the correct answer)—is a problem with all of the suggestions considered so far. They are all far too focused on single possibilities when, to repeat, what we are trying to establish is what makes it true that Blanking John could have thought of the right answer to the question when asked in the sense of having had a capacity to think of the right answer. Fluky John might even have had that fluky thought at the very moment he was asked the question. But the mere fact that he has the fluky thought does nothing to show that he could have thought of the correct answer at the time in the sense of having had the capacity to think of it.

What we need to add to the suggestions considered thus far is therefore some recognition of the fact that capacities are essentially general or multi-track in nature, and that they therefore manifest themselves not in single possibilities, but rather in whole rafts of possibilities. If Blanking John really could have thought of the correct answer to the question at the time he was asked, in the sense of having had the capacity to think of that answer, then (the idea is) he must likewise have had the capacity to think of the answer to a whole host of slight variations on the question that he was asked, variations in the manner in which the question was asked, and perhaps in the exact content of the question, and in the exact timing of the question, and so on. It is difficult to spell out exactly what these variations are in any precise way, but I take it that the basic idea is clear enough. (Think of how many philosophical conversations you need to have with students before you get a sense of their philosophical capacities, and of how often you are initially impressed by students, but then reconsider after becoming convinced that the good points that they made aren't evidence of an underlying capacity, but are rather just flukes.)

Once we see the need to recognize the multi-track nature of capacities, a quite different explanation of why the possible world in which Blanking John thinks of the correct answer to the question is closer to actuality than are the possible worlds in which Ignorant John and Fluky John think of the correct answer suggests itself. The crucial point is that this whole host of similar counterfactuals is true of Blanking John, but false of Ignorant John and Fluky John. In other words, we engage in a triangulation exercise. Begin from the fact that, abstracting away from all of those properties that could have an effect on what any of them thinks except the relevant properties of their brains, in those nearby possible worlds in which Blanking John is asked a whole host of similar questions he has the right thought in response to the similar questions when asked, whereas in the nearby possible worlds in which both Ignorant John and Fluky John are asked that whole host of similar questions they systematically fail to have the right thought in response. From this we draw the conclusion that, in that same nearby region of logical space, Blanking John is, whereas both Ignorant John and Fluky John are not, having the right thought in response to the question he was in fact asked at the time at which it was asked. This, accordingly, is why the possible world in which Blanking John has the right thought in response to the question when asked is nearer to actuality than is the possible world in which Ignorant John and Fluky John have the right thought in response to the question when asked. It is why Blanking John could, whereas Ignorant John and Fluky John could not, have thought of the right response to the question when asked.

Note that this suggestion, unlike the previous suggestion, is not vulnerable to the same sorts of empirical counter-example. Whether or not, as a matter of empirical fact, someone like Black with his devilish plans is present is irrelevant, because we abstract away from everything that underwrites the truth of the relevant counterfactuals apart from the relevant properties of Blanking John's, Ignorant John's, and Fluky John's brains. And whether or not, as a matter of empirical fact, Blanking John's actual brain is more or less similar to his brain in those nearby possible worlds in which he is thinking the correct thought in response to the question when asked, than are the actual brains of Ignorant John and Fluky John to their brains in the nearby worlds in which they are thinking the correct thought in response to the question when asked, is likewise irrelevant. It is irrelevant because the crucial question is whether the whole host of relevantly similar counterfactuals is true of Blanking John, Ignorant John, and Fluky John.

This provides us with a response to a more general worry that has in fact been in the background all along. For even if that whole host of counter-factuals described were true of Blanking John, we would surely still think that he lacked the capacity to think of the right answer to the question we asked him at the time if we discovered that there was no common structure to what underwrites the truth of that whole host of counterfactuals. For example, suppose that Blanking John was much like Ned Block's famous Blockhead (Block 1981), and each individual answer he gave to a question he was asked was the result of some aspect of his internal condition that was dedicated to

Recklessness, Weakness, and Compulsion / 29

giving exactly that answer in response to exactly that formulation of the question, an aspect that has nothing in common with any other aspect of his internal condition. In that case, even if Blanking John's internal nature was so complex that it could underwrite the truth of that whole host of similar counterfactuals, we would surely deny that he was intelligent at all. In other words, we would plainly resist the triangulation suggested, and so deny that he has any rational capacities at all.

As with the case of Blockhead, it seems to me that the right response to this more general worry is to insist that, if indeed Blanking John does have rational capacities, then there must be relevant structure in what underlies the truth of the various counterfactuals that we take to be true of him. After all, when Blanking John is asked the answer to a whole range of slightly different philosophical questions, he must exploit the very same capacities in order to answer many of those questions. The assumption must therefore be that what underwrites the truth of the counterfactuals that we take to be true of him is similarly structured. Spelling out what precisely this structure amounts to would be a mammoth task, one which goes way beyond the scope of the present chapter. However, I take it that the general idea should be plain enough, at least in the light of other similar responses to the Blockhead example itself (see, especially, Braddon-Mitchell and Jackson 1996). It is this structure in what underlies the truth of the various counterfactuals that are true of Blanking John that licenses our triangulation to the existence of a nearby possible world in which he doesn't blank. This, at any rate, is my conjecture.

Doubtless further refinements would be necessary for the present suggestion to be made completely convincing. However, even without these further refinements, it seems to me that it has already become plain, via the various responses we have been able to give to the counter-examples offered, that an analysis along the present lines is on the right track. The time has therefore come to see how the general idea can be applied to the reckless woman Watson describes.

As I said, what we blame the reckless woman for is having the wrong belief about what she should do in the circumstances of action that she faces. She believes that the value associated with having another drink makes it worthwhile risking being unable to fulfil some of her obligations. We disagree that that belief is supported by the evidence she considers. Blaming her is thus, as I said, appropriate just to the extent that she could have believed otherwise than that she should have another drink in the light of that evidence.

30 / **Michael Smith**

It would be totally inappropriate if she lacked the capacity to evaluate such evidence, or if, though she possessed that capacity, her belief were the product of (say) self-hatred which she could neither acknowledge nor get rid of. We can now explain what the difference is between these various possibilities.

To begin, we must determine whether or not a particular woman who fails to form the belief that is supported by the evidence she considers has the capacity to form the belief supported by that evidence. We must therefore abstract away from all those properties that could have an effect on what she believes except the relevant properties of her brain, and we must then ask whether a whole raft of counterfactuals is true of her. Would she have formed a whole host of similar beliefs in response to similar evidence? If she would have, then, the suggestion is—assuming that there is relevant structure in what underlies the truth of those counterfactuals—we can triangulate to the conclusion that, in that same nearby region of logical space, that same woman forms the right belief in response to the evidence she in fact considers. If all this is so then it follows that she has the capacity to form the right belief in response to the evidence she in fact considers.

Next we must determine whether her failure to form the correct belief is appropriately explained by her failure to exercise her capacity to form the correct belief in response to the evidence available to her. Is her failure to exercise her capacity the relevant explanation, or was her belief the product of (say) self-hatred which she could neither acknowledge nor get rid of? In order to answer this question we must ask whether the woman had the capacity to form the correct belief in response to the evidence available to her, but now instead of abstracting away from her various emotions, we take her emotions into account. If, for example, she does suffer from self-hatred, does her self-hatred undermine the truth of the relevant counterfactuals? If so then we conclude that her self-hatred was the explanation, rather than her failure to exercise her capacity. If not then we conclude that, since she had the capacity to form the correct belief notwithstanding her self-hatred, her failure to exercise her capacity was the relevant explanation.

So far so good. But now suppose someone asks us *why* the reckless woman failed to exercise her capacity to form the correct belief in response to the evidence available to her. Can we give an answer to this question? It seems to me that we might be able to give an answer, but that we might not. The important point I wish to emphasize here, however, is that the mere fact that

Recklessness, Weakness, and Compulsion / 31

we might not be able to give an answer to the question is of no real concern. Let me explain why.

Suppose that the reckless woman would have formed the correct belief about what she should do if she had first thought of something else that she didn't in fact think of. Perhaps she had made similar comparisons of the significance of alternatives in the past, and in those cases she had always come up with the correct answer about the relative significance of the value of drinking and failing to fulfil her obligations. Perhaps if she had only thought of those past decisions on this occasion, then she would have formed the correct belief this time as well. If all of this is the case, and if we suppose that she could have thought of those past decisions on this occasion, then, it seems to me, we do indeed have available an explanation of her failure to exercise her capacity to form the correct belief on this occasion. For we can explain her failure by citing the fact that she failed to think of the similar cases that she had considered in the past.

But, of course, as is perhaps already plain, perfectly good though this explanation is, it is an explanation of why the woman failed to exercise her capacity to form the correct belief which simply takes it for granted that she had the capacity, on this occasion, to think of those decisions that she made in the past. Perhaps we can explain why she failed to exercise this capacity as well. But perhaps we can't. In any case, at some point we will have to admit that our explanations simply come to an end. In other words, at some point we will have to rest content with explaining the reckless woman's failure to exercise her capacity to have a thought, or whatever, by saying that she simply blanked, and for that we will be unable to give anything by way of an explanation—not, at any rate, without retreating to brain science.

Importantly, however, this will give us no reason whatsoever to suppose that we cannot hold the reckless woman responsible for failing to think of whatever it is, and hence for blanking. For so long as we are right to assume that her failure of thought, or her blanking, occurs in a suitable context of nearby possible worlds in which she does have that thought, it thereby follows, analytically, both that she could have had that thought, or could have not blanked, in the sense of having had a capacity to have the thought, or not to have blanked, and that her failure to exercise her capacity is the relevant explanation of her failure to have the thought, or of her blanking. And this, in turn, is what legitimizes our holding her responsible. The fact that our explanations run out is neither here nor there.

Rational Capacities and Desire

We now have an account of what makes the 'could' claims true that we have to suppose to be true for it to be appropriate to hold the reckless woman responsible for her failure to have the right belief. The question is whether we can extend this to give an account of what makes the 'could' claims true that we have to suppose to be true for it to be appropriate to hold the weak woman responsible for her failure to have the right desire, and that we have to suppose to be false for it to be appropriate not to hold the compulsive woman responsible for her failure to have the right desire. At this point, however, a familiar problem arises.

The problem is, in essence, that whereas it is easy to see how the reckless woman's beliefs should and could have been the product of a rational capacity, it is difficult to see how the weak woman's desires should and could have been the product of a rational capacity. Since belief is a psychological state whose very nature is, *inter alia*, to be sensitive to evidence, it comes as no surprise that we are able to think of someone with beliefs as someone who possesses a capacity to revise her beliefs in a rational manner. But Hume, for one, thought that desires were, by contrast, 'original existences', and the point of his so labelling them was precisely to suggest that they were, by their very nature, a psychological state that is not sensitive to rational considerations of any sort (Hume 1740/1978). However, it seems to me that this Humean account of desire is radically mistaken (Smith forthcoming). Let me therefore briefly sketch a picture of evaluative belief which makes it clear how and why desires both should and could be the product of a rational capacity. Since I have spelled out the story in detail elsewhere (Smith 1994, 1997a, 2001), I will be brief.

What exactly is it that an agent believes when she believes some action to be desirable? It seems to me helpful, in answering this question, to begin from the more or less common-sense assumption that for an agent to believe it desirable to act in a certain way in certain circumstances is for her to believe that so acting is advisable: that is—and this is meant to be strictly equivalent—a matter of her believing that she would advise herself to perform that act in those circumstances if she were herself in circumstances in which she was best placed to give herself advice. If this is right, however, then two questions naturally spring to mind. First, what are these circumstances in which agents are best placed to give themselves advice, and secondly, what fixes the content of the advice that the agents in those circumstances would give themselves?

The answer to the first question is, I suggest, that agents are best placed to give themselves advice when their psychologies have been purged of all cognitive limitations and rational failings. And the answer to the second question, the question about the content of the advice that agents would give to themselves, is that the content of such advice is fixed by the contents of the desires that they would have, were their psychologies thus purged, about what they are to do in the circumstances of action about which they are seeking advice. In other words, when I believe that my performance of a certain action is desirable, that amounts to my believing that my performance of that act is advisable, where that, in turn, amounts to my believing that I would want myself so to act if I had a desire set that was purged of all cognitive limitations and rational failings.

If something like this is along the right lines, then all we need to do in order to get a full-blown analysis of desirability is to give an account of the conditions that need to be met by a desire set which is devoid of cognitive limitations and rational failings. My suggestion in this regard is basically a development of an idea of Bernard Williams's (Williams 1980). For a desire set to be devoid of cognitive limitations and rational failings is, I suggest, for it to be one which is maximally informed and coherent and unified. What it is desirable for an agent to do in certain circumstances is thus a matter of what she would want herself to do in those circumstances if she had a set of desires that was maximally informed and coherent and unified. The suggestion can be formulated more precisely as follows. Let's call the possible world in which the agent has the desires that she actually has in the circumstances of action she faces the 'evaluated' world, and the possible world in which she has that set of desires that is maximally informed and coherent and unified the 'evaluating' world. In these terms the suggestion is that what it is desirable for an agent to do in the evaluated world is fixed not by what, in the evaluated world, she wants herself to do in the evaluated world, and not by what, in the evaluating world, she wants herself to do in the evaluating world, but rather by what, in the evaluating world, she wants herself to do in the evaluated world. This, accordingly, is the property that an agent must believe her act to have when she values the performance of that act.

Once this is agreed it seems to me that there is no difficulty at all in seeing why the desires of the weak woman should and could be the product of a rational capacity. In order to see why, imagine a case in which, on reflection, a woman comes to believe that (say) she would desire that she abstain from drinking in the circumstances of action that she presently faces if she had a

34 / Michael Smith

maximally informed and coherent and unified set of desires, but imagine further that she doesn't have any desire at all to abstain. She desires to drink instead. Now consider the pair of psychological states that comprises her belief that she would desire that she abstain from drinking in the circumstances of action that she presently faces if she had a maximally informed and coherent and unified set of desires, and which also comprises the desire that she abstain from drinking; and compare that pair of psychological states with the pair that comprises her belief that she would desire that she abstain from drinking in the circumstances of action that she presently faces if she had a maximally informed and coherent and unified set of desires, but which also comprises instead a desire to drink. Which of these pairs of psychological states is more coherent?

The answer would seem to me to be plain enough. The first pair is much more coherent than the second. There is disequilibrium or dissonance or failure of fit involved in believing that she would desire herself to act in a certain way in certain circumstances if she had a maximally informed and coherent and unified desire set, and yet not desiring to act in that way. The failure to desire to act in that way is, after all, something that she disowns. From her perspective it makes no sense, given the rest of her desires. By her lights it is a state that she would not be in if she were in various ways better than she actually is: more informed, more coherent, more unified in her desiderative outlook. There would therefore seem to be more than a passing family resemblance between the relation that holds between the first pair of psychological states and more familiar examples of coherence relations that hold among psychological states. Coherence would thus seem to be on the side of the pair that comprises both the woman's belief that she would desire that she abstain from drinking in the circumstances of action that she presently faces and the desire that she abstain from drinking.

If this is right, however, then it follows immediately that if the woman is rational, in the relatively mundane sense of having a capacity to have the psychological states that coherence demands of her, then, at least when that capacity is exercised, she will end up having a desire that matches her belief about what she would want herself to do if she had a maximally informed and coherent and unified desire set. In other words, in the particular case under discussion, she will end up losing her desire to drink and acquiring a desire to abstain from drinking instead. The belief that she would desire that she act in a certain way if she had a set of desires that was maximally informed and coherent and unified would thus seem able to cause her to acquire a corresponding desire when it operates in conjunction with the capacity to have coherent psychological states. Put another way, it would thus seem to be in the nature of desires that they are psychological states that are sensitive to our beliefs about what we would desire that we do if we had a set of desires that was maximally informed and coherent and unified, sensitive in the sense of being psychological states that we would acquire in the light of such beliefs given that we have a capacity to have the psychological states that coherence demands of us.

We are now in a position to put this account of how desires can appropriately be seen as the product of a rational capacity together with the lessons that we learned earlier about what it means to say that someone has a rational capacity governing her beliefs, and thereby to tell a story about the difference between the weak woman and the compulsive woman. The suggestion is that both the weak woman and the compulsive woman are best interpreted as believing that they would want themselves to refrain from having another drink if they had a maximally informed and coherent and unified desire set. Both of them are therefore subject to coherence's demand that they desire to abstain from drinking. Both of them nonetheless desire to have another drink. The difference between them, however, lies in the fact that, notwithstanding her desire to drink, the weak woman could have desired to refrain from having another drink, in the sense of having a capacity to have that desire given that coherence demands that desire of her; and her failure to exercise that capacity is the explanation of her drinking. The compulsive woman, by contrast, given that she has a desire to drink, could not have desired to refrain from having another drink in the sense of lacking the capacity to have that desire, notwithstanding the fact that coherence demands that desire of her.

More precisely, we can explain the difference between them in the following terms. (Here we simply apply the account given in the cognitive case.) We begin by abstracting away from all those properties that could have an effect on what the weak woman and the compulsive woman desire except the relevant properties of their brains. We then note that the weak woman would, whereas the compulsive woman would not, have a whole host of counterfactuals true of her. She would desire to refrain from similar drinks, and the like—drinks of ever so slightly different kinds, in ever so slightly different circumstances, and so on—in those nearby possible worlds in which she believes that she would want herself so to act if she had a maximally informed and coherent and unified desire set. Assuming that there is relevant

36 / **Michael Smith**

structure in what underwrites the truth of these counterfactuals, we then triangulate much as before. That is, we conclude that in that same nearby region of logical space the weak woman does, whereas the compulsive woman does not, have a desire to refrain from having the very drink that she has in response to the very belief she has that she would want herself to refrain from having this drink if she had a maximally informed and coherent and unified desire set. This is what it means to say that the weak woman could, whereas the compulsive woman could not, have resisted her desire to drink.

If this is right, then note that though we can acknowledge both that the weak woman failed to exercise her capacity to desire in accordance with her belief, and that her failure explained her drinking, we must once again be careful not to suppose that we will always be able to give an explanation of why she failed. Of course, on certain occasions we might be able to give such an explanation (Pettit and Smith 1993; Kennett and Smith 1996). For example, suppose there is a routine that she regularly goes through when she desires a drink: perhaps she imagines her children looking at her pick up the drink and put it to her lips, and then homes in on the look of utter disappointment in their eyes. And suppose this routine has in the past reliably firmed her in her resolve to abstain from drinking. Then, if we in addition suppose that she could have gone through that process of imagination on this occasion, we may well have available an explanation of her failure to desire to refrain on this occasion. For we could then explain her failure to desire to refrain from drinking by citing the fact that she failed to go through the routine of imagining the look on her children's faces when she was about to take a drink. However, this explanation, like the earlier explanation in the cognitive case, simply takes for granted that she has another capacity that she failed to exercise at the relevant time—namely, the capacity to imagine the look on her children's faces when she was about to take a drink—and for this we have given no explanation at all. As in the cognitive case, it thus seems that at some point we will have to rest content with the fact that we cannot give an explanation of the weak woman's failure to exercise her capacity to desire to refrain from drinking—not, at any rate, without retreating to brain science.

Importantly, however, note that this gives us no reason whatsoever to suppose that we cannot hold the weak woman responsible for failing to desire to refrain from drinking. For so long as we are right to assume that that failure to desire to refrain from drinking occurs in a suitable context of nearby possible worlds in which she does desire to refrain, it thereby follows, analytically, both that she could have had that desire, in the sense of having a rational capacity to have the desire, notwithstanding the fact that she failed to have that desire in fact, and that her failure to exercise her capacity is the relevant explanation of her failure to desire to refrain from drinking. And this, in turn, is what legitimizes our holding her responsible. The fact that our explanations run out is neither here nor there.

Conclusion

I said at the outset that the 'could' claims we assume to be true (or false) when we describe someone as reckless, weak, or compelled, all mean much the same thing: specifically, they all signify the presence (or absence) of a relevant rational capacity. We can now see why that is so.

In the case of the reckless woman, we assume that, notwithstanding the fact that she has the incorrect belief about the relative value of drinking and risking failing to fulfil her obligations, she could have had the correct belief, in the sense of having a capacity to have that belief. As we have seen, this in turn means, *inter alia*, that she exists in a suitable context of nearby possible worlds in which, because she is suitably responsive to the evidence, she has not just this correct belief, but a whole host of similarly correct beliefs. In the case of the weak woman, we assume that, notwithstanding the fact that she desires, incorrectly, to have another drink, she could have had the right desire, in the sense of having a capacity to have that desire: that is, the desire to refrain. As we have seen, this in turn means, *inter alia*, that she exists in a suitable context of nearby possible worlds in which, because her desires fit coherently together with her beliefs about what she would want herself to do if she had a maximally informed and coherent and unified desire set, she has not just this right desire, but a whole host of similarly right desires. The compelled woman could not desire otherwise, in the sense of lacking this capacity.

In the case of both the reckless woman and the weak woman we have seen that this provides us with a plausible account of what it means to say that the women have capacities that they failed to exercise. The reckless woman has the capacity to believe correctly, but she failed to exercise that capacity. The weak woman has the capacity to desire otherwise, but she failed to exercise that capacity. Moreover, we have seen that though we might be able to explain their failure to exercise these capacities, we also might not be able to explain their failure to do so. Importantly, however, we have also seen that even if we are unable to explain those failures, that would give us no reason to be sceptical about the truth of such claims. For the truth of the claim that someone has a capacity to believe or desire correctly that she failed to exercise might simply be constituted by her failure of belief or desire in the context of a suitable raft of nearby possible worlds of the kind described.

2

How is Strength of Will Possible?

Richard Holton

Weakness of will is traditionally identified with akrasia: weak-willed agents, on this view, are those who intentionally do other than that which they judge to be best. This gives rise to the puzzle of how such failure is possible: how can an agent intentionally perform an action while believing a better option is available?

Suppose, however, that one were unconvinced by the traditional identification of weakness of will with akrasia. Suppose one thought instead of weakness of will as failure to persist in one's resolutions. And, correspondingly, suppose one thought of strength of will as success in persisting with one's resolutions. Then the interesting question would no longer be how *weakness* of will is possible. It is all too easy to see how an earlier resolution could be overcome by the growth of a subsequent desire. Rather, the interesting question would be how *strength* of will is possible. How do agents succeed in persisting with their resolutions in the face of strong contrary inclinations?[1]

Elsewhere (Holton 1999) I have argued for an account of weakness of will and strength of will along these lines; I shall summarize those ideas shortly.

This chapter was presented as a talk at the conference The Will in Moral Psychology, Edinburgh, July 2002. It is a précis of several chapters of an unfinished book, 'Aspects of the Will'. Issues skated over here just might receive a more adequate treatment there. Thanks to the Edinburgh audience, the editors, and especially to Rae Langton and Alison McIntyre; also to the Arts and Humanities Research Board for a grant that gave me a year free of teaching, during which this was written.

[1] Kent Bach (1995) makes much the same point. Note that in a case of weakness of will, the subsequent desires can affect the judgement about what is best; so it need not be a case of akrasia.

40 / Richard Holton

Here my focus is on the interesting question that follows: on how strength of will is possible. My answer, in brief, is that we standardly achieve strength of will by exercising will-power. I mean this as more than a pleonasm. My claim is that will-power is a distinct faculty, the exercise of which causally explains our ability to stick to a resolution.

To get some idea of what a separate faculty of will-power might be, let us contrast this approach with the two alternatives that have been dominant in recent philosophical discussion (alternatives first):

The Humean account (belief–desire account). This seeks to explain all intentional action in terms of the agent's beliefs and desires. Agents act on whichever of their desires are strongest.[2] An explanation of how agents stick by their resolutions must show how they thereby act on their strongest desires. (In so far as resolutions are understood as mental states at all, they must thus be reducible to beliefs and desires.)

The Augmented Humean account (belief–desire–intention account). This holds that beliefs and desires won't do the job. Intentions, of which resolutions are a species, should be seen as a third mental kind, irreducible to the other two. This second account thus involves an *ontological* revision of the first. However, when it comes to the *mechanism* that explains strength of will, there is no fundamental change. For this account keeps the idea that it is the relative strength of the conative inputs that determines what the agent will do; it is just that these now consist not simply of desires, but of desires *and* intentions. If a resolution is stronger than any contrary desires, the agent will stick to it; if the contrary desires are stronger, then the agent will act on them instead.

The will-power account. Like the second account, this keeps the idea that the basic mental states are beliefs, desires, and intentions. However, it differs radically in the mechanism by which the agent's action is determined. This is where the idea of will-power comes in. The claim is that the agent's decision is determined not just by the relative strength of the conative inputs, the desires and the intentions. Rather, there is a separate faculty of will-power which plays an independent contributory role. Agents whose will-power is

---

[2] More strictly we should factor in agents' beliefs about which of their desires can be realized: agents will be unlikely to act on their strongest desires in cases in which they think them probably unattainable, but think of other desires, nearly as strongly held, as readily attainable. To keep things manageable I ignore these complications here, though they are relevant to some of the motivational issues discussed below.

How is Strength of Will Possible? / 41

strong can stick by their resolutions even in the face of strong contrary desires; agents whose will-power is weak readily abandon their resolutions.

My project here is to develop an account of this third sort. Part of the ambition is simply to show that there is the necessary conceptual space for it: the recent dominance of the other two accounts has tended to obscure the very possibility of taking will-power seriously. But, of course, I want to go further than that. I want to argue that there are considerations, both philosophical and psychological, that show its advantages over the others. I start with a brief summary of the conception of strength of will that makes these issues pressing.

Akrasia, Resolutions, and Weakness of Will

Imagine someone who is convinced that all the arguments point the same way: he should give up meat. Yet suppose he does not. He is, therefore, akratic. But is he weak-willed? That, I contend, depends on other factors. Has he repeatedly vowed to give up, only to find himself succumbing time and again in the face of rare steaks and slow-cooked offal? Or does he unblushingly affirm while conceding practical inconsistency—that he has never had any intention of giving up, and never will? In the first case we surely would accuse him of weakness of will; in the second I think we would not. Although there is something very odd, indeed culpable, about his behaviour, it is not what we ordinarily think of as weakness of will.

If that is right, then central to the idea of weakness of will is an over-readiness to abandon one's resolutions. The weak-willed carnivore is the one who cannot maintain his resolve. How should that over-readiness be understood? Resolutions can be understood as a special kind of intention. Intentions themselves can play a number of roles; this is true whether or not we are reductivist about them. As Michael Bratman (1987) has shown, they serve to foreclose deliberation, and have an important function in enabling coordination. But they can also serve to protect the outcome of earlier reasoning from later temptation. I might judge that it will be better for me to work this evening than to do any of a number of other tempting things. Currently, moreover, working is what I most want to do. However, I know that when this evening comes, besieged by temptations, I will more strongly want to do one of those other things. What can I do to protect my current judgement—

42 / Richard Holton

that working is the thing to do—from the temptations that threaten to overwhelm it?

One thing I can do—indeed the most normal thing to do—is simply to *decide* now that I will work this evening. That is, I can form the intention to do so. But this is a special sort of intention. Its distinctive feature is that it is supposed to remain firm in the face of the contrary desires that I expect to have. This is what I take to be characteristic of a resolution. Resolutions are intentions part of whose function is to defeat contrary inclinations that I fear I might come to have.[3] Abandoning such intentions results in a special kind of failure. If new desires cause me to abandon my intention to eat in one restaurant in favour of an intention to eat in another, I open myself to the charge of being fickle. But when new desires cause me to abandon a resolution, I open myself to the more serious charge of being weak-willed.

However, not every case of abandoning a resolution in the face of the desires it was supposed to defeat is a case of weakness of will. Sometimes I might form a resolution for a very trivial reason. I might, for instance, resolve to go without water for two days to see what it feels like. And sometimes the contrary desires will be far stronger than I had imagined: perhaps, after a day, the desire for water will be enormous. In such cases we might be reluctant to say that those who revise their resolutions are weak-willed. Indeed, the failing would lie with those who persist. They would exhibit an unreasonable inflexibility or stubbornness. So weakness of will involves, I think, a normative element. It is the *unreasonable* revision of a resolution in the face of the contrary desires (or inclinations more generally) that it was supposed to defeat.[4]

We might expect strength of will to be the contrary of weakness of will. I think that it is. The central feature of strength of will is the ability to maintain one's resolutions in the face of the very inclinations that they were designed to overcome. In addition I think that it too involves a normative element. To show strength of will is not to maintain one's resolutions come

---

[3] In Holton 1999 I called these 'contrary inclination defeating intentions'; 'resolutions' is somewhat easier to say.

[4] Alison McIntyre showed me that, for it to be a case of weakness of will, the desire that defeats the resolution must be of the kind that the resolution was designed to defeat—a point which I missed in my earlier piece. Note too that there can be other reasons for revising a resolution that do not bring the charge of weakness of will. I might, for instance, become convinced (even unreasonably convinced) that the premiss on which the original resolution was based is false. Then revising the resolution (even unreasonably) would not exhibit weakness of will—provided that my conviction that the premiss was false was not, in turn, simply a rationalization triggered by the desires that the resolution was supposed to defeat.

what may. That, as we have seen, can sometimes be mere stubbornness. Rather it is *reasonable* maintenance that is required.

In the last section we shall return to this normative issue. But for the bulk of this chapter I shall be concerned with the descriptive issue of how strength of will is possible: how it is that we can maintain a resolution in the face of contrary desires. It is all too common to find that resolutions are overwhelmed by these desires; we need to know how it is that sometimes they are not.

Explaining Strength of Will in the Humean (Belief–Desire) Approach

My aim in this section is to describe what I take to be the most promising account of strength of will within the belief–desire framework, and to show that it fails. In so doing I hope to motivate the need for an alternative.

Let us start with a classic case of the need for strength of will. Suppose that you have a desire to give up smoking; that is, you prefer

(A) I give up smoking for good soon

to

(B) I don't give up smoking for good soon.[5]

However, you know that you will also strongly desire any particular cigarette that you are offered. 'And why not?', you might think: 'No single cigarette is going to do me much harm, yet the pleasure it will give will be great.' So you know that, for each cigarette at the moment before smoking it, you prefer:

(C) I don't resist this cigarette

to

(D) I resist this cigarette.[6]

---

[5] I put aside complications that come from the possibility that smoking is addictive. If that worries you, substitute an innocuous example.

[6] I say that these are the preferences *at the moment just before smoking each cigarette*. If you were to think *at all times* that it was preferable to smoke each cigarette than not to, then these preferences would be simply inconsistent with your preference to give up: in wanting to give up you would simply have failed to sum your individual preferences properly. In the situation I have in mind, you avoid that kind of inconsistency since your preferences change in the proximity of a cigarette.

44 / Richard Holton

It is easy to see where this reasoning will lead. It seems that if you act on your strongest desires, you will always put off giving up until after the next cigarette; and so you will never give up. This is true even if your desire to give up is greater than your desire for any particular cigarette (i.e. if you prefer A to C), since it seems that it is possible both to smoke any particular cigarette, and to give up in the near future.

It might appear then that the belief–desire account is in trouble right from the beginning. Given a pattern of desires that has this form—surely a very common one—it looks as though an agent who is motivated solely by desire will be unable to exercise strength of will. And that looks like a refutation of the belief–desire account, since surely agents with just this pattern of desires do sometimes display strength of will.

There are, however, two responses that the proponent of the belief–desire account can make. The first involves adding further desires; the second involves adding further beliefs. I take them in turn.

Adding a Further Desire

Although the belief–desire account makes do with just beliefs and desires, that does not mean that it can have no place for resolutions. They might be accepted as mental states, to be analysed as a form of belief, or a form of desire, or some combination of the two. Alternatively they might be seen, not as mental states at all, but as something like illocutionary acts. The obvious model here is promising. On this second approach, when a person makes a resolution she makes something like a promise to herself. This will typically give rise to a mental state: to the belief that she has made the resolution. But that belief isn't itself the resolution. The resolution is the illocutionary act that the belief is about.

Either of these ways of accommodating resolutions, the reductive or the illocutionary, now provides for a possible way out of the problem. For suppose that you do not simply *desire* to give up smoking; in addition you *resolve* to do so, forming a resolution that bears some particular date for its implementation. And suppose that you have *a strong desire to be resolute*: a strong desire to stick to your resolutions. Then, when the date for implementing the resolution comes, provided your desire to be resolute is stronger than your desire

In the terminology made famous by George Ainslie, you have hyperbolic discount curves. For Ainslie's account of such preferences, see Ainslie 1992, 2001. For a very clear presentation, see Rachlin 2000, ch. 2.

How is Strength of Will Possible? / 45

to smoke, you have a desire-driven way to give up. Unlike the desire to give up sometime soon, the desire to be resolute cannot be satisfied compatibly with taking the next cigarette after the resolution is to be implemented. The date on which you resolve to give up can be completely arbitrary, but it becomes significant because you choose it.[7]

Adding Some Further Beliefs

An alternative tack works by adding further beliefs rather than further desires. Recall that the initial difficulty got going because at each point you thought that it was possible both to take the next cigarette, and to give up smoking sometime soon. Suppose that you come to doubt that: suppose that at some point you come to believe that whether you give up smoking sometime soon is dependent on whether you smoke the next cigarette. Then you will be able to use your stronger desire to give up smoking soon (A) to overcome your desire to smoke the next cigarette (C). It is important to see what talk of 'dependent' here must mean. If the desire to give up smoking is to exert the requisite leverage, you must believe both

> *Effective*: If I resist this next cigarette, I'll give up smoking for good

and

> *Necessary*: If I don't resist this next cigarette, I won't give up smoking for good.

The names should make clear the functions of the beliefs, but let us spell them out nonetheless. If *Effective* is absent you will fail to think that resisting the next cigarette will have any effect on realizing your desire to give up soon, and so you will have no reason to resist. If *Necessary* is absent you can consistently think that you will be able both to smoke the next cigarette and to still give up, so again your desire to give up will provide no reason for resisting this cigarette.[8]

Why should you come to believe both *Necessary* and *Effective*? *Effective* might be justified on simple inductive grounds. If you feared that you would be

---

[7] For a discussion of an approach along these lines, see Sobel 1994: 249–50.

[8] This approach, though cast in a game-theoretic context which views agents as collections of (potentially competing) time-slices, originates with George Ainslie in the works mentioned above. For criticism of the time-slice framework, see Bratman 1995. For a reworking of the approach without time-slices, resulting in a position similar to that presented here, see Nozick 1993: 14–21 and Mele 1996.

46 / Richard Holton

simply unable ever to resist a cigarette, then resisting one now will show that your fear was ungrounded. Perhaps too it will be underpinned by some kind of sunk-cost reasoning. The more suffering you have endured to resist cigarettes, the more likely you will be to be motivated to resist them in the future: what a waste of effort otherwise! We can accept that people are in fact motivated in this way whether or not we think, with most economists, that there is something irrational about it.

Necessary is harder to justify. Presumably in forming a resolution to stop smoking you will have chosen some particular point as the one at which to give up.[9] Then your conviction in *Necessary* might be underpinned by some kind of *now-or-never* thinking. You can accept that the point which you chose is arbitrary. Nevertheless, you can think that, having chosen this point, you must stick to it: if you break your resolution to give up smoking now, you will never be in a position to stick to a similar resolution at any point in the future.

Moreover, we can see how this reason for believing in *Necessary* might interact with the phenomenon of wanting to be resolute that was discussed above. You might think that a failure to stick to this resolution to give up smoking would adversely affect your ability to stick to any other resolutions that you might form, resolutions about things quite unconnected with smoking. And so, in so far as that is an ability that you strongly want to keep, you have a further motivation for sticking to this particular resolution.[10]

Problems

So we have two attempts to explain strength of will within the belief–desire framework. Both involve ideas that have some plausibility. Yet neither, I think, will work as a complete account. For a start, both are vulnerable to serious problems of detail.[11] These, however, won't be my concern here. More fundamentally, both completely misrepresent the phenomenology of the exercise of strength of will.

---

[9] If you didn't, your resolution is unlikely to succeed; there is good evidence that resolutions without 'implementation intentions' are far less effective. See Gollwitzer 1996.

[10] The parallel again is with promising, understood in a broadly Humean way: resolutions are devices that enable you to stake your general reputation on each individual case.

[11] The *further desire* approach seems to involve attributing to the strong-willed agent a desire for resoluteness that approaches a fetish. The *further belief* approach faces difficulties in establishing

The central point is this. If these accounts were right, then sticking to a resolution would consist in the triumph of one desire (the stronger) over another. But that isn't what it feels like. It typically feels as though there is a struggle: that one maintains one's resolution by dint of effort in the face of the contrary desire. Perhaps not every case of maintaining strength of will is like that (we shall mention some that are not). But by and large, maintaining strength of will requires effort.

Moreover, the empirical evidence bears this out. The most straightforward comes from simple measures of the physical arousal to which the exercise of will-power gives rise. Ask agents to regulate themselves in ways that involve acting against contrary inclinations—to regulate their emotions, for instance, the expression of their emotions, their attention, or their thoughts—and they will show the standard signs of physiological arousal that accompany effort: increased blood pressure and pulse, changed skin conductance, etc.[12]

Of course it is true that cases only involving desires can give rise to a feeling of struggle: consider what it can be like trying to choose an option from a wide and attractive menu, even when there are no resolutions to which one is trying to keep. Here too we might speak of the *effort* of choosing. We might well think that this in itself shows that there is something wrong with the Humean picture: that in general it leaves insufficient space for the role of the active agent in making choices. However, my concern here is with the particular case of choice constrained by resolution. If the Humean account were right, we would expect the phenomenology of the effort of choosing to be the same as the phenomenology of the effort of maintaining a resolution that one has already chosen. But it is not. And the kind of regret that one can feel for an option not chosen is very different from the kind of regret—to say nothing of shame or guilt—that one feels when one abandons a resolution.[13]

---

that a reasonable agent would believe both *Necessary* and *Effective*. Why not think, for instance, that *Effective* would be undermined by the inductively sustained belief that, at least for the first few weeks, resolutions become harder to maintain as time goes on? It is easy enough to refuse the first cigarette; the difficult thing is to keep on refusing. Similarly, why wouldn't *Necessary* be undermined by the knowledge that many agents only give up smoking after several attempts to do so? In their cases the failure of one resolution didn't entail the failure of all subsequent ones.

[12] For a survey of this, see Muraven, Tice, and Baumeister 1998: 774–5.

[13] Although I say this so confidently, there is some empirical evidence that the effort of choosing has the same kinds of effect as the effort of maintaining a resolution. This might suggest that the same faculty is used in the two cases. I discuss this below, n. 26.

48 / **Richard Holton**

Intentions and Will-Power

How can we make sense of this idea of struggle? A first move is to distinguish resolutions from desires, for only then can we make sense of the idea of struggle involved in sticking with a resolution rather than bending to a desire. Resolutions, I have suggested, can be seen as a particular kind of intention. Having rejected the Humean account, we can follow Michael Bratman (1987) and others in treating intentions as mental states that are distinct from (i.e. not reducible to) beliefs and desires. Nevertheless, like desires, they are motivating states: an intention can move one to action. Intentions can thus work to preserve the motivational power of earlier desires: a desire can give rise to an intention, and this intention can result in subsequent action even when the desire is no longer present. Indeed an intention can result in subsequent action even when there are, by that time, contrary desires present. That, I suggested earlier, is precisely the role of resolutions. Resolutions are contrary-inclination-defeating intentions: intentions formed by the agent with the very role of defeating any contrary inclinations that might emerge.

Let us spell out some of the respects in which an approach that treats resolutions in this way departs from the Humean theory of motivation. It is not the case that to be motivated to act, an agent requires a belief and a desire. Nor is it true that agents will always act on their strongest desires. For an intention can serve as a motivation even when the desires that gave rise to it have been lost. Moreover, this intention can overcome the desires that are present at the time of action.

Once we introduce intentions in this way, how should we fill out the account? One possibility is to preserve something of the spirit of the Humean account. We might simply increase the class of motivating attitudes to encompass intentions as well as desires. Then, rather than saying that agents will act to satisfy their strongest *desire*, we might say that they will act to satisfy whichever is the strongest of their *desires and intentions*. Thus agents' actions will be determined by their beliefs, desires, and intentions. This takes us to the second of the accounts of strength of will that was mentioned at the outset: the Augmented Humean account.

Alternatively we could move further still, to the account I shall defend: the will-power account, which acknowledges beliefs, desires, and intentions but adds a distinct faculty of will-power as well. How does this change things? One obvious difference is that here the strength of the agent's desires and intentions is not the only determinant of what she will do. We also need to add the strength of her will-power as a separate factor. Putting things in these terms can, however, be misleading, for it suggests a picture in which will-power is simply a third input in the process that determines the agent's actions, a process on which the agent will seem like a spectator. I want rather to defend a picture on which will-power is a faculty that the agent actively employs. The extent to which this can be achieved will emerge, I hope, in what follows.

What, then, are the grounds for preferring the will-power account over the apparently simpler Augmented Humean alternative? My main contention is simply that it is better supported by the empirical evidence, both from ordinary common-sense observation, and from psychology. Indeed, the psychological literature does not just provide evidence for the *existence* of a distinct faculty of will-power which works to block reconsideration of past resolutions; it also provides some quite detailed evidence about the *nature* of that faculty. Roughly, it seems that will-power works very much like a muscle, something that it takes effort to employ, that tires in the short run, but that can be built up in the long run.

I shall present some of the psychological evidence shortly. But to see its relevance, first let us return to the commonplace observation that we used in rejecting the simple belief–desire approach: the observation that exercising will-power takes effort. Sticking by one's resolutions is hard work. This seems to count against the Augmented Humean account too. It certainly doesn't feel as though in employing will-power one is simply letting whichever is the stronger of one's desires or intentions have its way. It rather feels as though one is actively doing something, something that requires effort.

My suggestion is that effort is needed because one is actively employing one's faculty of will-power. What exactly does the effort consist in? It cannot be straightforward physical effort, since it is present whether the resolution is to perform an action—like starting on an exercise regime—or to refrain from performing an action—like giving up smoking. However much the desire might seem to drag one towards it, we cannot think that the effort of resisting literally consists in pulling back muscles that are straining for the cigarette. Rather, the effort involved has to be a kind of mental effort. It is the mental effort of maintaining one's resolutions; that is, of refusing to revise them. And my suggestion here is that one achieves this primarily by refusing to *reconsider* one's resolutions. On this picture, then, the effort involved in employing will-power is the effort involved in refusing to reconsider one's resolutions; and the faculty of will-power is the faculty that enables one to achieve this.

50 / **Richard Holton**

Before discussing the relevant empirical literature, we need to get a little clearer on the distinction between revision and reconsideration that is invoked here. We will also need to get clear on a further distinction between reconsideration and the simple rehearsal or reminder of the reasons for which one is acting.

Revision, Reconsideration, and Rehearsal

To revise one's intentions is to change them; that much is clear. Obviously reconsiderations differ in that they do not have to result in change. But I suggest that the full-blown reconsideration of a resolution does involve *suspension* of that resolution. Fully to reconsider a resolution is to open oneself to the possibility of revising it if the considerations come out a certain way; and that is to withdraw one's current commitment to it. Of course, one might say that the resolution remains in place pending the outcome of the revision. But such a claim does not carry conviction. For much of the point of a resolution, as with any intention, is that it is a fixed point around which other actions—one's own and those of others—can be coordinated. To reconsider an intention is exactly to remove that status from it (Bratman 1987: 62).

Although to suspend a resolution is not, *ipso facto*, to revise it, when temptation is great it is hard to keep the two separate. Very often the force of one's desire will akratically overwhelm one's judgement; or it will corrupt that judgement, so that while what one does is what one judges best, this is not what one would have judged best in a cooler moment; or it will move one so quickly to abandon one's resolution that one will never even carry out the judgement as to whether this is the best thing to do. Suspending a resolution can be like removing the bolts on a sluice: although one only meant to feel the force of the water, once the bolts are gone, there is no way of holding it back.

At the other extreme from full-blown reconsideration is the state of not thinking about one's resolutions at all: form them and then act on them, without so much as contemplating them or the possibility of acting other-wise. Perhaps this is the idea that we have of the very strong-willed individual who, as we might say, is never really tempted by the alternatives. It might seem then that this is what we should aim for with our resolutions. In fact in typical cases it would not work.

How is Strength of Will Possible? / 51

This kind of unthinking pattern best describes those actions that are automatic. Force yourself to get up at six every morning to go for a run, and after a while it will probably become automatic. The alarm clock will go, you will get out of bed, put on your running kit, and get outside without really giving thought to what you are doing. Much recent work in social psychology has shown just how widespread automatic behaviour is; there is even evidence to suggest that it involves quite different parts of the brain to those that are involved in volitional behaviour.[14] But the point at which an action becomes automatic is really the point at which will-power is no longer needed. There is good reason for this. At least to begin with, a resolution is typically a resolution to reform one's behaviour into paths that are not automatic. Indeed standardly the automatic behaviour is exactly the behaviour that one has resolved to stop—lighting up a cigarette for instance. If one is to be successful in resisting having a cigarette, and if cigarettes are around, one must constantly monitor whether or not one has picked one up; and one can hardly do that without thinking about cigarettes, and the possibility of smoking them. Successful resolutions cannot work unthinkingly.[15]

So to maintain a resolution like giving up smoking we need something in between full-blown reconsideration and unthinking action. Most resolutions are, I suspect, like this. What we need is a state that involves awareness of the resolution, and perhaps of the considerations for which it is held, but that doesn't involve reconsideration. The crucial factor here is that the resolution is not suspended. To remind oneself of one's resolutions is not, by itself, to bring them into question. (One can inspect the sluice bolts without removing them.) It is important that it is not suspended. For, as we have seen, once a resolution is suspended, it will all too easily be revised. We thus need a state of awareness that falls short of suspension: what I shall call *rehearsal*.

I speak as though the contrast between reconsideration and rehearsal is a sharp one. In fact, of course, there will be many states in between: what I have marked out are the extremes of a continuum. Moreover, very often mere rehearsal will lead one into reconsideration. This is unsurprising when one's rehearsal leads one to dwell on the benefits to be gained by yielding to

[14] On the former point, see, for instance, Bargh and Chartrand 1999. On the latter, see Jahanshahi and Frith 1998. (My thanks to Michael Scott for making me aware of the neuro-psychological literature.)

[15] The need for self-monitoring is central to Carver and Scheier's feedback account (1998).

52 / Richard Holton

temptation; but empirical work shows that the same effect will often come even when one's focus is on the benefits to be gained by holding out.[16]

Can we resist the slide from rehearsal to reconsideration by dint of mental effort? It might seem that this would require an ability to repress thought. The difficulty with such advice is that it is very hard to control one's thoughts directly. Indeed, the effort is typically counter-productive: attempting to repress a thought leads one to dwell on it all the more (Wegner 1989; Uleman and Bargh 1989).[17] But need it be that mental control involves such direct repression?

In seeing the possibilities it is useful to look to the advice given by those professionally concerned with the business of resisting temptation. Here is a representative passage from Ignatius of Loyola, founder of the Jesuits:

There are two ways of gaining merit when an evil thought comes from outside: the first . . . I resist it promptly and it is overcome; the second I resist it, it recurs again and again and I keep on resisting until the thought goes away defeated . . . One sins venially when the same thought of committing a mortal sin comes and one gives ear to it, dwelling on it a little or taking some sensual enjoyment from it, or when there is some negligence in rejecting this thought.

(Ignatius of Loyola, *Spiritual Exercises* (1996 edn.), ¶¶ 33–5)[18]

Quite what does 'resisting' a thought amount to? It does not seem that Ignatius is calling for outright thought suppression. Rather he talks of the risks of dwelling on a thought, or of taking some sensual enjoyment from it. The idea seems to be, not that we can keep certain thoughts out entirely, but that we can avoid focusing on them and developing them. Here it does seem far more plausible that we have some control.

I know of no studies on this, but some light might be shed by considering some parallel cases, even if the parallel is far from perfect. Suppose I ask you

---

[16] Focusing on the benefits to be gained from resisting temptation tends to make agents more likely to succumb, since, under the influence of the temptation, those benefits are judged less valuable. See Karniol and Miller 1983. Note that this effect only occurs when the rewards of holding out are broadly comparable to the rewards of yielding. When the rewards of holding out are judged to be much larger, focusing on them seems to strengthen resolve. Similar findings appear in the work of Walter Mischel discussed below, although here things are complicated by the fact that the reward for resisting temptation was just more of what one would have got had one succumbed. Hence it is hard to distinguish thoughts about the reward for waiting from thoughts about the reward for succumbing.

[17] Again, it has been suggested that this is connected with the idea of self-monitoring: in order to be sure that one is not thinking about something one needs to monitor that one is not (Wegner 1994).

[18] My thanks to Annamaria Schiaparelli for her advice to look at Ignatius.

not to think of the number 2. That is almost impossible, and the very effort of monitoring what you are doing makes your failure all the more certain. But suppose I ask you not to multiply 345 by 27. Unless you are extraordinarily good at mental arithmetic, so that the answer simply jumps out at you, you won't find my request hard to comply with at all. Nor will your monitoring of what you are doing undermine your compliance. Similarly, suppose I ask you not to think through, in detail, the route that you take from home to work. You might not be able to resist imagining the starting point; but I suspect, unless you live very close to work, that you will be able to stop yourself somewhere down the track. The point seems to be that there are quite a few steps needed to perform a long multiplication or to imaginatively trace one's route, steps that have to be taken in a particular order, and one is able to exercise some control over such a process.

I suggest that things are typically similar with the thoughts involved in the revision of resolutions. It might be impossible to control whether we entertain the thought of having a cigarette. But it might be possible to control whether or not we go through the procedure that is involved in revising one's resolution not to. This also seems to be the kind of thing that Ignatius has in mind. The sin does not consist in having the evil thought that 'comes from outside'; Ignatius accepted that that is inevitable. The sin comes with what I do with it.

Evidence for Will-Power

My suggestion, then, is that while rehearsal is needed for maintaining a resolution, reconsideration should be avoided. Let us turn to the empirical evidence for this. I start with a discussion of the developmental evidence that suggests that resolutions really do work to block reconsideration in the way I have said. I then turn to the other considerations which show that abiding by a resolution does involve the exercise of a distinct faculty of will-power, a faculty which the agent actively employs.

Developmental Evidence

Walter Mischel and his colleagues tested children on their ability to delay gratification to achieve greater reward.[19] For instance, they are told that they will receive one cookie if they ring a bell, which they are free to do at any time;

[19] For a summary of a large body of work, see Mischel 1996.

54 / Richard Holton

but that they will get two if they refrain from ringing the bell until an adult comes in. They found that ability to wait comes in around the age of 4 or 5. By the age of 6 almost all children have it, though to markedly different degrees. Strong self-control is a very good predictor of later success in a wide range of academic and social skills.

What are the strategies that children used? Mischel initially expected them to do better by being reminded of the rewards of waiting. In fact, however, those who could see the reward for waiting did far worse than those who could not. Those who could see the reward for not waiting did equally badly. Mischel's account is illuminating and entertaining enough to be worth quoting at length:

> Some of the most effective strategies that the children used were surprisingly simple. From time to time they reaffirmed their intentions quietly ('I'm waiting for the two cookies') and occasionally they reiterated the choice contingency aloud ('if I ring the bell I'll get this one, but if I wait I'll get those'). But mostly these 4-year-olds seemed able to wait for long periods by converting the frustrating waiting situation into a more tolerable non-waiting one, thus making the difficult task easier for themselves. They appeared to achieve this by purposely creating elaborate self-distraction. Instead of fixing their attention and thoughts on the rewards, as initially theorizing had predicted, they seemed to avoid thinking about them entirely. Some put their hands over their eyes, rested their heads on their arms, and invented other similar techniques for averting their gaze most of the time, occasionally seeming to remind themselves with a quick glance. Some talked quietly to themselves or even sang ('This is such a pretty day, hooray'); others made faces, picked their noses, made up games with their hands and feet, and even tried to doze off while continuing to wait. One of the most successful 'delayers' actually managed to nap during the delay time.
>
> (Mischel 1996: 202)

Here the children do seem to conform to the model I have proposed. They sometimes rehearse their resolution, and the reasons for having it (though in this case there is little benefit from so doing, since there is little need for self-monitoring). Seeing the cookies—whether the one to be gained by ringing the bell, or the two to be gained by waiting—radically undermined the children's ability to wait. It seems that this undermines resolve because it provokes reconsideration (Mischel 1996: 201–2).[20] In a further series of experiments Mischel found that being able to see the rewards did not undermine the resolution if the children were encouraged to see them as in some way

---

[20] This finding is corroborated by the Karniol and Miller study cited above.

unreal. A plausible explanation is that thinking of the rewards in this way does not encourage reconsideration, since they are not being thought of as the objects (or, at least, not as the objects with the salient 'hot' properties) about which the resolution was made (Mischel 1996: 203–7).

Mischel's findings do, however, raise one question. Consider the children who had very effective strategies for distracting themselves. Considered in a behaviouristic way these might be thought of as those exercising the greatest will-power, since they are the ones who are most successful at resisting temptation. This is how Mischel describes them. But in another sense we might think of them as the children who have least need for will-power; after all, these are the ones who are putting in little effort since their strategies are so effective (think of the child who took a nap). I suspect that our ordinary talk of will-power is ambiguous here. In this it is no different from our talk of many other virtues. Are they brave who distract themselves in the face of danger? Or need they fight to overcome their fear? I doubt that our ordinary usage provides an answer. Similarly, I doubt that our ordinary usage dictates whether to be exercising will-power an agent has to be involved in an effortful struggle. However, to avoid confusion, I will legislate. I will limit talk of will-power to situations of effortful refusal to reconsider a resolution. In some cases, then—such as the case of the automatic early-morning runner considered earlier—agents achieve strength of will without recourse to will-power at all. It is unlikely that any of the children in Mischel's experiments were in quite that situation. They all had to employ will-power initially. But some had no need to go on employing will-power, exactly because their initial employment had been so effective.

Evidence for Will-Power as a Separate Faculty

The considerations marshalled so far support the idea that one exercises will-power by refusing to reconsider an intention. This in turn suggests that the Augmented Humean account is going to be inadequate, for one's ability to refuse to reconsider is not going to be determined just by the strength of one's desires and intentions. One does not acquire a practical ability just by wanting it. But we might wonder whether this does much to show that will-power is a separate faculty. Here we need to turn to some evidence from social psychology.[21]

[21] For an excellent general survey of the relevant literature here, see Muraven and Baumeister 2000. Talk of *self-control* here, and elsewhere in the psychological literature, is, I think, roughly

56 / Richard Holton

Consider first the fact that the ability to abide by a resolution is affected by features that do not themselves seem to be desires or resolutions. Reformed alcoholics are far more likely to relapse if they are depressed, or anxious, or tired (Baumeister, Heatherton, and Tice 1994: 151 ff.).[22] Moreover, states such as these affect one's ability to abide by *all* of one's resolutions: resolutions not to drink, not to smoke, to eat well, to exercise, to work hard, not to watch daytime television, or whatever. Now of course it is possible to explain this by saying that these states (depression, anxiety, fatigue, etc.) systematically strengthen all of one's desires to drink, smoke, eat, etc., or weaken all of one's resolutions not to; but it is surely a more economical explanation to say that they affect one's ability to act in line with one's resolutions.[23] For why else would there be such systematic effects?

Consider next the remarkable empirical literature on what is known as 'ego-depletion'. It appears that will-power comes in limited amounts that can be used up: controlling oneself to eat radishes rather than the available chocolates in one experiment makes one less likely to persist in trying to solve puzzles in the next (Baumeister *et al.* 1998);[24] suppressing one's emotional responses to a film makes one less likely to persist, later on, in holding squeezed a handgrip exerciser (Muraven, Tice, and Baumeister 1998). Again it is possible to think that what happens here is that the strength of people's resolutions is affected: that maintaining one's resolution to suppress one's emotional responses weakens one's resolution to persist with handgrip exercises. But why should there be effects on such disparate resolutions? And why do some activities (those that involve will-power to act in the face of inclinations to the contrary) bring about these effects, while others (such as doing mathematical problems) do not (Muraven, Tice, and Baumeister 1998: 781–2)? And why do dieters whose will-power has been tested react by subsequently eating more, while non-dieters do not (Vohs and Heatherton

---

equivalent to my talk of *strength of will*. I would rather use *self-control* to describe the related but distinct phenomenon which is the contrary of akrasia: on this usage one lacks self-control if one does other than that which one judges best, even if one does not thereby violate one's resolve (and hence is not weak-willed).

[22] The same is true of those who are dieting (Baumeister, Heatherton, and Tice 1994: 184 ff.) or trying to give up smoking (Baumeister, Heatherton, and Tice 1994: 212 ff.) or taking drugs (Muraven and Baumeister 2000: 250).

[23] Moreover, while bad moods make dieters want to eat more, they tend to have the opposite effect on those who are not on a diet. So it seems that it is the resolution being affected, not the desire. See Muraven and Baumeister 2000: 251.

[24] The puzzles were in fact insoluble.

2000)?[25] A much better explanation is that one's action is determined not simply by the strength of one's desires and one's resolutions, but also by one's will-power; and that it is this component that is being affected by repeated exercise.[26]

A final piece of evidence is that one can apparently develop one's faculty of will-power by repeated exercise. Again, the idea that one becomes virtuous by behaving virtuously is a commonplace one, stressed by Aristotle and by many who have followed him: 'From holding back from pleasures we become moderate, and also when we have become moderate we are most capable of holding back from them' (Aristotle, *Nicomachean Ethics* (2002 edn.), 1104^{a}34–5).[27] Some recent research suggests that this might be right: subjects who undergo a regime of self-regulatory exercises—working on improving their posture for instance—show markedly less tendency to suffer ego-depletion (Muraven, Baumeister, and Tice 1999).[28]

---

[25] This finding parallels the finding of the effect on dieters of bad moods mentioned above.

[26] A note of caution is needed here. While these experiments do suggest that there is a faculty of will-power, they do not give any evidence for my conjecture that it works by blocking reconsideration. Indeed, one of the experiments might be thought to raise a problem for this conjecture, since it suggests that *all* choices give rise to ego-depletion (Baumeister *et al.* 1998, experiment 2, 1256–8). I cannot give a full description and discussion of this here: readers who are interested should consult the original article. However, two brief comments: (1) I am unconvinced that this experiment does lend support to the conclusion that *all* choice gives rise to ego-depletion, since the subjects make their choices under heavy moral pressure from the experimenters. It might well be this aspect (which is similar in kind to the pressure exerted by a resolution) rather than the choice per se, which gives rise to the ego-depletion. (2) Even if it does turn out that all decisions involve ego-depletion, I doubt that this would provide evidence against the hypothesis that will-power works by means of a refusal to reconsider. Rather, what it shows is that all decisions also involve a refusal to reconsider. But isn't that just what we should expect? On Bratman's account, intentions involve the foreclosure of deliberation. What is it to foreclose deliberation other than to refuse to reconsider? However, if this were true my earlier argument against the Humean theory would need revision. The Humean theory would still stand refuted, but not on the grounds that it makes exercises of will-power too similar to instances of choice.

[27] Aristotle is here talking about how we develop the excellences. He does not explicitly say the same about the development of self-control. He does say that lack of self-control can be cured, but he doesn't say how.

[28] Note that there was no effect shown on the *power* of the subjects' wills; only on their *stamina*, i.e. the degree to which they became fatigued. One thing that this research doesn't establish is whether the effect really comes from strengthening the faculty of will-power or from increasing the subjects' confidence that their resolutions will be effective. Indeed the further finding that attempts to implement resolutions in which it is hard to succeed (control of mood) don't have the same effect on will-power might be explained by the hypothesis that we are observing a self-efficacy effect. (In general *self-efficacy*—one's confidence in one's degree of control—is extremely

58 / Richard Holton

Once we think this way, a host more explanations become available. We have looked so far at intrapersonal differences: why do we sometimes stick by our resolutions, and sometimes not? But parallel explanations apply in interpersonal explanations: why do some people stick by their resolutions when others don't? It could be because their resolutions are stronger, or because the desires that they must overcome are weaker. Alternatively, it could be that their will-power is stronger: that having formed a resolution not to be moved by certain desires, they are better at acting in accordance with it, and at turning the corresponding intentions into action.

The approach employed here is a very general one. It has been a central feature of the cognitivist revolution that mental explanations, like explanations elsewhere, can be improved by positing further internal processes. Of course it is always possible to insist that wherever there is an intentional action, it is determined solely by the strength of our pro-attitudes, whether these are understood just as desires, or as desires or intentions; and then to read off the strength of those attitudes accordingly. But such an approach is not only untrue to our experience of sticking to a resolution; it also gives us, as the experiments I have cited show, inferior explanations of the behaviour that agents exhibit.

Motivation and Will-Power

I have argued that there is a faculty of will-power—something like a muscle—and that, when desires and resolutions clash, we can succeed in sticking to our resolutions by employing this faculty. Moreover, employing this faculty is hard work: it requires effort on the part of the agent. What implications does this have for our explanations of why people do and do not stick to their intentions?

Obviously one class of explanations becomes immediately available. If agents lack will-power, then they will not be able to stick to their intentions in the face of contrary desires. This might happen as a result of never having acquired a faculty of will-power (as in the case of a young child) or from having lost it temporarily (from stress or fatigue or whatever) or perhaps even permanently (from damage to the pre-frontal cortex).

important in explaining one's behaviour. For a general overview, see Bandura 1992. As the authors accept, we need more research here before any firm conclusions can be drawn.

So some cases of failure to stick by a resolution will be explained by the absence of sufficient will-power. Will all explanations be of this form? That would require that agents always stick by their resolutions when they possess the will-power to do so: that the presence or absence of sufficient will-power is the only factor. Yet that is most implausible. If will-power is a faculty which agents actively employ, then it should be something that they can fail to employ. Surely sometimes people have the will-power to stick by a resolution and yet decide not to do so. I have resolved not to have wine with my dinner, and I know full well that I could resist, but I decide to have it anyway: the wine appeals very strongly, and I am not much moved by the need to keep a clear head afterwards. Such cases are very common. Indeed, even in cases where will-power is depleted by stress or prior demand or whatever, it seems likely that I will typically abandon the effort to stick by the resolution before my will-power gives way completely. It is not that I could no longer resist; it is that the effort becomes too great and I give up the fight.

Here again the analogy of the muscle, and of muscular fatigue, is helpful. Recall the subjects in the ego-depletion experiments who were asked to hold squeezed a handgrip exerciser. We can easily imagine what it was like for them. The first few seconds were easy. Then, as the muscles got tired, they got more difficult. The hand started to ache, and the ache became more and more pressing, until the subject let go. We can imagine someone going on until the muscles literally could work no more. That is the kind of behaviour one sometimes sees in sporting competitions: grimacing, the competitor keeps on with the pull-ups, arms quivering uncontrollably, until, finally, the muscles give way. In such cases there is, quite literally, nothing more that the person could have done. In contrast, I doubt that any of the subjects with the handgrip exerciser pushed themselves so far. They got to a point where they said, perhaps even to themselves, they could go no further; but offered a large financial incentive, I suspect that they would have managed a few more seconds.

It is the ordinary handgrip subject rather than the competitive athlete who provides the better model for the typical defeat of will-power. Normally one does not find oneself literally powerless to resist a desire; rather, one *decides* to give in to it, since resistance is so hard (often, at the same time, convincing oneself that there is no good reason to resist). A subject whose will is weakened by fatigue or prior demand simply finds the effort of resistance greater, and so typically gives up earlier. It is as though the handgrip subject started with an already tired hand. Of course, in this case fatigue of the hand

60 / Richard Holton

muscles accompanied exhaustion of will-power (though the two processes didn't quite walk in step: those whose wills had been earlier depleted presumably didn't start with fatigued hand muscles). In other cases there will be no concomitant muscular fatigue. The effort of resisting a cigarette is not literally a muscular effort; but it is no less real for that.

In determining whether agents will stick with their resolutions we need then to factor in not just their immediately relevant beliefs, desires, and intentions, and the strength of their faculty of will-power, but also their motivation to employ that faculty. And this motivation will in turn be cashed out in terms of further beliefs, desires, and intentions. Does this mean that we are back with a Humean model, or at least with an Augmented Humean model, in which actions are determined by the strength of the beliefs, desires, and intentions? It does not. An analogy might be helpful. If you want to know how fast I can run a mile on a given occasion, you'll certainly need to know about my beliefs and desires. Have I been offered some reward for running it fast? Will an embarrassingly poor time be publicized? But you will also need to know about the state of my body: is it any good for middle-distance running? It is the same for sticking to resolutions. If you want to know whether someone will stick to a given resolution you'll need to know about her beliefs and desires, including her desires with respect to the content of that resolution and with respect to maintaining resolutions in general. But you'll also need to know about her will-power: how strong it is, how much it has been depleted, and so on.

At this point, however, proponents of the Humean model might object. Isn't saying that one must be motivated to use one's will-power tantamount to saying that one must desire to use it above all? And isn't that just introducing once again the *further desire* account within the belief–desire model? I think not. What this challenge fails to recognize is the radical difference between intentions and desires. Intentions motivate directly: to act on an intention one doesn't need a further desire to act on that intention. Similarly, in the special case of resolutions, to act on a resolution one doesn't need a desire to act on that resolution, or on resolutions in general. For many agents in many cases, a resolution will simply work on its own; the agent's desires will be irrelevant. However, agents will be tempted to revise resolutions when acting upon them requires a large amount of effort. Whether or not they will do so will depend on, among other things, the strength of their desire to maintain those resolutions in particular, and the strength of their desire to maintain their resoluteness in general. But even here, to be effective, these desires need not be the strongest. If the agent's will-power is sufficiently strong, a weak desire to be resolute might be all that is needed to keep it in place when it wavers in the face of a strong contrary desire.

It is here, I think, that the true importance of the considerations raised in attempting to defend the belief–desire account come in; and this explains their plausibility. A desire to be resolute does indeed help an agent to be resolute, but it needn't be the overwhelming desire that the further desire account held it to be. Similarly, belief in *Necessary* and *Effective* is highly relevant to whether agents will persist in their resolutions. An agent who has no confidence at all in *Effective*—an agent who fails to believe that if she refuses this cigarette then she will refuse others—will have little motivation to persist in her resolution. So even if she has the necessary will-power, it will not be used. Of course, an agent who knows that she has the necessary will-power will be far more likely to believe *Effective*, and so an absence of belief in *Effective* is likely to mark those who lack it. But it need not: will-power and self-knowledge need not go together.

The situation for *Necessary* is more plausibly the other way round. It is not that to be motivated one needs to believe *Necessary*: one can doubt it and still be resolute. It is rather that those who do believe *Necessary*—who believe that if they don't give up smoking now, they never will—are likely to be strongly motivated to maintain the resolution.

Is it Reasonable to Block Reconsideration?

So far I have been concerned predominantly with a descriptive question: what is the nature of will-power and of the strength of will that it supports? Now I turn to the normative question of whether it is reasonable to have and to exercise such a faculty. In fact, although I have not been addressing it, such a question has been implicit all along. On the account presented earlier, weakness of will is, roughly, the unreasonable revision of a resolution; strength of will is its reasonable maintenance. Thus, in giving this account of will-power I have been assuming that its employment is reasonable. If it is not, then it will never result in strength of will, but simply in stubbornness.

Giving a complete account of exactly when the employment of will-power is reasonable would be a big task; I cannot embark on it here. Besides, others have already made great progress. I hope that I shall be able to incorporate

62 / Richard Holton

much of what they say.[29] What I can do is to describe briefly how the normative issues appear when considered in the light of the account presented here, with its stress on the distinction between revision and reconsideration. In so doing I hope to sketch the lines of a defence against the obvious objection that it involves an unacceptable bootstrapping.

One natural account of the reasonableness of a procedure of practical rationality is pragmatic: people who live by it do better, in the sense of achieving their long-term goals, than those who don't. We might then defend the reasonableness of will-power by pointing to the advantages gained by those who have it: advantages well documented in the empirical literature. I think that such a defence is basically right. Yet there is a worry that accompanies any such pragmatic approach. Couldn't it be the case that the world is so arranged that the unreasonable flourish? To put the point picturesquely: Couldn't there be a perverse god who rewarded the unreasonable by making sure that they flourished, and penalized the reasonable by making sure that they didn't? Then flourishing would be no indication of reasonableness.

In fact it is far from clear that such arguments work. They are most effective in showing that pragmatic advantage is no guide to *theoretical* rationality: false beliefs can be more advantageous than true. But perhaps pragmatic advantage is a good guide to *practical* rationality. Perhaps the practically reasonable thing to do in the world of the perverse god is that which brings his reward, i.e. that which would *otherwise* be unreasonable. Nevertheless, it might seem as though there is particular reason to worry about will-power, its pragmatic advantage notwithstanding.

To see the worry we need a case in which someone has formed a resolution to resist a certain temptation, and where the refusal to reconsider that resolution will be, prima facie, reasonable (it isn't the kind of case in which the resolution was silly and the contrary desires justifiably strong). We also want it to be a case in which, had the agent never made the resolution and were now to consider what to do, she would, quite reasonably, choose to indulge (i.e. to do what, having formed the resolution, we describe as succumbing). In such a case it looks as though it is the resolution itself that is making all the difference: that it is the resolution itself that is making it reasonable not to succumb. But this seems to involve what Bratman has characterized as an unacceptable bootstrapping: the very fact that one has

---

[29] See especially McClennen 1990, and for a simple presentation of his view (contrasting it with Bratman's), DeHelian and McClennen 1993. For some proposed revisions to McClennen's conception of when resoluteness is rational, see Gauthier 1997 and Bratman 1998.

formed an intention to do something cannot by itself be a reason to do it. Otherwise we could give ourselves a reason to do something just by intending to do it; and that cannot be right (Bratman 1987: 24 ff.).[30]

A concrete example might be helpful: a suitably qualified case of a resolution to give up smoking will serve. We imagine a regular smoker who gains pleasure and comfort from cigarettes. She is young and fit: cigarettes are not going to kill her any time soon. Nevertheless, for the standard reasons, it is in her interest to give up smoking in the near future, and she desires to do so. So it is rational for her to form an intention to give up smoking soon. What should her attitude be towards today's habitual early-morning cigarette (a cigarette which would undoubtedly set her up nicely for the day)? It seems to depend on what resolutions she has made. If she has resolved to give up next week, there is no reason to forgo today's cigarette. If she has resolved to give up today, then there is. In short: it is reasonable to give up smoking soon; having resolved to do so, it is reasonable to forgo today's cigarette, and unreasonable not to; but had she not so resolved (had she resolved instead to give up next week) it would be unreasonable to forgo today's cigarette, and reasonable not to. It seems then that it is the existence of the resolution that makes all the difference. We have an instance of bootstrapping.

One response we might make is simply to insist that bootstrapping is acceptable for the special case of resolutions. Perhaps once we have resolved to do something, that does give us reason to do it. The justification comes from the need to maintain and develop the faculty of will-power, a need which does not apply to the case of intention more generally. If we fail to persist in our resolutions our faculty of will-power will be diminished. Equally importantly, since we will surely come to doubt instances of *Effective*, our confidence in the power of that faculty will be diminished.

I think that these are indeed important considerations. But they cannot give us a completely general defence of the reasonableness of will-power. For while it might sometimes be the case that the need to maintain and develop the faculty of will-power will outweigh the reason for succumbing to the temptation, there is no guarantee that this will generally be the case.

We need a different approach. It is provided, I think, by the distinction between reconsidering and revising a resolution. We have been talking as though the formation of a resolution provided a reason to perform the action which that resolution concerns. As such it would count in with the other

---

[30] For further discussion, see Broome 2001.

64 / Richard Holton

reasons for and against performing that action, and hence with the reasons for and against revising the resolution. However, prior to revision comes reconsideration: if the resolution isn't reconsidered it won't be revised. And a decisive reason against reconsideration need not be a decisive reason against revision once a reconsideration is made.

The basic idea is this: a resolution provides one with a reason against any reconsideration that is prompted by the desires that the resolution was designed to defeat. This reason has a special status: it will only be rationally defeated in very unusual circumstances (such as the example of water abstinence, when the resolution was trivial and the desires especially, and justifiably, strong). However, once a reconsideration is under way, things change. The fact that a resolution was made before is just one consideration among many. While it might be decisive (perhaps on the grounds of the need to maintain the faculty of will-power), it might well not be.

I suggest then that the exercise of will-power, understood as a block on reconsideration, need not be irrational in the way that it would be if we understood it as the requirement that the outcome of a reconsideration should always be the maintenance of a resolution. The rationale for will-power is indeed pragmatic; provided that it leads to pragmatic advantage in general (a condition that I have not explored), we need not fear that its bootstrapping features give rise to irrationality.

We might make a parallel with the case of a perverse god, this time one who, say, punished every correct long-division calculation. One might envisage two different responses to this from the understandably aggrieved populace. The first would involve training themselves always to get the calculations wrong. That clearly would require their learning to be (at least theoretically) irrational. The second response would simply involve refraining, whenever possible, from calculating long divisions. That would put a substantial constraint on their lives, but it need involve no irrationality. Teaching yourself always to decide reconsiderations in favour of maintaining resolutions corresponds to the first of these responses; teaching yourself to avoid the reconsiderations corresponds to the second.

We might wonder whether this approach can shed light on any of the puzzle cases that have concerned writers on intention. I suspect that it can; and seeing this will shed more light on the way in which the defence of will-power is indeed pragmatic. Consider first the toxin puzzle that Gregory Kavka (1983) devised. You are offered an enormous sum of money if you will form the intention to drink a toxin that will cause very unpleasant symptoms for a

How is Strength of Will Possible? / 65

day, but will not otherwise harm you. Let us suppose that you judge that the benefit of the money hugely outweighs the cost of the unpleasant symptoms, and so judge it rational to form the intention to drink the toxin. However, there is a catch. You will be rewarded simply for forming the intention (as indicated by a reliable brain scanner) and your reward will come before the moment to drink the toxin arrives. Can you still rationally form the intention to drink the toxin? There is an argument that you cannot. Suppose, for *reductio*, that you could. Then, once you have received the money, it will be rational to revise your intention, since you now only stand to lose by drinking the toxin. But knowing this, it will not be possible for you rationally to form the intention in the first place.

Much debate has centred on whether or not it is rational to revise the intention once you have the money. Some have argued that, given the pragmatic advantages that forming the intention brings, it is rational to do anything that is needed in order to form it. So if one needs to avoid revising it, it is rational to avoid revising it (Gauthier 1994: 707–9). Others counter that, pragmatic advantages notwithstanding, it must be rational to revise an intention whose realization will bring only costs: the best that can be said is that it is rational to make oneself irrational (Bratman 1987: 101–6; 1998).

On the approach suggested here, we can do justice to both of these thoughts. For there are now two questions: whether it is rational to reconsider the intention; and whether, once it is reconsidered, it is rational to revise it.[31] On the second of these questions, I side with those who argue that revision must be the rational course. The question of the rationality of reconsideration is harder. It seems that two different rules of practical rationality are engaged, and that they pull in opposite directions. You now believe that circumstances have changed in such a way as to defeat the purpose of the intention (you have the money), so you have grounds for reconsideration.[32] On the other hand, this is a resolution, and the desire to break it is the desire to avoid the unpleasant symptoms that it was designed to overcome, so in so far as there is a rational requirement to be strong-willed, there are grounds against reconsideration. We can thus understand why our reaction is so uncertain here.

We might argue that if the justification for the rules of practical reason is pragmatic, then the beneficial rule, urging non-reconsideration, should

---

[31] McClennen phrases his discussion in terms of the rationality of reconsideration rather than the rationality of revision (McClennen 1990: 227–31).

[32] This was one of the rules of thumb for revision of intentions that I gave in Holton 1999.

66 / Richard Holton

dominate. The difficulty here is that the toxin case is a one-off. It is, to say the least, unusual to meet cases of this form in daily life. So it is unlikely that there would be a general pragmatic advantage to be gained by refusing to reconsider resolutions in cases in which we believed them to be pointless. Nor, I suspect, could we rationally decide not to reconsider as a result of identifying something as a toxin case. Non-reconsideration has to be a non-reflective business, resulting from habits and tendencies that have been deeply ingrained.[33] Once we come to the point of deciding whether to reconsider it will be too late: by then we will already be reconsidering.

Nevertheless, we can bring out the pragmatic rationale for non-reconsideration in cases like these by considering situations in which there would be reason and opportunity for the relevant habits and tendencies to be laid down. Suppose that we lived in an environment in which almost every decision had the form of the toxin case. Suppose that, for his own mysterious ends, the perverse god arranged things so that the necessities of life were distributed to those who intended to endure subsequent (and by then pointless) suffering. Imagine how we would bring up our children. If resolute commitment to such intentions were really the only way to form them, that is just what we would encourage. We would inculcate habits of non-reconsideration of resolutions even when they seemed pointless. Such habits would, I suggest, appear perfectly rational.[34]

A more realistic instance of this comes with another set of cases that have been much discussed: those involving reciprocity (Gauthier 1994; Bratman 1998; Broome 2001). Suppose that I agree to do some onerous thing for you if you agree to do some onerous thing for me. Both of us would benefit from the exchange. Suppose that, by the nature of the case, you need to act first, and do so. I have got what I want. Why should I now bother reciprocating? But then we have a parallel worry to that which arose in the toxin case. For once you realize that I would have no reason to reciprocate, and so come to believe that I would not do so, you will not act either. So neither of us will benefit. It seems that we cannot get rational reciprocators; or, more accurately, that rational agents driven entirely by their self-interest cannot come to reciprocate in circumstances like these.

---

[33] For discussion, see Bratman 1987: 61.

[34] Although Bratman (1987) makes much of the distinction between the refusal to reconsider and the refusal to revise ('the two-tier theory'), he does not himself advocate this as providing a solution to the toxin puzzle. See Bratman 1998: 88–9 and 1999: 4, 8–9. His reason for rejecting this solution comes at least partly from his conviction that it must be irrational to persist in drinking the toxin.

Once again I suggest that the rational agents need to develop, and get others to recognize, a tendency not to reconsider their resolutions to reciprocate. And once again I suggest that this involves no irrationality. Moreover, it seems that this resonates with our moral expectations. We do not ask that those who have entered into reciprocal agreements should go on to consider whether to go through with their side of the deal, and conclude that they should. We rather ask that their compliance should come without further consideration. This is not to deny that compliance is defeasible: if something far more important comes up, or it is realized how wrong compliance would be, then it should be reconsidered. But where these factors don't intervene, reconsideration, even if it doesn't result in revision, provides an instance of a much discussed moral failing: the failing that consists in having one thought too many.

Conclusion

My contention, then, is that there is a faculty of will-power, which works, quite rationally, to block reconsideration of resolutions; and that strength of will is standardly achieved by its exercise. Moreover, this shows that the Humean theory of motivation, and the theory that results from simply adding intentions to it, are false. I do not pretend to have established these conclusions with certainty. I have drawn on our subjective experience, and on empirical work in social psychology. Subjective experience is notoriously misleading; and the empirical work is sufficiently recent, and sufficiently open to alternative interpretation, that its status is not yet secure. Whether or not my conclusions stand, I hope at least to have shown that the truth in this area cannot be settled a priori. There is conceptual space for many competing theories; it will take a lot of work to determine which is right.

3

Akrasia, Collective and Individual

Philip Pettit

Perhaps the most famous analogy in the history of philosophical argument is that which Plato draws in the *Republic* between the constitution of the city and the constitution of the soul. The analogy is justly famous, for it sheds light on many aspects of mentality and personhood. In particular, as I shall try to show here, the analogy—or at least something close to the analogy—sheds light on the nature of akrasia, or lack of self-control.

How to characterize akrasia? Without going into an analysis of our ordinary conceptions of the phenomena associated with this term, I shall assume that an agent is akratic when the following conditions are fulfilled. The agent holds by intentional states in the light of which he or she sees that a certain response is required; the states involved may be beliefs or desires, judgements or intentions, and the required response will typically be an action. The agent functions under conditions that are intuitively favourable, and within limits that are intuitively feasible, for acting as required; there is nothing abnormal about how things transpire within his or her constitution or circumstances— no malfunction, for example, or perturbation. But nevertheless the agent fails to act in the required manner.[1]

This chapter was presented at the Centre for Applied Philosophy and Public Ethics, Canberra, March 2001, at the conference Weakness of Will and Varieties of Practical Irrationality, Montreal, May 2001, and at the University of Michigan, April 2002. I benefited greatly from the various comments I received on these occasions, particularly from the remarks of my Montreal commentator, Tom Hurka. I was also helped by the comments of an anonymous referee.

[1] What is it for agents to see a certain response—say, an action—as something required of them? It means more than that the response is actually required, say under rational constraints; the agents must also recognize it as required. But recognizing it as required may mean one of two intuitively different things. Either that the agents notice that so far as they continue to entertain

Akrasia, Collective and Individual / 69

This conception of akrasia will pick out different phenomena if normal conditions are construed in different ways (Pettit 1999). But in practice it is going to be pretty stable, since most construals will agree on the sort of thing that makes functioning abnormal: blind spots, *idées fixes*, fallacious habits of reasoning, affective pathologies, ineradicable compulsions, mesmerizing intimidation or temptation, and so on. The important aspect of the conception is that it identifies akrasia with a mode of failure that is distinct from anything due to internal malfunction or external pressure. We track that general sort of breakdown in ordinary talk of weakness of the will, I believe, though I do not claim that all the nuances of such talk are reflected in my characterization of akrasia.

I look here at what is necessary for a group to constitute an agent that can display akrasia in this sense, and at what steps such a group might take to establish self-control. I do so, not just because the topic has some interest in itself, but—the Platonic message—because the discussion suggests some lessons about how we should think of akrasia in the individual as well as in the collective case. Under the image that the lessons support, akrasia is a sort of constitutional disorder: a failure to achieve a unity projected in the avowal of agency. This image fits well with the constitutional model of the soul that Christine Korsgaard (1999) finds in Plato's analogy, and her explication of the analogy offers a precedent—and indeed a prompt—for the line taken here.[2]

The chapter is in three sections. In the first I look at three sorts of groups that are incapable, so I argue, of akrasia: collections, cooperatives, and unified cooperatives. In the second section I introduce a further sort of group, the self-unifying cooperative, and I argue that this is capable of akratic behaviour. And then in the final section I draw out some lessons of the discussion that bear on individual as well as collective akrasia.

Groups Incapable of Akrasia

A group or collectivity will constitute an agent just so far as it is the bearer of intentional properties: just so far as it forms attitudes like beliefs and desires,

the requiring states, and perform up to standard, they must rationally display the response. Or that the agents explicitly or implicitly avow the requirement as something to which they hold themselves—and perhaps invite others to hold them—so that they must see any later failure, not just as a failure of rationality, but as a reason for self-rebuke. I do not need to rule here on whether avowal of the requirement flouted is necessary for akrasia.

[2] See too Adams 1985: 10. Another important source of ideas in this area is provided by Hurley 1989.

70 / Philip Pettit

or judgements and intentions, and acts on their basis. There are a number of different accounts, each progressively richer than the preceding, of what is required for a group to be an agent in this sense and, in particular, an agent capable of akrasia. I shall argue that only a group that satisfies the richest account is capable of agency and akrasia.

Collections

The least demanding account of what is required for a group to be an agent only ascribes agency in a very strained sense and need not detain us long. It is the sort of account suggested by Anthony Quinton (1975: 17) when he says:

To ascribe mental predicates to a group is always an indirect way of ascribing such predicates to its members. With such mental states as beliefs and attitudes, the ascriptions are of what I have called a summative kind. To say that the industrial working class is determined to resist anti-trade union laws is to say that all or most industrial workers are so minded.

According to this account, any number of individuals, no matter how arbitrarily related to one another, will be a bearer of intentional properties and will constitute an agent—albeit something less than an agent proper— just so far as the individuals in the group display a certain similarity in intentional properties. There is nothing to a group's being minded—being the bearer of mental properties—and to its revealing that mind in action than is already assured by the fact that it is a collection or set of individually minded agents.

This account is so generous that it amounts, as indeed Quinton intends, to an eliminativism about group agents. In the easy, summative sense in which a collection may hold a certain attitude—say, the belief that p—any subset is just as likely to hold an attitude, even a conflicting attitude, and so is any larger set of which the collection is a subset. The account makes it so easy for collectivities to hold attitudes that it represents them as agents only in a make-believe sense: 'only by figment, and for the sake of brevity of discussion' (Austin 1869: 364). No such fictive agents could display anything remotely like akrasia. Far from holding by attitudes which they might fail to live up to in action, they hold by no attitudes whatsoever (Pettit 2001a, ch. 5; 2002).

Cooperatives

The debunking account of group agency that Quinton represents has been roundly rejected in the recent literature and has served as a stimulus to the development of a family of much more demanding analyses. These analyses agree that a group cannot have intentional attitudes in a serious, literal sense, just in virtue of most of its members having corresponding individual attitudes. The members must cooperate in doing something in order to bring group attitudes into existence. They must form intentions about what is to transpire, they must reveal those intentions to one another, and they must adopt measures that give effect to relevant intentions: measures such as those involved in accepting a certain formula as a matter of joint belief or endorsing a certain authority as acting on behalf of the group. This style of analysis focuses on group intentions and group judgements, where judgements are beliefs associated, not just with a disposition to action, but with the acceptance of a formula. It suggests—and I shall go along with the idea—that those are going to be the principal kinds of intentional state that collectives exemplify.

The approach generally followed in this literature is to take a grouping of two or perhaps three agents and to try and identify the conditions under which we would ascribe a collective intention or judgement or action to them (Gilbert 1989; Meijers 1994; Searle 1995; Tuomela 1995; Bratman 1999; Miller 2001).The analyses all draw in some way on work in game theory and related disciplines, in particular on the idea that people in interaction will form beliefs about one another's dispositions, beliefs about one another's beliefs about such dispositions, beliefs about one another's beliefs about such beliefs, and so on.

The analyses generally agree that in order for joint intention to appear, for example, people must share in a mutual belief of this sort that bears on what each believes about the dispositions and beliefs of others, and on how each is ready to act in the event of others acting in a complementary way. Thus Michael Bratman (1999) argues that you and I will have a shared intention to do something just in case (a) you intend that we do it and I intend that we do it; (b) we each intend that we do it because (a) holds; and (c) those clauses are matters of which we are each aware, each aware that we are each aware, and so on in a hierarchy of mutual belief. The hierarchy will mean that each believes the matter in question—say, that p; each believes that each believes that p;

72 / Philip Pettit

each believes that each believes that each believes that p; and so on. And so on, most plausibly, in this mode: while not everyone may believe the required condition at each higher level, at least no one will disbelieve it at any such level (Lewis 1969).[3]

I am happy to assume that a common-belief analysis of some kind will give us a plausible story as to what is involved in a group's forming a judgement or intention, or performing an action. Common beliefs about the group's judgements and intentions will materialize fairly spontaneously among people in face-to-face groups of two or three. And they will materialize in groups with larger memberships on the basis of common beliefs as to the procedures to be followed in identifying the judgements and intentions of the group. Those procedures will typically involve voting among members— majoritarian voting in most plausible instances—or voting among those whom members elect as authorities. The votes required may be active or virtual. Someone will cast a virtual vote in favour of an arrangement or initiative to the extent that he could, as a matter of common belief, contest it—with whatever chance of success—but chooses not to do so. To vote for something in the active sense is to say 'Yea'; to vote in the virtual sense is to be in a position to say 'Nay' and to refrain from exercising that option.

We had no hesitation in saying that a group agent that is merely a collection of individually minded agents cannot display anything approximating akrasia. But what now of the collection whose members cooperate to derive judgements and intentions from their individual views, whether on the basis of some formal voting mechanism or in a more spontaneous manner? What of the sort of group that we can describe as a cooperative as distinct from a mere collection of individuals? Such a group will be minded on an indirect basis that allows the mind of the group—its pattern of judgements and

---

[3] There are a number of disputes that divide writers in this recent literature and they come up in particular with the analysis of group intention. One bears on the effect-of-intention question: whether it is necessary for collective intention that those who try to enact it are licensed— perhaps licensed on the basis of an implicit agreement—in rebuking those who fail to do their part in advancing or securing the intention. Another relates to the intended-content question: whether it is necessary that each of us in the group intend not just that I, this individual, behave in a certain way—presumably this is necessary—but also that we, the group, do so. And a third concerns the intending-subject question: whether in addition we, the group, must form an intention to do something—at whatever locus this is to be formed—such that this may not reflect anything that I or you intend that we do. I do not intend here to try to adjudicate any of these disputes, though the position adopted in the next section does have implications for how they should be resolved.

intentions—to come apart from the minds of its individual members. So does that mean that it will be capable of agency? I argue not.

The group will generate its group attitudes from the attitudes of individual members, forming on every issue an attitude that reflects the inputs of those members. In the typical, large-scale case it will tend to do this by relying on some explicit or implicit voting procedure. But the trouble with a group agent that operates solely by such moves is that it may not have the sort of rational unity or integrity that we require in an agent proper, and in particular in the agent that is capable of akrasia.

By a line of argument that has been widely endorsed in recent philosophical thought, a system will pass as an intentional agent only if it preserves intentional attitudes over time, and forms, unforms, and acts on those attitudes—at least within intuitively feasible limits and under intuitively favourable conditions—in a rationally permissible manner: only if it displays a certain rational unity (Dennett 1987; Pettit 1993, ch. 1). If the system believes that p and comes across evidence that not-p, it must tend to unform that belief. If the system believes that p and learns that if p then q, it must come to form the belief that q or to unform one of the other beliefs. If the system desires that p, believes that by Xing it can bring it about that p, and believes that other things are equal, then it must tend to X. Let the system fail in such ways—in particular, let it fail in ways that cannot be explained by departures from favourable conditions or by breaches of feasible limits—and it will not have the structure our conception of agency leads us to expect.

Even if we introduce the sort of complexity postulated in the cooperative, that will not guarantee that cooperatives have the rational unity associated with intentionality. For such cooperatives may operate by conventions that allow rational disunity. The convention established in the mutual awareness of members may ordain, for example, that the collectivity shall be deemed to judge or intend whatever a majority of members vote for its judging or intending in a given case. And it is demonstrable that if such a convention obtains—if the attitudes of the collectivity are required to be continuous in that majoritarian way with the current votes of members—then the collectivity may be guilty of grievous irrationality. The convention will enable the group to form putative judgements and intentions one by one, but it will allow the formation of judgements and intentions that fail to cohere with one another as a whole. It will allow the group to sustain such an irrational jumble of would-be judgements and intentions that it does not qualify as an

74 / Philip Pettit

intentional agent proper and the states formed do not count as the judgements and intentions of such an agent.

How to demonstrate the threat of such a failure of rational unity? I have written elsewhere on the problem involved—the discursive dilemma, I call it—and I shall summarize the line of argument briefly here (Pettit 2001a, ch. 5; 2002; List and Pettit 2002, forthcoming). The problem derives from a predicament noticed in jurisprudence (Kornhauser and Sager 1986, 1993; Kornhauser 1992a,b. See too Chapman 1998; Brennan 2001). In essence, it comes to this. If we take a set of rationally connected issues and then ask a group of people to determine its view as a group on each of those issues, a majoritarian pattern of voting may lead the group to endorse inconsistent positions. It may do this, in particular, without any members of the group being individually inconsistent in their votes.

Consider any set of logically connected propositions: say, p, if p then q and q; or p, q, p and q. With a group of three people, A, B, and C, it is always possible for A and C to support the first, B and C the second, giving a majority verdict for each. Will there have to be a majority in favour of the third proposition? Not necessarily, for the only one obliged to vote for the third will be C; he is the only one who has affirmed the first two. Thus a majority may record a vote that p, a majority that if p then q, and only a minority that q. Or a majority may record a judgement that p, a majority a judgement that q, and only a minority the judgement that p and q.

The predicament can be well expressed with the help of a matrix (Figure 3.1). Take the case where a group of three people, A, B, and C, has to determine its views on each of three propositions, p, if p then q, and q, and where the procedure they follow is to assent to a proposition in the event of a majority supporting it, and to dissent otherwise. It is entirely possible that the members of the group will cast their votes on the pattern involved in Figure 3.1, for each individual expresses a consistent set of views in the votes that he or she casts according to that matrix. But if they do cast their votes on that pattern, then a majority will support p, a majority support if p then q and yet a majority reject q. And in that case the group as a whole will be committed to an inconsistent set of judgements.

The discursive dilemma shows that it is possible for perfectly consistent and coherent individuals to give majority support to each of a set of inconsistent or incoherent judgements; the dilemma consists in the fact that there is a hard choice between such majoritarian responsiveness to individual views and the achievement of collective rationality. The members comprising the

Akrasia, Collective and Individual / 75

	p	if p then q	q
A	Yes	No	No
B	No	Yes	No
C	Yes	Yes	Yes

Fig. 3.1

different majorities may vary, so that there is no individual who belongs to the majority on each issue and who is guilty as an individual of irrationality. In the scenario depicted in Figure 3.1, for example, there is a majority in favour of p, a majority in favour of if p then q, and a majority in favour of not-q, but there is no individual who votes for each of the judgements in that inconsistent set. A votes against if p then q; B against p; and C, in effect, against not-q.

The lesson should be clear. In order for a collectivity to count as an intentional agent in a literal sense—and therefore as an agent capable of akrasia—not only must there be a basis in the cooperative disposition of members for ascribing judgements and intentions and actions to the collective; that is the point on which the mutual-awareness literature rightly insists. There must also be a basis for thinking of the collectivity as a subject that is rationally unified in such a way that, within feasible limits and under favourable conditions, we can expect it to live up to the constraints associated with intentionality; it will enter and exit putative states of belief and desire, judgement and intention, in a coherent, rational way, and perform in action as those states require. But the existence of discursive dilemmas means that there is no reason to expect a cooperative formed by individuals to display rational unity in the attitudes it aggregatively constructs, even in intuitively the most normal of circumstances: even, for example, when everyone in the group is rational, well-informed, and free to vote as he or she wishes. Thus there is no reason to treat the cooperative as an agent proper; there is no reason to think that it will have a single, unified vision by which to orient in the world.

This observation is enough on its own to ensure that the cooperative collection is incapable of akrasia; there can be no akrasia without agency proper. But the point in any case is palpable. Just as the group in Figure 3.1 asserts that p and that if p then q but denies that q, so a group might be led by voting—led even in the most normal of circumstances—to endorse propositions that make a certain action rational and yet to reject that action. Would it display akrasia in such a case? Of course not. The failure involved would be the failure to constitute an agent, not a failure—akratic in character—to perform as an agent should.

The discussion so far supports two negative results: first, that a mere collection of individual agents cannot constitute an agent capable of displaying akrasia; and, secondly, that a cooperative formed by such agents cannot do so either, so far as it is vulnerable to discursive dilemmas. But there is a third negative result that we can also derive from consideration of these cases and I turn now to this.

Unified Cooperatives

Suppose that a collection of individuals operates by voting on separate issues as they come up one by one. And now imagine that for some unconscious reason—maybe as a result of how the members are designed, maybe as a result of how their views happen to be structured—the voting gives rise to irrational results only under conditions that we can independently discount as abnormal conditions of functioning. The collection is rationally unified, though only in a more or less mechanical manner. Would such a group be an intentional agent? And, more particularly, would it be an agent that is capable of akrasia?

The sort of group agent envisaged—and I do not say that it is a plausible entity—would resemble the simple intentional system that most of us take non-human animals like cats and dogs to be. Dogs appear to form attitudes of belief and desire, to act on the basis of those attitudes, and to update them appropriately so that under most conditions of functioning they satisfy constraints of consistency and the like. Yet they do not do this through ever becoming aware of irrationalities as such and adjusting so as to avoid them. They are designed so that under normal conditions, as we intuitively think of them, such irrationalities just happen not to emerge. The unified cooperative envisaged under our current hypothesis would display a similar, blind disposition to avoid irrationality, at least under most circumstances, and it would make a similar claim to be regarded as an intentional agent.

I am happy to think of dogs and cats as intentional agents. They act in a manner that is well explained by the presence of intentional attitudes and they are disposed, however blindly, to display a degree of rational unity; or at least this is so under intuitively favourable conditions and within feasible limits (Pettit 1993; McGeer and Pettit 2002). For the same reason, then, I am happy to think that the unified cooperative envisaged in our thought experiment might count as an intentional agent too. But would it count as an agent capable of akrasia? As in the case of the mere collection and the cooperative, I argue not.

Suppose that the unified cooperative makes certain putative judgements, or forms certain putative intentions, apparently recognizing in light of those states that a certain response is required of it. And imagine now, as we might expect of an akratic agent, that it fails to display that response. Would we be entitled in these circumstances to ascribe akrasia to it?

By the account of akrasia sketched at the beginning of this chapter, we would be entitled to take the group as akratic if it were indeed an intentional agent and if conditions of functioning were normal. But if the unified cooperative failed to display rational unity under normal conditions, then that would provide evidence that undermined the attribution of agency as such, in which case there would be no reason to ascribe akrasia. We might save the attribution of agency by revising our view of its intentional attitudes. But to save the attribution of agency in this way, of course, would be to represent the agent as performing in the way required and to eliminate any appearance of akrasia.

The problem with the unified cooperative is that it passes as an intentional agent only so far as it reveals intentional attitudes in a rationally unified pattern of operation. There are states it enters and exits such that the ways they are formed and unformed—say, on the basis of voting—and the ways they operate in relation to one another, and ultimately in relation to behaviour, provide evidence that they are the intentional attitudes of a single agent. Let the unified cooperative fail on the operational side, therefore—let it fail to display rational unity under conditions that cannot be discounted as abnormal for functioning—and its title to being an intentional agent must falter. There will be no plausible evidence for the rather extravagant hypothesis that it is an intentional agent but one that is suffering akrasia.

This third result should be no surprise, given that the unified cooperative is an analogue of the non-human animal that achieves rational unity in a blind or mechanical way. For the argument just used will apply to non-human animals as well. Anything that might be taken as evidence of akrasia in such an animal will tend to undermine our confidence that it is an intentional system. Or it will lead us to revise our account of that creature's intentional attitudes,

78 / Philip Pettit

so that it no longer looks akratic. It is no surprise, therefore, that by our ordinary lights dogs and cats and the like do not display anything like akratic behaviour.

A Group Capable of Akrasia

We have seen that collective akrasia is not going to be realizable in a mere collection, in a cooperative, or even in a unified cooperative. But these three negative results point us towards a positive claim and I try to describe and defend this claim in the present section.

In order for a collection of agents to be capable of counting as an intentional agent in its own right, and therefore as an agent capable of akrasia, it is necessary for it to be able to form states that are fit for the role of intentional attitudes: say, the role of judgements and intentions. Call this *the cooperative requirement* of collective agency. But in order for those states actually to play the role of intentional attitudes it is equally necessary that the collection be able to unify them rationally with one another and with the behaviours that can be ascribed to the group. And if the collection is to be the sort of agent that can display akrasia, it is necessary that it be able to unify them rationally in something more than the mechanical manner of the unified cooperative. Call this *the self-unifying requirement* of collective agency.

With the cooperative and self-unifying requirements in mind, we can describe the profile of a group that transcends the three sorts of collections we have described. This will be a cooperative that takes steps to promote the achievement, as such, of its own rational unity or integrity. I think of this self-unifying cooperative as an integration of individuals or as a social integrate.

It is relatively easy to see how such a group might emerge. Let a collection of people establish or grow into a common purpose or purposes, on the basis of various levels of common belief. Let it face a variety of issues, perhaps at the same time, perhaps at different times, that it needs to resolve in order to pursue its purposes. Let it initially determine its view about each of those issues—taken separately—on the basis of some majoritarian form of voting, active or virtual. Let it baulk, however, in the event that the views thereby espoused—whether at the same or at different times—should prove not to cohere with one another, or not to cohere with the actions that it takes: let it be sensitive as such to the requirements of coherence, recognizing that they are grounded in the requirements of agency. And, finally, let it take steps in such an event that guard against rational disunity; let it strive to endorse only views that can be integrated with one another into a single rational vision of how things are and of how it is desirable that they should be.[4]

The integration of individuals established on the basis of such a mode of functioning would have an irresistible claim to being an intentional agent in its own right. It would embrace a rationally unified vision of things and it would act rationally on the basis of that vision. Moreover, it would show itself to be aware of the constraints that must be satisfied by a rational agent and it would be disposed to act so as to try to satisfy those constraints. It is hard to see what further credentials could be required in order to establish agency. True, the group envisaged will have no autonomous means of perception, no emotions in its own right, and no spontaneous inferential or other dispositions; it will exist and operate only by courtesy of individual contributions and only under painstaking procedures of aggregation and correction. But the group envisaged will have an intentionally unified vision of the world and will generally act as that vision requires (Rovane 1997). However bloodless and robotic it may be, there is no good reason to deny that it has the standing of an agent. So at any rate I shall assume here.

The elements required for the emergence of an integration of agents are all readily available in day-to-day life. The richest requirement is that the members of the group have to be aware as such of the constraints to be satisfied by a rational agent, so that they can adjust appropriately if they find that the constraints are breached. But this is not problematic. We have already assumed that in aggregating their views into collective beliefs the members rely on getting the group to accept relevant formulae. If people understand a formula, say 'p', then they have to know, more or less fully, what sort of thing provides inductive evidence in its favour and what provides evidence against; which propositions are consistent with it and which inconsistent; which

---

[4] Why suppose that the individuals consider the issues separately? Why suppose, for example, that they consider whether the group should endorse q, in abstraction from the question as to whether it has already endorsed p and if p then q? The argument could be run without this supposition, but two considerations make it a natural one to make. First, there will be no loss in having the individuals consider the issues separately, so far as they are capable of putting any resultant incoherence right. And secondly, it would seem to be better policy to let the incoherences emerge, and then to look at how they should be put right, rather than to have individuals privilege existing group commitments and avoid incoherences emerging in the first place; it may be the existing commitments that should rationally be revised and not the commitment most recently supported by individual voting.

80 / Philip Pettit

propositions entail it and which are entailed by it; and so on. But if they know this, then they know the constraints of rationality that a believer that p, or of course someone who intends to make it the case that p, will have to satisfy; what those constraints rule out are precisely responses that breach inductive coherence, deductive consistency, and the like.

Integrations of the kind described are perfectly familiar entities. Think of public bodies or business corporations or private associations or think of a few collaborators in some enterprise. Every such collection of people is going to have a more or less well-identified set of purposes to which its members have to subscribe. And every such collection is going to form judgements and intentions in the course of devising plans for the advancement of those purposes. The judgements and intentions are likely to be formed on the basis of explicit voting procedures, whether in the group as a whole or in one or another unit that it comprises. But the votes taken under such procedures will never be allowed to generate rational disunity. If they happen to support an irrational set of judgements or intentions then the group will take steps to revise or moderate the votes taken. Any group that regularly failed to do this would find itself unable to act systematically in pursuit of its goals; it would find itself trying to orient by an inconsistent map. And any group that failed to do this would be a laughing stock among its members and among the populace at large.

But would the integrated group of the kind envisaged be an agent capable of akrasia, or just an agent like the unified cooperative that we would never have compelling reason to treat as akratic? That is the crucial question for our purposes. I now proceed to argue, in positive vein, that there is little or no difficulty in thinking that an integration of individuals might prove to be an akratic agent, under the conception of akrasia used here.

There are three observations I make in the course of marshalling the argument. The first is that there is no problem of the kind that arose with unified cooperatives in acknowledging that integrations may be akratic. The second is that we can see why integrated collectivities might be subject, even in conditions that count as perfectly normal, to akrasia; we can see a difficulty in which akrasia might be sourced. And the third is that we can see strategies whereby an integrated group might hope to get over that difficulty and to avoid akrasia. This last observation is important because we would be loath to postulate lack of self-control in an agent that was incapable of making successful efforts to achieve self-control.

First Observation

The problem that would stop us from ascribing akrasia to the unified cooperative is that a condition necessary for doing this—that the agent fails to achieve rational unity under normal conditions of functioning—would deprive us of evidence to support the ascription of agency or the assumed characterization of the group's commitments. This problem will be overcome only where the failure to achieve rational unity does not undermine the claim to agency in this way. The potentially akratic group must be able to prove itself capable of agency, despite displaying the rational disunity associated with akrasia.

The integrated group characterized above will be able to meet this constraint. We can readily imagine such a group failing to behave in the way that the views it supports manifestly require, even under conditions that we have no independent reason to regard as abnormal. And we can imagine this happening in circumstances where we would have no lasting reason to doubt its status as an intentional agent. For the integrated group is capable, under our characterization, of recognizing rational constraints as such. And so it is capable of admitting, denouncing, and perhaps remedying the failure involved, recognizing it as a sort of failure that it should avoid.

If the group does this, and if it proves its sincerity in future behaviour or at least in behaviour in other domains, then there is going to be no problem in taking it to have intentional attitudes that it failed, despite conditions of functioning being normal, to act on. The fact that the group reaffirms the intentional states that it failed to live up to, acknowledging that failure as a failure, will make for a big contrast with the situation that might arise in the case of the unified cooperative. It will give us a powerful reason to countenance the group as an intentional agent, dismissing the counter-evidence that its behaviour constitutes. And if we do continue to take it as an intentional agent without revising our ascription of intentional attitudes, then we will have to ascribe akrasia to it.

The failure involved in akrasia means that the group does not satisfy the requirement of rational unity in the ordinary way that we would expect of an intentional agent. But the acknowledgement of failure will help to put right this shortfall from unity. When an integrated group admits such failure, then it can be seen as disowning the akratic action, denying it the status of a behaviour that reflects its intentional states: its presumptively unified way of seeing the world. It can be seen as laying claim to rational unity

82 / Philip Pettit

of a second-best sort: a unity that can exist in spite of the disunity displayed in actual behaviour.

Second Observation

The second observation I want to make is that the sort of failure associated with akrasia is perfectly intelligible in the case of the integrated group. There is a compelling reason why we might expect a group of the sort envisaged to find it difficult to get its act together and to manifest in action a unified understanding of what there is and what there ought to be. There is a compelling reason to expect such difficulty—and the possibility of failure—even when the group is functioning in intuitively normal conditions. This has to do with the fact that any integrated group is going to be plagued by discursive dilemmas.

Consider a simple group that operates by taking a majority vote on every issue that it confronts in the course of pursuing its purposes. The group may be the editorial committee of a journal, the workforce in some joint enterprise, a body that is commissioned to discharge a certain public duty, or whatever. Suppose that the group operates under intuitively normal circumstances: nothing stops members from debating fully and rationally the position that they ought to adopt on each issue, none of them is prey to any sort of irrationality in the votes that they cast, the voting procedures followed do not give rise to any particular difficulty, and so on. It is entirely possible, nonetheless, that the group will confront discursive dilemmas. And it is entirely possible that despite operating in normal conditions, and despite having and trying to exercise the self-regulative resources needed to promote collective rationality and unity, still it will fail to act as its official and continuing view requires it to act. It is entirely possible, in other words, that it will display akrasia.

The point is best established with reference to an example (cf. Blackburn 2001). Take a non-commercial academic journal with an editorial committee of three members that resolves all the issues it faces by majority vote and that is not subject to intuitively abnormal conditions of functioning. Suppose that the committee votes in January for promising subscribers that there will be no price rise within five years. Suppose that it votes in mid-year that it will send papers to external reviewers and be bound by their decision as to whether or not to publish any individual piece. And suppose that in December it faces the issue as to whether it should be prepared in principle to publish papers that involve technical apparatus and are quite costly to produce. The earlier votes will argue against its being prepared to do this, since a rise in the number of technical papers submitted and endorsed by reviewers—endorsed, without any eye to overall production costs—might force it to renege on one or other of those commitments. But nonetheless, of course, a majority may support the acceptance of technical papers, without any individual being irrational. The members of the committee might vote as in Figure 3.2.

Discursive dilemmas of this kind present a group with a hard choice. Members have to choose between, on the one side, letting the group be fully responsive to individual views, as recorded in majority voting, and on the other, ensuring that the group is collectively rational. Sometimes it will be hard for the group to determine where the demand for collective rationality leads: whether they should revise one of the earlier votes in Figure 3.2, for example, or the vote they have just taken. But even if there is no difficulty of this kind—even if it is clear what collective rationality requires of the group—they may find it hard to live up to that requirement; they may find themselves prey to akrasia.

They will not find it hard to live up to the requirement, of course, if they are individually devoted in a consuming, wholehearted way to the group and are in no way tempted to defect from what it requires of them. A group whose members were dedicated in this way would operate like a perfectly virtuous agent, always spontaneously supporting what the balance of available reasons requires of the group. But not all members need be so devoted to the group in which they figure; and when something less than full collective devotion is on offer, then it may prove very difficult for members to get their act together and ensure that the group lives up to the considerations that it endorses.

Suppose in the example just given that the group looks again at its votes in the first two columns and decides that they should stand, whether on their

	Price freeze	External review	Technical papers
A	Yes	No	Yes
B	No	Yes	Yes
C	Yes	Yes	No

Fig. 3.2

84 / Philip Pettit

own merits or because it is now too late to change them. In other words, suppose that the members quickly resolve the question as to what collective rationality requires of the group: it requires them to limit the number of technical papers to be accepted. Their shared judgement, perhaps unanimous, is that if the group is to affirm its claim to unity and agency, then the members have no choice but to limit the acceptance of technical papers. It is still possible in this event, and without conditions of functioning ceasing to be normal, that the group will find it hard to act on that determination: in effect, to act against the majority who support an open policy on technical papers.

That majority might remain individually and stubbornly inclined to support the acceptance of technical papers. And so we can imagine them turning their eyes from the group as a whole, and sticking to their votes when the issue is raised again. We can imagine them refusing to hear the call of the group as a whole and acting like encapsulated centres of voting who are responsive only to their own modular prompts. As we imagine this, we envisage the group taking an akratic line in the policy about the technical papers.

What might motivate the recalcitrant majority in the sort of case envisaged? They might be moved by a more or less selfish inclination or identification, being technically minded themselves; or they might be moved by a sense of fairness towards those who would be disadvantaged; or whatever. Personal virtue is as likely as personal vice to source recalcitrance towards a collectivity. Virtue in the individual members of a group may make for akrasia in the group as a whole.

But could it really be rational for the recalcitrant members to stick to a deviant pattern of voting, whether out of individual bias or virtue? I don't see why not. They would satisfy their private motives, partial or impartial, by doing so. And they might individually expect to get away with such voting, being outvoted by others; they might expect to be able to free-ride. Or they might hope that even if a majority remains recalcitrant, this will not cause problems: there will not be a deluge in the number of technical papers submitted and accepted, and the committee can get away with holding by all of the three commitments involved.

What, however, if it is clear to a recalcitrant member that if he or she doesn't change vote, then the group will indeed fail to avoid inconsistency? Could it be rational for that person to stick to the deviant pattern of voting? That would depend on how far it matters to the member in question that the group should retain an uncontroversial claim to unity and agency in the domain in question. If that does not matter in sufficient measure, then it will make rational sense for that person to refuse to go along with what he or she agrees is required of the group, thereby putting its status as a unified agent in jeopardy.

It is characteristic of akrasia that akratic behaviour does not actually undermine the status of a subject as an agent, even if it does put that status in jeopardy. Akratic agents will be able to retain that status so far as they prove capable of acknowledging and denouncing the failure and, ideally, reforming their behaviour in future—or if not actually achieving reform, at least establishing that the failure is untypical: while they may not get their act together in the domain in question, this is not characteristic of their performance in general.

As it is with akratic agents in general, so it can be with the sort of group agent envisaged. The group can fail to act as it agrees is required and yet retain its status as an agent by proving capable of admitting the failure involved and, in token of the admission, taking steps to reverse policy, or at least to insulate the failure and limit the damage it does. If it does not prove capable of this, then it cannot be represented, and cannot represent itself, as an agent that acts out of a rationally unified view of the world. It can be represented only as an aggregate of different agents, not as an agent unified within itself: only as many, not as one.

Third Observation

The final observation I want to make in support of my claim that integrated groups can display akrasia is that there are strategies available to any such group whereby it might seek to guard against this sort of failure. One way in which a group might be protected against akrasia, of course, would be through its members being individually so devoted to the collectivity that it inevitably behaves in the fashion of a virtuous agent. But short of such a radical alternative to akrasia, there are a number of means whereby a group might try to ensure that it achieves continence: that is, a form of self-control that does not require virtuous devotion (Pettit and Smith 1993).

The strategies I have in mind often serve two purposes: first, to show the group a salient way out of a discursive dilemma, by identifying a course of action whereby coherence can be achieved, and secondly, to guard against the unwillingness of some members to go along with that course of action. The first purpose is associated with self-direction, the second with self-control.

86 / Philip Pettit

Here we are only concerned with the strategies as means of achieving the second, self-controlling effect (see List and Pettit 2002).

The first and most obvious strategy for promoting self-control in a collectivity would be for the group to ensure that the costs of failing to achieve such self-control are significant. The members might pre-commit themselves to being collectively rational, for example, exposing themselves to a cost that all will have to bear in the event of failing to achieve such rationality. Or the members might lay down procedures under which those who remain recalcitrant in the attempt to achieve collective rationality will be expelled or punished in some way.

A second sort of strategy for achieving collective continence would have the group seek, not to raise the costs of failing to achieve self-control, but to restrict the opportunities for such failure. Thus the group might restrict the range of matters in respect of which it acts, recognizing that troubles loom outside the boundary thereby imposed. This strategy is likely to be of limited use, since the group may not be able to impose an effective boundary without compromising its ability to advance its purposes. Or, alternatively, the group might take steps to try and ensure that differences of the sort that give rise to discursive dilemmas do not emerge. The group might seek, by whatever means, to bring members of the group together in their views as to what the group should judge and on how it should act. The means adopted could involve an increase in deliberative discussion—though that could backfire by sharpening rather than moderating differences (Sunstein 2002)—or a resort to less savoury ways of shaping and homogenizing people's opinions.

A third sort of strategy whereby a group might achieve self-control—and indeed self-direction—is probably more promising. The members of the group might follow a procedure whereby the decision on problematic issues is taken out of their individual hands. They might arrange to have such matters decided by more or less automatic procedures. This sort of self-denying ordinance comes in two particularly salient versions.

Under the first version of the strategy, the group would agree in advance that should different majorities support incoherent positions on certain sets of issues, then the positions adopted on some of those issues will dictate, independently of majority vote, the position that the group should adopt on others. Thus the group might decide that in the event of majorities having endorsed in the past positions that dictate a position on an issue that arises later, the earlier votes will rationally dictate the group position on that later issue. Or a group might decide that the positions adopted on more general, principled issues will rationally dictate the position to be adopted on matters of greater detail. Or whatever.

Under the second version of this strategy, the group would agree that, in the event of recalcitrance causing a problem—or indeed more generally—the group position will be determined by some designated officer, or perhaps by a small committee that is not so likely to be affected by discursive dilemmas. This strategy would enable the group to transcend the difficulty raised by such dilemmas in a smooth and unproblematic manner, though it would compromise the participatory character of the collective. As the first version privileges certain considerations in the formation of group views, this second version would privilege certain members.

These remarks should be sufficient to indicate that not only are integrated collectivities likely to be plagued by a malaise resembling akrasia. The malaise in question looks to be well deserving of the title of 'akrasia', so far as those groups are also likely to have access to strategies of self-control: strategies whereby the group can keep itself collectively rational, even though its members may not be wholeheartedly devoted to it.

The Lessons

The fact that akrasia in collectives takes the form described in the last section tells us something about akrasia as such, and in this final section I mention some lessons that we can draw from the discussion. I concentrate on three lessons in particular: first, that akrasia is not mechanical in character; secondly, that it is not essentially a hierarchical phenomenon in which lower-level elements revolt against a higher; and thirdly, that it is not exclusively action-centred in its manifestations: it can affect attitudes as well. In defending these lessons, I give support to something close to what Christine Korsgaard (1999) describes as a constitutional model of the role that reason plays in the person, though I do not defend the distinctively Kantian views with which she is associated.

Akrasia is not Mechanical in Character

The first lesson, according to which akrasia is not mechanical in character, derives from the discussion in the first section, where we saw that akrasia has no place in the mere collection, the cooperative, or even the unified cooperative. The unified cooperative represents a collective agent that operates in a more or less mechanical way, paralleling the mode of operation most of us ascribe to non-human animals like dogs and cats. It relies on voting and other mechanisms that generate candidate states for the role of judgements and intentions. And the psychology or organization of its members ensures, without anyone necessarily being aware of the fact, that those states will actually implement that role, at least under intuitively favourable circumstances and within intuitively feasible limits. They ensure that the unified cooperative will achieve and maintain rational unity in the way it forms and unforms such states and in the way the states lead to action.

I argued earlier that the unified cooperative cannot be indicted with akrasia because any failure to achieve rational unity would put its status as an agent in question, so that there would be no reason to think that it is an agent but one that is akratic. I supported that observation by pointing out that something very similar is going to be true of the non-human animal. Let such an animal behave in a way that makes no sense in the light of the intentional states ascribed to it, and let conditions be intuitively normal. We will naturally conclude in such a case either that it is not an agent proper or that our initial ascription of intentional states was mistaken. We will not have any good reason for regarding it as an akratic agent.

The lesson drawn in our discussion of collectives was that if a group agent is to be capable of akrasia then it must be an agent that can be aware as such of the constraints of rationality and that it must be able to regulate itself in the light of those constraints. Only an agent of that kind could fail to achieve rational unity in action, even in intuitively normal conditions, and yet count as an intentional agent proper. Only an agent of that kind would be able to establish its status as a rationally unified subject through recognizing and admitting the failure, representing the action in question as something that it does not endorse or own and as something, therefore, in which it was not really present as an agent.

The point made here would seem to apply more generally, as indeed we saw in the case of non-human animals. What it establishes is that akrasia presupposes a sort of agent that is not just brutely disposed to achieve a certain rational unity in action but that has the capacity to work intentionally at the achievement of such unity. The agent must be able to recognize the constraints that have to be satisfied by any system that holds by certain profiles of belief and desire and the like. And it must be able to identify the requirements of those constraints in its own case and, in principle, to regulate its performance so as to meet those requirements (Pettit 1993; McGeer and Pettit 2002). In short, it must be able to make normative judgements about the constraints it ought to satisfy in different cases, not just be disposed to satisfy those constraints in a more or less unthinking manner.

This lesson, to put it a bit more sharply, is that the agent that is capable of akrasia has got to be something more than just a decision-theoretic system in which states of belief and desire mutate and materialize in action according to standard requirements of rationality (*pace* Jackson 1984; see Pettit and Smith 1993). It has got to be able to express such states in assertions about what is the case and about what would ideally be the case, recognizing in virtue of that ability that this or that action is required of it: and recognizing this, despite the occasional failure—even in intuitively normal conditions—to act in the required way. No failure in a decision-theoretic system would give us compelling reason to ascribe akrasia if the subject in question did not have this sort of ability; it would only give us reason to posit a malfunction or to think again about our initial ascription of intentional states.

Akrasia is Not Necessarily a Hierarchical Phenomenon

The second lesson that I derive from our discussion is that akrasia is not an essentially hierarchical phenomenon. Traditional discussions of akrasia suggest that it has a deeply hierarchical aspect, representing it as the failure of a higher self to subdue a lower self, or the failure of the superior faculty of reason to suppress the base passions. 'Every rational creature, 'tis said, is oblig'd to regulate his actions by reason; and if any other motive or principle challenge the direction of his conduct, he ought to oppose it, 'till it be entirely subdu'd, or at least brought to a conformity with that superior principle' (Hume 1740/1978: 413).

The striking thing about the akrasia that I identified in collectives, however, is that it does not have a hierarchical aspect at all. The elements that are in conflict when akrasia strikes may be coordinate factors, not factors that are arranged in any order of power or authority. They are simply the different individuals involved, as in the example of the editorial committee that I discussed. Each of these has his or her own view as to what the group should judge and do and each is generally disposed to play his or her part in the integration of the group as an agent proper. But even when the demands of integration are discerned among the members, and even when conditions of functioning are normal, each is subject to the possibility of a certain

90 / Philip Pettit

recalcitrance of motivation: a modular encapsulation that blocks the achievement of harmony with the voices of others. When that recalcitrance surfaces on a wide front, the individuals fail to get their act together and the group fails to act as its commitments require. And that failure is precisely what constitutes akrasia.

If we agree that there is collective akrasia of this kind, then we must agree that akrasia is not necessarily hierarchical in character. The solution may involve subordinating some elements to others, as we saw, but the problem arises in the first place, not because of insubordination, but rather because of a failure of coordination. Does the collective case suggest, however, that akrasia in the individual may also take a non-hierarchical form? This question takes us into uncertain, speculative realms, but I cannot resist sketching a possibility under which at least some forms of individual akrasia would have a non-hierarchical character.

The individual who escapes akrasia, like the collective that does so, will prove thereby to be a creature of reason. But that this is so does not mean that reason is itself a faculty that has to impress its rule on more rebellious elements in the personality, subordinating them to its control. It may be, as in the collective case, that reason is a pattern to be achieved among the elements that go to make the agent, not itself one of the elements involved. Discourse with others or with themselves will make clear to agents that this or that action is required of them if they are to count as coherent and conversable. But consistently with an agent as a whole recognizing what coherence and conversability require—in parallel to how the group as a whole might recognize this—there may be different voices within his or her make-up that continue to register dissent and continue to prove recalcitrant. We may often think of akrasia materializing as a result of precisely that sort of recalcitrance triumphing.

What might be the voices that go to constitute an individual agent, in the way in which different individuals constitute a group? One possibility would be to conceive of the voices required as the different modalities of cognition and motivation—the different perspectives—between which individuals often describe themselves as being undecided. There are longer-term and shorter-term perspectives, for example; altruistic and egocentric, or social and personal perspectives; perspectives that are relatively warm or involved and perspectives that are relatively cool or detached; perspectives that differ so far as they are associated with substantively different sets of desirability characteristics; and so on. We might think of these perspectives all being engaged in decision-making, with the engagement being regulated by the agent's sense of what reason overall requires. And we might think of akrasia appearing so far as some of the perspectives prove resistant to the adjustments that overall reason dictates—so far as they perform like encapsulated, modular units (Fodor 1983)—and yet prove capable of affecting action.

There is no problem in seeing how the different voices in a person might give counsel that offends against reason, where we conceive of reason as a certain unified sort of pattern. As there are discursive dilemmas that arise for any group, so there will be dilemmas that arise among these voices, even if the voices are each consistent in their own recommendations.

Imagine that a person confronts the issue of whether or not to buy a Volvo, where it is assumed that the decision turns on two questions: one, whether it would be good to have a car; and two, whether a Volvo is the best sort of car to have. And suppose that the relevant voices in a person are: A, the economic voice of self-interest; B, the ecological voice of the environment; and C, the voice concerned with what will impress the neighbours. These voices, which represent rival sets of desirability characteristics, may give rise to the pattern shown in Figure 3.3, where the support provided for a given judgement can be thought of as a sort of voting.

The pattern of support represented in the matrix is entirely intuitive. The economic self A recommends getting a car, because of the saving of time involved, but recommends against the relatively expensive Volvo. The ecological self B votes against a car, for standard environmental reasons, but registers that a Volvo is the best sort of car, given its low emission levels. And the status-oriented self C recommends both in favour of getting a car and in favour of getting the particularly impressive Volvo. But the result is that while there is a majority of voices that think it would be good to get a car, and a majority that think a Volvo is the best car, there is also a majority against

	Good to have a car?	Is Volvo the best car?	Buy a Volvo?
A	Yes	No	No
B	No	Yes	No
C	Yes	Yes	Yes

Fig. 3.3

getting a Volvo. We might imagine the person who operates under the influence of such voices coming to the view that he or she should buy a Volvo but proving akratic when it comes to phoning the dealer.

The picture of individual akrasia that this suggests is attractively egalitarian and emphasizes, intuitively, that the recalcitrant elements in the akratic agent need not be voices of temptation but voices that make a serious claim on the person. It would enable us to avoid the downgrading of inclination and emotion that typifies more standard approaches, for example, and allow us to enfranchise the affective as well as the intellectual voices within us. The most admirable human beings, according to the picture projected, would be those who let the voices of the heart as well as the voices of the head each have their say on every issue. They would be committed to achieving rational unity in themselves but not at the cost of suppressing any such voices. They would renounce the sort of ideal sometimes imagined in traditional moral theory: that of being someone in whom only one voice speaks, and in whom all elements have been drilled into marching to the beat of one drum.

My discussion of collective akrasia not only makes an egalitarian vision of akrasia available, it may also help to explain why the hierarchical picture remains so prominent. We saw in discussion of how collectives achieve self-control that one way of doing so is by giving over control, in the event of any rational dissension, to certain considerations or to a certain individual or set of individuals. One way in which individuals may achieve self-control is by giving over control, in parallel fashion, to privileged sorts of considerations or to a privileged sort of voice. The most plausible version of this strategy would be to give control to more general, principled considerations or to give control to the cool voice that marshals such considerations in our reasoning. And that is precisely the sort of strategy supported in traditional religious and moralistic writings. So far as this strategy of self-control has been the most salient one around, it may have given life to the hierarchical conception of akrasia. For if that strategy is taken to be the only one available, then the essential problem in akrasia will be traced to the fact that more particularistic considerations push us away from the rule of the principled considerations that govern by right, or that the warmer voices of feeling and emotion rebel against the cool, detached voice that is properly placed in authority above them.

These remarks should help to show how akrasia in the individual might allow of a revisionary, egalitarian representation. So at least I hope. But I hasten to add that the representation depends on an analogy between

Akrasia, Collective and Individual / 93

individual and group that is only very partial. To make the analogy detailed, we would need to have an account of how the different voices in a subject are to be distinguished. We would need to be told more about how those different voices speak to the subject: how, for example, emotions and sentiments represent things to a person (Pettit 2001*b*). And we would need a model of how such voices can contribute to a personal decision when, clearly, they do not operate as voters, let alone as voters who can only say 'Yea' or 'Nay'.

Still, it is worth emphasizing that even if it is only suggestive, the metaphor has an intuitive appeal and that it has also proved attractive to others. Thus R. M. Adams (1985: 10–11) gives expression to a similar image of the soul.

What I think is and ought to be the order of the soul is not a pure democracy, and certainly not mob rule, but something more like the American system of representative government with 'divided powers', with opposing tendencies and competing interests retaining an independent voice and influence—with state and federal governments, legislative and executive and judicial branches, public and private sectors, all acting in their own right in ways that directly affect the moral character of the nation and its relations with other peoples. It is important for the individual, as for the state, to be able to act fairly consistently over time in accordance with rationally coherent policies subjected to ethical reflection. But it is also important for the individual, as for the state, to have potential sources within—to have, as it were, organs that can take positions that the chief executive wishes they would not take. The ever present possibility of internal conflict is not only a vexation and a potential hindrance to resolute action; it is also a wellspring of vitality and sensitivity, and a check against one-sidedness and fanaticism.

Like Korsgaard, Adams thinks that this image of the soul is broadly Platonic in provenance. And in that connection it is perhaps worth quoting what another scholar says about Plato's views on the unity of the person. 'Being one, on this account, is something to which we aspire; "one" is an honorific title. The inquiry that leads to that unity, however, is an inquiry conducted by the active mind, the syllogizing soul endeavouring to maintain consistency in its beliefs and to produce proper explanations . . . Self-identity and unity are what we aim for' (McCabe 1994: 300).

Akrasia is Not Exclusively Action-Centred in Manifestation

According to the account given of collective akrasia, the malaise involved has a distinctively practical aspect (Pettit and Smith 1993). The group fails to achieve rational unity despite operating within feasible limits and under

94 / Philip Pettit

favourable conditions. Specifically, the group fails to achieve rational unity as a result of a divergence among its members on the question of what it ought to do and a failure on their part to come into line with the demands of reason on the group overall. But though the sort of failure involved has this practical aspect, it is a striking feature of the malaise described that it can affect, not just what the group does or forms the intention of doing, but also what it judges to be the case and thereby comes to believe. Collective akrasia is not exclusively action-centred.

The reason this is so is that the difficulty that gives rise to akrasia—the difficulty made vivid in the discursive dilemma—can affect the formation of judgement as well as the formation and enactment of intention. In our original example of a discursive dilemma, the three members of a group give majority support to p and to if p then q but not to q; under the rules described, indeed, they effectively deny that q. Just as the failure of the group to intend or to act as certain commitments require can be explained by the recalcitrance of a relevant majority, so such recalcitrance may explain the failure of the group to form such a judgement. And if it does explain that sort of failure, then we have to see the group's not making that judgement as a manifestation of akrasia.

Nothing in this line of thought should be surprising. The making of a judgement that s—the acceptance of a corresponding formula—involves the formation of a belief that s, so far as the agent becomes disposed thereby to act as if it were the case that s. But the making of any judgement constitutes an action. The group acts in making a judgement on the question 's or not s?'; it decides to put the matter to a vote. And the group acts in actually forming the judgement that s; it goes through the process of voting. Akrasia can affect the group's performance in regard to those actions and so it can affect its performance in regard to the formation or non-formation of an associated belief. Even if the group is required by its own lights to believe that s, it is clearly going to be possible for it to fail to form any belief on the matter or to come to form the belief that not s; and this is clearly going to be possible, moreover, in intuitively normal conditions of functioning.

The lesson is that akrasia is not exclusively action-centred in its manifestations. And that lesson, it transpires, may apply in the individual as well as in the collective case. Assume, uncontroversially, that one of the ways in which individuals form beliefs is by making judgements: by endorsing relevant formulae, taking them to be well supported, and by becoming disposed at the same time to act as if they were true. If an individual can be conceptualized as a forum where different voices speak, and where the achievement of agency and personhood requires their continuing orchestration, then akrasia may strike here in the same way as with the collectivity. Despite agreed evidence as to what reason requires the individual to judge on some issue, the voices within the person may fail, akratically, to get their act together.

There may be reason why the individual is required to make a judgement on some matter like '*s* or not *s*?', and yet he or she might fail to address or resolve it. Or there might be reason for someone to judge that *s*, and yet the person might fail to get his or her voices in unison and so might not support that judgement. All the evidence might suggest that a friend has been disloyal, for example, and yet the voices of affection and nostalgia might refuse to go along, leading the agent to report, akratically: 'I know it's a compelling conclusion; but I just can't believe it.'

While this line on the possibility of belief-related akrasia is controversial, it is not unprecedented and it is not implausible (Mele 1987, 1995). It is supported, for example, by the fact that we hold people responsible for the things they believe in domains where we think they are capable of judgement (Pettit and Smith 1996; Scanlon 1998; Pettit 2001*a*). How could we hold people responsible in this way unless we thought that their beliefs were subject to personal control and yet that sometimes they failed, akratically, to exercise that control?

Conclusion

The upshot of our discussion is tantalizing. We have seen that groups, but only groups of a distinctively self-unifying kind, can manifest akrasia. And that observation has sponsored three fairly well-pointed lessons for the nature of akrasia in general. It argues that akrasia is not mechanical in character but supposes a capacity to recognize the demands of reasons and to regulate in the light of them. It supports an image of akrasia in which the problem is not essentially a failure of the higher elements in a hierarchy to subdue lower elements but a failure among more or less equally ranked elements—equally ranked voices—to get their act together. And it suggests that akrasia is not exclusively action-centred in its manifestations, being a malaise that can affect the formation of judgement as well as the performance of action. None of these claims will prove irresistible, of course, but they should each make a serious claim on our attention.

96 / Philip Pettit

They should make a claim on our attention, I have suggested, not just in relation to collectives but also in relation to individuals. The image of the individual as an amalgam of different voices is only a metaphor, of course, and there is no suggestion that those voices have the autonomy of different persons or contribute to the views of an individual in the procedurally procrustean manner of voters. But the point it conveys is surely engaging: that there may be profit in thinking of the individual as a plurality of perspectives that interact in a continuing search for the unity of a single, reasoned vision. And if we do think of the individual in that way then akrasia will have to be seen in the individual as well as the collective case as a phenomenon that is non-mechanical and non-hierarchical in nature and that is not exclusively action-centred in its manifestations.

4

Emotions and the Intelligibility of Akratic Action

Christine Tappolet

As is clear from the writings of Plato and Aristotle, emotions have traditionally been regarded as largely responsible for irrational actions and, more specifically, for akratic actions, which are taken to be paradigmatic of practical irrationality.[1] Consider Paolo and Francesca, the two unlucky lovers described by Dante.[2] On the traditional conception, their passionate love is to blame for their adultery, an act which we can suppose they committed against their better judgement, that is, in spite of judging that, all things considered, it would have been better to abstain. Recall that Francesca's jealous husband promptly killed the two lovers, thereby sending them to hell and eternal turpitude. Following Plato, one could say that Francesca's behaviour is compulsive: her emotion forced her to act against her better judgement.[3]

I owe special thanks to Sarah Stroud for extensive and extremely valuable written comments. I am also grateful to Ronnie de Sousa, Maite Ezcurdia, Daniel Laurier, Duncan MacIntosh, Alison McIntyre, Martin Montminy, Martine Nida-Rümelin, Ruwen Ogien, Philip Pettit, Fabienne Pironet, Michael Smith, Xavier Vanmechelen, and Ralph Wedgwood for their questions and suggestions, and also for the helpful comments of two anonymous referees. My work was supported by grants from FCAR (Fonds pour la formation de chercheurs et l'aide à la recherche) and the Social Sciences and Humanities Research Council of Canada, which I gratefully acknowledge

[1] See Plato, *Protagoras*; Aristotle, *Nicomachean Ethics*, bk. VII.

[2] See Dante, *La Divina Commedia*, *Inferno*, canto V.

[3] This would at least seem to follow from the claim that 'no one willingly goes to meet evil or what he thinks to be evil' (Plato, *Protagoras* (1961 edn.), 358c–d). For a more recent defence of the claim that emotions force us to act against our will, see Hare 1963: 78–9.

98 / Christine Tappolet

Alternatively, one could think with Aristotle that, given her emotion, Francesca was not in a position fully to take into account the danger that was involved; her emotion prevented her from forming the full-fledged judgement that the planned action was to be avoided (*Nicomachean Ethics* 1147^b).

At first glance, the traditional way of conceiving akrasia seems to contrast with most contemporary accounts. On those accounts, it is thought possible freely to act against a full-fledged better judgement. Moreover, emotions seem to play no role at all in such accounts. As is clear from the definitions of akrasia one finds in the contemporary literature, the only mental states that are generally taken to be involved are judgements, desires, and possibly intentions. At best, emotions are claimed to have a causal role: they are among the different possible causes of the akratic break. Given this, most contemporary philosophers working on akrasia seem happy to accept the traditional claim that emotions are nothing but blind and potentially disruptive forces.

As recent work on emotion shows, however, emotions should not be thought of merely as factors which tend to interfere with reason. The general recent trend has been to stress their indispensability for both practical and theoretical rationality.[4] My main aim here is to determine what role, if any, emotions actually play in akratic action. I shall develop my view by contrasting it with the account offered by one of the only contemporary philosophers to claim that emotions have an important role to play in akrasia, namely Ronald de Sousa (1987).[5] Given that de Sousa presupposes Donald Davidson's conception of akrasia, I will start with a presentation of that conception. After having raised a number of questions about the arguments de Sousa offers, and after having presented what I take to be its main problem—a problem that actually comes from the Davidsonian framework it presupposes—I shall present an alternative conception.

As will become apparent, my approach is quite close to de Sousa's, for it also makes use of the important insight that emotions involve patterns of attention. However, it gives emotions a more than merely causal role. I shall argue that since emotions can be seen as perceptions of values—a view that de Sousa actually shares—they have the capacity to make akratic action intelli-

---

[4] De Sousa 1987 was a principal milestone of this new trend. See also the essays by de Sousa, Rorty, and Greenspan in A. Rorty 1980*a*, as well as Damasio 1994 and Frank 1988.

[5] Frank Jackson distinguishes between passionate and non-passionate cases of akrasia and gives an account of the passionate cases (Jackson 1984). Peter Goldie claims that emotions 'can ground a certain sort of weakness of the will' (Goldie 2000: 110). See also Jones forthcoming.

Emotions and Akratic Action / 99

gible, as distinct from merely causally explainable. Given this, the role of emotions with respect to action is not merely that of a disruptive force. Indeed, akratic actions based on emotions can actually be more rational than actions that follow the agent's better judgement. Moreover, it will turn out that akratic actions that do not involve emotions are more of a puzzle than the ones involving emotions. Or so I shall argue.[6]

Davidson's Account of Akrasia

Akratic actions can be defined as free and intentional actions performed despite the judgement that another course of action is better, all things considered. Following Davidson, such actions can be characterized more precisely as follows:

(1) An action x is an akratic action iff the agent judges at time t that, all things considered, it is better to do some alternative action y rather than action x at time t, and the agent is or believes herself to be able and free to do y at time t, but she freely and intentionally does x at time t.[7]

As Davidson points out (1970a: 22), there seem to be actions corresponding to this definition. We can quite easily imagine Francesca's action along these lines. It certainly seems that her making love with Paolo could have been both free and intentional. We can suppose that though Francesca was aware that some risk was involved, she did not expect that they would be discovered and killed. Had she known that this was likely and nonetheless committed the adultery, it might have been suspected that her action was compulsive. But if we imagine that she was only considering that some kind of risk was involved, there is no reason not to suppose that she could have refrained. Moreover, we can imagine that at the very moment she committed the adultery, she judged

[6] It should be noted that I concentrate on akratic action, thereby leaving aside what Richard Holton argues is properly called 'weakness of will', namely cases in which agents fail to act on their intentions (Holton 1999).

[7] Davidson's own definition is the following: 'In doing x an agent acts incontinently if and only if: (a) the agent does x intentionally; (b) the agent believes there is an alternative action y open to him; and (c) the agent judges that, all things considered, it would be better to do y than to do x' (Davidson 1970a: 22). The main difference with my definition is that Davidson does not require that akratic action be free. Note also that it might be sufficient that the agent believe that the akratic action is an alternative one.

100 / Christine Tappolet

that, all things considered, it would have been better to refrain. There seems to be no reason to suppose that she could not have formed such a judgement.

The problem is that such an action appears to conflict with the idea that intentional actions are done in the guise of the good, or, to put it in Davidson's words, that 'in so far as a person acts intentionally he acts in the light of what he imagines (judges) to be the better' (1970a: 22). More precisely, the existence of akratic actions seems incompatible with what could be called the *principle of intentionality*:

> (2) If an agent judges at time t that it is better to do x than to do y at time t, and she is able and free to do x at time t, then she will intentionally and freely do x at time t, if she does either x or y intentionally at time t.[8]

As Davidson argues, both this principle and the claim that there are akratic actions are plausible. Davidson's solution to the puzzle is to argue that the evaluative judgements involved in (1) and (2) are of different kinds. According to Davidson, the evaluative judgement that plays a role in the definition of akrasia is not simply a judgement that tells us what to do and is the outcome of deliberation. Rather, the judgement in question is relational. The logical form of such a judgement is $pf(x$ is better than y, $r)$, where the 'pf' operator is a relational one positing a relation between a set of reasons, r, and the comparative judgement (cf. Davidson 1970a: 38–9). One can paraphrase such a judgement as follows: in light of the set of reasons r, action x is better than y. The judgement bears on what is better relative to a given set of reasons—all the reasons that the agent judges relevant in the case of an all-things-considered judgement—and not on what is better *tout court*. It tells us not what we ought to do, but what our reasons indicate we should do. It has the same structure as an evidential judgement, such as the judgement that what I perceive indicates that p.

Relational evaluative judgements are different from what one could call unconditional evaluative judgements. Davidson speaks of judgements *sans phrase*, which he contrasts with conditional or prima facie evaluative judgements. An unconditional evaluative judgement bears on what is better independent of the reasons the agent has. One can suppose that such a judgement is the outcome of deliberation; this is at least what is often the case. However, even if it is based on the different reasons that are available, as a conclusion it is so to speak detached from these reasons.

---

[8] This principle brings together the two principles put forward at Davidson 1970a: 23.

Emotions and Akratic Action / 101

According to Davidson, the principle of intentionality concerns the unconditional judgement, not the relational one. It is the former, and not the latter, which is tied to action. One can say that, for Davidson, what happens in cases of akratic action is that the agent makes the two following judgements:

(1) the reasons I have indicate that this other action y is better than action x;

(2) action x is better than y.[9]

If the principle of intentionality is true, that is, if it is true that the second kind of judgement results in action, the agent will do x if she does either x or y; she will be akratic.

On this account, the error of the akratic agent is that although she judges that her reasons indicate that the alternative action is better, she does not judge that this is the better action. As Davidson points out, this is not a logical mistake. The two judgements are logically compatible. For, quite unfortunately, the fact that the reasons we have indicate that one action is better than another is perfectly compatible with the fact that, in reality, the reverse is true. Nonetheless, once an agent has judged that her reasons indicate that action y is better than action x, she clearly ought to make the unconditional judgement that y is better than x. As Davidson puts it, an agent ought to judge, and hence act, on the basis of all available reasons (Davidson 1970a: 41). This is what the so-called *principle of continence* requires. Thus, the akratic agent makes an error in her reasoning; she fails to abide by the principle of continence.[10]

The question is whether this account of akrasia is fully convincing. I shall return to this question. But first, let us consider where emotions would fit into this picture.

Emotions and the Reasoning Error

According to de Sousa, it is an emotion which is responsible for the reasoning error that characterizes akrasia on the Davidsonian picture. The reason why

---

[9] In Davidson 1970a, Davidson never claims that the akratic agent explicitly makes these judgements. However, this follows from the thesis that intentional action is done in the light of what is judged to be better, when put together with the thesis that akratic action is intentional.

[10] Actually, given this interpretation of Davidson, the breach of the principle of continence is an epistemic failure. Although the akratic agent judges that all the reasons he has indicate that p, he makes a judgement which is incompatible with p.

102 / Christine Tappolet

the agent comes to the erroneous conclusion that the akratic action is better than the other one is that she does not ground her conclusion on the relational evaluative judgement, which involves all available reasons, but on a partial judgement, that is, a judgement which only takes into account a limited number of reasons. According to de Sousa, this error is due to the presence of an emotion. To echo de Sousa, one could say that an emotion plugs the partial judgement into the motor system (de Sousa 1987: 200). Thus, if Francesca commits adultery contrary to her better judgement, it is her passionate love that is to blame. We can suppose that her emotion causes her to move from the relational judgement that sexual intercourse with Paolo is better than abstinence relative to a subset of reasons—its being exceedingly pleasant, say—to the unconditional judgement that that action is better than abstinence.

As it stands, this claim about the role of emotions is very strong, given that it requires that some emotion be involved in every case of akrasia. Thus, in cases where there is apparently no emotion involved, we have nonetheless to suppose that some emotion is at work. Consider Davidson's famous tooth-brushing case (Davidson 1970a: 30). Don relaxes in bed after a hard day when he realizes that he has forgotten to brush his teeth. He comes to the conclusion that, all things considered, it would be better to stay in bed: getting up might spoil his calm, for instance. Still, he gets up and brushes his teeth. Where is the emotion? One could surely come up with some suggestion—maybe it is an emotional concern for his teeth or a mild fear of feeling guilty which is at work. But it has to be acknowledged that, in such cases, there is a difficulty for the claim that all cases of akratic action involve an emotion.[11] There seem to be both cases of emotional akrasia and cases of what could be called 'cool akrasia', namely, akrasia that does not involve emotions.

The question is why we should believe that akratic actions involve emotions. As far as I can see, de Sousa offers two arguments for this claim. The first is an argument that works by eliminating all other possibilities, and the second is based on a claim linking emotions to attention. I shall consider them in turn, starting with the first.

De Sousa's first argument. Let me introduce a bit of terminology. I shall call whatever is responsible for the reasoning error Davidson postulates the 'akratic cause'. Now the important premiss in the first argument is that the akratic cause can be neither a 'merely physiological factor that is in

---

[11] In conversation, Ronald de Sousa suggested that habit might be the cause of such actions.

itself arational', nor a desire, nor a belief (de Sousa 1987: 200). Thus, what is needed to fit the bill is a cause that is neither a belief nor a desire, but that nonetheless allows for rational assessment. Emotions, which are states that cannot be reduced to beliefs and desires, are just what we need—or so we are told.

Why couldn't the akratic cause be a belief or a desire? De Sousa argues as follows. The akratic cause cannot be a belief or a desire, for, by hypothesis, all reasons, be they cognitive or desiderative, have been taken into account. De Sousa concludes that 'whatever tips the balance cannot be another reason' (de Sousa 1987: 200). This argument seems less than convincing. It is difficult to see why any of the beliefs or desires that have been taken into account by the agent could not cause the reasoning error. The fact that a mental state plays a role in the justification of an all-things-considered better judgement, and thus possibly has a causal effect on that judgement, hardly seems to prevent that same mental state from having other causal roles. Thus Francesca's belief that making love with Paolo would be exceedingly pleasant could well cause the reasoning error. Moreover, it could also be the case that some belief or desire which is not among the reasons the agent considered could be the cause of the error. Maybe it is the belief that she is about to become 30 that causes her to judge that intercourse with Paolo is better than abstinence, a belief which we can suppose did not play any role in her deliberation.

As for the idea that the akratic cause is not rationally assessable, we are told that this is wrong because, first, this is not the kind of thing which can cause a judgement in the appropriate way. The claim is that only states that are rationally assessable can be the proper causes of judgements, that is, causes that result in rational judgements. Simplifying a bit, this is what de Sousa calls *Elster's principle of autonomy*.[12] It may be that there is indeed a principle along these lines, though one would need to be careful not to exclude cases in which judgements are caused by perceptual experiences. However, the problem is that, as far as I can see, nothing prevents us from saying that the akratic agent's unconditional evaluative judgement fails to satisfy this requirement. The judgement is in any case claimed to be irrational given that it violates the principle of continence. There is no harm in supposing that it also falls foul of (some plausible version of) the principle of autonomy. For this surely does not

---

[12] See de Sousa 1987: 200, 174; Elster 1983: 15–16. Elster's suggestion is to 'evaluate the broad rationality of beliefs and desires by looking at the way in which they are shaped', beliefs or desires counting as irrational if 'they have been shaped by irrelevant causal factors' (Elster 1983: 15–16).

104 / Christine Tappolet

entail that the unconditional evaluative judgement fails to be a genuine judgement.

This brings us to the second reason to believe that the akratic cause cannot be non-rational. The claim is that 'it becomes unclear whether the action is an intentional act of the subject's at all' (de Sousa 1987: 200). This is far from obvious. The thought is probably that if a judgement is caused by a non-rational state, such as a sensation, perhaps, it cannot serve as a proper reason for the action. To accept that such an improperly caused judgement could make an action rational would be akin to saying that an unjustified belief can justify another belief. It might well be that this is false—that only justified beliefs have justificatory force. However, it is less than clear that such a principle applies in the case of intentional action. Even if a judgement is inappropriately caused, and hence irrational, it is not clear that it has to be ruled out as a reason for the action.

All in all, this first argument to support the thesis that the akratic cause is an emotion hardly seems effective.

De Sousa's second argument. Let me now consider a second argument for the claim that the akratic cause is an emotion. Actually, this is more a quick suggestion in de Sousa than it is a full-fledged argument. However, I believe it contains the seed of a convincing case for the claim that at least some akratic actions involve emotions. De Sousa's suggestion is that emotions are 'perfectly tailored for the role of arbitrators among reasons' because 'their essential role lies in establishing specific patterns of salience relevant to inferences' (de Sousa 1987: 200). The thesis de Sousa advocates is that emotions direct our attention, in that they involve what he calls 'species of determinate patterns of salience among objects of attention, lines of inquiry, and inferential strategies' (de Sousa 1987: 196).[13] In short, the emotions we experience determine the content of our beliefs and desires. In de Sousa's words, 'emotions limit the range of information that the organism will take into account, the inferences actually drawn from a potential infinity, and the set of live options among

---

[13] A similar hypothesis has been put forward by the neurologist Antonio Damasio. On his view, what he calls *somatic markers*, that is, emotions and feelings that 'have been connected, by learning, to predicted future outcomes of certain scenarios' (Damasio 1994: 174), make up for the shortcomings of pure reason. These somatic markers assist the deliberation and decision process by highlighting options as dangerous or favourable; they function as a 'biasing device' (Damasio 1994: 174) which forces attention on the negative or positive outcomes of options, so that the number of considered options is reduced. As Damasio puts it: 'a somatic state, negative or positive, caused by the appearance of a given representation, operates not only as a *marker for the value of what is represented, but also as a booster for continued working memory and attention*' (Damasio 1994: 197–8).

which it will choose' (de Sousa 1987: 195). In this way, emotions can be seen to have an important practical function. According to de Sousa, it is in virtue of emotions that we can avoid the sad destiny of the robot sitting outside a room containing a bomb, busily analysing an infinity of irrelevant information, such as the impact of its options on the price of tea in China, instead of running for what it would consider its life.[14]

Intuitively, the suggestion that emotions involve a particular focus of attention is highly plausible. Suppose you encounter a wild and fierce-looking dog while alone in the woods. You will register every movement and sound it makes, waiting for it to attack you. Your attention will be almost entirely concentrated on the object of your emotion and its fear-inspiring features, such as its rolling eyes and bared teeth. Moreover, the claim that emotions and attentional phenomena are closely related is also supported by empirical evidence. A great number of psychological studies tend to confirm the claim that emotions and, more broadly, affective phenomena such as anxiety or depression influence attention.[15]

Moreover, it is natural to think that the pattern of attention that comes with an emotion could have an important role to play in akrasia. It seems plausible that given Francesca's passionate love, her attention is focused on certain aspects of her situation—Paolo's charms, the expected pleasure of sexual intercourse with Paolo, and so on. More precisely, her attention will be focused on the positive traits of the akratic action. No wonder she will fail to abide by the principle of continence; thoughts about danger or duty are surely not salient in her mind.[16]

As this example suggests, and as many philosophers have underlined, it seems true that akrasia at least often involves a particular attentional bias.[17]

[14] See de Sousa 1987: 192–4. The example is from Dennett 1984.

[15] The psychologists Gerald Matthews and Adrian Wells write that 'states of emotions influence both the contents of consciousness and performance on tasks requiring selection of stimuli or intensive concentration' (Matthews and Wells 1999: 171). See also Wells and Matthews 1994 and Mogg and Bradley 1999, as well as Faucher and Tappolet 2002, for a survey.

[16] As Dante tells us, the two lovers were reading a book narrating the story of Lancelot and Guinevere. It is clear that this activity was instrumental in the production of the pattern of attention characteristic of their passionate love.

[17] See Bratman's claim that the reasoning error which the akratic agent is guilty of is due to the fact that his attention is focused on the positive aspects of the akratic action (Bratman 1979: 168). Similarly, Peacocke notes that some imaginative or perceptual asymmetry related to attention makes the akratic action more intelligible (Peacocke 1985: 55–6, 72); and Mele claims that many strict akratic actions can be explained in part by the perceived proximity of the rewards of the incontinent alternative and the agent's attentional condition (Mele 1987: 92).

106 / Christine Tappolet

Given this, there is good reason to think that emotions have an important role in at least some cases of akrasia. However, one should be careful not to overstate the claim that the akratic agent is focused on what speaks in favour of the akratic action. For it has to be kept in mind that the agent also makes a better judgement in favour of the alternative action. The emotion does not achieve a complete blackout of the reasons that speak against the akratic action. Still, it can be agreed that the reasons in favour of the akratic action are in the foreground.

But why should we conclude that emotions are involved as causes of the reasoning error postulated by Davidson? The question is whether emotions and the focus of attention they involve are bound to come into the picture as akratic causes or whether they could play a different role. Before I address this question, let me first present a deeper worry with de Sousa's approach. Once we have cleared away this problem it will be easier to see where emotions fit into the picture.

In fact, the real problem with de Sousa's approach comes from the Davidsonian framework he makes his own. As many have argued, Davidson's conception of akrasia seems wrong. Akratic action is better conceived of as action contrary to an unconditional evaluative judgement.[18] The agent acts while judging that an alternative action is better, or at least while judging that, all things considered, there is good and sufficient reason for her not to perform the action she performs, where this all-things-considered judgement results from her deliberation, but does not merely state what the reasons she has indicate.[19]

Why should we believe this? The best method to argue for this conception of akrasia—and it might well be thought that it is not an absolutely compelling method—is by way of examples. There seems to be nothing wrong with imagining a case like that of Francesca along these lines. On the contrary, it is quite natural to describe Francesca's case in this way. Francesca has reasons both for and against making love with Paolo. She not only judges that her reasons speak in favour of refraining from making love with Paolo, but also

[18] Cf. Mele's definition of what he calls 'strict incontinent actions' (Mele 1987: 7). The possibility of someone's making the reasoning error postulated by Davidson cannot be denied. Moreover, given the impact of emotions on attention, it is likely that they are the source of this kind of error. However, such an agent simply seems bad at reasoning, rather than akratic in the strict sense.

[19] As David Wiggins says, the expression 'all things considered' has here its ordinary sense (Wiggins 1980: 241 n. 4).

judges that it would be better to refrain. However, as the story goes, she nonetheless opts for having intercourse with Paolo.

Moreover, and more importantly for our purpose, it seems plausible to suppose that she does not judge that it would be better to make love with Paolo. As Michael Bratman notes, it seems quite false to suppose with Davidson that the akratic agent judges it better to perform the action she actually performs (Bratman 1979: 160; Charlton 1988: 124). If we asked her, she would certainly deny that she judges that making love with Paolo is a better course of action than abstinence. And there seems to be no reason to hold that she is insincere. What happens in akratic action is that the agent judges that another course of action is better, but the desire for the akratic action turns out to be the strongest from the point of view of its motivational force. Briefly put, the judgements that are involved would seem to be the following:

(1) the reasons I have indicate that action y is better than x;
(2) action y is better than x (all things considered).

And yet the agent does not choose y, but the alternative action x. Contrary to what Davidson seems to claim, it is false to suppose that this requires that the agent judges that action x is better.

If this is on the right track, we have to conclude that emotions are not to be identified with akratic causes. And the reason for this is simply that there are no such causes. Obviously an akratic action will always be caused by something or other. But what does not necessarily exist is something causally responsible for the reasoning error which Davidson postulates. Even though the agent surely judges that, in some respects, action x is better than action y, she does not wrongly infer that the akratic action is better than the envisaged alternative *sans phrase* (to use Davidson's formulation). Hence, it is not necessary to postulate a mechanism that could explain the error of making this judgement rather than a judgement that would conform to the principle of continence.

It follows that the second argument I considered, the one which was based on the claim that emotions involve specific patterns of attention, cannot be taken to show that emotions are akratic causes. However, it would be wrong to infer that emotions do not play any role at all. If at least some akratic actions are characterized by a certain pattern of attention, and if emotions involve such patterns of attention, then there is good reason to believe that

108 / Christine Tappolet

emotions at least sometimes have a role to play in akrasia. The question is what role that could be.

The first suggestion that comes to one's mind is that although emotions are not involved as the causes of the reasoning error, they can nonetheless play a causal role with respect to akratic action. There are different points at which an emotion could have a causal influence. It could be an emotion that causes the agent to act on the reason she considers to be insufficient for the action. Francesca's love might ensure that the thought that the envisaged action is exceedingly pleasant is acted upon. A slightly different possibility is that the emotion directly causes the akratic action: Francesca's love might simply get her to perform the fatal deed. It could also be that the emotion causes a lack of motivation. Consider a depressed agent, Anna. Given her sadness, Anna might lack any motivation to act in accordance with her better judgement. In all these cases, the emotion is hypothesized to have a merely causal role; it either brings about the akratic action or interferes with the agent's motivational set so as to prevent the action which corresponds to her better judgement. And in all these cases, the causal influence of the emotion could be explained in terms of the impact of emotions on attention. Though these seem to be the main possibilities, there might be other possible causal routes from emotions to akratic action.

Now there is no doubt that emotions could have a causal role with respect to akratic action. The question is whether this is the only role emotions could have. As I shall argue in the next section, the answer is 'no'.

Emotions as Perceptions of Values

As is often underlined in recent work, emotions can be the objects of rational or cognitive assessments. These assessments can be of quite different kinds. Emotions can be more or less rational from a strategic point of view: some emotions interfere with our ends, while others are essential to furthering those ends.[20] Emotions can also be more or less rational depending on the rationality of the beliefs or judgements upon which they are based. A feeling of joy based on an irrational belief, such as a belief caused by wishful thinking, will be deemed no more rational than the belief that gave rise to it. More

---

[20] Robert Frank argues that being prone to some emotions, like anger, can make for an advantage in interactions with rational agents (Frank 1988).

importantly for our purposes, an emotion can be said to be more or less appropriate with respect to the evaluative features of its object: an emotion of fear directed towards something completely innocuous would be inappropriate, whereas fear felt with respect to something dangerous would be judged to be appropriate. Depending on the importance of the danger, the intensity of the fear can also be more or less proportionate: intense fear would be disproportionate with respect to a minor threat, which only warrants mild fear.[21]

The fact that emotions can be evaluated in terms of their appropriateness and proportionality invites us to think of emotions as we think of perceptual experiences. In particular, it is natural to understand the appropriateness conditions for emotions as analogous to the correctness conditions for perceptual experiences. In the same way that perceptual experiences are assessed with respect to what they represent, it seems emotions can be assessed in terms of how they fit evaluative facts.[22] Emotions could have the same function with respect to values as perceptual experiences have for colours and shapes, so that we could say emotions are perceptions of values.[23] Consider again fear. When nothing interferes with its proper functioning, that is, when the conditions in which it is felt are favourable, my fear allows me to track danger.

Moreover, there is reason to think that the evaluative content of an emotion is of the same kind as the content of perceptual experiences in that it is non-conceptual.[24] This is suggested by the fact that emotions are to a large extent isolated from our higher-order cognitive processes and thus from our

---

[21] Though they disagree on how to understand this claim, almost all philosophers who write on emotions accept that emotions can be assessed in terms of their appropriateness. See, among others, Brentano 1889/1969: 22 ff.; de Sousa 1987: 122; Mulligan 1998; D'Arms and Jacobson 2000a. For the claim that an emotion's *intensity* can be also be assessed, see Broad 1954: 293; and more recently D'Arms and Jacobson 2000a: 73–4 and Jones forthcoming.

[22] This claim goes back to the moral sense theorists Shaftesbury (1711/1964), Hutcheson (1738/1971), and possibly Hume (1740/1978), and to the turn-of-the-century philosophers Scheler (1913–16/1973) and Meinong (1917/1972). More recently, see McDowell 1985b; Wiggins 1987; de Sousa 1987: 45, 2002; Tappolet 1995; 2000, ch. 6; d'Arms and Jacobson 2000a,b; Johnston 2001; and Wedgwood 2001b.

[23] This claim is obviously compatible with value realism, but it does not entail it; it is even compatible with the claim that there are no evaluative properties out there.

[24] See Tappolet 1995, 2000. See also Johnston 2001 for the claim that what he calls 'affect' involves 'pre-judgmental disclosures of values' (Johnston 2001: 182). Work in neuroscience by LeDoux shows that the brain structure responsible for an emotion such as fear, the amygdala, receives crude stimulus information directly from the sensory thalamus (what LeDoux calls the 'low road'; LeDoux and Phelps 2000: 159), that is, before it is processed by the sensory cortex.

110 / Christine Tappolet

deliberative faculty.[25] As we all know, it is possible to experience fear while judging that what one is afraid of is not dangerous. One can thus say with Karen Jones that 'our emotions can key us to the presence of . . . reason-giving considerations without necessarily presenting that information in a form available to conscious articulation and even despite our consciously held and internally justified judgement that the situation presents no such reasons' (Jones forthcoming).

More should be said to explain and defend this conception of emotions as perceptions of evaluative facts, but this would take us too far afield from the topic of akrasia. Instead, I shall simply assume that such an account is broadly on the right track.

As should be obvious, the claim that emotions are perceptions of values is compatible with the thesis that emotions influence our attention. Indeed, these two claims go hand in hand.[26] For if anything can be said to attract and also in general to merit our attention, it is whatever falls under some evaluative concept or other, such as the concepts of the dangerous, the disgusting, the shameful, the irritating, the attractive, the admirable, or the love-worthy. It is thus to be expected that (one of) the mechanisms that get us to focus our attention on certain features of our environment is involved in our grasp of the evaluative aspects of that environment.[27] Indeed, it is difficult to imagine how fear could begin to make us aware of the danger in some situation without also directing our attention to the object of our fear.

Now if emotions are perceptions of values, actions caused by emotions can be explained in terms of the perceived value.[28] The value that is perceived, whether correctly or not, makes the action intelligible. Suppose a bear attacks me. The fear I experience does not only save my life when it causes my

---

[25] See Greenspan's arguments against the claim that emotions are evaluative judgements (Greenspan 1988). And see Griffiths 1997 for the claim that emotions are cognitively encapsulated.

[26] As we have seen, Damasio claims that 'a somatic state . . . operates not only as a *marker for the value of what is represented, but also as a booster for continued working memory and attention*' (Damasio 1994: 197–8).

[27] One way to see the relation between the perception of the evaluative fact and the focusing of attention is to claim that the former is the source of the latter. See Johnston 2001, n. 2, for this suggestion.

[28] See Johnston 2001 for the claim that the special intelligibility that 'affect' confers on desires and actions can only be explained if one adopts a perceptual model of such affective states. Note that the claim that the value in question makes the action intelligible is neutral with respect to the issue of whether reasons are internal or external. The danger I perceive can be a reason to flee either because the danger is a reason to flee whatever my beliefs and desires, or because given my desires (or, more broadly, my motivational set) and my beliefs, that fact is a reason for me.

running away; it also makes the action intelligible. The danger which my fear allows me to track explains why I run away. And this is so even if there is actually no danger involved: although I haven't realized this, the bear is behind a thick glass wall, for instance. Given my fear, my action is still intelligible. The reason why I run away is that, although there is no danger, I nonetheless perceive the situation as dangerous. Things appear to be the same in cases where there is a conflict between the emotion and what the agent judges to be the case. Suppose I judge, be it correctly or incorrectly, that there is no risk involved and that my fear is irrational. It would seem that my running away could still be explained in terms of the danger I perceive, be it correctly or incorrectly. Again, the reason why I run away is that although I judge that there is no danger, I perceive the situation as dangerous. Given its relation to evaluative facts, the emotion thus plays an important role, in that it makes the action intelligible.

This claim can be generalized to cases of akratic action. Suppose I am about to cross a narrow rope bridge hanging high up on a deep shaft. Though I feel fear, I judge that all things considered I ought to cross the bridge; I judge it to be sufficiently safe and going back would make for a much longer hike. If I end up not crossing the bridge, it will not be difficult to make sense of my action: the perceived danger, be it real or not, readily explains why I didn't cross the bridge. Or consider again Francesca and her passionate love for Paolo. On the claim under consideration, this love consists in the perception of Paolo as a worthy object of love. Now this cannot directly make Francesca's action intelligible, for it does not involve a perception of the value of the action itself. But it is surely an important part of what makes it intelligible. The value that Francesca perceives makes her desire to make love to Paolo intelligible and thus indirectly makes her action intelligible. If this is right, emotions are not only causally involved in cases where we act against our better judgement; they make the action intelligible, even though we judge that another course of action would have been better all things considered.

If this is on the right track, cases of akrasia caused by emotions involve a conflict between a value perception and an evaluative judgement that can be compared to perceptual illusions such as the Müller-Lyer illusion, in which one sees the lines as being of a different length even though one judges or even knows that they are of the same length. This is particularly easy to see in cases in which one judges that one's emotion is not appropriate, such as when I fear something while I judge that there is no danger and nonetheless act on my fear. But even in cases where the agent does not judge that the emotion is

112 / Christine Tappolet

inappropriate—the agent might realize that the planned action is dangerous but judge this to be insufficient reason to refrain from performing it—the value that is experienced conflicts with the agent's better judgement. Given her emotion, the agent experiences the akratic action as being the one to be performed while she also judges that there is insufficient reason for this action all things considered. Note that contrary to the case of perceptual illusion, it need not necessarily be the emotion that gets things wrong. Maybe the fear was appropriate and the judgement that there is no danger utterly wrong. If so, the fear that the agent felt, and which made her refrain from the action judged to be better all things considered, could well have saved her life.

Some Objections

Some will think that the claim that emotions can make akratic action intelligible given that they are perceptions of values is nothing more than an emphatic way to put something rather trivial. Emotions are what Davidson calls 'pro-attitudes' (Davidson 1963). Now pro-attitudes in general (plus appropriate means–end beliefs) rationalize actions; they make actions intelligible. Thus, it might seem that there is a much faster and philosophically safer route to the claim that emotions can make actions intelligible. And then there is really no surprise in finding out that emotions can also make akratic actions intelligible. Since akratic actions are intentional, we already know that they are susceptible of an explanation which makes them intelligible; though there is no reason to choose the akratic action instead of the option judged to be better all things considered—or so the agent believes, at least—the akratic action is done for a reason.

The problem with this reasoning is that it is not clear that all of the very different items that are in general counted as pro-attitudes—Davidson mentions desires, urges, promptings, moral views, aesthetic principles, economic prejudices, social conventions, goals, emotions, sentiments, moods, motives, passions, and hungers—really have the power to make an action intelligible. As Warren Quinn's example of an urge to turn on radios shows, a mere behavioural disposition does not make the behaviour it causes intelligible.[29] A tendency to behave in a certain way is of no help in understanding why an action is undertaken. Things seem different in the case of what we ordinarily

---

[29] Quinn 1993: 236–7. See also Scanlon 1998, ch. 1; Dancy 2000b, ch. 2; and Johnston 2001.

call a desire, such as my morning desire for an espresso. Such a desire is an attitude characterized by its felt qualities and which thus counts as an affective or emotional state. There is no doubt that such a desire can make an action intelligible. The lesson to draw is that in so far as a state makes an action intelligible, it is more than a mere behavioural disposition. In any case, if one counts behavioural dispositions among pro-attitudes, a state can be a pro-attitude without being of any help with respect to the intelligibility of actions. Thus, the above-mentioned line of argument starts with a false premiss. Given this, the argument I gave to the effect that emotions can make actions intelligible is not dispensable.[30]

Another objection is that the claim that emotion can make akratic action intelligible is based on an unbalanced diet of examples. What about mad and disruptive emotions, it will be asked? As Michael Stocker has underlined (Stocker 1979), emotions such as anger, envy, jealousy, frustration, and despair can make us feel less motivated to seek both what is and what is believed to be good; indeed, such states can get us to desire both what is and what is believed to be bad. When Othello kills Desdemona out of jealousy, his action aims not at a good, but at something he knows to be bad. So how could it be claimed that jealousy makes the killing intelligible? The jealousy, it would seem, is just a causal factor that explains Othello's madness.

One should, I think, grant that some emotions are just too insane to make any behaviour intelligible. But this is no less true of judgements. One's practical judgements might be so insane that they hardly make any behaviour intelligible. However, it should be clear that in many cases in which an action is and is believed to be bad, and in which the emotion which motivated the action was inappropriate, the action is nonetheless made intelligible at least in some minimal sense. Given his emotional state, destruction and death seemed desirable to Othello, and though we cannot applaud his action, it seems we can understand it. Perhaps there are people whose emotions fire off so randomly that these latter can no longer be thought of as perceptions of values. Such emotions would just be too unreliable to make sense of anything. But in most cases, it seems that we better understand even an action as mad as Othello's if we know that it was caused by an emotion such as jealousy.

---

[30] One might reply that only states which can rationalize action should count as pro-attitudes. In that case the route to the conclusion that emotions can make akratic action intelligible could start with the thesis that emotions are reasons. The problem is that this would not be a quick route: one would have to argue for the claim that emotions can be reasons.

114 / Christine Tappolet

Another worry that might arise is whether akratic action grounded in emotion could be free. There is, of course, a debate about whether action against one's better judgement can be free or whether there is no difference between such actions and compulsion.[31] Given that the issue is the role emotions play, let me assume for the sake of argument that action against one's better judgement can indeed be free. Now the first important point to note is that non-akratic action caused by an emotion need not be unfree. Though some behaviour caused by emotion is certainly compulsive—one might think of flight behaviour caused by panic, for instance—most cases of emotional action are such that an agent could have resisted the emotion's pull. I could have resisted the fear I experienced and crossed that bridge, for instance. Given this, there is no more reason to think that an akratic action caused by an emotion is unfree than to think that an akratic action caused by some other state, such as a desire or a judgement, is unfree. One can well suppose that Francesca, to go back to our example, could have acted otherwise. For even if emotions, like judgements and desires, are not directly subject to the will, it is nonetheless true that one is often able to take the steps necessary to resist them. Like Ulysses, Francesca could have asked to be tied to a ship's mast during her encounter with Paolo. In a more realistic vein, she could have tried to concentrate on the danger that she and Paolo were in.

Another possible objection would be to question whether actions caused by emotions are really intentional. Such a charge could be based on the idea that only actions which result from deliberation are intentional. As Nomy Arpaly puts it, 'we routinely assume that acting for reasons necessarily involves deliberation' (Arpaly 2000: 505). Thus, an action caused by an emotion could never be intentional. Of course, Francesca does deliberate. The problem, it could be claimed, is that her passionate love is neither a part, nor an outcome, of such deliberation. However, we can agree with Arpaly that this seems too strong a requirement on intentional action. The person who turns on the light when she comes home at night can be said to act intentionally even if no deliberation is involved. She need not think that she wants to see her way around her living room and reflect that the best way to do that is to turn on the light, perhaps mentally comparing that action with other ways of achieving the same end, such as lighting a match or putting fire to the house.

---

[31] See Plato, *Protagoras* 352b–358d; Hare 1963, ch. 5; Pugmire 1982; Watson 1977; Buss 1997; as well as Mele 2002.

It is not even necessary that she reflect that if she desires to turn on the light, the best way to achieve this is to turn on the light. To count as intentional, it is sufficient that her action be responsive to the reasons she has. Given this, the action is performed for these reasons. The mistake is to think that for this she needs not only to be responsive to her reasons, but also to have certain propositional attitudes, such as judgements about these reasons.[32]

The Rationality of Emotional Akrasia

I have argued that akratic action based on emotion—emotional akrasia—can be made intelligible by the emotion in question. There are two further claims I wish to defend here. The first is that akratic actions based on emotion can actually be more rational than actions which conform to one's better judgement. The second is that akrasia that does not involve emotion—cool akrasia—is much more of a puzzle than emotional akrasia.

It is easy to see that, far from being only disruptive, emotions can also help us to behave more adequately than if we only trusted our deliberative faculty. My belief that there is no danger and that I thus ought to behave in a certain way might be simply wrong, so that it would only be thanks to my fear that I am able to escape the danger that threatens me. As is often noted, the fact that fear allows us to react rapidly and quite independently of higher cognitive processing and deliberation makes for its adaptiveness.

However, there is also reason to think that emotions can be helpful in quite a different way. They can, it seems, make us more rational, in the sense of allowing us to track reasons which we have but which we have neglected in our deliberation. As Alison McIntyre argues, akratic action sometimes seems more rational than action that is in line with our better judgement.[33] One of the examples she uses is Mark Twain's character Huckleberry Finn, who after having helped Jim to run away from slavery decides to turn him in, but when he is given the opportunity, finds himself doing just the contrary.[34] Now it can be agreed that it is more plausible to say that Huck's decision not to turn Jim in (although he judges that this is what he ought to do all things considered) is not only morally more admirable, but also more rational, than acting on

---

[32] This claim is incompatible with an intellectualist conception of rational agency, a problem I discuss in the next section.

[33] See McIntyre 1990, as well as Audi 1990 and Arpaly 2000.

[34] The example is from Bennett 1974.

116 / Christine Tappolet

his all-things-considered judgement. This is the case because his all-things-considered judgement neglects important considerations, such as Jim's being his friend, Jim's trust and gratitude, Jim's desire for freedom, etc. Those considerations might have produced a change of mind in Huck had he taken them into account, for he would have considered them to be reasons had he properly deliberated. Maybe Huck just overlooked those considerations when making up his mind, or maybe he didn't realize that they were reasons for him. Now, as the story goes, it is his emotional state that leads him to disregard his moral principles. It is his feeling of friendship and sympathy for Jim that prevents Huck from turning him in. Thus, his emotional state can be seen as a response to considerations that militate against turning Jim in, namely, Jim's being his friend and thus making his feelings of friendship and sympathy appropriate, for instance. By interfering with his better judgement, the emotion enables Jim to track reasons he would have neglected had he followed the conclusion of his deliberation.

In the course of her argument for the claim that akrasia can be rational, Nomy Arpaly describes a similar case (Arpaly 2000: 504). Emily's feelings of restlessness, sadness, and ill-motivation, which cause her to abandon a chemistry Ph.D. against her better judgement, are in fact responses to the fact that the programme is ill-suited for her. These feelings can be seen as a response to factors which, given Emily's beliefs and desires, are in fact good reasons for her to abandon the programme. Thus, her emotional states not only make her decision to abandon intelligible, but indeed lead her to act in a more rational way, something which she recognizes later. As Karen Jones says when commenting on this example, such cases show that 'an agent's emotion can be keyed-to her reasons in such a way that they enable the agent to track those reasons, while her all-things-considered judgement does not' (Jones forthcoming).

But how can acting against one's all-thing-considered judgement be more rational than acting on such a judgement? Perhaps we should take issue with Arpaly's claim that 'a theory of rationality should not assume that there is something special about an agent's best judgement. An agent's best judgement is just another belief, and for something to conflict with one's best judgement is nothing more dramatic than ordinary inconsistency between beliefs, or between beliefs and desires' (Arpaly 2000: 512).

As Jones underlines, Arpaly's claim is at odds with an influential conception of rational agency, one according to which an agent can be said to be committed to guiding her action according to the best reasons only if she is committed to following her all-things-considered judgements.[35] On this intellectualist conception, rational agency is not simply a matter of correctly tracking reasons; it involves *thinking* that we are properly responsive to reasons. There is, however, an alternative and quite plausible picture which is compatible with what is suggested by the above-mentioned examples. As Jones argues, the commitment to rational agency can be understood 'as the commitment to the cultivation and exercise of habits of reflective self-monitoring of our practical and epistemic agency' (Jones forthcoming). The important point here is that the cultivation and exercise of our emotional dispositions is arguably part of what expresses this commitment to rational agency. Given this, acting on the basis of our emotions can be expressing our commitment to rational agency. This will be so when our emotional dispositions are shaped by a process of self-formation; they are not simply mechanisms we happen to find in ourselves, but the outcome of a conscious self-educational process that aims at experiencing emotions when and only when they are appropriate.

One could say that in so far as our emotional dispositions are our own, acting on the basis of our emotions can be expressive of rational agency. And such action can be expressive of our commitment to rational agency even when it conflicts with the conclusions of our deliberation. For on some occasions such a conclusion would have been distrusted had our self-monitoring dispositions worked properly. As Jones claims, 'the functioning of such sub-systems does not stop being expressive of our commitment to rational guidance just because there is now an opposing all-things-considered judgement. In many cases that all-things-considered judgement may be such that the agent would distrust it, if her self-monitoring capacities were functioning as they should' (Jones forthcoming). Thus, though emotions quite often get us to act irrationally, and though this irrationality often involves acting against our better judgements, they can also help us to overcome the shortcomings of our deliberative faculty. And they can do so without making us less than agents committed to guiding our actions according to our best reasons. Thus emotional akrasia can be more rational than acting on a better judgement.

---

[35] See Korsgaard 1997: 222; Raz 1999: 16; Scanlon 1998, ch. 1, esp. p. 25; Wallace 1999*b*.

Cool Akrasia as Surd

By contrast, there are grounds to think that akratic action that does not involve emotions lacks intelligibility. For what happens in cool akrasia is that some consideration which has been judged to furnish insufficient reason for action is supposed nonetheless to be the reason for the action, thus making the action intelligible. The question is how such a consideration can be seen as the reason for the action, given the context. Consider the case of an akratic smoker. Let us suppose she agrees that smoking this cigarette would be pleasant, but judges that this is not a sufficient reason to smoke it, given all the reasons she has not to smoke it. How then can the fact that smoking is pleasant be the reason for her having the cigarette? It is clear that her belief that smoking this cigarette is pleasant can be part of what *causes* her smoking. But what is not clear is whether this belief can help to make sense of her action. The question is how her smoking can be seen as being done in light of the pleasantness of the action, given her overall verdict. The difficulty can be seen if we think of what the agent would say if asked why she is smoking the cigarette. She cannot really say that she is doing it for the pleasure involved, given her other beliefs. It is simply not clear that an agent can aim at a value that she considers to be a bad or insufficient reason for performing the action. It seems in short that a consideration can make an action intelligible only if it is considered to be sufficient (cf. Walker 1989: 670).

But how then can an emotion—or, more precisely, the value that is perceived when we experience an emotion—make an akratic action intelligible? What is the difference between (for instance) *perceiving* the action as pleasant, and *believing* that the action is pleasant, which would allow us to say in the one case that the action has been made intelligible, and in the other not? The difference is simple. In the case of a perception of value, what we have is the workings of a subsystem, that is, of something that works independently of higher-order cognitive faculties, whereas in the case of evaluative beliefs or judgements, we have a state of the same kind as the better judgement. Given this, the reason that is given in one's perception is immune, so to speak, from the overall verdict one makes. That one considers one's fear or the danger to be insufficient reason does not change the fact that an action based on that fear will be intelligible.

Note that if the evaluative belief were itself the outcome of a properly shaped subsystem, such as the agent's emotional dispositions, things would be different. The agent's attraction to the pleasure of smoking might make the

Emotions and Akratic Action / 119

desire to smoke and hence the smoking intelligible. And merely judging, whether correctly or incorrectly, that this attraction is inappropriate or simply keyed to an insufficient reason would not necessarily change this fact. But the evaluative belief alone does not seem to throw any light on why she smokes the cigarette, given her overall verdict on the action.

It might be claimed that everything depends on how the action is described.[36] As is generally acknowledged, it is under a description that actions are made intelligible. Given this, one could say that under the description 'smoking this cigarette though refraining is supported by better reasons' the action cannot be made sense of, whereas it *can* be made sense of under the simple description 'smoking this cigarette'. This is perhaps what Davidson has in mind when he writes 'but if the question is read, what is the agent's reason for doing *a* when he believes it would be better, all things considered, to do another thing, then the answer must be: for this, the agent has no reason' (Davidson 1970*a*: 42), adding that the agent has of course a reason for doing the action *a*. Now it is true that the agent has a reason for her action under the description 'smoking this cigarette'—it is the reason judged insufficient. What I dispute is that this reason is the reason why the action, so described, is done. Even though there is a reason for the action described as 'smoking this cigarette', it is not clear that this reason is sufficient to make sense of the action under this description, given the smoker's overall verdict.

If this is correct, one can conclude that there is an important difference between cases of emotional akrasia and cases of cool akrasia. In contrast with the latter, emotional akratic actions are not really puzzling. Echoing Peacocke's claim that 'we do find akrasia especially puzzling when there are no imaginative or perceptual asymmetries' (Peacocke 1985: 72), it can be said that cool akrasia is particularly puzzling. Not only is it not clear that the attentional focus that comes with emotions is present, but the puzzle is that such actions are supposed to be intentional while there seems to be nothing that makes them intelligible. As we have seen, it is difficult to believe that the mere judgement that the action has some attractive feature is the reason for the akratic action, given the agent's overall verdict. So in the absence of an emotion, there seems to be nothing that can help make sense of the action. Maybe the simple desire to perform the action is sufficient. But then it would have to be shown that that desire is not merely the cause of the action, but

---

[36] I owe this objection to Sarah Stroud.

120 / Christine Tappolet

also a state that can make it intelligible. And it would also have to be shown that that desire is not in fact an emotional state. In so far as it is not clear that acts of cool akrasia are done for a reason, the question of the possibility of cool akrasia still seems to be an open one.

Conclusion

Let me pull the threads together. I raised a number of problems with the argument presented by de Sousa for his claim that emotions get us from some relative better judgement based on a subset of reasons to the unconditional, or *sans phrase*, judgement and thus to action. The main difficulty with this claim is that it assumes Davidson's conception of akratic action. If emotions have a role to play in akrasia, it cannot be that of the akratic cause. For since there is (at least typically) no reasoning error in akrasia, there is nothing which causes such an error. Instead, I suggested that emotions have a more direct and more positive role to play in at least certain cases of akrasia. Emotions can both cause and make intelligible akratic actions. In so far as it makes sense to say that emotions are perceptions of values, we can say that akratic actions caused by emotions are performed in light of the perceived value. Moreover, I argued that akratic action grounded on emotion can be more rational than action that conforms to our better judgement. This is so at least when our emotional dispositions are the result of a process of self-formation. Finally, the comparison between cases of emotional akrasia and cases of cool akrasia suggests that unlike the former, it is not clear that the latter are really done for a reason. The upshot is that it is not clear whether there really is such a thing as cool intentional action done against one's better judgement.

5

Weakness of Will and Practical Judgement

Sarah Stroud

I shall be concerned in this chapter with a certain thesis about practical reasoning, and with the implications of weakness of will for that thesis. These implications merit careful study. For it seems at first glance that the phenomenon of weakness of will would threaten or even falsify the view of practical reasoning which I shall describe, and thus that weakness of will (if indeed it exists) motivates moving to a different, indeed radically opposed, conception of practical reasoning. I shall however argue to the contrary. First I shall try to defuse the apparent conflict between the existence of weak-willed action and the abstract conception of practical reasoning which will be my concern. Then I shall present other considerations also having to do with weakness of will which, I suggest, actually *favour* that conception over the rival view which will serve as its foil here.

Earlier versions of this chapter were presented at the conference Weakness of Will and Varieties of Practical Irrationality, Montreal, May 2001, and at the Second Annual Bellingham Summer Philosophy Conference, Bellingham, Washington, August 2001. My thanks to those present on those occasions, and to my commentators (respectively Xavier Vanmechelen and Rob Epperson), for useful discussion and comments. I am also grateful for written comments from Christine Tappolet and from anonymous referees which were very helpful in revising the chapter. My work on this chapter was supported by a grant from FCAR (Fonds pour la formation de chercheurs et l'aide à la recherche), which I gratefully acknowledge.

122 / Sarah Stroud

Practical Judgement, and Other *Dramatis Personae*

Practical Judgement

The basic thesis about practical reasoning which will be at issue throughout the chapter is that it characteristically yields what I shall call *practical judgements*. Through deliberating, I want to suggest, an agent can reach a conclusion—a judgement—which has an internal, necessary relation to subsequent action or intention.[1] Further, an agent's having reached a practical judgement in favour of φing is normally sufficient explanation of her (intentionally) φing, or intending to φ (when she does, of course). (This latter claim about the explanatory role of practical judgements is to be contrasted with the idea that an explanation of her action in terms of her practical judgement is incomplete or merely enthymematic.) These are the two central features of the judgements whose existence I mean to assert: their internal or necessary relation to subsequent action or intention, and their special explanatory role with respect to same. As a gloss on these two features, I'll call such judgements *practical* judgements.

Now my primary concern is simply the very abstract claim that there exist judgements which have these qualities. I am less concerned to identify any particular judgement as a practical judgement (i.e. as a judgement which has these qualities). However, I do have a tentative identification to offer, which will play some role in the argument to come: that such practical judgements are judgements of the form 'I have most reason to φ'.[2] The primary thesis at issue, then, is that practical reasoning characteristically yields judgements which have an internal or necessary relation to subsequent action or intention, and which normally constitute sufficient explanation of such subsequent action or intention. The classification of such putative practical judgements as judgements of the form 'I have most reason to φ' is a secondary suggestion (which could, of course, be wrong without the more general idea's thereby being impugned).

---

[1] We need to add 'or intention' because we sometimes deliberate about future actions, in which case the immediate product of our deliberation is not an action (now) but rather an intention to pursue a particular course of action in the future. Thus, it is possible for practical reasoning to have completed its work, and for our course to be settled, without our (yet) *doing* anything in accordance with that decision.

[2] Here—and in much else I say about practical judgements—I have been influenced by Scanlon 1998, ch. 1; and also by Nagel 1970, ch. VIII (see esp. §4).

Of course, even with this additional suggestion, this thesis about practical reasoning is very abstract, and leaves many questions about the latter unanswered. The view that we characteristically reach practical judgements through deliberation is certainly not intended as a complete portrait of the complex process of practical reasoning. Its scope is limited in a number of other important respects as well. First, you will notice that the thesis as formulated thus far is quite vague, in that I haven't as yet given any account of key terms such as 'internal' or 'necessary'. However, for now we can leave the thesis vague in this way. I shall later discuss how exactly these terms—and thus this thesis—might plausibly be interpreted. In any case, the opposing view of practical reason which I shall present shortly wishes to deny that there are judgements which enjoy an internal or necessary connection to action in *any* sense. Secondly, note that our thesis does not claim that *all* intentional actions are preceded by practical judgements.[3] (It does not even imply that all instances of practical deliberation issue in such judgements.) It holds only that when we do make judgements to the effect that we have most reason to ϕ, those judgements enjoy the special features mentioned. Thirdly, the thesis of the explanatory sufficiency of practical judgement does not entail that explanations in terms of the agent's practical judgement are the only acceptable explanations of intentional actions, even in cases in which the agent did indeed reach such a judgement. It merely asserts that if one *does* offer an explanation in those terms, that explanation is sufficient as it stands (as opposed to being incomplete or merely enthymematic).

A final remark about our thesis. The view that there are practical judgements in this sense is not the same as the thesis of ethical (judgement) internalism. However, it has the same form as the latter. (Those familiar with the debates over ethical internalism will thus recognize, in this chapter, some structural analogues of points and arguments made in that context.) It is an internalist thesis of a similar stripe, in terms of what it claims on behalf of a certain kind of judgement; it is just that the kinds of judgement at issue are different. The ethical internalist claims a necessary or internal relation between ethical judgements and action; the believer in *practical* judgements makes a claim of the same kind with respect to *his* favoured judgement (which is not distinctively ethical). Indeed, having noticed the two different types of judgement which are at issue, one might well think that the type of

---

[3] Cf. Scanlon 1998: 47: 'One can have an intention without having gone through a conscious process of assessing the reasons for following this course of action and judging them to be sufficient.'

124 / Sarah Stroud

internalism proposed by the defender of practical judgements is in fact the most plausible there could possibly be—the internalist thesis which is most likely to be defensible if any is.[4] For if internalism is false about first-person, present-tense conclusions about what one has most reason to do, one might well wonder what *better* case for internalism could be made for judgements from a different domain, one less transparently linked to the basic practical question facing any deliberating agent.

Weakness of Will

Now enter akrasia. Suppose we grant that weak-willed action, or action contrary to one's better judgement,[5] is possible and indeed actual. What implications for general conceptions of practical reasoning does this admission have? I wish to explore here whether the mere existence of such 'defective' cases forces us to change the way we might have been inclined to view the 'successful' or 'normal' case. My concern is that the mere existence of such defective cases might put paid to an otherwise attractive general account of what is going on in normal cases of deliberation, intention, and action.

In particular, the existence of akratic action seems to threaten the idea that we make practical judgements in the sense I have identified. It does so because it seems plausible that the 'better judgement' contrary to which the agent acts in cases of akrasia is precisely a conclusion of deliberation of the type mooted above, and thus a would-be practical judgement. (It is a striking fact that many weak-willed decisions are made after deliberation which seems to issue in a judgement of what one has most reason to do, which the agent then ignores and contrary to which he acts.) But if the akratic agent does indeed act contrary to what we would have thought was his practical judgement, then this seems to undermine the two central claims made on behalf of practical judgements. How can there be an internal relation between an alleged practical judgement and the agent's subsequent action if there are cases in

---

[4] Indeed, a number of writers have hoped to use internalism about reason-judgements as the basis for an extension of internalism to further cases, notably including moral judgements. See, for example, Nagel 1970, Korsgaard 1986b, Foot 1995 (see also 2001, esp. chs. 1 and 4), and Scanlon 1998.

[5] I operate throughout with a standard conception of weak-willed or akratic action as (free, intentional) action contrary to one's better judgement. I use terms such as 'akrasia', 'weakness of will', 'akratic action', and 'weak-willed action' interchangeably to refer to this phenomenon.

Weakness of Will and Practical Judgement / 125

which the latter does not even correspond to the former? Furthermore, how can the former serve as a sufficient *explanation* of a subsequent corresponding action when it is evidently not *sufficient for* such subsequent corresponding action?

For the purposes of our investigation into the implications of akrasia, I am just assuming here that akrasia exists. Furthermore, I am granting the plausibility of supposing that the akratic agent's 'better judgement' is indeed a (would-be) practical judgement. One could of course reject either of these suppositions, in which case akrasia would pose no threat to the view that there are practical judgements. One could hold, first of all, that akrasia does not exist: that an agent's subsequent intentional action never diverges from the practical judgement he reached in deliberation. On this view, his φing is sufficient proof (despite whatever he may say to the contrary) that any practical judgement he may have reached was in fact in favour of φing. Alternatively, one could admit the existence of akrasia, but deny the conflict between its existence and our thesis about practical judgements. The idea here would be to deny that the 'better judgement' contrary to which the akratic agent acts could indeed be plausibly identified *as* a practical judgement.[6] I mention these possible moves only to set them aside; in fact I don't consider either attractive on substantive grounds. But in any case I'd like to explore what happens if we do admit both the existence of akratic action, and the apparent conflict between that admission and the idea that we make practical judgements.

What happens, I think, is that we may be tempted to move to a different conception of practical reasoning, one according to which we do *not* make practical judgements in the sense I have defined. One way of denying my thesis concerning practical judgements would be to take a line, with respect to such 'judgements', that is analogous to expressivism or non-cognitivism in ethics. That is, one could grant the internal relation to action and even the explanatory sufficiency claimed for practical judgements, but deny that the

---

[6] This is Davidson's strategy in Davidson 1970a. According to Davidson, the agent who akratically ψs although his better judgement favours φing never in fact reaches a fully *practical* judgement in favour of φing. He reaches only a 'conditional' judgement of the form '*all things considered*, φing is the (better) thing to do', a judgement which—crucially—does not involve a *commitment* to φing's being the (better) thing to do. Such a judgement, Davidson says, is thus 'practical only in its subject, not in its issue' (1970a: 39). In the 'normal' case, however, in which the agent does do φ, he reaches not just a 'conditional' judgement in favour of φing, but indeed an 'unconditional', and thus fully practical, judgement of the form 'φing is the (better) thing to do'.

126 / Sarah Stroud

'judgements' enjoying those features are in fact genuine *judgements* at all. Again, I mention this possibility only to set it aside. While such an expressivist view would indeed be a rival to the more cognitivist proposal which I have in mind, its 'internalist' commitments seem no less threatened by the phenomenon of weak-willed action. My focus here will be a different way of denying that there are practical judgements as I understand them: an alternative which, unlike the 'expressivist' one, *can* be seen as a response to the challenge posed by weakness of will, and which indeed seems positively to draw support from the latter's existence.

Humean Externalist Practical Reasoning

That alternative is a broadly 'externalist', 'Humean' conception of practical reasoning which denies that deliberation can issue in genuinely practical judgements as understood here.[7] The 'Humean externalist', as I shall call him, offers an externalist construal of allegedly practical judgements (on analogy with an externalist view of moral judgements). Whereas the expressivist approach questioned whether so-called 'practical judgements' are really *judgements*, the Humean externalist attacks their title to be considered *practical*. (Thus the phrase 'practical judgement' is apt, in neatly suggesting the two main ways in which their existence can be denied.)

All sides grant, I assume, that practical deliberation often—or at least sometimes—issues in a conclusion about what one has most reason to do. Further, all sides presumably grant that when someone does reach such a conclusion, he then *usually* acts accordingly. So it is incumbent on the Humean externalist, no less than the defender of practical judgement, to say something about these deliberative conclusions and their relation to action. In light of the existence of weak-willed action, in which an agent acts contrary to his deliberative conclusion as to what he has most reason to do, the Humean externalist denies that there is an internal, necessary relation between the reaching of such a conclusion and subsequent action and intention. Furthermore, he denies that the agent's having reached such a

---

[7] I got the idea of calling this view 'externalist' from Bratman 1979, which described (and sought to reject) a form of externalism about judgements concerning what it would be best to do (Bratman 1979: 159 ff.). In general, one is an externalist about a type of judgement if one holds that there is no necessary or internal connection between such judgements and action (or intention or motivation).

conclusion can be a sufficient explanation of subsequent action and intention, even when these do conform to the conclusion reached. He thus denies both of the claimed features of practical judgements.

These two denials are linked. The Humean externalist reasons as follows: because the same allegedly practical judgement is present in both 'defective' and 'successful' cases, it cannot serve as a full explanation of action even in the latter class of cases. Rather, such judgements can constitute at best *part* of the explanation of an agent's ϕing, even in 'successful' cases. Clearly a further factor must be present in the 'successful' cases which is not present in the akratic cases. But then the presence of this further factor must be a necessary ingredient in the full explanation of the 'successful' case. Explanations which simply cite an agent's putative practical judgement are therefore strictly speaking incomplete or enthymematic, and the alleged practical judgement, on its own, cannot be said to enjoy a privileged or necessary link to intention or action. A 'bridge' between the two must be built by this further, independent factor which may or may not be present in an individual case. (More on this 'further factor' in a moment.)

Such an 'externalist' solution to the problem posed by akratic action may well draw strength from a general Humean commitment to the motivational inertness of (genuine) beliefs or judgements (whence the rubric '*Humean externalist*'). Recall the analogue of non-cognitivism or expressivism already mentioned, which secures the internal connection between practical 'judgements' and action by reclassifying the former as not in fact genuine judgements at all. The Humean externalist—here siding with the defender of practical judgements against the non-cognitivist—grants that such deliberative conclusions about what we have most reason to do *are* genuine judgements. Indeed, he may use that very fact to motivate his view. If these are genuine judgements, then for that very reason they cannot, on their own, motivate or lead to intention or action. Beliefs and judgements are motivationally inert; motivation, intention, and action can only result from the combination of a judgement or belief and a desire. The Humean externalist will thus argue in particular that the 'gap' which he sees between the putative practical judgement on the one hand, and intention or action on the other, can only be bridged by the independent presence of a *desire* (understanding this latter in the broad sense usually adopted by Humeans).[8]

---

[8] Cf. Robert Brandom: 'pro-attitudes must be included...on this account, to *bridge the gap* between what one believes and what one decides to do' (Brandom 1994: 247; my emphasis).

128 / Sarah Stroud

What desire will he propose? On analogy with the most natural (although not the only) way of developing ethical externalism, I shall imagine our Humean externalist as appealing to a supposed general desire *to do what we have most reason to do*. I shall imagine him as claiming that most of us, most of the time, have such a standing desire. Most of us, in short, desire to comply with something like Davidson's 'principle of continence' (Davidson 1970a: 41), which directs us to perform the act judged best in light of all relevant reasons.[9] The claimed prevalence of this standing desire allows the Humean externalist to grant that it is *normal* or *common* for people's deliberative conclusions to be followed by corresponding action. Indeed, the prevalence of this desire explains, for the Humean externalist, the (otherwise mysterious) reliable correspondence between our actions and our judgements concerning what we have most reason to do.

Before continuing to consider this proposal, I should pause to acknowledge that a Humean externalist need not, simply as such, take this specific line (i.e. that of attributing to us this particular standing desire). What is crucial for the Humean externalist is that an agent's action—even in a 'successful' case—is explained in part by appealing to a desire (or set of desires) which is independent of her putative practical judgement. More generally, what is essential to the Humean approach is that an agent's action be explained in part by desires she has which are independent of the judgements she makes. Now just as there is no absolute necessity for the Humean ethical externalist to appeal to a general desire to do what is right, there is no absolute necessity for the Humean externalist about putative practical judgements to appeal to the particular desire I have just proposed. As has by now become evident in the debates over ethical externalism, there are other possible strategies by which a Humean externalist could try to secure and explain the reliable connections which we seem to observe between certain judgements and behaviour.[10]

Nonetheless, I shall continue to focus here on the particular development of the Humean externalist line which I have proposed, for two reasons. My aim is to draw out the contrasts between a Humean externalist conception of practical reasoning and the view that we make genuinely practical judgements. In order to isolate those contrasts, I would like to consider a version of the former which makes as much common cause as possible with the latter.

---

[9] I here ignore the complication that for Davidson that judgement is merely 'conditional', as explained in n. 6 above.

[10] For representative debate on this point spawned by Smith 1994, see Brink 1997, Copp 1997, Smith 1997a, and Dreier 2000.

And the particular Humean line which I have proposed seems (in comparison with other possible Humean strategies) to be a good candidate. After all, the defender of practical judgements wants both to assign a privileged status to an agent's judgement concerning what she has most reason to do, and to offer that judgement as sufficient explanation of her acting accordingly (if indeed she does). The particular Humean externalist line which I have suggested seems to meet those wishes halfway.

For this Humean approach, while baulking (of course) at the claimed explanatory *sufficiency* of putative practical judgements with respect to corresponding intention and action, at least grants pervasive explanatory *relevance*— and thereby a kind of privileged status—to those judgements. Our Humean externalist is happy to say that the putative practical judgement plays a role in the generation and explanation of corresponding action or intention, rather than being a mere coincidence with respect to same.[11] He simply insists that strictly speaking a further desire is also necessary—one which, as it happens, we generally have. Now if the Humean externalist wishes to have the 'belief' slot in any action-explanation filled by this particular belief—the belief that one has most reason to ϕ—then it seems the only desire he can add is the general desire to do what one has most reason to do. Only this particular Humean line will be in a position to hold that the agent's deliberative conclusion (when she reaches one) is at least *part* of the explanation of her subsequent action, thus bringing the Humean conception closer to the practical-judgement view itself.

There is a second reason for considering this particular Humean strategy in preference to ones which assign no role to the agent's putative practical judgement in explaining her action (even when the action conforms to the judgement). It is that the former seems prima facie better able to explain why the agent has gone to the trouble of determining what she has most reason to do. If an agent desires to do what she has most reason to do, this furnishes an economical explanation both of her ϕing when she judges that she has most reason to ϕ, and of her having taken the time and effort to figure out what she has most reason to do.

I return, then, to the proposal which I have put in the mouth of the Humean externalist. This proposal seems easily able to offer an explanation of

---

[11] Jeanette Kennett complains, of an alternative Humean approach, that on such a view 'th[e] concurrence of judgement and action seems purely fortuitous. The judgement itself, that a course of action is better or best, is doing no work' (Kennett 2001: 51). Such a charge would not be justified against the Humean externalist line developed here.

130 / Sarah Stroud

the 'normal', 'successful' case in which someone who deliberates to the conclusion that she has most reason to φ then forms the intention to φ. What has happened is that the purely theoretical conclusion that she has most reason to φ has 'hooked up' with her standing desire to do what she has most reason to do, to yield a decision or intention to φ. Furthermore, this proposal is also compatible with—indeed entails—the possibility of someone's *not* forming the intention to φ on the basis of the conclusion that she has most reason to φ. On the Humean externalist picture, that transition requires, as it were, a second, independent 'input' (in the form of a desire) in order to go through. So whenever that desire is not present, the inference will not be made. This means the Humean externalist view in effect predicts the possibility of akrasia.[12] From the point of view of the Humean externalist, the phenomenon of weakness of will simply serves as a convenient reminder that there is indeed a gap between any putative practical judgement and action or intention—something to which our Humean is committed in any case. Weakness of will is in this sense a friend of the Humean externalist picture.

Our *dramatis personae* are now on stage. The practical-judgement view holds that deliberation characteristically issues in practical judgements which enjoy some sort of necessary link to subsequent action and intention, and which normally constitute sufficient explanation of such subsequent action and intention. These theses, however, seem threatened by the phenomenon of weak-willed action, in which the correspondence between the agent's apparent practical judgement and his subsequent action is broken. The

---

[12] This does not mean it is transparent what exactly is happening (in Humean externalist terms) in cases of akratic action. It is not very plausible to say that a desire which we typically have, and which works most of the time to secure the connection between our deliberative conclusions about what we have most reason to do and our subsequent action and intention, suddenly vanishes entirely for the short time in which the akratic decision is taken, only to return a few minutes later when the agent returns to normal, non-akratic functioning. However, I leave it to those more attracted to the Humean externalist line to work out what exactly is missing in cases of akrasia that is present in normal, successful cases of deliberation and action: there are presumably options other than saying that this general desire disappears entirely for a short time. (Mele 1995: 25–30 might be the basis for an alternative story, for instance.)

Incidentally, the *ethical* externalist may have an easier time explaining 'defective' cases, because in the ethical domain those are usually understood in terms of a particular figure, the amoralist, who (according to the externalist) simply lacks the general desire to do what is right which most of us have. The problem of weakness of will, however, does not concern people who seem systematically different from the rest of us, but, rather, episodic failures on the part of people who, most of the time, are normal in this regard.

Humean externalist offers a rival picture of practical reasoning which seems perfectly compatible with the possibility of akrasia, while entailing a different understanding of 'normal' or 'successful' cases of deliberation and action. Unlike the defender of genuinely practical judgements, the Humean externalist casts the 'normal' case as a compound of two separable elements: a motivationally inert judgement about what one has most reason to do, and an independent desire to do what one has most reason to do.

The Rational Sufficiency of Practical Judgement

In the rest of this chapter I would like to develop two important points of contrast between the view that we make practical judgements and the Humean externalist strategy. These contrasts are meant to persuade you that we should not move to the Humean externalist conception, despite the apparent problems posed by weakness of will for the practical-judgement view.

The first contrast is this. The believer in practical judgement sees the agent as having, and the Humean externalist sees him as not having, sufficient grounds—simply on the strength of his practical judgement—rationally to form a certain intention. The agent makes a sort of inference: he draws a certain further conclusion (in the form of an intention) from his deliberative conclusion about what he has most reason to do. The believer in practical judgements accepts this transition or inference as enjoying a kind of legitimacy as it stands. The Humean externalist, by contrast, rejects this inference (as thus far described). He considers it, as it were, *invalid* unless we add a further 'premiss': a further input to practical thought which is required in order for that output to count as a warranted conclusion. The Humean externalist sees a gap which the defender of practical judgement doesn't see, a gap between the premiss already mentioned (the agent's judgement of what he has most reason to do) and the conclusion drawn (his eventual intention or decision). And in order to justify the agent's inferentially crossing that gap, the Humean externalist thinks we must attribute to him an additional 'premiss'. By contrast, the believer in practical judgement rejects the need for any 'help' from additional 'premisses' (in the form of other independent judgements or mental states of the agent). He is willing to go 'express' from premiss to conclusion: to attribute the transition solely to the *structure* of rational practical thought.

132 / Sarah Stroud

I would now like to point out two things about this aspect of the Humean externalist picture. First, let me briefly flag the asymmetry between the practical case (as the Humean externalist construes it) and the case of belief. It would be very natural to say, concerning belief, that someone who comes to see herself as having sufficient reason to believe that p will normally therefore come to believe that p, and that the former judgement is sufficient explanation of the latter belief.[13] The transition from judging that one has sufficient grounds to believe that p to believing that p seems intelligible and justified as it stands; no further premiss seems to be required in order for this to constitute an acceptable update of one's epistemic stance.[14] In particular, this transition certainly does not seem to require the assistance of a desire, such as a desire to believe that which one has sufficient reason to believe. If the Humean externalist agrees with these points about belief, it follows that he is willing to countenance as a legitimate transition in the theoretical domain something which he is unwilling to accept as such in the practical realm. I do not pretend that this is a decisive objection, but, all the same, we may find this disanalogy striking. It will be all the more striking to the extent that we see theoretical and practical reasoning as broadly structurally similar: in so far, for instance, as we see both as involving a review and comparative assessment of what we take to be the relevant reasons for believing or doing something, which normally culminates in a corresponding belief or intention.

Now on to the second point I wish to make about the 'gap' which the Humean externalist sees in the agent's transition from practical judgement to intention. The Humean externalist's refusal to see that transition as simply part of the structure of practical reasoning, and his corresponding insistence that a further premiss is required, is reminiscent of the difficulties Achilles had with that rather odd fellow the Tortoise (Carroll 1895). Recall that the Tortoise agreed to accept, as premisses, p and $<$if p then $q>$. But he baulked at drawing the conclusion that q (while not retracting his acceptance of either premiss). The Tortoise saw a yawning gap between acceptance of those premisses and the drawing of the conclusion that q, and he wondered whether or how he could be compelled to cross that gap. In response, Achilles

---

[13] Scanlon makes these points about belief at Scanlon 1998: 33; see also 23. (Scanlon himself holds that analogous claims are true in the practical domain; see Scanlon 1998: 24, 33–4.)

[14] I am not suggesting that such an update would be rationally mandatory, only that it would be rationally legitimate. Here, as elsewhere, the possibility of modus tollens goes hand in hand with that of modus ponens: one's unwillingness to conclude that p might lead one to contrapose and decide that the reasons to believe that p must not after all be sufficient.

Weakness of Will and Practical Judgement / 133

asked the Tortoise whether he accepted the following principle: $<$if p, and if $<$if p then $q>$, then $q>$. The Tortoise said he would gladly accept that principle if Achilles wanted him to; why didn't Achilles just add that proposition to the list of premises the Tortoise accepts. So began a long day. As one can quickly see, it won't help to add this premiss to those which the Tortoise accepts.

General, sweeping moral of this story: structural elements of reasoning—facts about the outputs which a rational system yields given certain inputs—should not be confused with additional inputs (premises). To use or follow an inference rule is not simply to have an additional premiss acting as an input to an inferential system. Yet in apparent defiance of this general moral, the Humean externalist seeks to account for the transition from practical judgement to intention precisely by attributing to the agent an additional 'input' or premiss which licenses or legitimizes the transition in question.

Let me now explain this parallel between Achilles and the Humean externalist (as well as the limitations thereof). Achilles was faced with someone unwilling to make a certain inference. He hoped he could transform that person into someone *willing* to make that inference by adding a further premiss, in this case $<$if p, and if $<$if p then $q>$, then $q>$. This strategy failed. Someone unwilling to make the original inference cannot be transformed in this way; he will still be unwilling to make the inference even after he has accepted the new premiss and added it to the original premises (p and $<$if p then $q>$). The addition of the new premiss is *otiose* with respect to his rational grounds for drawing the conclusion.

Similarly, imagine the Humean externalist faced with an akratic agent—someone who does not make the 'inference' from his deliberative conclusion as to what he has most reason to do to a corresponding intention. Like Achilles, the Humean externalist thinks that this condition can be cured by adding another 'premiss'. However, in this case the new 'premiss' will have to be not a belief, but a *desire*: roughly, a desire to comply with the principle of continence. Despite this asymmetry between the cases, though, it remains the case that the contents of both premises share a similarity of form. Both are conditionals; and, indeed, each conditional takes the form of a principle which explicitly licenses or enjoins the making of precisely the inference at issue. On the one hand we have, as the content of the Tortoise's new *belief*,

if p, and if $<$if p then $q>$, then q.

The principle which Achilles urges on the Tortoise thus explicitly enjoins the making of precisely the inference which the Tortoise had been resisting. And

134 / Sarah Stroud

on the other hand we have, as the content of our akratic agent's new *desire*, something like

> if I judge that I have most reason to ϕ, I form an intention to ϕ.

The principle of continence instructs one to make precisely the transition which our akratic agent—before he was given a desire to comply with the principle of continence—was unwilling to make.[15]

One difference between the two cases does emerge at this point. Unlike the Tortoise, it seems the new and improved practical agent will now be willing to make the inference to an intention to ϕ.[16] Achilles is still left where he always was with the Tortoise; whereas the agent who now both judges (as he did before) that he has most reason to ϕ, *and* (now) wants to do what he has most reason to do, will indeed go ahead and form the intention to ϕ. It thus seems as if the Humean externalist's strategy for 'closing the gap' *worked*, while Achilles' didn't. And the Humean externalist may well say that this is a major difference!

However, notice that the Humean strategy works only in so far as our agent complies with a further structural element of practical reasoning which we might call *the basic instrumentalist principle*. It works, that is, only in so far as our agent complies with the principle:

> form an intention to ϕ when you want to ψ and believe that by ϕing you will ψ.[17]

Our agent (now) wants to comply with the principle of continence; he believes that by forming the intention to ϕ he will comply with the principle of continence; straightaway he forms the intention to ϕ. This transition requires no help from further premises. But it reflects—is an instance of— the structural aspect of practical reasoning just mentioned. Someone who does not 'use' the basic instrumentalist 'inference rule' will still see a gap

---

[15] Ariela Lazar also discusses the principle of continence in relation to the Tortoise; see Lazar 1999, esp. 390.

[16] I omit for simplicity, here and wherever pertinent, the qualifications (about this being the agent's strongest desire all things considered, for example) which would be necessary in order to explain his going all the way to an intention based on the considerations already cited.

[17] Compare the formulation of Michael Smith's P1 (Smith 1994: 92); and, again, note the qualification expressed in the previous footnote. Note also that, despite its name, the basic instrumentalist principle is not in my formulation limited to means–end reasoning narrowly construed (although it includes the latter). For example, it also applies in cases (such as this one) in which ϕing would *constitute* ψing.

between *these* 'premises' and that 'conclusion'. A gap is still there; it is just being bridged by a distinctively Humean claim about the structure of practical reasoning.[18]

A new, and interesting, moral now emerges. Humeans may once have been inclined to contrast their own supposedly modest commitments with those of their rationalist opponents, who (they say) are forever making grand claims about the 'structure of practical reasoning', i.e. positing transitions or conclusions that are allegedly mandated by Reason independent of one's particular aims and desires. In contrast, the Humean might have thought, he himself eschews such 'categorical' structural claims by always requiring the cooperation of a desire in any transition to intention. But as we now see, the Humean does *not* eschew structural claims about practical reasoning, and in particular claims of rational requirements which are independent of one's aims or goals.[19] Like the practical-judgement view, an instrumental conception of practical reasoning also makes structural claims, in holding out as rationally privileged certain transitions which do not depend for their authority on one's particular aims or desires. The Humean thus in effect makes a categorical, structural claim about the transmission of reason-giving force from ends to means. The bindingness of the hypothetical imperative is itself categorical.[20]

Both sides therefore see practical reasoning as containing structural elements. Both sides see the agent as following what might grandly be called a 'categorical imperative of practical reason' in making the transition from deliberative conclusion to intention. The two views disagree only about which structural claims are true: about which 'categorical imperative of practical reason' is at work here. Whereas the defender of practical judgement grants the agent the inferential licence to go 'non-stop' from deliberative conclusion to intention, the Humean externalist insists on appealing to a larger cast of characters and on covering the distance via a more roundabout route. In that respect the Humean externalist strategy does remind one of the troubles Achilles had with the Tortoise.

---

[18] The Humean externalist does fare better than Achilles in the following sense. The gap that remains once Achilles has added his further element is exactly the same gap that was there originally, whereas the gap that remains once the Humean externalist has added *his* favoured additional element is a *different* gap. But in both cases a gap remains.

[19] Jamie Dreier (1997) also points out this Humean commitment. As he says elsewhere, this means 'there aren't any metaphysical grounds for preferring a Humean ... account of practical rationality to a Kantian ... one' (Dreier 1994: 521).

[20] See Railton 1992 for this point.

136 / Sarah Stroud

Different Interpretations of Constitutive Principles

As I shall now argue, not only does the Humean instrumentalist believe that practical reasoning has a constitutive structure; he may well make a claim of the same *kind* about this structural element as the believer in practical judgement makes about his. How ought we to interpret the Humean instrumentalist's 'categorical imperative of practical reason', which conducts one from wanting to ψ, and believing that by φing one will ψ, to intending to φ? Though we may do so, we need not interpret the Humean as claiming that this rational transition is a matter of absolute necessity—as if someone's having an end *entailed* his being motivated to pursue means to that end. That would make it impossible to will the end without willing the means. But the Humean may well think that someone could fail to will the means while willing the end. That is, someone could fail to make the transition identified by the Humean instrumentalist as a structural element of practical reasoning. This is not impossible, he may think, but rather *irrational*.[21] On this interpretation, the basic instrumentalist principle articulates not an entailment, but rather a constitutive element of rational practical thought.[22] If he takes this line, the Humean allows us to see his instrumentalist claim as a norm of practical reason, rather than a definitional point about willing or desires; for only a principle that it is possible to violate can be a norm.

We can take a hint from this interpretation of the characteristic Humean instrumentalist structural claim in considering how best to interpret the corresponding structural claim advanced by the believer in practical judgements. If akrasia exists, the defender of practical judgements would be most unwise to suggest that forming a genuine practical judgement is literally a sufficient condition for subsequent corresponding action or intention. For it would then be impossible to act contrary to a genuine practical judgement— something which akrasia renders doubtful. (As we have seen, the weak-willed

---

[21] It would be an instance of what Korsgaard calls 'true irrationality' (Korsgaard 1986*b*). Dreier (1997) and Korsgaard (1986*b*) both make this point, agreeing (from, respectively, pro-Humean and anti-Humean perspectives) that Humean instrumentalism should be interpreted in such a way that violations of its central structural claim about practical reason are possible (though irrational). (See also Kennett 2001: 91–2, 115.)

[22] Consider Kant's qualification: 'whoever wills the end also wills (*in so far as reason has decisive influence on his actions*) the indispensably necessary means to it that are within his power' (Kant 1785/ 1996, Ak. iv. 417; my emphasis). As Dreier notes (1997: 90), that qualification marks the difference between the strong-entailment reading and the constitutive-norm reading of the principle to which Kant refers.

Weakness of Will and Practical Judgement / 137

agent seems to reach a practical judgement in favour of φing before going on, intentionally and deliberately, to do something incompatible with φing.) In short, it seems the defender of practical judgement is not best advised to present his claim as an entailment. Fortunately, as we have just seen, this very strong interpretation of claims about the structure of practical reasoning is not the only one available, or even the most attractive. The defender of practical judgement may well also wish his claim to be understood as an articulation of a constitutive element of rational thought in a more normative sense. Such a normative interpretation positively *requires* the possibility that the principle could be violated—a possibility conveniently made actual by the akratic agent. So the existence of weakness of will is actually a boon for the believer in practical judgement when the latter is interpreted as a constitutive norm rather than as an alleged entailment.

Such an interpretation proposes a particular way of understanding the 'necessary' or 'internal' link to subsequent action or intention which is one of the central claimed features of practical judgements. The relevant conception of necessity here is not one of strict entailment or nomological sufficiency. Rather, a certain transition within practical thought is said to be 'necessary' in the sense that it is a *rational* transition: an inference which is characteristic of, or part of the structure of, rational practical thinking.[23] I emphasize the word 'rational' in order to underline the normative element of this claim. Rational practical thought constitutively involves moving from certain conclusions (those about what you have most reason to do) to intention; this transition is sufficiently grounded as it stands, and requires no assistance from further premisses.

If we read it this way, the claim that there are practical judgements can be seen simply as an expression (or, at least, as an interpretation) of some uncontroversial and indeed compelling ideas about rational agency. Consider the following thoughts: that it is constitutive of rational practical thought to be motivated by (your judgement of) good reasons; that rational practical thought constitutively connects recognition of (practical) reasons with intention and action; that reason-judgements have as it were automatic practical pertinence with respect to intention and action. It seems hard to

---

[23] Kennett seems to share the *substance* of the view I have just sketched about the relation between 'judgements about what we have reason to do' and motivation or action (Kennett 2001: 105). Yet she makes an opposite terminological choice: she says the connection between the two is not a 'necessary' one, but 'is best described as a contingent *rational* connection' (Kennett 2001: 91; cf. 105).

138 / Sarah Stroud

object to the claim that we make practical judgements in so far as it is simply an expression of ideas like these. What *is* a rational agent, if not, in the first instance, one who perceives, responds to, and indeed acts on the basis of reasons?[24] Even the verbal relation between 'rational' and 'reasons' makes it very difficult to deny that some such constitutive connection holds.

I have been sketching an interpretation of the first thesis which the believer in practical judgements advances: that practical judgements enjoy an internal or necessary connection with subsequent action or intention. One advantage of this kind of interpretation is that it seems to marry nicely—indeed, as nicely as the Humean externalist view does—with the existence of weakness of will. However, if we assume the existence of akratic action, we may still wonder whether we are entitled to the second central claim made on behalf of practical judgements: that an agent's having reached an appropriate practical judgement can serve as a sufficient explanation of her corresponding action or intention. It is obviously not *sufficient for* the latter.

The question of what is (or can be) a sufficient explanation of my forming the intention to ϕ depends partly, of course, on general issues in the theory of explanation. One such issue is whether it is part of our best general conception of explanation that any sufficient explanation of something must also be a sufficient condition for that thing, in the strong sense of its being impossible for the supposed explanans to occur or to exist without the explanandum's following. Now in fact I very much doubt that such a requirement is part of our best accounts of explanation in general.[25] For it certainly *seems* to be a perfectly good explanation for the building's having burned down that I doused the whole thing with gasoline and then set the gas alight—even if such actions are not invariably sufficient for a building's burning down. Suppose this is right: that a good explanation is not constrained to offer as explanans something which is literally a sufficient condition for the expla-

---

[24] Cf. Scanlon 1998: 'a rational creature is, first of all . . . one that has the capacity to recognize, assess, and be moved by reasons' (23); '[I simply] assum[e] that rational agents are capable of making and being moved by judgments about reasons' (19); 'it is central to being a rational creature that one's attitudes are responsive to one's judgments about reasons' (62).

[25] Jonathan Dancy rather tentatively agrees that it would not be, arguing (at Dancy 2000*a*: 151–6) in favour of the following hypothesis: 'an explanation can be perfectly good without being "complete" , where a complete explanation is one that is inconsistent with the non-occurrence of the explanandum. . . . The idea that non-complete explanations are enthymematic is a mistake' (Dancy 2000*a*: 151). I say 'rather tentatively' because he views this as 'a highly debatable doctrine in the theory of explanation' (Dancy 2000*a*: 151), albeit one to which his views about reasons for action commit him.

nandum. Then the claimed explanatory sufficiency of practical judgements is not after all threatened by their not entailing subsequent corresponding action.[26] There are resources internal to the general concept of explanation to rebut that charge.

However, I do not wish simply to rely on aspects of the general theory of explanation in defending the explanatory sufficiency of practical judgement. For even if the suggestion I made above is false, there could yet be resources internal to the explanation of intentional action in particular which would help to bolster that claim. Such explanations might have special features which the defender of practical judgements could profitably exploit. And indeed it seems that the actions[27] of rational agents admit of a particular *kind* of explanation to which phenomena outside that domain are not subject. For when we explain such actions, we generally do so in terms of reasons. We typically offer a particular type of explanation, which I shall call 'rational explanation,' which does not apply outside the context of rational agency.[28]

Without pretending here to offer a detailed catalogue of the distinctive features of this special style of explanation, I do wish at least to take advantage of its existence. I propose in particular that we gloss the thesis of the explanatory sufficiency of practical judgement in the following way. A rational agent's action is sufficiently *rationally* explained by her having made a practical judgement in favour of acting in that way. A rational agent's practical judgement constitutes sufficient *rational* explanation of her subsequent corresponding action or intention. These riders emphasize the special type of explanation being deployed—rational explanation—and thus the special conceptual context within which these explanations in terms of practical judgement are held to be sufficient. They thus reinforce the close connection of our claims about practical judgement to constitutive norms of rational agency. By so doing, they further bolster our rejection of the idea that

---

[26] Cf. Nagel: 'the acceptance of such a judgment [a first-person present-tense practical judgement] is by itself sufficient to *explain* action or desire in accordance with it, although it is also compatible with the non-occurrence of such action or desire' (1970: 109).

[27] And, in general, their 'judgment-sensitive attitudes,' as Scanlon would have it (Scanlon 1998, ch. 1).

[28] To say that rational explanations are a special type of explanation is not necessarily to hold that they are *sui generis*, or to rule out their being a subset of a broader category of explanation. For example, Davidson seeks 'to defend the ancient—and common-sense—position that rationalization [explanation in terms of the agent's reasons] is a species of causal explanation' (Davidson 1963: 3). Rationalization could thus be a distinctive *species* of explanation—a type of explanation to which not every event which admits of causal explanation is subject—without being *sui generis*.

claims of explanatory sufficiency require the nomological sufficiency of the explanans. After all, rational agents can be irrational on occasion. But when their reasoning and their actions depart from the patterns constitutive of rational thought and agency, their susceptibility to that distinctive style of explanation which is rational explanation is thereby attenuated.[29]

In case you are inclined to find dubious the moves I have made to preserve the explanatory sufficiency of practical judgements in the face of their admitted nomological insufficiency, note that the Humean externalist will have to make exactly the same moves if he admits that it is *possible* (albeit irrational) not to be motivated in accordance with the basic instrumentalist principle. The Humean externalist's favoured account of the 'successful' case (in which an agent's action corresponds to her deliberative conclusion) cites (*a*), the agent's judgement that she has most reason to ϕ, and (*b*), her desire to do what she has most reason to do, in explaining her having formed the intention to ϕ. This explanation is supposed to be complete in a way that an explanation simply in terms of (*a*) is held not to be. But if it is possible to fail to be motivated in accordance with the basic instrumentalist principle, then it seems the Humean externalist explanation is not complete after all. For in that case it is possible for someone to judge that she has most reason to ϕ, and want to do what she has most reason to do, and yet *fail* to form the intention to ϕ.

The Humean externalist explanation is thus threatened with exposure as incomplete or insufficient just as the explanation in terms of practical judgement was. In response, the same moves are available to the Humean as were available to the defender of practical judgement. He can press the point about explanation in general which I raised earlier. And to bolster his argument, he can add a similar rider about rational explanation to his claim of explanatory sufficiency. That is, he can specify—on strict analogy with the corresponding move by the defender of practical judgements—that what he meant was that a rational agent's intentional ϕing is adequately *rationally* explained by his desire to ψ and his belief that by ϕing he would ψ.

Let us take stock. The first point of contrast which I have been developing between the practical-judgement view and the Humean externalist picture concerns the rational sufficiency of practical judgement. The Humean externalist and the defender of practical judgement disagree about whether

---

[29] Davidson suggests that akratic action may well admit of a *psychological* explanation while resisting *rational* explanation (Davidson 1970a: 42).

an agent has sufficient grounds, simply on the strength of her practical judgement, rationally to form a certain intention. Yet in the course of our investigation, we have seen that both the defender of practical judgements and the Humean instrumentalist advance what we may call structural theses about practical reasoning. Both propose general principles that are held to be constitutive transitions within rational practical thought and that can thus underwrite claims of explanatory sufficiency. The two views are on a par in that respect. Furthermore, now that we have seen better how to interpret the special features claimed for practical judgements, the threat that the existence of weakness of will seemed to pose to their existence has receded, leaving the Humean externalist without that apparent advantage over the practical-judgement view. Finally, we may now have a better appreciation of just how plausible the practical-judgement view is, once it is understood in the appropriate way. So Humean dreams of clear superiority over the practical-judgement view—especially in so far as such hopes were nourished by the existence of akrasia—ought by now to have faded away.

The Possibility of Global Akrasia

I wish to close by developing a second general observation about the Humean externalist picture, one which I think constitutes a definite *dis*advantage for that conception in comparison with the practical-judgement view. It concerns the possibility of global akrasia.

The Humean externalist response to the existence of akrasia is an instance of a strategy that philosophers have found tempting in many contexts. Suppose one notices that in addition to the 'normal' or 'successful' case of a given phenomenon, there exists also a 'defective' or 'non-standard' case. The phenomenon of this sort which has most exercised philosophers is of course perceiving a physical object versus hallucinating or dreaming. A very natural response to an observation of this kind is to understand the successful case as a *compound* of two or more independent or separable elements: one which it has in common with the defective case, and others which serve as the additional elements which make it successful.[30] One thus effectively takes the defective

---

[30] For penetrating discussion—far more subtle than that offered here—and a useful catalogue of several areas of philosophy within which such analyses have proved tempting, see Dancy 1995; see also Dancy 2000b: 138 ff.

142 / Sarah Stroud

case as the base case, and considers what needs to be added in order to arrive at the successful case.

Take for instance the view that normal or successful ('veridical') perception is to be analysed as consisting of two elements. The first constitutes that which the successful and defective cases have in common, namely the having of a certain sense-datum or sensory experience. Crucially, this common element is to be defined or identified in terms that do not presuppose the existence of objects in the world (e.g. purely in phenomenological terms, or ostensively). It is thus independent of the successful case: as noted above, we have in effect taken the defective case as our starting point. The second element is the further fact that the object actually exists, or caused the aforementioned perception, or some such 'success' condition; this second element is what distinguishes the successful from the defective case.

Notice that any view which sees the successful case as a compound of this kind implies the following possibility: that what we currently consider to be the 'defective' or 'non-standard' case is in fact the *only* case, rather than the rare exception. (It *could* be that all our sense-data or sensory experiences are illusory.) This conceptual possibility must exist if the normal case is simply a compound of two logically independent elements. If the element which the successful and defective cases share is defined in terms which make no reference to success, then we need only imagine that the further element which constitutes success never in fact obtains. We would then have a world in which what we now consider to be failure is in fact universal.

Simply *distinguishing* between 'successful' and 'defective' cases of a particular phenomenon does not bring with it commitment to this alleged possibility. For there are other ways of conceiving the relation between standard and non-standard cases which do not entail the possibility of global 'failure'. Consider, for example, counterfeit bills. Counterfeit bills constitute a sort of defective or non-standard case in comparison with genuine or authentic bills (legal tender). But here it would not be plausible to analyse the 'successful' case in the way sketched above.[31] It would not be plausible to take the counterfeit bill as the base case and figure out what we need to add to it to get a genuine bill. For what the two have in common cannot easily be defined without referring to the 'successful' case. Counterfeit bills are parasitic on the institution of genuine bills; it couldn't actually be the case that *all* bills were

---

[31] Cf. Geach's observation that ' "x is a forged banknote" does not split up into "x is a banknote" and "x is forged" ' (Geach 1956: 33). Thanks to Christine Tappolet for pointing out to me that Geach mentions this very example.

counterfeit. So the possibility of global failure is forced on us not by the mere distinction between success and failure, but specifically by construing the 'successful' case as a compound of *logically independent elements* in the way I described.[32]

The Humean externalist view concerning putative practical judgements exemplifies the 'compound' strategy which I have just been limning. The Humean externalist grants that normally agents form intentions in keeping with—not contrary to—their deliberative conclusions about what they have most reason to do. In that sense we have a 'normal' or 'successful' case with which we can contrast the 'defective' cases (of akratic action) which have preoccupied us here. The Humean externalist sees both the successful and the defective cases as involving the making of a particular motivationally inert judgement, which can be defined or identified independently of any connection to action (that is, without presupposing anything about success). What distinguishes successful from defective cases is the additional and independent presence of a *desire* of a certain type. Each of these elements—the motivationally inert judgement, and the desire—can exist without the other; the successful case is the happy product of their pairing. On such a view, the successful case is indeed the defective case *plus*. We add some further elements to the defective case to turn it into a successful case.

Because it is an instance of this 'compound' strategy, Humean externalism will similarly entail the possibility of global failure. It will entail the possibility, that is, of our *never* acting in accordance with our judgements of what we have most reason to do: of our *always* manifesting only the 'defective' behaviour, and never the 'successful' sort. Indeed, on the Humean picture, it is easy to see how such a possibility would be realized. Judgement and desire are 'distinct existences' for the Humean: we could have either without the other. Suppose then that we continued to make motivationally inert judgements about what we have most reason to do, but we never wanted to do what we have most reason to do (or that desire was always too weak to win the day). We might then always act akratically—*always* act contrary to our judgement of what we have most reason to do. If the Humean externalist approach is correct, such a state of affairs—a world of global akrasia—must be coherent, intelligible, and conceptually possible.

But here, I think, we have arrived at a real objection to the Humean externalist picture, for such a world does not clearly seem conceivable or

---

[32] Dancy rightly stresses the independence of the elements in his 1995 discussion; see esp. 433.

144 / Sarah Stroud

coherent.[33] We are asked to imagine our *always* acting contrary to judgements (which we continue to form) of what we have most reason to do. But this state of affairs seems to resist formulation even in the imagination; our conception of these matters does not seem to be open to the alleged 'possibility' which the compound approach forces on us. Rather, we seem naturally to have some sense in this context—as we did in the case of counterfeit bills— that the degenerate case is necessarily a degenerate case, that its occasional existence can be granted only against a background of general success.[34] The Humean externalist strategy entails the existence of a possibility which we find difficult to accept.

The Humean externalist may seek to intervene at this juncture, pointing out that even on his view, a world of global akrasia would be a very strange world relative to our own—very different indeed. For, he may remind us, he holds that it is a widespread, pervasive fact among human beings that they do generally want to do what they have most reason to do. To imagine beings who systematically lack any such desire is thus to imagine beings whose characteristic desires are very different from our own—beings who for that reason may be hard for us to understand, or even fully to conceptualize. In this way, if we report a feeling of resistance to the possibility of absolutely global akrasia, the Humean may rush to meet us halfway.

Note, however, the following important fact about the Humean picture of this alternative universe. These beings who are completely uninfluenced by the conclusions they reach about what they have most reason to do are still *practically rational agents*; they are simply rational agents with a different inven-

---

[33] Indeed, as Gary Watson and Christine Tappolet have suggested to me, this possibility is not clearly coherent even in the case of a single person. It is not clear that even a single agent, let alone a whole world of agents, could exhibit 'global' akrasia.

[34] Compare what Robert Brandom says about reliabilism as a general model for knowledge: 'the sorts of examples of knowledge to which [reliabilism] draws our attention ... are in principle exceptional. Knowledge based on reliability without the subject's having reasons for it is possible as a local phenomenon, but not as a global one' (Brandom 2000: 106). Such examples 'are *essentially* fringe phenomena. Their intelligibility is parasitic on that of the reason-giving practices that underwrite ordinary ascriptions of knowledge—and indeed of belief *tout court*' (110). (Thanks to David Davies for drawing these passages to my attention in this context.) Compare also the following remarks of Anscombe's: 'The occurrence of other answers to the question "Why?" besides ones like "I just did" , is essential to the existence of the concept of an intention or voluntary action.... This ... means that the concept of voluntary or intentional action would not exist, if the question "Why?" , with answers that give reasons for acting, did not. Given that it does exist, the cases where the answer is "For no particular reason" , etc. can occur ... but it must not be supposed that ... that answer ... could be the only answer ever given' (Anscombe 1963, §§20, 21).

tory of desires than is typical of human beings hereabouts. On the Humean picture—in contradistinction to the practical-judgement view—it is not constitutive of rational agency to be influenced by such considerations. So the fact that such influence is completely absent in that world does not take us out of the domain of rational agency altogether. It simply means that these practically rational agents lack certain desires which we have. Our practical reasoning has as it were more 'premisses' to operate on than theirs does— notably a desire, which they lack, to do what we have most reason to do. But on the Humean externalist picture, the fundamental mode of rational operation given the inputs to the system is the same in the two worlds.

The defender of practical judgement will give a different diagnosis of our reluctance to admit the conceivability of this world. He may, although he need not, say that a world in which no beings ever did what they judged they had most reason to do is flat-out impossible. From his perspective, it is, at a minimum, unclear whether such beings could still be said to make such judgements. But in fact he need not establish a negative answer to that question in order sufficiently to distinguish his position from the Humean externalist's. For even if the defender of practical judgement admits the logical possibility of such a world, he will claim that in such a world we are no longer dealing with beings who exhibit rational agency.[35] He will say that this is simply not a world of practically rational agents. To suppose that we might be completely and systematically uninfluenced by our judgement of what we have most reason to do is not merely, as the Humean would have it, to alter the inventory of mental states which can serve as premises for rational practical inference. Rather, we feel that there is a deeper unintelligibility or inconceivability in trying to suppose this. This need not be construed as absolute impossibility, but rather as impossibility *within the framework of rational*

---

[35] Ralph Wedgwood's conceptual role semantics for moral terms (Wedgwood 2001*a*) could concur with either position. On Wedgwood's version of conceptual role semantics, 'the meaning of a term is given by the *basic rules of rationality* governing its use' (6); one can thus be said to understand a term only if one masters those rules. Wedgwood's analysis in fact centres on terms which could figure in practical judgements, such as 'what we have most reason to do' (14). According to Wedgwood, the basic rule of rationality governing the use of such terms is a rule of practical reasoning according to which (roughly) acceptance of a first-person-singular, present-tense sentence involving such a term commits one to forming a corresponding intention. Violations of this rule—such as are regularly exhibited by agents in our imaginary world of global akrasia—are irrational in those who understand such terms. So, at best, our imaginary world is filled with agents who are systematically irrational. And at worst—given their seeming lack of mastery of this rule—it is questionable whether the agents in such a world even understand those terms, and thus even make practical judgements.

146 / Sarah Stroud

agency. If the 'degenerate' case became the standard, indeed the universal, case, we feel we would no longer be within that framework as we understand it. The Humean externalist must deny this: he is committed to the possibility, *within the framework of rational agency,* of this alternative universe.

This chapter has been devoted to the question of the implications of weakness of will for our conception of practical reasoning, and in particular for the existence of practical judgements. It might have seemed that the very existence of weakness of will favoured the Humean externalist model over the view that deliberation characteristically issues in practical judgements. Through my exploration of the question of the rational sufficiency of practical judgement earlier, I hope to have neutralized that apparent advantage. And in this latter part of the chapter I have introduced a further consideration having to do with weakness of will which, I have argued, constitutes a definite liability for the Humean externalist picture in comparison with the practical-judgement view. In dealing with *this* question about weakness of will—not whether it is possible, but whether it could be 'global'—the practical-judgement conception, I submit, is clearly superior.

6

Accidie, Evaluation, and Motivation

Sergio Tenenbaum

Accidie seems to be a phenomenon in which evaluation and motivation come completely apart; someone who suffers from *accidie* supposedly still accepts that various things are good or valuable, but is not motivated to pursue any of them. This kind of phenomenon seems to be devastating for theories of practical reason that aim to maintain a tight connection between motivation and evaluation, and, in particular, for any theory according to which judging something to be good or valuable necessarily gives rise to a corresponding desire in the agent.[1] In this chapter I will look into what I call 'scholastic views' of practical reason, views that postulate quite a strong connection between motivation and evaluation. I will actually focus on an 'extreme' version of the view, one according to which motivation and evaluation are somehow *identified*. I will argue that phenomena such as *accidie* do not pose a threat even to such an extreme version of the scholastic view. I will argue that these versions of a scholastic view can not only account for the phenomenon, but they might help us understand in which ways *accidie* may be a form of irrationality. If all this is correct, there is no reason to think that such phenomena present a threat to the general view that motivational states

I would like to thank Joe Heath, Jennifer Nagel, Sarah Stroud, Christine Tappolet, Daniel Weinstock, and two anonymous referees for Oxford University Press for comments on this chapter. An early version of this chapter was read at the conference Weakness of Will and Varieties of Practical Irrationality, Montreal, May 2001. I would also like to thank the members of the audience at that conference for interesting questions and discussion.

[1] The *locus classicus* of this kind of criticism of theories according to which 'only the good attracts' is Stocker 1979.

148 / Sergio Tenenbaum

such as desires always aim at the good or to the view that we only desire *sub species boni*.

The Scholastic View

In the *Critique of Practical Reason* Kant discusses what he calls the 'old formula of the schools':[2] 'We desire what we conceive to be good; we avoid what we conceive to be bad.'[3] I will call any view that accepts some version of the 'old formula of the schools' a 'scholastic view', but I will be mostly concerned with a particular strong version of the scholastic view. In this section I will present a brief overview of the motivations for accepting a scholastic view. I'll start with relatively weak versions of the scholastic view, and then work up to the reasons to accept a stronger version.

Let us start with the following 'minimal' scholastic claim:

(S1) If α desires X, then α conceives X to be good.

If one thinks that the old formula of the schools should also be understood as a biconditional, one also accepts the converse of (S1):

(S2) If α conceives X to be good, then α desires X.

We can introduce (S3), the conjunction of the two conditionals:

(S3) α desires X if and only if α conceives X to be good.

(S3) should be distinguished from the stronger claim that desiring X and conceiving X to be good are just one psychological state:

(S4) To desire X is to conceive X to be good.

I'll often refer to the agent's desires as pertaining to his 'motivation', and the agent's conceiving of various things to be good as pertaining to his 'evaluation'. S1–S4 are various theses regarding how motivation and evaluation are connected. The most extreme claim, S4, takes the difference between 'evaluation'

---

[2] I have adapted the formulation of the 'old formula of the schools' which is found in Lewis White Beck's translation of Kant 1788 (Kant 1788/1956: 61). Beck cites Wolff and Baumgarten as Kant's sources for the formula.

[3] The Latin phrase that Kant uses is 'Nihil appetimus, nisi sub ratione boni; nihil aversamur nisi sub ratione mali'. To avoid too many awkward constructions, I will often speak only of pursuing good, instead of pursuing good and avoiding evil.

and 'motivation' to be what Descartes would have called a 'distinction of reason'. Evaluation fully determines motivation and vice versa. S3 doesn't quite make that claim. If S3 is true, then, indeed, if an agent positively evaluates X, then the agent must be motivated to do X, and vice versa. But S3 allows for significant gaps between evaluation and motivation. S3 does not rule out the possibility that an agent will be strongly motivated to do something that she finds to be only slightly valuable, or that the agent is weakly motivated to do something that she finds immensely valuable. All these possibilities are ruled out by S4. I will start by looking into the reasons for accepting S1. I will then try to show that the reasons that motivate accepting S1 also provide a good case for accepting S4, and thus a fortiori, S2 and S3.[4] My aim here is not to provide a conclusive argument for a scholastic view, but to present it as an attractive option in the field. Indeed, I think much of the resistance to scholastic views comes from cases in which it seems that one must concede that evaluation and motivation have come apart. Since *accidie* seems to be a case in which we have an agent finding things valuable but having *no* motivation to pursue them, and thus to exemplify a particularly extreme version of this kind of phenomenon, if we can show that scholastic views can explain *accidie*, we will have taken a major step towards establishing the cogency of scholastic views.[5]

However, before we look into the reasons for accepting any of the above claims, it might be worth saying a few words about the notion of desire that's in question. Many philosophers have distinguished between two senses of 'desire': a broader sense, which is supposed to include any pro-attitude towards an object, and 'desire' in a narrower sense, which is often accompanied by a more vivid phenomenology. When one says, for instance, 'I don't have any desire to go out in the rain and vote, but I have to', one would be using 'desire' in the second sense.[6] 'Desire' here is meant in the broader sense. However, the

---

[4] For an independent argument in favour of a claim roughly equivalent to S2, see Arkonovich forthcoming.

[5] Michael Smith, for instance, takes the possibility of *accidie* to pose a major obstacle to John McDowell's account of the virtuous agent. See Smith 1994, §4.7. What seems to be a problem there is exactly the 'scholastic' character of the view (the claim that the evaluation of the agent can't leave her unmoved). See McDowell 1979. Akrasia seems to be another serious stumbling block for scholastic views. In Tenenbaum 1999 I argue that scholastic views can provide better accounts of akrasia than non-scholastic views. I look into other kinds of recalcitrant phenomena in Tenenbaum forthcoming *a*. Some of the points made in the following paragraphs are also made in these papers.

[6] See Schueler 1995. For similar points, see also Scanlon 1998, esp. pt. i, and Nagel 1970.

150 / Sergio Tenenbaum

scholastic view, as I understand it, is interested in the notion of desire only in so far as it does work in deliberation[7] or intentional explanations.[8]

Many philosophers have argued for the claim that a desire must have an intelligible object of pursuit.[9] To use Anscombe's example, if someone wakes up with an inexplicable impulse to put all her green books on the roof, it would seem at best misleading to consider putting all her books on the roof as something she wants. And one could expect that such an impulse would not enter her deliberations unless she could, at some stage, see *a point* in moving the books to this location.[10] Moreover, if she did proceed to put books on top of the roof, and someone were to ask her why she was doing this, it would seem that no proper intentional explanation would be given if the agent responded by saying, 'I simply wanted to put the green books on the roof' or 'for no particular reason'. As Anscombe puts it:

> If someone hunted out all the green books in his house and spread them out carefully on the roof, and gave one of these answers to the question 'Why?' his words would be unintelligible unless as joking and mystification. They would be unintelligible, not because one did not know what *they* meant, but because one could not make out what the man meant by saying them here.

> (Anscombe 1963, §18)

Let us now make a first attempt at trying to turn these remarks into an argument for the scholastic view. In a proper intentional explanation, the agent (or a third person) will be able to explain the point of engaging in such an activity; in other words, he will be able to explain what good he sees in the pursuit of this activity. On this view, a desire for an object as it typically appears in, for instance, an intentional explanation in the form of a belief–desire explanation must show what the agent found attractive in the choice of this action. But if the desire is not for something that one can intelligibly conceive to be good, or if it is not for something that the *agent* conceives to be good, we would not know what point the agent could see in such an action,

---

[7] This does not mean that the deliberations must be *about* the desire rather than its content. See Pettit and Smith 1990.

[8] For the sake of simplicity, I will talk mostly about intentional explanations, and leave deliberation aside. All I say, however, should also apply to deliberation.

[9] See, for instance, Raz 1996: 70 ff., Tenenbaum 1999, and, to some extent, Quinn 1994. Cf. G. E. M. Anscombe's claim that one can want an object only under a desirability characterization (Anscombe 1963, §§37, 38).

[10] Of course, *the fact that she has that impulse* might enter her deliberations, since it can be, for instance, something bothersome that she would like to get rid of.

Accidie, Evaluation, and Motivation / 151

and we would therefore not have made the agent intelligible. We would be left, in this case, unable (to use Anscombe's words) to 'understand such a man' (Anscombe 1963, §18). Thus, we come to the conclusion that desire, in so far as it has a role to play in deliberation and intentional explanations, must involve a positive evaluation of its object, or it must conceive it to be good.

If this reasoning is sound, it establishes S1, but it certainly does not establish S4. All that this shows is that in explaining the agent's behaviour in this particular manner, one needs to appeal to what the agent found good in the end she was pursuing; we need to provide what Anscombe calls a 'desirability characterization'. But it does not show that it is impossible for an evaluation the agent makes to leave her completely unmoved, let alone that the motivational and evaluative elements in the agent's psychology have to be simply identified.

The reasons to accept S4 will be clearer if we look into an objection to S1, and see how a defender of S1 can respond to this kind of objection. Suppose one grants that one finds somewhat awkward that an agent gives the answer above when asked 'why are you putting the books on the roof?' However, the objection goes, this says more about how we expect agents to behave than about the nature of intentional explanations. It is true that agents rarely have an 'unmotivated' [11] or basic desire to put books on rooftops, and it would thus come as a surprise that an agent is so motivated. But, suppose we found no other source of motivation for the agent's actions. We would surely want to say that the impulse was what brought the action about. And that would mean that in this case the impulse does explain the action. If one is attached to a scholastic view, one might be tempted to insist that in this case the impulse is not a desire or that the explanation is not properly speaking an explanation, but this might now seem completely ad hoc. Is there any essential difference between an explanation that mentions an unmotivated or basic desire that has this kind of odd content, and one that mentions an unmotivated desire that has an 'intelligible content'? Would there be any reason not to see the desires of the 'odd' agent as working in any way differently from the desires of the 'normal' agent?

If the defender of S1 is going to answer the above questions affirmatively, she must appeal to a conception of intentional explanation that can make sense of treating these cases differently. An attractive possibility is to appeal to a broadly 'Davidsonian' conception of intentional explanations, a conception

---

[11] I am using this expression in Thomas Nagel's sense. See Nagel 1970.

152 / Sergio Tenenbaum

according to which intentional explanations are guided by what Davidson calls 'the constitutive ideal of rationality' (Davidson 1970*b*). One way to understand this idea is that intentional explanations aim to display the agent's behaviour as aspiring to conform the norms and ideals of rationality.[12] Given that we are imperfectly rational beings, intentional explanations will not always make agents fully *rational*, but they should make them at least *intelligible*;[13] we should at least be capable of seeing how the agent could have *taken* this kind of behaviour to be rationally warranted. Putative 'desires' whose objects cannot be understood to be intelligible objects of pursuit (and thus could not be conceived of as good) will not be able to throw any light on how the behaviour was intelligible, and explanations that cite such 'desires' would thus not serve the same explanatory aims as intentional explanations do.

This way of understanding a commitment to S1 will make it dependent on accepting this broadly Davidsonian conception of intentional explanations. I will not try to defend this conception here.[14] What matters to us is that if we accept S1 on those grounds, it will be plausible to accept S4 on the same grounds. For suppose there is a gap between motivation and evaluation. Suppose we find that there is an element of brute motivation (or lack thereof) in desire that can work to some extent independently of the agent's evaluations, independently of how the agent conceives or judges things to be good. Since this element would not help to make the behaviour intelligible, it would be extraneous to the aims of intentional explanations. In so far as these elements could cause the agent's body to move, they would be better conceived as *interfering* with activity that could be the subject of intentional explanations; mentioning those causal influences would be better understood as an explanation for the lack of availability of a proper intentional explanation. Assimilating unintelligible impulses into intentional explanations would be a mistake akin to assimilating body tics, jerks, and paralyses to those explanations;[15] the mental origin of the behaviour would not contrib-

---

[12] Cf. John McDowell's claim that 'the concepts of propositional attitudes have their proper home in explanations of a special sort: explanations in which things are made intelligible by being revealed to be, or to approximate to being, as they rationally ought to be' (McDowell 1985*a*: 328).

[13] I put the point in this way, partly because I think that this Davidsonian picture is not far from Anscombe's understanding of intentional explanations in Anscombe 1963.

[14] See McDowell 1985*a* and Hornsby 1998 for some arguments for similar views.

[15] However, those impulses can give rise to rather complex behaviour (for instance, in those who suffer from obsessive-compulsive disorders), and it would be implausible to claim that no instances of such behaviour admit of intentional explanation. I try to show that a scholastic view

Accidie, Evaluation, and Motivation / 153

ute any further to its intelligibility.[16] Since, on this view, the *point* of intentional explanation is to show how an action appeared reasonable to an agent, it will be difficult to find room there for brute motivation.[17]

Of course, given that human agents are imperfectly rational, we must make room for the possibility that the behaviour explained is irrational. But there is no reason to think that this should proceed by finding some kind of brute motivation in the agent. Theoretical irrationality is generally understood not in terms of brute dispositions, but rather in terms of conflict of judgements, or incoherent conceptions, or the improper formation of judgements, etc. There is no reason to think that the same should not be true of practical reason.

However, if practical irrationality resists those kinds of explanations, we might need to revise this understanding of practical irrationality; and if that puts too much pressure on the scholastic view, it might force us to abandon this view. Indeed cases of practical irrationality often appear to be cases in which postulating a gap between motivation and evaluation is the only way to account for the phenomenon. Moreover, the Davidsonian framework seems particularly unsuited to accommodate explanations of purported cases of practical irrationality, given that it understands intentional explanations as essentially rationalizing explanations. Thus showing how a scholastic view can accommodate *accidie* and related phenomena, as well as the possibility of irrationality in these cases, is indispensable for establishing the plausibility of this kind of view.

The Problem with *Accidie*

A scholastic view seems to be at its best when dealing with reasonable persons engaging in normal behaviour under calm and controlled conditions. However, problems seem to abound when we look at various human failings and unfortunate circumstances. Evil, weakness of the will, and dejection, just to

can allow for some explanations of this kind of behaviour to count as intentional explanations in Tenenbaum forthcoming *a*.

[16] Anscombe gives examples of other mental causes that do not contribute to making behaviour intelligible in the same way. See Anscombe 1963, §§9, 10.

[17] To say that it is 'difficult' does not mean that it is impossible. One might try to find a way to accommodate this possibility within the Davidsonian framework (perhaps by appealing to a notion of 'partial intelligibility'). But part of the point of this chapter is to argue that there is no need to take this route since apparent counter-examples to S4 can be explained without abandoning a scholastic view.

154 / Sergio Tenenbaum

cite a few examples, seem to threaten the equation of desiring and conceiving something to be good. In a famous paper Michael Stocker argued that looking at these kinds of phenomenon should do away with any temptation to identify motivation and evaluation. According to Stocker, *accidie* and other similar cases of 'lack of will', in particular, cannot be accounted for in terms of shifts in one's conception of the good:

> Through *accidie*...through general apathy, through despair...and so on, one may feel less and less motivated to seek what is good. One's lessened desire need not signal, much less be the product of, the fact that, or one's belief that, there is less good to be obtained or produced...Indeed, a frequent added defect of being in such 'depressions' is that one sees all the good to be won or saved and one lacks the will, interest, desire or strength.
>
> (Stocker 1979: 744)

'Good' is said in many ways, and one could try to argue here that the objection Stocker is raising is based on confusing a formal notion of good employed in the scholastic view, a notion of the good that does not commit us to any particular answer to the question 'what is good?', and a more substantive notion of good. Suppose someone says 'I want to be bad' when she is about to engage in morally dubious behaviour. This kind of assertion need not be seen as a counter-example to the scholastic view, as an expression of the agent's lack of interest in the pursuit of any good. An agent who makes such a statement is claiming that she wants what is morally bad, not what is bad *simpliciter*. The scholastic view can say in this case that the agent conceives that which she considers to be morally bad as good.

However, one cannot account for the dejected agent in the same way. Indeed, Stocker's apt description of the dejected person seems to pose a particularly difficult challenge. The person in a state of *accidie* is not rejecting a particular conception of the good in favour of other, perhaps socially devious, goods. The dejected person seems to be simply lacking in the will to do *anything* she finds good or valuable, however generously we conceive of goodness or value; she seems to be unmotivated to act *from any conception of the good*. It would seem indeed odd to come to the conclusion that in some sense, however attenuated, she conceives inaction to be good, and thus it seems hard to avoid the conclusion that there is a purely motivational element in intentional action here that is independent of evaluative considerations.

It is worth putting forth the following tentative characterization of the dejected agent, or the agent who suffers from *accidie*. We can say that the dejected agent is an agent who, for some period of time, is not motivated to do anything in particular, or someone who has very little motivation to pursue ends that she herself would recognize she would pursue if she were not in a 'dejected state'. However, she also denies (sincerely) that she no longer understands the value or importance of the things she no longer pursues; she does think that it is in her power (at least in some sense) to pursue these things; and she does not think that she is pursuing anything of greater importance at the moment. Moreover, we have no reasons, or at least no prima facie reasons,[18] to think that her self-description is systematically mistaken. Persons in a state of *accidie*, under this description, might range from the 'average' person who at times might lack the motivation to get out of bed, or engage in meaningful activities, to some cases of clinical depression.[19] If this is an apt description of the dejected person, it seems hard to deny that he conceives, for instance, his own health to be good, but just does not desire to pursue it.

We can present this challenge to the scholastic view as follows: the scholastic view assumes that our judgements of the good will issue in action without any interference from any purely motivational sources. *Accidie* presents a rather stark counter-example to this assumption; one's motivation to pursue the good in this case is simply absent. Under a simplistic under-standing of the scholastic view, the objection is indeed devastating. Suppose the scholastic view takes each desire of the agent to be something that she judges to be good, and deliberation consists in 'adding up' the good to be found in each of the options open to the agent. Then a scholastic view could only account for *accidie* in terms of the agent finding that there is more good in 'staying put' than in doing anything else. This is certainly not a very plausible account of the phenomenon. However, I will try to show that a more sophisticated version of the scholastic view will be able to account for the phenomenon in a quite different manner. In particular, instead of trying to show how the dejected agent finds some good in staying put that other agents don't, or finds some kind of 'disvalue' in acting, I will argue what is distinctive in *accidie* is how the agent in such a state moves from particular

---

[18] Of course, we might end up having theoretical reasons to conclude that her self-description is mistaken.

[19] Certainly not all cases of clinical depression can be described in this manner or pose any particular threat to scholastic views. In many cases, patients simply 'don't care' about anything in such a way that it would be hard to say that they still value anything. See the *DSM-IV-TR* (American Psychiatric Association 2000) entry on major depressive disorders.

156 / Sergio Tenenbaum

desires to a general conception of the good. My claim is that a scholastic view can account for *accidie* by understanding the agent in this state to be putting certain constraints on the formation of a general conception of the good. In so far as *accidie* is irrational, its irrationality should be accounted for in terms of a judgement of the legitimacy of those constraints, in our eyes and in the agent's.

I want to argue that a certain version of the scholastic view can account for *accidie* in this way. A central feature of this view is that desires are 'appearances of the good' from certain evaluative perspectives. Whether or not one should pursue an object that appears to be good in a certain way will depend in part on whether and how one thinks that the relevant evaluative perspective should be incorporated into one's general conception of the good, and into one's unconditional judgement of the good. This will in turn depend on whether one holds that a certain relation, which I call a relation of 'conditioning', obtains between certain states of affairs and the evaluative perspective in question, and whether one believes that these states of affairs obtain. My claim is that *accidie* can be understood as accepting a relation of conditioning of this kind and a belief to the effect that the condition does not obtain. The rationality of *accidie* would then be a function of the rationality of accepting the relation and forming the belief in question.

Appearances of the Good and Evaluative Perspectives

Since a scholastic view claims that we desire only what we conceive to be good, a natural way to start looking into our favoured version of the scholastic view is to spell out how it understands the 'good'. As I suggested above, the notion of the good employed by such a plausible scholastic view is a quite general notion. Attempts to incorporate a more substantive notion of the good will typically render the scholastic view wholly implausible. For example, if we take 'good' to stand for 'morally good', we will be committed to the insanely optimistic claim that we only want what we regard to be morally good. Reading it as 'aesthetic good' or 'gastronomic good' can have only worse results. So the good here is to be understood as a formal notion. Saying that desire aims at the good is akin to saying that the desire presents the object to us as worth pursuing, as having a point, and saying this does not rule out the possibility that there might be a number of irreducible substantive goods. It does imply, however, that desire is not a blind impulse, as, for instance, one

Accidie, Evaluation, and Motivation / 157

might feel if one were possessed by a random impulse to switch around copies of the *Republic* in the various offices in one's department. To say that desire aims at the good is not unlike saying that belief aims at the truth:[20] the latter does not imply a particular conception of *what* is true, but it does seem to be in tension with a conception of belief as a mere disposition to assert.[21]

Moreover a desire should be identified not with *judging* or *believing* something to be good, but rather with *conceiving* it to be good from a certain evaluative perspective. Desires are not 'all-out' attitudes. That is, it is possible without any irrationality or inconsistency to desire incompatible things. I may have a desire for sweet foods (because they are tasty) and a desire for abstaining from sweet foods (because they are unhealthy). Since a desire commits me at most to pursue its object *all other things being equal*, this pair of attitudes is perfectly coherent. The same is not true of beliefs. A rational agent ought to revise her beliefs when she finds out that they are incompatible.[22] Thus desires and beliefs are improperly regarded as analogous notions in their realms.

If anything, desire under this view is the practical counterpart of an 'appearance', as in 'This conclusion appears to follow from these premisses' or 'This shirt appears to be yellow'. Rather than appearances of what is the case, desires are appearances of the good.[23] Desiring X thus would amount to *conceiving* X to be good in a certain manner, but not necessarily *judging* it to be good. The analogy with theoretical appearances can be helpful here. No doubt appearances can be deceptive. But, more importantly, appearances can continue to be deceptive, even when I understand that they are merely appearances. This is, for instance, the nature of visual illusions. If certain dots are flickering on my computer in the right way, I will see something that appears to be in 3D, even though I know that the computer screen is flat. My awareness that this is an illusion will not, however, make things appear different from the perspective of my visual experience; the image still *looks* to be in 3D.[24] And despite the fact that I know that the image is not in 3D, when it appears to me that it is so from a visual perspective, it appears, from

---

[20] But see below for some caveats.

[21] See, for instance, Gareth Evans's remarks on the problems of understanding belief as a disposition to assert in Evans 1982: 224–5.

[22] I am ignoring here complications that might arise from cases in which revising beliefs in the face of inconsistency might be extremely costly.

[23] For a similar view, see Stampe 1987.

[24] For a remarkable example, see Donald Hoffman's web site, especially <aris.ss.uci.edu/cogsci/personnel/hoffman/cylinderapplet.html>. These illusions are discussed in Hoffman 1998.

158 / Sergio Tenenbaum

that perspective, that it is *true* that the image is in 3D; in fact, one can hardly distinguish between 'appearing' and 'appearing true' in the theoretical realm.

In the same way, there will be cases in which something appears good in a certain way even when I 'know' it not to be so. I might want a new BMW when my car contrasts so poorly with the neighbours' car, even if I am convinced that there is no value in trying to 'keep up with the neighbours'. My 'awareness' that there is nothing good in owning a BMW[25] does not change the fact that from what we could call 'the perspective of envy' owning a BMW still appears to be good. The scholastic view, understood in this manner, does not prevent us from seeing agents as desiring what they know to be bad; this would be no different from the fact that, in the theoretical realm, often certain contents will appear to be true in certain ways when the agent knows them to be false. Following the analogy with a visual perspective, we can say that desires are appearances of the good from certain evaluative perspectives. Envy, as I pointed out above, could be considered to be an evaluative perspective, and for the envious person, various things will appear to be good; in other words, this perspective will provide the agent with various desires (like wanting to do harm to the neighbour's lawn, to buy a nicer car, etc.). Similarly, our gastronomic sensibilities could also be viewed as constituting an evaluative perspective. From that perspective, the consumption of sweets, heavy cream, etc. appears to be good, but the consumption of cough syrup appears to be bad. Evaluative perspectives thus generate various desires, and *eo ipso* various appearances of the good. However, in this version of the scholastic view, desires should be identified not with how the agent *judges* things but with how various things *appear* good to the agent.[26]

Forming General Conceptions of the Good

Since from different perspectives different things appear to be good, an agent should be capable of forming a general conception of the good by reflecting upon and assessing these various perspectives. Of course, an agent could just embrace an evaluative perspective and ignore all others; one could live just to satisfy one's gastronomic inclinations. However, an agent who did not try to form a reflective conception of the good would hardly be recognized as an

[25] I am assuming that I see no putative good in owning a BMW other than the higher status it would grant me.

[26] Similar points are made in Tenenbaum 1999, forthcoming *a*.

agent. We can say that what appears to be good within this general conception of the good is what the agent desires from a reflective perspective. A reflective being tries to form a general conception of the good, and if she does not always act on it, she is at least *committed* to acting in accordance with what upon reflection she deems to be good.

We should not understand a general conception of the good to be a large-scale plan of life in which one delineates one's life goals, and possibly ranks all possible alternative lives with respect to their desirability. Although such a large-scale conception of the good may function as a regulative ideal of some kind, it is hard to believe that any agent has in hand such a blueprint of the ideal life and a whole host of contingency plans. So a conception of the good should be understood here as an 'all-things-considered' evaluative conception that is substantive enough to justify the choices that the agent makes in a given situation when her decision does not manifest any kind of practical irrationality. The agent must try to find a way to adjudicate between the various 'claims' made by distinct perspectives, from which various objects appear to be good, and the considered view that emerges from this attempt is the agent's general conception of the good.

But in what kinds of relations can an appearance of the good stand to the agent's general conception of the good? The most obvious relation is that the fact that an object is deemed good from a certain evaluative perspective will make a positive contribution to the value of the object. So, for instance, that I greatly enjoy the taste of chocolate makes it the case that in the absence of any stronger desire to avoid chocolate, I'll choose to consume it when the opportunity comes. However, although on a purely 'hydraulic' theory of motivation[27] this is the *only* relation between a desire and the eventual choice or intention of the agent, a scholastic view does not need to subscribe to the view that one should always take the claim of an appearance of the good in this manner. Another obvious possibility is that some appearances will be, upon reflection, deemed illusory. So, for instance, my impulse to 'teach the driver who cut me off a lesson'[28] might be one that is not merely overridden by my interest in getting home alive and well. I might, upon reflection, come to the conclusion that the appearance that there is value in such actions is

---

[27] I am borrowing this notion of a 'hydraulic' theory of motivation from John McDowell. See McDowell 1995.

[28] The same would hold, for instance, for the agent that Gary Watson describes who is tempted to smash her racket into her opponent's head after losing a game. See Watson 1975. On this issue, see Tenenbaum 1999.

160 / Sergio Tenenbaum

completely illusory; as much as I am sometimes tempted by it, there is really nothing to be said for punitive driving.

Conditioning and Value: Happiness and Virtue

I want to explore a third relation between an evaluative perspective and a conception of the good, the relation of *conditioning*: a certain perspective is conditioned by X if what appears to be good from this perspective could only be correctly judged to be good if X obtains.[29] I think the clearest statements of such a relationship obtaining appear in Kant's discussion of the relationship between happiness and virtue. I will thus start by looking into Kant's account of this relation. I will outline the way in which Kant sees the relationship and try to show that this is a plausible understanding of how one can come to see the value of one's happiness as dependent on one's character. I will then try to generalize this relation in two ways. I will try to show that the relevant relation can hold of a number of conditions and evaluative perspectives, and also that we can talk about a less stringent relation between certain conditions and evaluative perspectives of which this kind of relationship will be just a particular case. I will then argue that we can make a plausible case for understanding cases of *accidie* as particular instances of a general relation of conditioning. I will finally examine the ways in which loss of will can be a form of irrationality on this account.

So this detour through Kant's views serves various purposes. First, it will help us understand the nature of the relation of conditioning. Secondly, it will help us avoid looking as if we are introducing an ad hoc modification to accommodate *accidie*. If I am right, *accidie* is a particular case of a relation that obtains in various other contexts. Finally, the relation between virtue and happiness as Kant understands it displays the relation of conditioning in a setting in which no irrationality is involved. This will help us in understanding what kind of irrationality may or may not be displayed in *accidie*.

Kant famously argued that a relation like this obtains between virtue and happiness, and that a virtuous disposition is what makes one worthy of being happy. Kant often describes the relationship between virtue and happiness from the point of view of an impartial spectator, who cannot be pleased by disproportion in the unhappiness of the virtuous person or the happiness of

---

[29] See the more precise definition in the next section.

the vicious person.[30] This claim implies at least that if one's ends are evil, they should not be satisfied, and thus to that extent the person should be unhappy; the object of the happiness of the evil person is often itself morally objectionable.[31] No doubt when one imagines a vicious person being happy, one will include in the conception of his happiness the satisfaction of evil ends (such as, for instance, the *schadenfreude* of seeing other people humiliated). These are certainly ends that an impartial spectator could not consider to be good. However, this doctrine also implies something about how a virtuous person conceives of happiness brought about by (or conjoined with) evil, *even when there is nothing untoward about the object of one's happiness*. This point might be clearer if we move from 'an impartial spectator' to the virtuous agent's own conception of the worth of her happiness when brought about, or accompanied, by evil. How would a virtuous agent conceive of possible cases in which she could obtain something genuinely valuable through immoral means?

Suppose Isabel can spend a weekend in New York (which she very much wants to do), but only if she betrays her friend Ralph (suppose Ralph's enemies offer the trip in exchange for breaking Ralph's confidence). No doubt the fact that the weekend can be obtained only by this means does not affect the fact that Isabel's representation of vacationing in New York is the representation of a genuine form of value. However, one might say, the value of loyalty overrides the value of any other enjoyment afforded by such a vacation. This is certainly true, but here again this seems to fail to capture appropriately what it would be for Isabel (a virtuous person for our purposes) to betray Ralph. For what Isabel imagines when she sees herself in New York at the expense of her friend is not just that she settled for a lesser good. It seems plausible that Isabel will see her stay in New York as not worth having at all rather than something that would be a second best to staying loyal to her friend.

It would certainly be wrong to say that when Isabel represents herself spending time in New York owing to an immoral act, something changes in the content of the representation; it is not the case that she now represents New York as noisy, chilly, and consumerist, or that she suddenly remembers that crowded places can be unpleasant. We would naturally describe this situation as a case in which Isabel is so disgusted with herself that she would not enjoy her trip. However, we must be careful here in reading this descrip-

---

[30] See, for instance, Kant 1788/1996, Ak. v. 110.

[31] See Kant's examples of what an immoral person would want in Kant 1797/1996, Ak. vi. 481.

162 / Sergio Tenenbaum

tion. For it is not the case that we would merely be making a psychological prediction. Isabel would find her character wanting if she realized that were her happiness brought about by evil, she would nonetheless have no problem enjoying herself. She would probably not think that if she succumbed to temptation, she should at least try to find some kind of therapy that would allow her to enjoy the trip. What would be lacking here is not the capacity to appreciate the good, as might be the case if someone were to face an exquisite dessert after having had too much of the main course. The problem is not in what is available in New York or with her sensibilities; the problem is just that the trip was made possible by those means.

Of course one might say that the fact that she cannot enjoy the trip saddened by the fate of her friend can be fully accounted for by the fact that she recognizes that the betrayal is a much greater loss than anything that can be gained by it. But this, again, fails to capture the situation. No doubt the trip might not be enough *to compensate her for* the fate of her friend, either in the sense that she will think that overall it all worked out for the best, or in the sense that the trip will suffice for her to check the 'yes' box after the question 'Are you happy?' in a welfare survey. But if her happiness is not *conditioned* by her disposition not to betray her friend, there is no reason to say that she could not enjoy the trip, for the fate of her friend would not make it the case that she would be *indifferent* to the prospect of a weekend in New York. Her friend's well-being and her being in New York would make just two independent contributions to her well-being. It might be worth comparing Isabel's fate with the fate of the person who just before embarking for her trip to New York learns that a pretty good friend has been fired from his job. It might be the case that the person would have gladly given up her trip if it could have saved her friend's job. But it would be perfectly reasonable for her in these circumstances to continue as planned, thinking that—given that nothing will be gained by staying home—she might as well enjoy the trip (even if her friend's loss of a job would be enough for her not to check the 'yes' box in the welfare survey).[32]

Suppose now Isabel, in a moment of weakness, does betray her friend. Now in an important sense, Isabel still sees the value of spending time in New York at the same time that she cannot judge this to be good. If asked, 'Don't you think that enjoying art is one of the greatest things in life, and that it's just

---

[32] Of course, he might find that it is his duty to stay and support his friend. But it is easy to assume that no such duty obtains, if, for instance, the friend goes back home (and home is miles away) to cope with the situation, or decides to spend the next few weeks in isolation.

Accidie, Evaluation, and Motivation / 163

wonderful to take walks in Central Park?', she might respond that she does agree with those things. She can say all those things and still refuse to go to New York because she thinks that her betrayal of her friend makes this end no longer worth pursuing. We can distinguish between judging that X is worthy of pursuit (and thus 'good' in our sense) in situation S, and judging that X is valuable in this more general sense,[33] by saying that an agent judges that something is worth pursuing in situation S if she would judge it to be good if she were to find herself in S.

Following the above cases, we can say that an agent finds X valuable if the agent would find X worthy of pursuit if certain conditions obtained, and these conditions are such that the agent finds it desirable that they obtain. In Isabel's case, she would find going to New York something that is worth pursuing if she could travel there without having to engage in vicious behaviour, and she certainly wishes she could travel there without engaging in vicious behaviour. Of course this is not the only case in which an agent might find something valuable but not worth pursuing. One might find that a valuable object is not worth pursuing because of overriding values or because the agent cannot reasonably expect that it is in his power to bring about the object. However, all that matters to our present purposes is to note that there are at least some cases in which an agent does not find a valuable object worth pursuing because a condition on an evaluative perspective does not obtain. In an important and clear sense, even when Isabel no longer thinks that her trip is worth pursuing, she still retains her understanding of the value of engaging in such a trip. As one might have guessed, this point will be crucial in allowing us to understand how the agent who suffers from *accidie* still values, in at least some sense, the things he does not pursue.

Generalizing Conditioning

If we talk about virtue being the condition of happiness in the sense that no worth will be attached to happiness when conjoined with a disposition that is not virtuous, we had better have relatively low thresholds for virtue. For minor failings certainly will not, and should not, do all that much damage to how I conceive the worth of my happiness. A few trivial lies, a broken promise to my grandmother to visit her more often, and my occasional dumping of a

---

[33] From now on I will just use 'valuable' in this more general sense.

164 / Sergio Tenenbaum

recyclable bottle in the nearer garbage bin will not make the prospect of going to New York seem much less worthy of pursuit to me. This is not just a fact about the uncaring beings we are, but seems perfectly justified: only an extremely gloomy person would be incapable of enjoying life as a result of some minor vices. A relaxed notion of conditionality can make room for an attitude to the relation between virtue and happiness that falls in between these two cases. Let us distinguish between the following:

> *Strong conditionality.* C strongly conditions an evaluative perspective for an agent A if and only if, for every O conceived to be good from that perspective, A should judge O to be good (or O should be considered desirable in A's reflective conception of the good) only if C obtains.

> *Weak conditionality.* C weakly conditions an evaluative perspective for an agent A if and only if, for some O conceived to be good from that perspective, A should judge O to be a lesser good (or O should be considered less desirable in A's reflective conception of the good) if C does not obtain than if C obtains.

So we can think of an interpretation of Kant's claim that the highest good is happiness *in proportion* to virtue that seems to make it into a plausible requirement on conceptions of the good, if we allow that at most only the absence of a thoroughly vicious disposition strongly conditions our happiness (or the evaluative perspectives from which we consider various elements of our happiness to be good). Although there is nothing here that approximates mathematical exactitude in the calculation of proportionality, we may say that one's ethical disposition is relevant to how we conceive our happiness to be good, and, of course, the worse the vice the less we should see our happiness as desirable.

It is important to note that conditionality cannot be incorporated into the evaluative perspective itself. It is not the case that when we learn that the worth of our happiness suffers those bruises from our disposition, we should conclude that being virtuous is part of the good that one enjoys when one goes to, say, the Rockies. It would be ludicrous to suggest that as I see the beautiful landscape, I am appreciating something like the mereological sum, or the 'organic whole', of my virtue (such as it is) and the beauty that surrounds me.[34] What I enjoy is just the beauty itself; that is what constitutes

---

[34] G. E. Moore defines the relevant notion of an 'organic whole' in Moore 1903: 27–31. My discussion of conditioning, and especially this point, is obviously indebted to Korsgaard 1983.

Accidie, Evaluation, and Motivation / 165

this happy aspect of my existence. Whatever relation there is between my virtue on the one hand, and my enjoyment and its worth on the other, it can't be a part–whole relation. It is important to note that I am not pressing here a general criticism against the idea of an organic whole. Let us grant that the notion of an organic whole provides a good account of the nature, for instance, of aesthetic goods. Here it is plausible to say that one's experience and the art object are both relevant parts of what is being appreciated when one appreciates art. We do talk about a certain piece being 'moving', for instance, which suggests that we appreciate both the piece and its effect on us.

But let us look back at the New York example. Suppose Isabel has now gone to New York by unimpeachable means, and that she is now fully enjoying a stroll in Central Park. Would it be plausible to say that what Isabel appreciates is the organic whole formed by the stroll in Central Park combined with her virtue? Certainly Isabel could be enjoying the stroll in Central Park without any thought whatsoever of her virtue. If Isabel were asked to describe what she finds so good about strolling in Central Park, no matter how articulate she were, she would never mention her virtue. Moreover, suppose a completely vicious person is walking alongside Isabel, undisturbed by the effect that his lack of virtue ought to have on his appreciation of this activity. He strolls along having more or less exactly the same reactions that Isabel does. Trying to appeal to the notion of an organic whole would have the implausible conclusion that Isabel and this vicious person are enjoying two completely different kinds of good.[35]

Are these relations of conditioning more general? If we accept Kant's proportionality requirement, we can think that the contribution that an element in a certain evaluative perspective makes to a conception of the good can be *affected* by a certain condition without fully depending on it. That is, even if being *thoroughly* vicious might make one's happiness not worth having, more common human vicious dispositions can affect the worth of one's happiness without rendering it an object that can no longer be judged to make any contribution to the good.

---

[35] Of course, if one has a purely dispositional understanding of 'desire', there would be no reason not to think that the object of Isabel's desire is her strolling in Central Park while being virtuous. But this understanding of 'desire' is incompatible with the Davidsonian understanding of intentional explanation sketched above, since not just any disposition to behave would be capable of picking out an intelligible object of pursuit (as, for instance, Quinn's example of an agent who is disposed to turn on radios for no particular reason; see Quinn 1993).

Further, there is no reason to think that what conditions an evaluative perspective has to be a disposition to act, or anything for which the agent is responsible. The representation of the pursuit of one's happiness after a tragic event will share many of the features of the representation of this pursuit conjoined with the awareness of a vicious disposition. Moreover, certain conditions might not have such a general impact on one's conception of happiness. The loss of a loved one might dampen one's appreciation for sports, but make one's commitments to other people all the more important. Also, Kant's conception makes one's happiness depend on a very specific condition. However, one could think that the general structure of the relation of conditioning does not require anything that specific. One might have just a vague conception that 'the way one's life is going' cannot leave untouched one's conception of what is worth pursuing.

On the other hand, there might be more specific relations of conditioning. Suppose that as I was growing up I spent time around my grandfather's home town, where I would often go fishing, sometimes with him. I might find that after the death of my grandfather (say, from natural causes when he was already advanced in his years) I cannot see much point in fishing in that area or fishing any more. It might not be the case that I liked fishing just because I was doing it, at least at times, with my grandfather. However, even if fishing there is very good, the prospect of driving there and fishing without my grandfather might seem meaningless. It need not be the case that I find these memories painful; quite the opposite, I might cherish my memories of those days. It is just, as one might say, not the same without him there (although the sense of 'its not being the same' can't be that one no longer understands the point of fishing; one might still otherwise be an avid fisherman and recognize that this was a prime spot for fishing). It is natural to say that the value of fishing in this area was conditioned by my grandfather being around.

Of course, this shows that conditioning judgements need not have, as might be the case for the relation between virtue and happiness, objective purport. I might not find that other people need to have the same attitude towards fishing in that area or anything else in relation to my (or their) grandfather being alive. In fact, it might not even be the case that I would find myself wanting if this relation were to fail to obtain in my case. I might consider the counterfactual situation in which I still value fishing in that area despite the loss of my grandparent as a case in which my evaluative outlook would be different, but not necessarily defective. Moreover, relations of conditionality can also be much more frivolous than anything I have presented so far. One might think, for instance, that certain goods are conditioned by one's age: one might think that it does not become a middle-aged man to rollerblade around town, or a young fellow to have tea and cookies in the afternoon.

Conditioning and *Accidie*

It should be obvious now that I think the best way for a scholastic view to accommodate *accidie* is by means of this relation of conditionality. We can say that the agent in a state of *accidie* takes certain evaluative perspectives to be conditioned by certain states that do not obtain. In extreme cases, *all* evaluative perspectives are taken by the person suffering from *accidie* to be conditioned, and to be such that the particular condition is violated.[36] But what could this condition be? The account does not need to be committed to a particular condition, or to assume that the same condition will apply to every case. However, it would be plausible to think that the condition will have something to do with the agent's own state of mind or with his assessment of himself. Plausible ways in which we could express the violation of the condition on the evaluative perspective would be the following: 'Given that I feel this way', or 'Given the kind of person I am', or 'Given that my life has turned this way', or 'Given all that has happened around me', etc. No doubt all of these are vague characterizations of why conditions on evaluative perspectives do not obtain, but, as I said above, there is no need to think that only precisely characterized states of affairs can serve as conditions on evaluative perspectives.[37] But one can say that although the dejected agent judges certain things to be valuable, he thinks that some of the above facts constitute a violation of a condition of his evaluative perspective, and thus a violation of a condition of their being worth pursuing.

How plausible is it to see the dejected agent as committed to taking a certain evaluative perspective to be conditioned by something? To bolster my case I shall start by the advantages. First, we need not claim that the depressed

[36] As will be clear below, this needs elaboration.

[37] Although sometimes a more specific condition could be seen to be at work in clinical depression. See, for instance, the following description in *DSM-IV-TR* (American Psychiatric Association 2000), under the heading 'Major Depressive Episodes': 'The sense of worthlessness or guilt associated with a Major Depressive Episode may include unrealistic negative evaluations of one's worth or guilty preoccupations or ruminations over minor past failings.'

168 / Sergio Tenenbaum

agent, for instance, has completely lost touch with the value of the things he does not pursue, and thus deny his own assessment of his situation. Doing justice to this assessment is important not just because of philosophical squeamishness about overriding an agent's report of his state of mind. As Stocker points out in the passage quoted earlier, we cannot very well describe the awful predicament of the person suffering from *accidie* if we do not ascribe to him a certain appreciation of the values in question. Part of the predicament, as Stocker describes in the passage quoted earlier, 'is that one sees all the good to be won or saved and one lacks the will'. We also do not need to postulate newly acquired desires or evaluative perspectives counteracting the usual course of the old evaluations. It is not as if *accidie* were the result of sudden heightened sensitivity to the value of staying put. Finally, we need not see *accidie* as the result of a surd lack of 'oomph' on the part of our evaluations, as the result of something completely external to how the agent views the world.

However, not all seems to fall so neatly in place. It seems that *accidie* does not take the form of any particular judgement, and it is certainly not necessarily connected to the awareness that a certain fact renders much that is valuable no longer worth pursuing. But even if there were such a fact, the agent who suffers from *accidie* might resist the claim that she thinks that the fact conditions the value. After all, the depressed person often tries to work against her depression in an apparent recognition that the value is still worth pursuing.

As I said earlier, the relation of conditionality does not preclude the possibility that what conditions a certain evaluative perspective is rather vague. Now if my proposal is correct, we should see the agent who suffers from *accidie* as *committed* to a certain relation of conditionality. The proposal does not require that the agent can immediately describe or even assent to the attitude ascribed to her. The conditions of adequacy of the explanation are given by whether it can help make the agent intelligible, or, in certain cases, whether it helps us better place the origin of a certain lack of intelligibility in the behaviour of the agent.[38] Nonetheless, distinguishing various different

---

[38] Any view of intentional explanations that is committed to the constitutive role of the ideal of rationality will have to make room for the fact that these explanations do not always work by making the agent fully intelligible, but rather by locating or describing an agent's failure to live up to the ideal of rationality. One is no less than the other part of the more general enterprise of evaluating an agent. Intentional explanations can make agents look not only intelligent, good, and perceptive, but also vicious, ignorant, and insensitive.

Accidie, Evaluation, and Motivation / 169

forms of *accidie* in light of this account can help us see the extent to which the scholastic view can explain the agent's view of her situation. Moreover, these distinctions will also help us see to what extent the scholastic view can take *accidie* to be a form of irrationality.

On this account, we can distinguish at least three kinds of agents suffering from *accidie*: the full-blown, the hesitant, and the inconsistent.[39] In the first case, the agent's commitment to the absence of a condition that makes a certain value worth pursuing will be stable and not challenged by any of her other practical commitments; that is, the agent simply accepts that a general condition of value does not obtain. This is not to say, of course, that there is nothing that the agent considers regrettable about her situation; it would be hard to describe the case as a case of *accidie* if the agent were completely contented with her situation. Rather, what she finds regrettable in this case is the fact that the condition does not obtain: that she is the kind of person she is, that things came down this way, etc. In the full-blown case the agent is not inconsistent, nor does she fail to act in accordance with how she thinks she should act. This does not mean that there is nothing amiss with her practical standpoint. We might think that at least in some cases it would not be completely warranted, for instance, for an agent to think that various pleasures are no longer worth having on account of the fact that, for instance, she finds (perhaps also unwarrantedly) that she has failed so miserably in her life. But in so far as these are judgements that she fully endorses, whatever her cognitive failings are, her practical attitudes are coherent.

Indeed it might be worth noting that the agent who engaged in vicious behaviour in the past, but now, on account of accepting some kind of Kantian view of the relation between virtue and happiness, does not find her happiness worth pursuing, would be suffering, on this account, from full-blown *accidie*. And if one accepts the Kantian view in question, there would be nothing wrong with her attitudes; her happiness would, on this view, indeed not be worth pursuing.[40] It might also be worth remarking that the fact that this agent turns out to fall into our classification of *accidie* is *not* an unwelcome consequence. Suppose, for instance, an agent in this predicament let a good opportunity significantly to improve her happiness pass by. Her explanation

---

[39] Here of course it is a matter of conceptual space. I am not arguing that we will necessarily find abundant cases of all these three kinds.

[40] I am not sure that the view this agent endorses is properly Kant's view. In so far as she recognizes her past as vicious and no longer acts in this manner, it is unclear to what extent she is still vicious, and whether her happiness is worth pursuing or not.

170 / Sergio Tenenbaum

for passing it up could be something like: 'Of course it is a good thing when people are happy, and, of course, I see the value of having all those things. However, after what I have done I can't just live like anyone else.' Just as with other cases of *accidie*, she would still be capable of appreciating the value of those things that would make her happy, but she would be incapable of pursuing them.

But the full-blown case need not be the only case of *accidie*. Another possibility is that the acceptance that the value is not worth pursuing will not be so 'full-blown', but rather the agent will waver between this view and the view that the value is worth pursuing, as well as other intermediate positions allowed by the weaker notion of conditionality. Again, depending on one's theory of rationality, one might or might not see these cases of *accidie* as failures of rationality. If one thinks that there are substantive restrictions on relations of conditionality, one might come to the conclusion that this kind of attitude could not be rationally justified. And one could also think that wavering and hesitation are themselves marks of an irrational disposition.

But one can also be divided, as it were, in relation to the very judgement of conditionality. That is, one might think that one ought to judge that nothing conditions the value that one fails to pursue, but yet find oneself judging otherwise. In this case, I think the agent suffering from *accidie* is, in this respect, much like the akratic agent, who does not have his reflective understanding of how he ought to judge lined up with the way he judges.[41] And just as with akratic behaviour, the agent in this case would be manifesting a form of irrationality. Indeed this would be a rather paradigmatic form of irrationality, the irrationality of judging or acting in a way that we ourselves recognize to be unwarranted.

But here it might seem that one could raise a new objection. For if the agent recognizes that he ought to judge that the value is still worth pursuing, and that nothing about him or the world around him makes it the case that there is no unmet condition on the relevant evaluative perspective, then what could be missing? How could there be a gap between thinking that one ought to judge that p and judging that p? Although a detailed discussion of this issue would take us far beyond our topic, I think it is a misconception about the nature of cognition that leads one to think that there could be no gap here. In particular, I think one is led to this conclusion by the view that there could be

---

[41] I defend this view of the akratic agent in Tenenbaum 1999.

no significant differences among ways in which one grasps that there is conclusive reason to accept p.[42] However, if there are significant differences, and if one's grasp of these reasons can be defective, clouded, or in any way imperfect, one's judgement might be swayed by more vivid appearances that one recognizes ought not to sway one's judgement. No doubt a person who forms judgements this way is irrational, but this irrationality does not make her a conceptual impossibility.

One might argue that this account still falsifies the agent's self-understanding; after all, on this view, the person suffering from *accidie* does not accept the unconditional judgement that she should act in the relevant ways. At best, in the case of the 'divided' dejected agent, she recognizes that this is a judgement she *ought* to make. And this, one might claim, is not enough to make sense of the phenomenon. But here the lines between the phenomenon and our philosophical understanding of it start to fade. Any understanding of the phenomenon must preserve the obvious fact that the agent suffering from it takes himself to be in a predicament, and this predicament should be understood in terms of the fact that the agent recognizes that he has no motivation to promote ends that he recognizes to be valuable. But this phenomenon is preserved on our account by the fact that something that in normal conditions is valuable cannot be incorporated into one's conception of the good owing to undesirable circumstances. And in the case of the divided agent, the predicament is made worse by the fact that the very judgement of conditionality is recognized to be one that the agent ought not to make.

Of course, if one understands the scholastic view as holding that desires are judgements of value and that forming a conception of the good amounts to no more than adding those up, the scholastic view will not be able to make sense of much human behaviour that clearly falls within the purview of intentional explanations. However, that would be to conceive of the scholastic view as simply mirroring a hydraulic conception of human action, rather than as a genuine alternative to it: an alternative in which the rational structure of human agency can come to light, even if human agents fall far short of being perfectly rational.

[42] For more detail, see Tenenbaum 1999.

7

The Work of the Will

Gary Watson

Not so long ago, talking about the will aroused widespread suspicion in English-speaking philosophy. Brian O'Shaughnessy was going against the grain in 1980 when he declared his belief 'in the existence of the contentious psychological phenomenon, the will', which he took to be 'a *sui generis* psychological phenomenal something whose existence philosophers have in recent years tended to deny' (O'Shaughnessy 1980: i. 30). For reasons that are not fully clear to me, the concept is nowadays taken more seriously. This shift does seem to be correlated with two other (independent but overlapping) trends in which a notion of the will tends to be featured: with a developing sympathy for one or another Kantian account of agency, and with the revival of libertarian theories of freedom. However, there are influential discussions of the will that don't represent either of these movements, notably Harry Frankfurt's and Brian O'Shaughnessy's.[1]

The first version of this chapter was presented at the conference Weakness of Will and Varieties of Practical Irrationality, Montreal, May 2001. I learned a lot from the participants, and especially from David Owens's commentary, on that occasion. Subsequent presentations and drafts have benefited from comments by Lilli Alanen, Richard Arneson, Sarah Buss, Pamela Hieronymi, Paul Hoffman, Bryan Lee, Sara Lundquist, Gideon Yaffe, Andrew Youpa, Linda Zagzebski, and participants in the Agency Dissertation Workshop at Riverside. Finally, I am most grateful to Sarah Stroud and Christine Tappolet for organizing the Montreal conference, for their editorial work on this volume, and in particular for their help with drafts of this chapter.

[1] Whether these are discussions of the same concept of the 'will' is another question.

The Work of the Will / 173

This revival is not always signalled by the use of the term 'will'. Some writers speak mainly of decisions or choices.[2] Thomas Pink explicitly equates the will with the capacity to decide: 'We ... believe ourselves to have a *will*—a capacity for decision-making or intention formation' (Pink 1996: 16). What matters is not of course the terminology but the thought that the corresponding phenomenon is a primary locus of human agency.[3] This thought is also developed in some recent work by R. Jay Wallace:

> By volition here I mean a kind of motivational state that, by contrast with ... given desires ... are [*sic*] directly under the control of the agent. Familiar examples of volitional states in this sense are intentions, choices, and decisions ... intentions, choices, and decisions are things we do, primitive examples of the phenomenon of agency itself. ... This line ... marks a distinction of fundamental importance, the line between the passive and the active in our psychological lives.
>
> (Wallace 1999*a*: 636–7)

It is this idea of decision as an especially central, if not unique, case of agency that is the subject matter of this chapter.[4] Although I will try to respond to a few objections along the way, for the most part I will proceed on the assumption that the idea is correct. I shall be pursuing two sets of questions about the will, understood as the capacity to decide. In Section I, I ask: is the will the same thing as practical reason or judgement? If not, how are they related? Section II is concerned with decisions in the realm of belief. For instance, after studying the matter, I conclude—that is, come to believe—that creationism ('creation science') is false. The earth is much, much older than 7,000 years. Should we take such decisions (decisions *that* as distinct from decisions *to*) to be instances of our agency as well? If so, should we speak, too, of a doxastic will? As we shall see at the end, these two sets of questions are connected.

---

[2] I shall mostly speak of deciding rather than of choosing. There are, however, revealing differences between 'decision' and 'choice' that will become important later.

[3] As we will see, however, one of the philosophers whose name is linked with philosophical renewal of interest in the will—Brian O'Shaughnessy—denies that decision itself has these features.

[4] The idea of the will in question here is not to be confused with the notion of will as 'will-power'. As Robert Roberts points out, we often use the term 'will' to pick out 'a family of capacities for resisting adverse inclinations' (Roberts 1984: 227). These capacities are 'skills of self-management', as Roberts puts it (238). This notion is less basic than the capacity to form decisions, as we can see by noting that one can decide to exercise one's will-power or not. For another discussion of will-power, see Richard Holton, 'How is Strength of Will Possible?', Ch. 2 this volume.

174 / Gary Watson

There is some dispute about the extension of the term 'deciding', so I should say a few words by way of clarification. We ordinarily restrict the term to contexts in which there is prior uncertainty and an attempt to make up one's mind by deliberation.[5] The active phenomenon that I am concerned with, however, need not involve such doubt or deliberation. Perhaps the following case will illustrate what I am after. Suppose I am walking along a residential street when I notice, across the way, a frail, elderly person struggling to pull a very heavy piece of luggage up a steep set of stairs. Noticing his need, I put down my packages and cross the street to offer my assistance. In this case, I am not in a state of uncertainty that requires resolution by deliberation. The thing to do is clear at once. So on the aforementioned criteria, this is not strictly a case of deciding what to do. But it does exhibit the activity that concerns me. What matters for my purposes is not whether we call this deciding; what matters is the active phenomenon that also occurs in explicit deciding, namely, adopting and forming an intention, in other words the settling on this course of action. In this example, I claim, without the need for prior deliberation, I form or adopt an intention to help, and this is itself an instance of agency.[6]

It might be objected that in this case there is no need to distinguish any such special prior activity. Perhaps my agency consists solely in my *attempting* to help in some way, say, by my giving him a hand. No doubt in some cases it will be artificial to distinguish adopting the intention to x and $x$ing (or attempting to x). But in my example, and in many others, the distinction seems real. Prior to actually helping, or offering to help, I do certain things, such as setting down what I am carrying and crossing the street, in preparation to help, and therefore with that intention. Preparing to help is not yet attempting to do so. The distinction is especially clear where there is a significant time lag—if, for example, I form the intention to help once I deliver my packages down the street. So I am not claiming (or denying) that all instances of intentional

---

[5] Cf. O'Shaughnessy: 'Thus, decidings form a sub-class of comings-to-intend. Namely: the class of those comings-to-intend events that resolve a state of uncertainty over what to do' (O'Shaughnessy 1980: ii. 297).

[6] I do not suppose that talk of decisions assumes an awareness of discrete episodes of intention formation, any more than talk of perceptions and thoughts does. We could also say that (implicitly) I judged that lending a hand was more important than proceeding with my business, though nothing like that 'crossed my mind'. I agree with Larry Wright: 'Most of the judgements we make in the course of our lives we reach without deliberating on them at all. The stream of life is filled with learnings and decidings that we do not even pick out of the smooth flow as articulated episodes, much less as the objects of deliberation. Usually, it is only after the fact, and for particular purposes, that we break out the thoughts or decisions . . . ' (Wright 1995: 567).

The Work of the Will / 175

bodily movement are preceded by intention formation. Nor am I claiming (or denying) that all intention acquisition is active. (I assume that there are ways of acquiring intentions besides *adopting* them.[7]) What matters for the purposes of my investigation is that: (1) adopting intentions in the way just illustrated is an ubiquitous instance of agency, namely a case of setting oneself to act in a certain way, whether or not there was prior uncertainty or an immediate attempt; and (2) the sort of activity illustrated here is especially central to what it is to be a rational agent, so that a human being who never engaged in such activity would be an agent only in a very truncated sense.[8]

I

Deliberating and Deciding

With these points in mind, then, I will focus on deciding in what follows, since that is a clear, if not unique, case of the phenomenon. My first question, as I vaguely posed it, was about the relation of deciding to practical reason.

Practical reasoning, in the sense of deliberation, is a species of normative reasoning about action. It is characterized not just by its content—what should be done by certain agents, including oneself, under certain circum-stances—but by its aim.[9] Practical deliberation, as I think of it, is *reasoning about what is best (or satisfactory) to do with a view to making up one's mind about what to do*.[10] This connects practical reasoning with *decision* because it connects it with making up one's mind. If we identify the will with deciding to act, then we can say that practical reasoning is reasoning about what to do with a view to determining one's will.[11] One's aim in deliberation is to make a commitment to a course of action by making a judgement about what is best (or good

[7] This issue is explored in Mele 2000.

[8] Although the active formation of intention is not typically preceded by deliberation, I do think that such agency presupposes the general capacity for deliberation, so that there could not be a creature without practical reason who decided in this way. I think the active status of the phenomenon under consideration has to do with its sensitivity to reasons, which depends on the capacity for critical reflection. I return to this briefly at the end.

[9] Contrast a discussion of the general conditions under which going to war is justified with the question of whether to go to war. Both involve practical reason, but only the latter is deliberative. (Of course the former might be part of the latter.)

[10] Compare Richard Moran: 'The aim and conclusion [of deliberation] is the binding of oneself to a certain course of action (or proposition) ...' (Moran 2000: 95).

[11] We could also say that practical reasoning is reasoning about what is most choiceworthy with a view to choosing.

176 / Gary Watson

enough) to do.[12] This commitment—the adoption of an intention—is the conceptual terminus of reason when it's directed to action.

Although nothing crucial to my aims in this chapter depends on it, I shall assume in what follows that judgements about what is best can be true or false. If theoretical deliberation is concerned to arrive at true beliefs, it follows that (quite apart from the empirical premisses upon which it relies) practical deliberation involves theoretical reasoning. This implication doesn't render practical reason a kind of theoretical reasoning, since true belief is not its ultimate end. Rather, these forms of reasoning necessarily intersect (on this so-called cognitivist view). One could avoid this conclusion, without abandoning the assumption, simply by excluding beliefs about choiceworthiness from the province of theoretical reason. But this stipulation would have no philosophical purpose, as far as I can tell. Such judgements are not usefully to be contrasted with something called theoretical or 'factual' judgements, unless these terms are given an artificially limited sense.[13]

Notice that, when things go as intended, practical deliberation involves making up my mind *twice*. Making up my mind about what is best to do is coming to a judgement: deciding *that* such and such is the thing to do.[14] Making up my mind about what to do is forming an intention: deciding *to* do such and such. (Adapting T. M. Scanlon's useful terminology, we might call these 'assessing' and 'opting', respectively; Scanlon 2002: 169–70.) Both moments of resolution are part of the enterprise of practical deliberation. Although they typically coincide, these are importantly distinct forms of commitment. The distinction manifests itself in at least two familiar ways: first, when we fail to reach a decision about what is best to do because the reasons are unclear or indeterminate but we still must decide to do *x* or to do *y*; and, secondly, when we fail to follow our decision about what is best.

Suppose I receive an offer of an attractive faculty position in another part of the country, away from my birthplace and extended family. One of three things might occur. Perhaps, after reflection, I arrive at a definite conclusion

---

[12] Cf. David Velleman: 'the object of theoretical reasoning is to arrive at true belief' (Velleman 1996: 180).

[13] For a discussion and brief defence of this view, see Scanlon 1998: 55–64. Although David Owens agrees that practical judgements are true or false, he denies that they are beliefs or comings to belief; see Owens 2000: 110 ff.

[14] I assume, too, that in the contexts that we have in mind, judging that *p* is coming to believe that *p*. Thus just as 'decision to' is an intention-forming process, 'deciding that' is a belief-forming process. But the relation of judging to believing is probably more complicated than this. See Cohen 1989.

(say, that it is best to decline the offer) and so decide to do so. Or I might be unable to decide what's best, because the considerations on both sides seem equally compelling or perhaps incommensurable. Still, I must decide what to do, if only by default. Or, I might conclude, unequivocally, that I should decline, say. Even though I have made up my mind on the normative question, I might remain unsettled about what to do. It is plausible to say that what is in evidence in the second and third cases is the distinction between practical judgement and will.[15]

Two Conceptions of Agency

Contrast two conceptions of how human agency is oriented towards practical reason or the good. What I shall call *internalist* conceptions of agency regard the will (in so far as they make use of this concept) as having some kind of necessary connection or concern with the good or the choiceworthy. (Here the classical statement is the opening line of Aristotle's *Nicomachean Ethics*: 'Every craft and every investigation, and likewise every action and decision, seems to aim at some good'; Aristotle, *Nicomachean Ethics* (1985 edn.), $1094^{a}1$.) Internalists take the link between intention and the good to be analogous to the connection of belief with truth. Just as no attitude that wasn't to some extent regulated by truth-relevant considerations could be the attitude of belief, so nothing could count as intending (or willing) if it were totally unguided by the good. Externalists deny any such connection of intention to the good. On their view, the will comes most prominently into play once the question of what is good to do is settled.

The contrast, to put it very crudely, is between the Greeks and the Christians.[16] On the Greek view, the human 'capacity' to oppose the good is a liability (rather than a power) we should work to overcome. It is an imperfection that limits our powers rather than underwriting our agency. For Aristotle, there are three (or four) characters whose behaviour has different relations to the good: the virtuous, the vicious, and the incontinent (or continent). In much modern philosophy, another type comes to the fore,

---

[15] Since, according to me, judgement is a form of decision, why shouldn't we speak of it as an exercise of will? This is part of the second set of questions distinguished in my opening remarks. I venture an answer to this question towards the end.

[16] Crudely (to mention only one reason) because obviously there are Christian thinkers on both sides of this issue. But it is a generalization worth making because the question becomes a preoccupation in Christian thought. (I suspect that a certain conception of sin requires externalism.)

178 / Gary Watson

he who would challenge the good. (I don't say that this type was beyond the ken of Greek philosophy.) On all accounts, this capacity indeed makes us liable to evil, but the modern tendency is to see that liability as a necessary condition of self-governance. This is only a tendency, however. As heirs of both traditions, most of us feel the tension between them, and find both conceptions, unadorned, deeply problematic in their own ways. My aim is not to adjudicate this large issue here, but to investigate whether the idea of the will can have a prominent place only in externalist accounts. But some development of this issue will be necessary to set up the later discussion of 'cognitive agency'.

A rather pure contemporary version of internalism about agency (though without the language of 'will') is defended by Sarah Buss, who argues that

if we ever do anything intentionally, then evaluative beliefs must play a direct, independent motivating role in our behaviour.... We do nothing intentionally to achieve [our] ends unless we act as we do because we accept certain practical norms; our actions are not self-directed unless they reflect our beliefs about how it is rational, or appropriate, or right, or good, or desirable, or acceptable to behave.

(Buss 1999: 400–1)[17]

Rogers Albritton defends the opposing view:

But having to do a thing [in that one has compelling reasons to do it] does not settle magically the question whether to *do* it or not. Reasons, of whatever species, can't close that question. It's a question of a different *genre*, and is not relative to any system of reasons. It isn't for *reasons*, in the end, that we act for reasons.

(Albritton 1985: 248)[18]

For the externalist, it is the difference between these questions that indicates the work of the will: to determine whether to comply with the outcome of normative reflection. Unlike practical judgement, or belief in general, volitional commitment is not, in R. Jay Wallace's phrase, 'an essentially normative stance'.[19] Accordingly, it is not necessarily guided by the norms of practical reason.

---

[17] Christine Korsgaard is an internalist who explicitly appeals to volition. The analogue of belief, Korsgaard claims, is 'volition or choice', and willing is a normative commitment. See Korsgaard 1996*b*, 1997. For a formulation of a Kantian version of internalism, see Herman 2002.

[18] Robert Kane emphasizes the difference between these two questions as well. See Kane 1996: 21.

[19] See Wallace 2001. (My treatment of the issues in this chapter is much indebted to this essay.) After citing Albritton's discussion approvingly, Wallace writes, 'The question of what action we are going to perform is not necessarily answered by our having determined to our own satisfaction what it would be best to do' (Wallace 2001: 11).

Externalism must be true, Wallace argues, if we are to make sense of our capacity for self-determination. Further, he thinks that this view of intention is supported by reflection on Moore's Paradox. Wallace observes that 'I believe that p, but p is not true' is paradoxical in a way that 'I intend to x, but $x$ing is not choiceworthy' is not. In the first case, the endorsements expressed in the two conjuncts cancel one another out in such a way that it seems impossible coherently to attribute either of these attitudes to me. This does not seem to be so in the second case. This shows that whereas the capacity to form beliefs must be regulated by truth-relevant norms, the capacity to form intentions is not constrained by the norms of choiceworthiness.[20] Thus, Wallace accepts internalism for belief but not for intention.

On this account, the internalists' mistake is to conflate these two types of commitment. Hence the notorious difficulty of understanding akrasia (and all that). They can allow, in various ways, for the possibility of knowingly behaving contrary to practical judgement, but the problem is to account for our sense that such counter-normative conduct[21] is voluntary or an exercise of agency at all.[22] If the will follows normative commitment, then an individual cannot willingly go against practical judgement. On Aristotle's account of akrasia, for example, it is hard to see why the akratic individual acts voluntarily as distinct from having her agency hijacked or bypassed by the brute forces of desire.[23] What is missing, it seems, is the idea of the akratic individual consenting to or forming the intention to depart from practical reason. What is missing, in other words, is the very idea of the will.

This leads to a second complaint. The objection is not just that the internalist conception of the will seems inadequate for an understanding of the agency that is displayed in akrasia (and the like); the point is that this inadequacy is due precisely to the absence of any notion of the will distinct from practical judgement. So the fact that we *have* a concept of the will at all, a distinction between deciding to and deciding that, is implicitly a rebuke to the internalist picture. (See Appendix 7.1.)

---

[20] For an alternative view of practical versions of Moore's Paradox, see Moran 2000, esp. ch. 2.

[21] By this phrase, I refer to conduct that is in the ordinary sense weak-willed, as well as choices made in indifference to or defiance of what the agent takes to be best, if these are possible.

[22] I do not say that the only recourse for internalists is flat denial of weakness of will. Indeed, quite a lot has been said along these lines to accommodate common sense. But to remain internalist, the account will have to imply that in akrasia we are less fully agents than otherwise.

[23] This implication—that the akratic's agency is overcome or compromised—would not entail that the individual could not be held responsible for this failure, in so far as it was a failure of character.

180 / Gary Watson

The primary appeal of externalism, then, is just the failure of internalism to make sense of counter-normative agency. But I don't think we can be happy with this view, either. The idea that the question 'What shall I do?' is always left open by practical reason[24] threatens to sever the notions of choice and choiceworthiness in an incoherent way.[25] If making up one's mind what to do is not 'an essentially normative stance', is just different in this way from making up one's mind about what is best to do, then there would seem to be no more than a contingent connection between these two moments of resolution. But then agency would be located, as O'Shaughnessy says, 'in the motion of the will, understood as an explanatory ultimate' (O'Shaughnessy 1980: ii. 341). It would make sense to suppose that such commitments could become unhinged from reasons in a quite general way.[26] Absurdly, it would then seem a wonder why we ever bothered about the good at all.

Something is wrong with the externalist picture. What requires explanation is disregarding the good, not seeking it. This point blunts the force of Wallace's claim about Moore's Paradox. Believing something one regards as false is indeed less incoherent than intending to pursue what one takes to be the inferior option. Just the same, 'I *never* intend to do what I decide is best to do' *is* incoherent. The externalist owes us an explanation of why the global

---

[24] It might be tempting to construe the open question in this way: 'What kind of self shall I be? A self that responds to such-and-such considerations or to others?' This doesn't provide the 'shall' with a non-normative sense, however; it just poses the deliberative question at a different level. Kane seems to construe the question in this way in the case of akratic struggles: '*qua* agent and practical reasoner, she has the general purpose of resolving the conflict in one way or the other and thereby deciding (for the present at least) what sort of person she wants to be—which of her internal points of view . . . she wishes to have prevail' (Kane 1996: 139). Kane speaks of such moments as occasions 'when agents are torn between conflicting visions of what they should become' (Kane 1996: 130). If the question about what kind of person to be is a normative question, then in the cases we are discussing it has already been settled. If it's a volitional question, what is its content?

[25] David Velleman proposes a mixed externalist position. He objects to the conception of an agent 'as being capable of intentional action—and hence as being an agent—only by virtue of being a pursuer of value' (Velleman 1992: 99). But in contrast to Albritton and Wallace, Velleman *is* an internalist regarding the connection of agency with *reason(s)*. He manages this unusual juxtaposition, of course, by disconnecting reason from value.

[26] For reasons indicated in the previous note, Velleman would object to this way of putting it, since he thinks reasons don't necessarily come from value. Note also that in going against practical judgement one might still be responding to the specific (prima facie or *pro tanto*) considerations that favour this sub-optimal choice.

case makes no sense, if intending has no internal connection to what is choiceworthy.[27]

Moreover, for the same reasons, externalism is problematic even where we would expect to find it most helpful: in its treatment of weakness of will. The internalists' problem is to make sense of weakness as genuine agency. In contrast, externalists have trouble explaining what is, after all, *weak* in akratic behaviour. In weakness of will, properly so-called, one goes against the grain of one's own commitments, and this is an appropriate description only if practical judgement constitutes a commitment *to act*.[28] On the externalist view, however, going against reason must always come down to a choice among possible commitments. Externalism is therefore in danger of conflating weakness and 'radical choice'.

For these reasons, neither (unqualified) internalism nor (unqualified) externalism is satisfactory. The truth must lie somewhere in between. An adequate view must provide for a 'non-contingent' connection between normative and volitional commitment and at the same time make sense of the possibility of sometimes deliberately opting for the lesser good. Obviously, the issue is too undeveloped and complex to adjudicate here. My main concern is with a much narrower but still significant question. Does the notion of the will have a distinctive role only in views that want to make room for counter-normative assertions of agency?

The Executive Function of the Will

A positive answer to this question would predict that internalist philosophies of action have no use for the concept of will except as another name for practical judgement. But that would be wrong. (See Appendix 7.2.) For as noted at the end of the section 'Deliberating and Deciding', the distinction between practical judgement and will is not motivated exclusively by the need to account for counter-normative agency. The distinction is also revealed in circumstances of normative uncertainty or indeterminacy. In these contexts, the question 'What shall I do?' is clearly different from the question 'What

---

[27] Wallace writes: 'In practice, of course, cases of non-normative choice are the exception rather than the rule' (Wallace 2001: 14). But why 'of course'?

[28] For an understanding of weakness of will as irresolution with respect to one's volitional commitments, rather than as going against one's normative judgements, see Holton 1999 and Holton's contribution to this volume (Ch. 2).

182 / Gary Watson

should I do?' The issue here is not 'Shall I comply with my judgement?' but 'What shall I do in view of the fact that the reasons, all things considered, are not decisive?' Here there is a need for volitional commitment that can and should be recognized by the most robust version of internalism. This is sometimes called the 'executive' function of the will.[29] (See Appendix 7.3.)

Even when reason is not entirely silent, uncertain, or indeterminate, the will has constructive work to do. Judgement may leave open the constitutive or instrumental means to responding to certain reasons. Moreover, as many writers have stressed (including Thomas Pink and especially Michael Bratman[30]), practical commitment has a planning and coordinational role that is needed for coherent action over time.[31] In this way, decisions might be in the service of rational agency even when they are not carrying out substantive demands or recommendations (at whatever level of generality). They might be said in these contexts to be constrained by the formal aims of practical reason. Furthermore, as Bratman emphasizes, adopting intentions to serve this planning role then gives us reasons for additional intentions and actions.

The political image here is suggestive. The will comes into play on an internalist view only when intention is not completely scripted in advance by reasons. 'Deciding to' typically involves shaping priorities among a structure of reasons and thereby giving certain considerations a special reason-giving force.[32] And this is precisely what is required for a substantive executive role: that the executive have latitude for its own operation within a legislative framework to which it is subordinate. On the other hand, the will would not be carrying out practical reason if it went against its mandates. When

---

[29] 'A decision', Thomas Pink says, 'is a second-order executive action—an action by which we ensure that we subsequently perform the first-order actions which, as deliberators, we have judged it desirable to perform' (Pink 1996: 5). For the bearing of Kant's distinction between *Wille* and *Willkür* on this idea of an executive function, see Appendix 7.3.

[30] See Bratman 1987. As David Owens puts it, following Bratman and Pink, the function of intention 'is simply to perpetuate the motivational force of practical judgement over time' (Owens 2000: 105).

[31] Frankfurt proposes a similar view: 'a function of decision is to integrate the person both dynamically and statically. Dynamically insofar as it provides...for coherence and unity of purpose over time; statically, insofar as it establishes...a reflexive or hierarchical structure by which one person's identity may be in part constituted' (Frankfurt 1987: 175). This identity-constituting function can be seen as serving the interests of reason, since without it one lacks any standpoint as a practical reasoner. Nonetheless, Frankfurt, here and especially in later work, rejects the idea that the function of reason is to enable one to act well—that, he says, is the business of deliberation (Frankfurt 1987: 174).

[32] See Michael Bratman's discussion of decision as 'treating something as a reason' in Bratman 1996.

The Work of the Will / 183

intention fails to be guided by judgement, it fails to operate in its executive capacity—it fails to operate *as* a will. For the internalist, intentional activity that is not under judgemental control is not an exercise of agential control, or of full-blooded agency.[33]

Recall the comparison of will and belief. For the internalist, the will is like belief in this respect: just as total indifference to truth is not compatible with belief, so nothing that operated indifferently to the aims of practical reason could count as the operation of the will. Externalists insist on a sharp disanalogy here. They agree that the function of the will is executive, if this is taken in a strictly normative sense. Trivially, we misuse our volitional powers when we form intentions that flout practical norms. But the capacity for misuse is not a defect in those powers themselves; on the contrary, it is integral to them.[34] In contrast, the capacity to violate the norms of theoretical reason constitutes an imperfection in our cognitive faculties.

Deliberation in the Service of Intention

I have been contrasting two ways of thinking of the relation between practical judgement and the will. Before I turn to the second set of questions about agency and belief, I want to note an important qualification to my characterization of deliberation. I have been assuming that the aim of deliberative practical reason is to make up one's mind on the basis of one's determination of which available option is best. The question I have just been exploring is whether the idea of a power to make up one's mind that is distinct from normative assessment has a role only in an externalist theory. My answer is 'no'. But this description of deliberation is surely idealized. Counter-normative conduct often involves deliberation as well. So, it might be objected, practical reasoning is no more 'internally connected' to the good than the will is.

---

[33] Cf. David Owens: 'the mere fact that something is produced by my will, that my will motivates it, does not put me in control of it. I am in control of it only when my judgement as to whether it ought to be produced at will can determine whether it is produced at will. I am in control of the products of my will when the will itself is under my reflective control' (Owens 2000: 80).

[34] For an interesting argument for this claim, see Wallace 2001: 10. His argument is that the capacity for rational self-guidance necessarily contains the potential for self-alienation, because it requires a capacity of motivational transcendence that can be turned against the disposition to be guided by normative conclusions. This argument might show that our capacity for rational action is contingent upon certain skills that also make us liable to practical irrationality. But it

184 / Gary Watson

This observation reminds us to beware of linking practical reasoning too tightly with unconditional judgements about what is best to do, but it doesn't show that deliberation is not always concerned with what it is good to do. Perhaps I have akratically resolved to have an affair, or to take up (or continue) smoking, or to steal some morphine from a pharmacy to quiet my addiction. I will sometimes, and perhaps typically, engage in practical reasoning in executing these aims. And these deliberations needn't be purely strategic. For example, in the most obvious kind of case, I might carry out my sub-optimal intention to smoke in a way that mitigates its destructive effects (e.g. 'low tar' tobacco). In a more interesting kind of case, I might seek (perhaps self-deceptively) to be unfaithful in a way that is less rather than more disrespectful to my spouse, or choose ways of stealing the drugs that minimize the risk to others' lives and property. In these ways, I employ genuinely normative, sometimes even moral, thought in the pursuit of unworthy aims.[35] Intending to do the forbidden thing need not mean kicking over all the moral traces. In some cases, normative constraints might lead me to give up my akratic project altogether. We are often trying to act as well as possible given our defective aims, treating those ends as part of the background scene, as though they were someone else's or those of ourselves in the past.[36]

There is a need in the theory of moral reasoning for an analogue to John Rawls's distinction in political philosophy between 'full' and 'partial' compliance theory. From the moral point of view, there can be better and worse ways, right and wrong forms of carrying out impermissible maxims, just as there can be just and unjust ways of responding to injustices. In Kantian terms, for example, obviously I can be responsive to hypothetical imperatives in the employment of maxims that violate the categorical imperative. But

doesn't follow, as Wallace seems to think, that when these enabling capacities are misused their manifestations are themselves instances of self-determination. They are at most, as he himself puts it, 'hazardous by-products' of the contingent conditions of self-determination.

[35] See Wallace 2001 for an insightful discussion of the role of 'instrumental rationality' in akratic action. My point here is that the reasoning in question need not be just instrumental.

[36] Cf. O'Shaughnessy 1980: ii. 342: '... there are ways of relating to the past that are "in bad faith". Thus a man can relate to his previous decisions as to the decrees of an authority he dare not question. Thereby he places his present self in subjection, as to a destiny, to a tyrannical past self. Now this is a loss of freedom—akin to the compulsions of the obsessional—and rationality. For the "authentic" and rational relation to one's past decisions is that they are perpetually open to review.... In short, something between uncertainty and fate, viz., *commitment.*'

The Work of the Will / 185

distinctively moral judgement could also be involved in the execution of a maxim that I know to be non-universalizable. The reasoning involved here would be conditional upon my having adopted that maxim, but it would not be strictly hypothetical in Kant's sense. Of course I should abandon my adulterous project, but given that I am not going to, there is room for reasoning about which sub-maxims are permissible (taking the project as fixed).

In sum, akratic commitments are not just a matter of bypassing or rejecting one's evaluative capacities and judgements. Those capacities and judgements are often engaged in that counter-normative conduct. What follows, though, is not that deliberation can proceed in indifference to the good, but that this concern can be qualified and compromised in the ways just indicated. I am not saying that all deliberation in the service of objectionable ends is *morally* mitigating in this way. Using the hypothetical imperative without any concession to the moral point of view, or even to prudence, is still a restricted kind of deliberation, and hence a restricted kind of concern for reasons. Deliberation remains an inherently normative process.

II

Deciding as an Active Phenomenon

> Judging, making up our minds what to think, is something for which we are, in principle, responsible—something we freely do, as opposed to something that merely happens in our lives.... This freedom, exemplified in responsible acts of judging, is essentially a matter of being answerable to criticism in the light of rationally relevant considerations. So the realm of freedom, at least the realm of the freedom of judging, can be identified with the space of reasons.
>
> (John McDowell)

> Belief and other attitudes [unlike the sensations]... are stances of the person to which the demand for justification is internal. And the demand for justification internal to attitudes involves a sense of agency and authority that is fundamentally different from the various forms of direction or control one may be able to exercise over some mind or another.
>
> (Richard Moran)

186 / Gary Watson

I turn at last to the second set of questions I posed in the beginning. Should we regard 'doxastic' decisions—our making up our minds what to believe on a certain matter—to be instances of agency, as I (with Wallace and some others) have assumed volitional commitments to be? If so, should we speak of the will in this domain?[37]

I won't attempt anything like a sustained defence of my initial assumption that practical decision, 'deciding to', is an active phenomenon. In the rest of the chapter, I will be concerned mainly with whether there is any good reason to deny the same status to doxastic commitments. Thus my case in what follows is more or less an *ad hominem* to those who agree with this assumption but refuse to admit doxastic agency. If you insist on David Owens's definition of activity as 'events subject to the will, events whose justification lies in how desirable their occurrence would be' (Owens 2000: 85), you will dismiss the possibility of this sort of agency from the start.[38] But it is important to note that this definition precludes not only doxastic agency, but the agency of practical decisions as well. For in general the decision or intention to x is justified by the choiceworthiness of xing, not by the independent desirability of so deciding or intending.[39] So anyone who regards volitional commitments as instances of activity will need another understanding of the basic idea. My question is whether doxastic commitments are active in the very same sense. As far as I can see, they are.[40]

Unfortunately, it is beyond my powers to say anything very helpful here, but I should try to say something about the basic notion, as I understand it. I think that both 'deciding that' and 'deciding to', assessings and optings, are exercises of agency because they are forms of *assenting or rejecting*. The idea of agency seems to me bound up with the sense in which these are instances of practical or cognitive *commitment*. We are answerable for our decisions because they are attributable to us in these ways.

Before we take up the specifically doxastic case, it is crucial for my purposes to distinguish deciding as a basic form of activity from trying. If 'deciding to' is an activity, it is peculiar in some respects because of its relation to intentionality. My deliberation about whether to accept the offer of employment is of

---

[37] As Descartes does. See App. 7.2.

[38] Not that Owens himself dismisses the possibility by definition. His book is a sustained argument for this conclusion.

[39] As Owens himself emphasizes (Owens 2000: 81–2). So does Pink (1996, *passim*).

[40] I hasten to make the same qualification I made about practical decision. I am not saying that all belief acquisition is an instance of forming a belief or making a judgement; therefore I am not saying that all believing is active.

course intentional, guided by the aim of making up my mind on the question of whether to go. However, it cannot target its specific terminus; I cannot aim to make up my mind, specifically, to decline. For, typically anyway,[41] to aim to commit myself to *x*ing, with a view to following through on that commitment, I must already intend to *x* and hence must already have made up my mind on the matter.[42]

If I understand him correctly, Brian O'Shaughnessy is led by these features of decision to conclude that deciding (as distinct from deliberating) is not intentional[43] and so is not an instance of activity. Deliberation is intentional activity, on his view, because it consists in trying to make up one's mind. But the culmination of this activity—deciding to decline the offer—is not.[44] For O'Shaughnessy, deciding signals the activity of the will only to the extent to which it is the termination of the activity of trying, namely trying to make up one's mind.[45] If trying were the root of all activity, then that would be a reason for denying that decisions of any kind are instances of agency.

Someone who shared O'Shaughnessy's view that trying is the basic form of intentional activity might insist that decidings to act should still be called active and intentional in virtue of being the realizations of the attempt to settle on a course of action.[46] Whether or not this is a plausible thing

[41] Typically. But there are circumstances, for example, of irresolution, in which I might set out to bring about a state of conviction on my part. Thanks to Pamela Hieronymi and Dana Nelkin for pressing me on this point. Hieronymi discusses some of the subtleties of this issue in 'Controlling Attitudes' (unpub. ms).

[42] There is a performative or behavioural sense in which deciding is not opaque in this way. A judge can decide in favour of the plaintiff, intending in advance to do just that. That is because 'decide in favour of' denotes here a public declaration of some kind. In the sense under consideration in this chapter, if she is to intend to find in favour of the plaintiff, the judge must already have decided so to find.

[43] Hugh McCann disagrees: 'It is impossible to make a decision without intending to decide, and without intending to decide exactly as we do' (McCann 1986: 142).

[44] He puts it this way: in deliberation, 'an active procedure, that . . . falls essentially under [the description] "trying to decide whether to do" and inessentially under "deciding what to do", is followed by an essentially inactive event of "deciding to do" ' (O'Shaughnessy 1980: ii. 300).

[45] O'Shaughnessy thinks that decision is always subsequent to uncertainty but that it needn't result from an attempt to make up one's mind. So decision needn't even be the upshot of activity. He thinks 'a man can go to bed undecided and wake to a state of decision . . . All that may be required is that the mental dust should settle. In any case, that practical uncertainty should give way to practical commitment' (O'Shaughnessy 1980: ii. 301). For criticisms of O'Shaughnessy on this point, see Magill 1997: 92.

[46] Mele's view is something like this, but he doesn't emphasize trying. He proposes that 'practical decidings are intentional actions' in virtue of being 'produced' by 'an intention to decide what to do' (Mele 2000: 93).

188 / Gary Watson

to say,[47] I do not think that the active character of forming intentions is just derivative in this way from the activity of trying to decide. These are, in my view, distinct modes of agency.[48] As I said at the beginning, on many occasions (indeed, typically) we form intentions without attempting to make up our minds to act. In these cases, what O'Shaughnessy says of (what he calls) 'willing'—that it is 'something such that its happening *in* one is never its happening *to* one'—seems clearly to apply (O'Shaughnessy 1980: ii. 345). Like tryings, my deciding to decline the offer or my forming the intention to help the man with his luggage do not 'just happen' to me along the way, in the way that receiving the offer or encountering a man in need do; they are (more or less) intelligent responses that I make as I move around in the world. Practical commitment, to use O'Shaughnessy's term,[49] is just as much an 'essentially active phenomenon' as trying. It is an exercise of agency not because it is an instance or product of trying but because, as I said, it is a case of *assenting or rejecting*.

Cognitive Agency

The same seems to me to be true of 'cognitive' commitments.[50] Philosophers resist this idea because they think that in the realm of belief we don't have the necessary kind of *control*. Recall Jay Wallace's view:

[47] O'Shaughnessy thinks it is not (O'Shaughnessy 1980: i. 299). The relation of deciding to decline the offer to deliberating about whether to decline, he suggests, is analogous to the relation between finding and seeking.

[48] See Pink 1996 for a very helpful discussion of O'Shaughnessy's views, and for defence of the claim that trying and deciding are distinct forms of agency.

[49] This way of characterizing intentions raises questions about non-reflective creatures. O'Shaughnessy certainly thinks they have intentions, but calling these states 'commitments' doesn't ring true. It might be thought that 'prior' intentions are commitments and that the other animals do not have these. However, if the concept of intention applies to animals at all, the occurrence of preparatory activity on their part seems to require the attribution of prior intentions. If the dog is digging the hole in order to bury the bone, and if one thinks that the dog both digs the hole and buries the bone intentionally, what grounds would one have for denying that it digs the hole with the intention of burying the bone? Alternatively, as I am inclined to think, perhaps it is appropriate to speak of intentions as practical commitments only in case the creature has *formed* those intentions, as distinct from acquiring them in other ways. In that case, we could allow for prior intentions in non-reflective beings without attributing practical commitments to them. I would want to make a parallel claim about cognitive commitments.

[50] Unsurprisingly, O'Shaughnessy disagrees: 'Believing is in itself essentially inactive' (O'Shaughnessy 1980: i. 28). So does Bernard Williams, who agrees 'with Hume against Descartes that belief is an essentially passive phenomenon' (Williams 1978: 177).

The Work of the Will / 189

By volition here I mean a kind of motivational state that, by contrast with . . . given desires . . . are [sic] directly under the control of the agent. Familiar examples of volitional states in this sense are intentions, choices, and decisions. . . . intentions, choices, and decisions are things we do, primitive examples of the phenomenon of agency itself. . . . This line . . . marks a distinction of fundamental importance, the line between the passive and the active in our psychological lives.

(Wallace 1999a: 636–7)

Does a criterion of direct control mark 'decidings to' as active in a way in which judgements (practical or otherwise) cannot be?

To begin with, no one denies that we have at least *indirect* control of our beliefs in so far as it is up to us to undertake to gather or evaluate evidence. When I conclude, after weighing the evidence, that the Earth is more than 5,000 years old, my belief comes about as a result of my intentional activities. The dispute is whether we have a form of control or agency with respect to judgement or belief that is not derivative in this way. John Heil thinks not. We select our 'belief-generating procedures', he says, but we don't select our beliefs. 'We believe, not because on reflection a certain thing seems worthy of belief, seems epistemically *valuable*, but because in reflecting we become vulnerable in certain ways to beliefs of certain sorts.' In this respect, Heil concludes, 'We are largely *at the mercy* of our belief-forming equipment' (Heil 1983: 358). David Owens agrees. 'In the end, it is the world that determines what I believe, not me.' Once we decide to attend to the evidence, he supposes, 'the evidence takes over and I lose control' (Owens 2000: 12).

These descriptions seem scary, suggesting a distance (if not dissociation) from my epistemic faculties from which I witness their 'output'. Indeed, Heil and Owens draw here a false contrast. Doxastic control is not opposed to being determined, in accordance with some 'belief-relevant norms',[51] by the 'world'. On the contrary, that is what such control amounts to. Our cognitive lives would be out of control to the extent to which we were incapable of responding to norms of coherence and relevant evidence, that is, were not normatively competent in this way.

To be sure, often, as we say, I 'can't help' making certain judgements given the reasons available to me. When I stand in the garden, eyes open, I can't just choose whether or not to believe that the sun is shining, although I might have been able to avoid encountering the overwhelming evidence in the first place. This lack of choice is not to be deplored. Everyone admits that

---

[51] I borrow this phrase from Pettit and Smith 1996.

190 / Gary Watson

judgement must answer to evidence or reason in a way that is not true of practical commitment. I cannot, transparently, form the judgement that 'creation science' is true merely because I suppose that its truth, or believing in its truth, would serve my ends or would be otherwise desirable.[52] Yet that is possible, with transparency, in at least some if not all cases of forming intentions to act. Nothing that was subject to my particular ends in this way could count as 'belief'. Again, this means that some version of internalism must hold in the case of cognitive agency.

This contrast might seem to entail straight away that beliefs couldn't be under your 'direct control'. And yet the point about the irresistibility of certain reasons holds for practical decision as well. Just as I am powerless to believe that the Earth came into existence just a few thousand years ago, given what else I know, in the very same sense, it seems to me, I am powerless to form the intention to lop off my leg, given my other (non-destructive) doxastic and practical commitments. Do I have the power to adopt the intention to do what seems to me pointless or crazy? Perhaps in some sense I do. But I doubt that it is a sense that is *both* inapplicable to the formation of judgements and clearly a condition of agency.

If agency is exercised by assent to propositions or courses of action, then the relevant notion of control is the notion that is appropriate to the mode of assent in question. So I don't concede that the absence of a certain kind of dependency on your ends that often obtains in the case of intentions means that, in the case of our cognitive commitments, we lack control in the relevant sense. Again, such dependency, if systematic and thoroughgoing, would undercut the capacity for judgement, so it can hardly be part of the pertinent notion of cognitive agency. Nor do I concede that our beliefs are things that happen to us, are mere effects upon us of the world.

Is there a Doxastic Will?

So far I have been speaking in favour of cognitive agency, but what about the related question I raised earlier: if doxastic commitments are instances of

---

[52] But compare this exchange between Charles Ryder and Sebastian Flyte in Waugh 1945/1967: 83:

> 'But my dear Sebastian, you can't seriously *believe* it all.'
> 'Can't I?'
> 'I mean about Christmas and the star and the three kings and the ox and the ass.'
> 'Oh yes, I believe that. It's a lovely idea.'
> 'But you can't *believe* things because they're a lovely idea.'
> 'But I *do*. That's how I believe.'

The Work of the Will / 191

activity, should they be regarded as exercises of the will? There are good reasons, prima facie, to deny the consequent. In common speech, we don't naturally speak of 'voluntariness' outside the practical realm.[53] Doesn't this suggest the fundamental asymmetry I have been (perhaps stubbornly) resisting? In accordance with the etymology of the word, ordinary language suggests that there is no use for the notion of the will beyond that realm. This tells against cognitive agency, it might be argued, since where there is no will, there is no agency.

Perhaps, though, this fact about ordinary language is philosophically superficial. Notice, for one thing, that we don't speak of forming intentions voluntarily or involuntarily either. Something is voluntary, it seems, when it is appropriately related to intention.[54] So this observation can't be the basis for any special contrast of belief with intention. More significantly, judgement generally has some of the central features that Aristotle, for example, associates with the voluntary.[55] I don't know what views Aristotle had about the status of belief. But he suggests in book 3 of the *Nicomachean Ethics* that not only actions but also feelings and 'decisions' (in his special sense of deliberative desires) are voluntary. We don't speak this way in common English, but the core feature of Aristotle's idea applies here as well: the 'origin', or 'moving principle', is in us.[56] Far from being 'at the mercy' of those faculties, coming to believe (or intend) is attributable to me as its author because (and if) it is

[53] For good discussions of 'the voluntariness of belief', consult Code 1987 and Zagzebski 1996: 61–73.

[54] An alternative explanation of the oddity of speaking of intentions as voluntary might be that they couldn't fail to be voluntary. Hugh McCann thinks intentions are 'essentially voluntary'. 'Volition [which includes for McCann forming intentions] can be voluntary in the way water can be wet—that is, essentially, in a way that does not require some means as explanation' (McCann 1974: 92). The idea is that water isn't wet in the same sense that the streets are wet; that is, it isn't covered with water. Rather water is wetting, productive of wetness; it is what makes things wet. In this sense, I would agree that intending is voluntary: it is the (or a) source of voluntariness.

[55] Thanks to Barbara Herman for emphasizing to me the relevance of Aristotle's treatment of the voluntary.

[56] Consider the following paradigm of involuntary reactions: 'Facing [Oakland A's batter] Johnny Damon in the first inning, [the Seattle Mariner pitcher John] Halama stuck his bare hand up and deflected Damon's comebacker. "I keep telling myself not to do that," Halama said, "but it's just a reaction. I say I am not going to do it, and wind up doing it.' (Jim Street, MLB.com, 11 Apr. 2001). The origin of movement is not, in the relevant sense, in Halama. To adapt Heil's remark, Halama is at the mercy of his intention-forming equipment. Something like this can happen in the cognitive realm as well. Unreflective cognitive reactions can go against one's reflective judgements (though not as transparently). I keep telling myself that the fact that seven heads in a row have come up doesn't increase the probability of tails on the next flip, but I wind up

192 / Gary Watson

related in the right way to my adjudicative (and executive) capacities. In this sense, we can (and do) say that my beliefs are 'up to me': they are subject (potentially at least) to my decision-making powers, my normative competence.[57] What is up to me in this sense is what I am (potentially) responsible for. What is up to me[58] is what falls within the range of my responsibilities.

All the same, I think there is an insight embodied in ordinary usage. As we have seen, there are two grounds for distinguishing between the will and judgement. One is the need, emphasized by externalists, to account for counter-normative exercises of agency. This ground can have no application to belief, since it is agreed by virtually everyone that one can believe only under the guise of truth. The other ground is that we need a notion of the will as distinct from judgement where there is executive work to do. And there is work of this kind only because practical judgement doesn't fully determine practical commitment. That's why there is a further question, 'What shall I do?', to which the adoption of an intention is an answer. And this answer is often tantamount to giving certain considerations reason-giving force that they otherwise wouldn't have.[59] For practical purposes, then, we need a capacity for commitment that is distinct from judgement.[60] The non-practical case looks different, however. Once I have assessed the evidence, it seems, there can be no remaining question about what to believe, no place for an epistemic 'opting' that goes beyond the relevant assessment.[61]

But we must be careful to distinguish assessing the evidence regarding p from believing that p. This distinction complicates our issue. My assessment of the evidence may not always yield conviction, either because of theoretical akrasia,[62] or, more importantly for our purposes, because the evidence is not decisive. Consider the moderate form of voluntarism defended by William James in 'The Will to Believe' (James 1896). James considers cases in which theoretical reason doesn't and perhaps can't decisively favour p or not-p. In

---

expecting tails anyway. Perhaps we shouldn't think of this expectation as a belief, exactly— perhaps just a 'hunch'. But a parallel qualification seems equally apt in the case of intention.

[57] For a helpful discussion of attributability, responsibility, and being up to us, see Scanlon 1998: 18–22 and ch. 6; 2002.

[58] An explicitly normative application of this phrase is apparent in 'it was [or will be] up to you to see to it that the doors are locked'.

[59] Again, see Bratman's discussion of decision as 'treating something as a reason' in Bratman 1996.

[60] Owens 2000 is very helpful on this topic.

[61] It is revealing that 'choose' is a rough synonym for 'decide' in 'deciding to', but not in 'deciding that'. Choosing is 'opting', not 'assessing'.

[62] For discussions of theoretical akrasia, see Hurley 1989, Scanlon 1998, and Wallace 2001.

The Work of the Will / 193

some of these cases, he thinks, it is not unreasonable to be influenced by non-epistemic considerations, for example, regarding the kind of life to which believing that *p* might contribute. The issue between James and W. K. Clifford is precisely over whether our assessment of the evidence always settles the question of what *to* believe (Clifford 1866). If James is right, there is latitude for 'opting' in the cognitive realm as well, precisely where theoretical reasons run out.

It is an important question here whether the will to believe in these cases is indeed a will to *believe*, as distinct from a determination to live as if one believed *p* were true, or to accept *p* as true for the purposes of improving one's life.[63] Certainly, this is contestable. Unlike extreme voluntarism, though, we can't dismiss James's position out of hand. Someone who sincerely utters, 'I believe *p*, though not-*p* is equally supported by the evidence', might or might not be irresponsible, as Clifford urges. But unlike 'I believe *p*, but *p* isn't true', the utterance is not Moore-paradoxical. Indeed, the debate between James and Clifford—whether such believing could be reasonable—presumes that the endorsement of this conjunction of attitudes can be coherently attributable to someone.

Thus, our initial explanation of why there is no cognitive version of the will—namely, that there is no occasion for doxastic commitment that goes beyond the epistemic reasons—was flawed. Even so, a fundamental disanalogy remains. Intending and acting in the face of uncertainty or indeterminacy can serve the ends of practical reason. But believing (as distinct from some weaker form of acceptance) on insufficient evidence cannot serve the ends of theoretical reason. Hence, in the kind of case on which James focuses, doxastic commitment is merely an instrumentally valuable result of the operation of practical reason, rather than a cognitive form of the will. This conclusion should lead us not to reject cognitive agency but to question the idea that where there is no will, we are inactive.[64]

Agency and Responsibility

My case for cognitive agency has relied a good deal on the thought that we are as responsible for the judgements we make as for the intentions we form. In

[63] Michael Bratman distinguishes belief from acceptance in Bratman 1992. See also Cohen 1989.

[64] Joseph Raz also defends the thesis that we are active in believing even though we don't (in any straightforward sense) believe voluntarily (Raz 1999). Linda Zagzebski (2001) thinks that an individual's epistemic achievements are 'up to her', though not voluntary.

194 / Gary Watson

both cases I am open to normative appraisal and answerable for my commitments. It makes sense to press me on my reasons, and to say of me, 'You should have reached a different conclusion (formed a different intention).' But some philosophers, for example, David Owens, deny the assumption that responsibility requires agency or control in any sense.[65] I find this denial extremely puzzling, because responsibility for particular attitudes seems to me to require a kind of attributability that is sufficient for agency of the kind I have been at pains to articulate. When, in the passage quoted earlier, Owens insists that 'it is the world that determines what I believe, not me', he is making a claim about control, but that claim would equally deny my responsibility. If the world, or my cognitive equipment, *and not I*, determines what I believe, then it is inapt to attribute the outcome to me, to credit or fault me for these attitudes.

Not surprisingly, the disagreement here turns on what kind of control is required for agency. Since Owens thinks we don't have that kind of control, and yet agrees that we are responsible for our epistemic commitments, he thinks responsibility does not presuppose agency. I think that Owens is wrong about agency but right about responsibility. I have nothing more to say in support of this position here. But I would like to conclude this part of the chapter with a slight concession to those who think that Owens is right about agency but wrong about responsibility.[66] I have stressed important parallels between epistemic and practical responsibility. But there are striking differences as well, differences that might lead some to deny that we are directly responsible for our beliefs in the same sense in which we are responsible for our conduct. Both epistemic and moral responsibility involve a kind of accountability. But there are dimensions of moral accountability for intention that have no counterpart in the epistemic case. We can put this by saying that we have notions of culpability and guilt that don't apply to responsibility for belief. There is no such thing as epistemic guilt, really—just various forms of fault. The notions I have in mind are thought to ground various reactive attitudes, blame, and other hard treatment of the culprit. Now the kinds of capacity for responsiveness to reasons to which I have alluded here account

[65] This is one of the targets of Owens 2000; see esp. chs. 1 and 8.

[66] Linda Zagzebski (1996: 68) notes the 'dependency of our responsibility for our acts on our responsibility for the beliefs providing our reasons for acting', an observation she attributes to Edmund Pincoffs. Some might be tempted to see this responsibility as reducible to responsibility for earlier evidence-gathering, and hence as reducible to (or traceable to) act-responsibility. But that seems just to push the question back to the individual's responsibility for her earlier beliefs relevant to the evidence-gathering decisions.

The Work of the Will / 195

for the possibility of various sorts of normative criticism, but they hardly ground the thought that the agent deserves to be subject to retributive sanctions in virtue of her rational shortcomings. It might be supposed, then, that accountability of this further kind makes sense only if we have a kind of control—volitional control, perhaps—that goes beyond the kind of reasons-responsiveness that is involved in belief (something called free will). Indeed, it is common to suppose that what is required is just the capacity for counter-normative agency.

My concession, then, is that there might be dimensions of responsibility that have no epistemic counterpart because there is a kind of control over conduct that is absent in the cognitive realm. I said that this was a *slight* concession for two reasons. First, I don't in fact see how this further, counter-normative form of control is supposed to ground the retributive practices in any case. But obviously this is a larger question than I can take on here. Secondly, to deny that we are 'really' responsible in the cognitive realm on the foregoing grounds is to overlook the multidimensional character of responsibility. Even if there are valid forms of calling people to account that require different kinds of control from those we could have over our beliefs, it remains true that some significant facets of responsibility apply to us equally as epistemic and as moral beings.

Conclusion

The two main topics of this chapter—the issue of cognitive agency and the dispute between internalists and externalists—are linked in an important way. Externalism about practical decision is at odds with the idea that there is distinctively doxastic activity.[67] As we have seen, suitably qualified, internalism about the cognitive realm is uncontroversial. This means that belief is an attitude that is constituted in part by its subjection to norms of relevant evidence. It is controlled by considerations of truth. But, as we have seen, externalism about practical decision rests on the thought that, if intention stands to goodness as belief stands to truth, there is no place here for control or (hence) for agency. What opens up the possibility of agency, according to this idea, is precisely that intention is not a 'normative stance'; if it were, it would be controlled by the good (or by the individual's 'normative

---

[67] I don't say that these are strictly contradictory. Rather, the natural lines of thought supporting each position are opposed to one another.

196 / Gary Watson

equipment') rather than by the agent. As Wallace says, the 'normative aspect of believing . . . is connected with the further fact that there are clear limits, of a conceptual nature, on the possibility of believing at will' (Wallace 2001: 10). If I can adopt a certain attitude 'at will', the attitude in question can't be an 'essentially normative stance'; it can't be part of what it is to be that attitude that it be regulated by certain norms. For those regulatory limits would be limits on agency. On the other hand, those who allow for agency or control in the doxastic realm are apt to do so on the basis of an understanding of control as normative competence. Given this understanding, the case for thinking that something different in kind is necessary for intention and action seems less than compelling.

I have found no convincing reasons to think that adopting intentions and making judgements belong on different sides of a line dividing our agency from what merely happens to us. The capacity to assent to and be guided by relevant reasons is central to what it is to be an epistemically and morally responsible being, and this normative competence involves a fundamental kind of agency. Making up one's mind—'deciding that' or 'deciding to'—is a basic mode of activity that pervades our theoretical and practical lives. Nevertheless, I have argued, there is no straightforward analogue of the will in cognitive contexts. What follows from this, in my view, is not that there is no cognitive agency, but that the boundaries between the active and the passive are not marked by the will.

APPENDIX 7.1. ARISTOTLE AND THE WILL

The idea that the will plays no role in internalist philosophies of mind is arguably borne out by Aristotle's work. Many readers are led to conclude that Aristotle lacks the concept of will precisely because they don't find in his philosophy an unambiguous acknowledgement of counter-normative agency. Although 'prohairesis' is usually translated as 'choice' (or less often 'decision'), Aristotle glosses it as 'desiring in accordance with the good as the result of deliberation'. So akratic behaviour is plainly not an exercise of 'choice' in this sense. This problem is part of what worried Elizabeth Anscombe regarding 'prohairesis':

> At any rate, 'choice' cannot do all the work Aristotle wants to make it do. The uncontrolled man who has further intentions in doing what he does, whose actions are deliberate, although the deliberation is in the interests of a desire which conflicts with what he regards as doing

well—to describe his action we need a concept (our 'intention') having to do with will or appetition.

(Anscombe 1965: 150)

According to Terence Irwin, the Greeks are often thought to lack a notion of the will because they worked with a belief–desire model of behaviour that appears to treat 'agents as passive subjects of their desires, and in doing so they seem to leave out an important aspect of their agency'. Of course, this is just the externalist thought that without the will you don't have agency at all, but only motivational states like desires and beliefs that lead to action without the need for an agent. However, Irwin argues that

it would be both a historical and philosophical mistake ... to claim that Greek philosophers lack a concept of the will, if we simply mean that they are not voluntarists,[68] for the debate between voluntarism and intellectualism[69] is a debate between two views of the will among disputants who share a concept of the will.

(Irwin 1992: 468)

Irwin himself suggests a way of characterizing the will in a way that is neutral between internalist and externalist conceptions, such that Aristotle and 'voluntarists' have different views about the nature of the will, and not different concepts. What is common, Irwin suggests, is the idea of something that performs the regulative function of critical reflection on our desires in order to adjudicate among them. This general concept is sufficient to imply agency, Irwin thinks, because it implies rational control. So we are agents because we are capable of rational choice among different desires in so far as we are capable of deliberating about them 'in the light of our views of the overall good, and capable of choice in accordance with the result of this deliberation' (Irwin 1992: 467).

This rebuts the charge that an internalist conception can't account for agency, but it doesn't suffice to provide a notion of the will as something distinct from judgement. For what plays the adjudicating role here is practical reason, not *prohairesis*. (For further historical discussion, see Kahn 1985 and Normore 1998.)

APPENDIX 7.2. DESCARTES AND INTERNALISM

Descartes defines the will as 'the ability to do or not do something (that is, to affirm or deny, to pursue or avoid)' (Meditation IV, in Descartes 1641c/1984: ii. 40). Two points

---

[68] In my terms, roughly, externalists.　　[69] In my terms, roughly, internalists.

198 / Gary Watson

are especially noteworthy in his treatment: it has definite internalist tendencies, and it applies to intellectual judgement and intention alike. His conception appears to be to some extent internalist, for it is in the nature of the will to be drawn to the good: 'The will of a thinking being is borne, willingly indeed and freely (*for that is of the essence of will*), but none the less infallibly, towards the good that it clearly knows' (Descartes 1641a/1967: ii. 56, my emphasis). In the following passage from Descartes 1649 (Article 177), Descartes even suggests that the normative orientation of the will doesn't depend on clear and distinct perception (on what one *knows*): 'For if we were wholly certain that what we are doing is bad, we would refrain from doing it, since the will tends only towards objects that have some semblance of goodness' (Descartes 1649/1984: i. 392). Note, however, that the idea that we are drawn only to courses of action that bear the 'semblance' of good is consistent with a moderate form of internalism, for it allows for the possibility of willing akrasia. That we are attracted only to options *qua* good doesn't entail that we can't be attracted to an option we take to be *less* good than an alternative.

Descartes explicitly rejects the 'indifference' to reason that is implied by strong externalism: 'In order to be free, there is no need for me to be inclined both ways; on the contrary, the more I incline in one direction—either because I clearly understand that reasons of truth and goodness point that way, or because of a divinely produced disposition of my inmost thoughts—the freer is my choice' (Meditation IV, in Descartes 1641c/1984: ii. 40). Indifference, he says, 'does not belong to the essence of human freedom, since not only are we free when our ignorance of the right renders us indifferent, but we are also free—indeed, at our freest—when a clear perception impels us to pursue some object' (Descartes 1641b/1984: ii. 292). For Descartes, only God's will is 'indifferent', for his will is the source of the true and the good and hence is not guided by them. 'Thus the supreme indifference to be found in God is the supreme indication of his omnipotence' (Descartes 1641b/1984: ii. 292). It is not far off, then, to characterize acts of the externalist will as God-like, if we conjoin that view with a Cartesian conception of God.[70] The freedom of finite beings, in contrast, requires responsiveness to norms that are not of their own creation:

> But as for man, since he finds that the nature of all goodness and truth is already determined by God, and his will cannot tend towards anything else, it is evident that he will embrace what is good and true all the more willingly and hence more freely, in proportion as he sees it more clearly. . . . Hence the indifference which belongs to human freedom is very different from that which belongs to divine freedom.
>
> (Descartes 1641b/1984: ii. 292)

It is noteworthy that, at least in the first edition of the *Essay Concerning Human Understanding*, Locke takes the same line on God's freedom as Descartes here takes

---

[70] It is this idea of the will that O'Shaughnessy ridicules when he writes of those who 'conceive of self-determination as akin to the whims of a Deity responsible to nothing. . . . But that would banish intelligibility from all action'; O'Shaughnessy 1980: ii. 341.

The Work of the Will / 199

on human freedom: 'God himself cannot choose what is not good; the Freedom of the Almighty hinders not his being determined by what is best' (Locke 1690/1975: ɪɪ. xxi. 49). For an illuminating recent treatment of Locke on freedom, see Yaffe 2000.

There are passages that create difficulties for this internalist interpretation. For example (and I'm sure there are others), in a letter to Mesland in 1645 Descartes says this: 'when a very evident reason moves us in one direction, although morally speaking we can hardly move in the contrary direction, absolutely speaking we can'.[71] This remark suggests that the constraints on willing against the good are merely normative.

There is a question, finally, about what makes Descartes's will a unified capacity, as Bernard Williams takes it to be: 'the operation of the will is the same, whether one is concerned with reasons of "the true" or of "the good"' (Williams 1978: 169). The power to assent to proposals to believe or act might be said to be a general capacity with two sub-capacities or sub-functions, depending on whether it is concerned with the issue of the true or the good.[72] But suppose someone said that vision and hearing were functions or sub-capacities of a general capacity of sense-perception. That would seem artificial. Is it any less so in the case of the double function of Descartes's will? Alternatively, unity might result from an intellectualist construal of the good. Exercises of the will are *always* affirmations or denials; the 'practical' will involves affirmations of ideas with practical content, that is, ideas about the good. (I am not suggesting that this is Descartes's own view.) But then the problem is to see what such affirmations have to do with *intention*.

APPENDIX 7.3. KANT AND INTERNALISM

Is Kant an internalist or externalist? As usual, he is difficult to put into conventional categories. Initially, one might be inclined to see his distinction between *Wille* and *Willkür* as marking a familiar externalist distinction between practical reason and volition. In the following passage, though, Kant speaks with the internalists, but, of course, the distinction between 'phenomenon' and 'noumenon' significantly complicates the exegesis:

But freedom of choice [*Willkür*] cannot be defined—as some have tried to define it—as the capacity to make a choice for or against the law (*libertas indifferentiae*), even though choice as a *phenomenon* provides frequent examples of this in experience. . . . Only freedom in relation to the internal lawgiving of reason is really a capacity; the possibility of deviating from it is an incapacity. How can that capacity [namely, freedom] be defined by this incapacity?

(Kant 1797/1991, Ak. vi. 226–7)

[71] Quoted in Youpa 2002; I have learned a lot from Youpa's discussion of Descartes.

[72] Here I am indebted to communications with Paul Hoffman.

200 / Gary Watson

Kant's distinction between *Wille* and *Willkür* is suggestive in connection with the idea of the executive will. According to Henry Allison, 'Kant uses the terms *Wille* and *Willkür* to characterize respectively the legislative and executive functions of a unified faculty of volition, which he likewise refers to as *Wille*' (Allison 1990: 129). Allison says that this distinction identifies a 'duality within unity' (Allison 1990: 130). It is in these terms, he suggests, that the idea of autonomy (understood as the will's giving laws to and for itself) must be construed, 'since this is just a matter of *Wille* giving the law to, or being the law for, *Willkür*. Strictly speaking it is only *Wille* in the broad sense that has the property of autonomy, since it is only *Wille* in this sense that can be characterized as a law to itself' (Allison 1990: 131). The duality is clear, but I'm not sure why the unity is anything more than nominal. The claim seems rather like saying of the master–servant pair that *it* is self-determining.

For an internalist discussion of the Kantian conception of the will, see Herman 2002.

8

Choosing Rationally and Choosing Correctly

Ralph Wedgwood

Two Views of Practical Reason

Suppose that you are faced with several different options (that is, several ways in which you might act in a given situation). Which option should you choose?

Let us take an example that Bernard Williams made famous (Williams 1980: 102). Suppose that you want a gin and tonic, and you believe that the stuff in front of you is gin. In fact, however, the stuff is not gin but petrol. So if you drink the stuff (even mixed with tonic), it will be decidedly unpleasant, to say the least. Should you choose to drink the stuff or not?

It seems to me that there are at least two ways of interpreting this question. If we interpret the question in one way, 'what you should choose' depends on what the available options are *really like* (not just on what you *believe* about what these options are like). For example, it may depend on the actual causal consequences of those options, or on other external facts that are quite

This chapter is an extensively revised restatement of the arguments of an earlier paper (Wedgwood 2002*d*), which was based on the talk that I gave at the conference Weakness of Will and Varieties of Practical Irrationality, Université de Montréal, May 2001. This restatement of those arguments was presented to audiences at Oxford and at the University of Arizona in February 2002. I am grateful to all those audiences (and especially to my commentator in Montreal, Josée Brunet), and also to Carla Bagnoli, John Broome, Alex Byrne, Philip Clark, Ned Hall, Elizabeth Harman, Sally Haslanger, Richard Holton, Leonard Katz, Kathrin Koslicki, Jim Pryor, Susanna Siegel, David Velleman, and the editors of this volume, for helpful comments.

202 / Ralph Wedgwood

independent of your state of mind. In this case, the option of drinking the stuff involves drinking petrol, and so giving yourself a decidedly unpleasant experience, while many of the other available options have no comparable drawbacks. So, when the question is interpreted in this way, you 'shouldn't choose' to drink the stuff. We could call this an 'external', or 'objective', 'should'. I shall express this external 'should' by saying that in this case, choosing to mix the stuff with tonic and drink it is an *incorrect* choice for you to make. As we might say, in choosing to mix the stuff with tonic and drink it, you have got things *wrong*; your choice was a *mistake*.

If we interpret the question in another way, however, 'what you should choose' depends only on your *overall state of mind* (not on external facts that could vary while your state of mind remained unchanged). Even though you mistakenly believe that the stuff in front of you is gin and not petrol, it could still be that there is an impeccable process of reasoning that leads from your current state of mind to your choosing to mix the stuff with tonic and drink it. In that case, the choice to mix the stuff with tonic and drink it fits perfectly with your current overall state of mind. So in this case, when the question is interpreted in this way, it would be wrong to say that you 'shouldn't choose' to drink the stuff. We could call this an 'internal', or 'subjective', 'should'.[1] I shall express this internal 'should' by saying that in this case, choosing to mix the stuff with tonic and drink it is a perfectly *rational* choice for you to make.[2]

The central topic of this chapter is the relationship between these two kinds of 'should', the 'internal' and the 'external' 'should'—or, in other words, between choosing 'rationally' and choosing 'correctly'. It would be odd if these two kinds of 'should' were completely independent of each other; it seems more likely that the truths involving one of these two kinds of

---

[1] I need not claim that the term 'should' is simply *ambiguous*. It may be that 'should' is *context-sensitive*. Perhaps, for example, 'should' is always implicitly relativized to a contextually determined parameter of some sort. Then we could say that the external, or objective, 'should' is relative to the parameter of this sort that is determined by certain contexts, while the internal, or subjective, 'should' is relative to the parameter of this sort that is determined by other contexts. Unfortunately, I cannot go further into these semantic issues here.

[2] That is, I am assuming that something like the thesis that epistemologists—such as Fumerton (1995: 60–9)—call 'internalism' holds of rational choice just as much as of rational or 'justified' belief. I should emphasize that in using the terms 'internal' and 'external' to indicate this contrast between two ways of evaluating choices, I am following the usage that is standard among epistemologists. I am *not* following the usage that is most common among meta-ethicists. So it should not be assumed that what I am here calling the 'internal "should"' has any relation to the so-called 'internal "ought"' that has been discussed by Stephen Darwall (1995: 9–12) and others.

'should' are in some way *explained* by truths involving the other. But in which direction does the order of explanation go? Are the truths about which choices are (internally or subjectively) *rational* ultimately explained by more fundamental truths about which choices are (externally or objectively) *correct*? Or does the order of explanation go in the other direction?

This issue marks a crucial disagreement between two views of practical reason. In effect, it is the issue that underlies the disagreement between what Garrett Cullity and Berys Gaut have called the *recognitional* and the *constructivist* views of practical reason (Cullity and Gaut 1997*b*: 1–6).[3]

As I shall understand them, 'recognitional' views of practical reason take as fundamental some principle about when a choice is (externally or objectively) *correct*. For example, such recognitional views might take as fundamental the principle that a choice is correct if and only if the option chosen really is in a certain way a *good thing to do*—where whether or not an option is a good thing to do in this way may depend, at least in part, on external facts, such as the actual causal consequences of the available options, and the like.

These recognitional views rely on this fundamental principle in giving an account of what it is for a choice to count as (internally or subjectively) *rational*. Proponents of these views cannot say that a choice is rational just in case the option chosen really is a good thing to do. Whether or not a choice is rational is, I am assuming, an 'internal' matter, determined by the agent's overall state of mind alone, whereas whether or not an option is a good thing to do is an 'external' matter, which may depend, at least in part, on external facts. Instead, proponents of these recognitional views could say something like this: a choice is rational just in case the agent *believes* that the option chosen is (in the relevant way) a good thing to do. But this would not be a very plausible thing to say: if the agent's belief that the option chosen is a good thing to do is a grossly irrational belief, then surely the choice will be equally irrational. So it would be more plausible to say this: a choice is rational just in case it is *rational for the agent to believe* that the option chosen is (in the relevant way) a good thing to do. As many epistemologists agree, whether or not it is rational for the agent to hold a certain belief is also an 'internal' matter in the relevant sense, determined by the believer's overall state of mind, and not by facts that could vary while that state of mind remained unchanged. According to this conception of rational belief, what makes it rational for

---

[3] Christine Korsgaard (1996*b*: 35) calls these two views of practical reason 'realism' and 'constructivism' respectively.

204 / Ralph Wedgwood

one to hold a certain belief are internal facts about one's experiences, memories, intuitions, background beliefs, and so on.[4]

The first task for any version of the recognitional view, then, is to identify a certain concept that represents the property of being in the relevant way a 'good thing to do'. Then this view will give an account of what it is for a choice to be rational in terms of the rationality of holding certain *beliefs* that involve this concept. For example, according to the version of the recognitional view under consideration, whenever it is rational for one to choose a certain option, what makes it rational for one to choose this option is the fact that it is rational for one to hold a certain belief involving this concept—namely, the belief that the option is in the relevant way a 'good thing to do'.

Intuitively, if the fundamental principle applying to choices is that one 'should' (in the external or objective sense of 'should') choose options that really are good things to do, then this seems to *explain why* there is also a subsidiary principle applying to choices, to the effect that one 'should' (in the internal or subjective sense of 'should') choose options that it is rational for one to believe to be good things to do. But what exactly is the nature of the explanatory connection between these two principles? It may be that the explanatory connection is this.[5] The fact that an option is a good thing for one to do is an external fact about that option; it is not determined by facts about one's state of mind alone. So one cannot *directly* comply with the requirement that one should choose options that really are good things to do. One can only comply with this requirement *indirectly*, by means of complying with an internal requirement that one should adjust one's choices to some internal fact about one's mental states. The best internal requirement of this sort to comply with, in order to achieve the external result of choosing options that really are good things to do, is the requirement that one should choose options that it is rational for one to believe to be good things to do. In this way, then, a recognitional view may not only give an account of the feature that makes rational choices rational; it may also help to *explain why* one 'should' make choices that have that feature, rather than choices that lack it.

---

[4] So, if one has sufficiently misleading evidence, it might be rational for one to believe an option to be a good thing to do, even if it is not in fact a good thing to do. In this case, according to this account of rational choice, it is rational to choose the option, even though the option is not a good thing to do. Conversely, misleading evidence might prevent it from being rational to believe an option to be a good thing to do, even though in fact it is a good thing to do. In this case, it is irrational to choose the option, even though the option is a good thing to do.

[5] I have developed this approach to understanding the relation between internal and external uses of 'should' in other work (Wedgwood 2002*b*).

Choosing Rationally and Correctly / 205

A recognitional view of this sort can also give an explanation of why akrasia is irrational. Let us assume that akrasia involves choosing to do something that one believes not to be a good thing to do. Now, one's belief that a certain option is not a good thing to do is either a rational belief for one to hold or it is not. If it is not a rational belief for one to hold, then one is being irrational in one's beliefs. If, on the other hand, it is a rational belief for one to hold, then it cannot simultaneously be rational for one to believe that the option *is* a good thing to do. So, one is choosing the option even though it is not rational for one to believe the option to be a good thing to do; hence—according to the recognitional view of rational choice—one's choice is irrational. So akrasia necessarily involves irrationality, either in one's beliefs or in one's choices.

We might express the recognitional view, metaphorically, by saying that rational practical reasoning 'aims' at choosing options that really are good things to do. In this way, the recognitional view of rational choice parallels a certain claim that is often made about *belief*. According to this claim about belief, if one forms and revises one's beliefs rationally, one's reasoning 'aims' at believing the truth and nothing but the truth about the question at issue.[6] In this sense, the recognitional view holds that rational choice 'aims at' options that are good things to do, just as rational belief 'aims at' the truth.[7]

I have only given a crude sketch of the recognitional view of practical reason here. The recognitional view might be refined in many ways. For example, the recognitional view could be generalized so that it applies not just to *choices* (which are mental events involving the formation of a new intention), but to all kinds of *intention revision* (including mental events in which one reaffirms or abandons an old intention). It could also be generalized so that it even applies to one's *failing* to revise one's intentions on a certain occasion, since intuitively failing to revise one's intentions can also sometimes be a serious mistake.

---

[6] In other work (Wedgwood 2002*a*) I have suggested that the slogan that 'belief aims at the truth' is best interpreted as making a claim about belief that is analogous to the claim that the recognitional view makes about choice. The fundamental principle applying to belief is that a belief is correct if and only if the proposition believed is true. This fundamental principle of correct belief explains the principles of rational belief. Roughly, the formation of a belief is rational if and only if, in forming that belief, the believer was following the appropriate rules and procedures—namely, those rules and procedures that it is rational for the believer to regard as reliable ways of reaching the truth.

[7] Proponents of the recognitional view need not maintain that the good is the 'constitutive aim' of all desire or of all action as such. They can agree with David Velleman (1992: 117–22; 1996: 190–1) that it is quite possible for one to desire states of affairs, or to perform actions, that one

206 / Ralph Wedgwood

This view might also be revised to give a more refined account of when exactly a choice is rational. According to the simple account that I am currently considering, a choice is rational if and only if it is rational for the agent, at the time of choice, to believe the chosen option to be a good thing to do. But suppose that one has to make a choice in an emergency, in which one does not have enough time or information for it to be rational for one to hold an outright belief about whether any of the available options is a good thing to do. In cases of this sort, one's choice can surely still be rational, even though it is not rational for one to believe the chosen option to be a good thing to do. This suggests that the account must be refined so that it requires one to adjust one's choice to the *evidence* that one has in favour of beliefs about whether or not the available options are good things to do, even if that evidence is not good enough to make it rational for one to hold an outright belief to the effect that the chosen option is a good thing to do.

I shall return to the task of refining the recognitional view of practical reason in the final section of this chapter. In most of this chapter, however, I shall ignore all these refinements to the recognitional view. To simplify the discussion, I shall just focus on the simple version, according to which a choice is correct if and only if the chosen option is a good thing to do, and a choice is rational if and only if it is rational for the agent to believe the chosen option to be a good thing to do. All the arguments that I shall make in the next four sections could be adapted to apply to the more refined versions just as much as to this simple version.[8]

This simple version makes it particularly clear why it is appropriate to call this a 'recognitional' view of practical reason. According to this view, there are simply truths about which of the available options are good things to do and which are not; and the central or canonical method of practical reasoning is just to attempt to *recognize*, or to *form rational beliefs about*, these truths, and then

believes not to be good in any way. Proponents of the recognitional view only insist that if one performs such actions, one is akratic and therefore irrational.

[8] John Broome has objected to me that in presenting the issues in this way, I am conflating two separate questions: the question of the relative priority of the 'internal' and the 'external' 'should', and the question of the relation between the terms 'should' and 'good'. But as I explain in the next section, there is a 'formal' way of using the term 'good' such that to say that a certain option is 'not a good thing to do' in this way just *is* to say that it is something that one (in the external sense) 'should not choose'. There are also many more 'substantive' ways in which something can be good: for example, something can be good for me, or good for Oxford University, or morally good. The question of how these substantive ways of being good are related to what one (in the external sense) 'should' choose is one that I shall not be addressing here.

to make one's choice accordingly.[9] Something like this conception of rational practical reasoning is suggested by Aristotle's claim that practical wisdom involves both the 'practical intellect'—that is, sound reasoning about action based on a true understanding of the human good—and choice in accordance with what the practical intellect asserts.[10]

Proponents of the *constructivist* view of practical reason, on the other hand, take as fundamental certain internal requirements that a choice must meet in order to be rational. They deny that these internal requirements of rational choice are explained by any principle about when a choice is (externally) 'correct', or when an option is (externally) a 'good thing to do'. Thus, the constructivists deny that these internal requirements of rationality are explained by the good external results to which complying with these requirements either will actually lead, or may reasonably be expected to lead. According to the constructivists, these internal requirements either require no explanation at all, or else are explained in some other way.

For this reason, according to the constructivists, there is no external concept of an option's being 'good' in some way such that it is a basic requirement of rationality that one must choose options that it is rational for one to believe to be good in that way. (If this were a basic requirement of rationality, it would be all but irresistible to conclude that the reason why one should choose actions that it is rational for one to *believe* to be good in that way is because of a more fundamental principle that one should choose actions that really *are* good in that way.) Instead, constructivists typically propose that the requirements of practical rationality are either purely *procedural* require- ments, or else pure requirements of *formal coherence* among one's choices or preferences.

There are two main versions of constructivism that are defended by contemporary philosophers. One version is *decision-theoretic* constructivism, according to which one's preferences are rational if and only if they satisfy certain conditions of coherence or consistency. Typically, the idea is that

---

[9] I describe this as the 'central or canonical' method of practical reasoning because strictly speaking, according to this view as I formulated it, it may also be rational to take certain *short cuts* in one's practical reasoning. So long as it is rationally permissible for one to believe that the chosen option is a good thing to do, and one's choice is suitably sensitive to whatever considerations make it the case that it is rationally permissible for one to believe this, then one's choice may be rational even if one has not actually formed any belief at all about whether or not the option in question is a good thing to do.

[10] See Aristotle's definition of 'practical wisdom' (*phronēsis*) in *Nicomachean Ethics* 6. 5, 1140[b]5 (repeated at 1140[b]22); and compare also 6. 2, 1139[a]24, and 6. 9, 1142[b]34.

208 / Ralph Wedgwood

these preferences must satisfy the 'axioms' (transitivity, monotonicity, independence, and so on) that are necessary to make it possible to represent those preferences by means of a 'utility function' (Joyce 1999: 84–9). For an agent whose preferences are coherent in this way, it is rational to choose an option if and only if no alternative option is preferred.[11]

The other main version of constructivism is *Kantian* constructivism, according to which the fundamental principle of rational choice requires that in making choices, one should follow a procedure that meets certain formal conditions of consistency and universalizability. Specifically, according to Kant (1788, Ak. v. 30–1), to be rational, one must always make one's choice through following some 'maxim' or general rule, which it must also be consistent for one at the same time to will to be a universal law.[12]

In these constructivist theories, then, these internal requirements of rational choice are fundamental. Constructivists have made many claims about these requirements: some constructivists have compared them to the requirements of logical consistency among our beliefs;[13] and some constructivists have claimed that these requirements of rational choice are a priori.[14] But they all deny that the external notions of a choice's being 'correct' or of an option's being a 'good thing to do' play any role in the explanation of the requirements of rational choice. The external notions are either denied to have any necessary connection to the notions of rational practical reasoning or of reasons for action, or else they are simply *defined* in terms of what it is

---

[11] I tentatively suggest that the broadly procedural account of rational practical reasoning sketched by Bernard Williams (1980: 104–5) is also a version of constructivism. Williams seems to think that it is just intuitively clear that certain procedures of deliberation are rational. He certainly does not try to explain why these procedures are rational by appealing to the good external results that complying with these procedures may be expected to have.

[12] This interpretation of Kant—which is basically due to Korsgaard (1989)—is controversial, and rejected by some philosophers, such as Wood (1999), who regard themselves as Kantians. But for present purposes, it does not matter whether this interpretation of Kant is correct. All that matters here is that the view that I am calling 'Kantian constructivism' is worthy of serious examination.

[13] For example, Richard Jeffrey talks of the principles of rational choice as the 'logic of decision' (Jeffrey 1983); and Korsgaard claims that, just as 'if I am going to think I must think in accordance with the principle of non-contradiction', so too, in essentially the same way, 'if I am going to will at all I must do so universally ... The requirement of universality is in this way constitutive of willing' (Korsgaard 1996b: 235).

[14] Kant repeatedly insists that the fundamental principle of practical reason must be a priori (Kant 1785, Ak. iv. 388–90, 406–12, 425–7). Some decision-theoretic constructivists, such as Gauthier (1985) and Dreier (1997), also seem to suggest that the fundamental requirements of rational preference are a priori.

'rational to choose'. For example, according to some of these philosophers, for an option to be a good thing for one to do just is for it to be an option that it *would* be rational for one to choose, if one were ideally well informed about the relevant facts.[15] According to this definition, all truths about which choices are correct, and about which options are good things to do, are 'constructed' out of the internal requirements of rational choice.

Paraphrasing Christine Korsgaard (1996*b*: 36–7), we can express the difference between constructivism and the recognitional view as follows. Constructivists believe that there are truths about what is a good thing for one to do *because* there are rational procedures for making choices—whereas according to the recognitional view, there are rational procedures for making choices *because* there are truths about what is a good thing for one to do, which it is rational for one to expect those procedures to track. For the constructivists, these rational procedures—or more generally, the internal requirements of rational choice—are fundamental. Everything else that has any necessary connection to reasons for action must be explained on the basis of these internal requirements of rationality. This is why both the Kantian constructivists, such as Korsgaard (1996*b*), and the decision-theoretic constructivists, such as David Gauthier (1986), seek to construct the whole of ethics on the basis of their account of these internal requirements of rational choice.

In this chapter I shall consider some of the objections that the constructivists have directed against the recognitional view. Ironically, as I shall argue, these objections apply just as much to constructivism as to certain versions of the recognitional view. Then I shall argue that there is a version of the recognitional view that is immune to constructivist objections. This, it seems to me, provides considerable support for this version of the recognitional view.

'Formal' and 'Substantive' Versions of the Recognitional View

As I explained in the previous section, the simple version of the recognitional view that I am focusing on here first identifies a certain concept that

---

[15] Compare Christine Korsgaard (1986*a*: 122): 'what makes the object of your rational choice good is that it *is* the object of a rational choice'. Here Korsgaard is broadly speaking following Kant, who appears to believe that an option is a good thing to do (not merely good in relation to

210 / Ralph Wedgwood

represents the property of being an option that is in a certain way a 'good thing to do', and then claims that a choice is rational if and only if it is rational for the agent to hold a certain *belief* involving this concept—namely, the belief that the chosen option is in this way a 'good thing to do'.

But which way of being a good thing to do is 'the relevant way'? As Judith Thomson (2001: 17–19) and others have pointed out, there are many different ways in which something can be good: it may be good for me, or good for Oxford University, or morally good, and so on. Perhaps there can also be more than one concept that represents the very same property (such as the concepts 'good for Cicero' and 'good for Tully', perhaps). If so, then even after the recognitional view has identified the relevant way of being good, it must still identify the relevant *concept* that represents the property of being in this way a good thing to do. So exactly *which*, out of all the concepts that can be expressed by the term 'a good thing to do', is the one that the recognitional view is employing here?

According to David Velleman (1996: 176–7), there are two main types of concept that proponents of the recognitional view can employ here. They could employ a concept that gives a purely 'formal' specification of the 'object of practical reasoning'; or they could employ a concept that gives a 'substantive' specification of the 'object of practical reasoning'.

As Velleman explains, a concept gives a 'formal' specification of 'the object of an enterprise' if it is simply the concept of the object of that enterprise. For example, the concept 'winning' gives a formal specification of 'the object of a competitive game', since the concept ' "winning" just is the concept of succeeding in competition' (Velleman 1996: 176). Similarly, Velleman suggests, one concept that could be expressed by the term 'a good thing to do' is simply the concept of the 'object' of practical reasoning.

Velleman believes that practical reasoning literally has an 'object' or 'aim'. I shall not assume this here. Instead, I shall suppose that a purely 'formal' concept of a 'good thing to do' is a concept such that it is a conceptual truth that an option is a 'good thing to do' in this sense if and only if it is an option that it is *correct* to choose—in precisely the same sense of the term 'correct' that I explained in the previous section. One such concept, which can be expressed by describing an option as a 'good thing to do', is as I have argued elsewhere (Wedgwood 2001*a*) a concept the content of which is determined by the special 'conceptual role' that it plays in rational practical

some end, but good *simpliciter*) just in case it is an option that no well-informed agent can reject without violating the fundamental internal requirement of rationality.

Choosing Rationally and Correctly / 211

reasoning. Specifically, if a rational agent makes judgements using this concept, about which of the available options fall under this concept and which do not, then she will choose one of the options that she judges to fall under the concept, and not one of the options that she judges not to fall under it. I have argued that if the content of a concept is determined by its having a conceptual role of this kind, then it follows that an option falls under the concept if and only if it is correct to choose it.

To judge that an option is a 'good thing to do', in this formal sense, then, is not to make a specific value-judgement, such as that the option is *morally* good, or good *for the agent*, or good *as a means to a certain end*. It is simply to judge that it is an option that it is correct to choose. This judgement could also be expressed in many other ways. For example, this judgement could also be expressed by saying that the option is 'choiceworthy' or 'OK'. The judgement that an option is in this formal sense *not* a good thing to do could be expressed by saying that the option is something that one had 'better not' do, or that there is a 'conclusive reason' for one not to do, or simply that one 'should not' do.[16]

One version of the recognitional view, then, would use the term 'a good thing to do' to express this purely formal concept. I shall call this the 'formal' version of the recognitional view. The formal version of the recognitional view is distinct from the constructivist view, because whether or not something counts as a 'good thing to do', in this formal sense, is typically determined not by internal facts about the agent's overall state of mind, but at least in part by external facts which could vary while the agent's overall state of mind remained unchanged.

Alternatively, the recognitional view might use the term 'a good thing to do' to express a more *substantive* concept of an option's being good in some specific way. I shall call views of this sort 'substantive' versions of the recognitional view. For example, one such substantive version of the recognitional view would use the term 'a good thing to do' to mean *optimal for the agent's happiness*. This version of the recognitional view would in effect be what Derek Parfit (1984: 1–2) has called the 'Self-interest Theory of Rationality'. According to this theory, a choice is correct if and only if the chosen option maximizes the agent's happiness (that is, there is no alternative to the chosen option that will make a greater contribution to the agent's happiness); and a

---

[16] To say that X is a 'good thing to do' (in this 'formal' sense) does not imply that one *should* do X. One might be in a 'Buridan's ass' case, in which both X and Y are good things to do, but it is impossible to do both. In this case, it is not true that one should do X or that one should do Y. Still, they are both good things to do.

212 / Ralph Wedgwood

choice is rational if and only if it is rational for the agent to *believe* that the chosen option maximizes her happiness.

Another 'substantive' version of the recognitional view would use the term 'a good thing to do' to mean *optimal for satisfying the totality of the agent's present desires.* This would in effect be what Parfit (1984: 92–4) has called the the 'Instrumental version of the Present-aim Theory'. According to this theory, a choice is correct if and only if the chosen option optimally satisfies the totality of the agent's present desires; and a choice is rational if and only if it is rational for the agent to believe that the chosen option optimally satisfies the totality of his present desires.[17]

A Problem for 'Substantive' Versions of the Recognitional View

Let us start by considering 'substantive' versions of the recognitional view. For example, consider the *egoistic* version of the recognitional view (Parfit's 'Self-interest Theory'). This view interprets the notion of a 'good thing to do' as *optimal for the agent's own happiness* (where the term 'happiness' expresses a substantive concept of some sort—not simply the purely formal concept of a life of the sort that it is correct to choose). According to this view, if one makes a choice, one's choice is correct if and only if the chosen option maximizes one's happiness; and one's choice is rational if and only if it is rational for one to believe that the chosen option maximizes one's happiness.

As I shall argue here, this egoistic version of the recognitional view faces a problem that Christine Korsgaard (1996*b*: 9–21) has called 'the normative question'. According to this egoistic view, it is irrational—indeed akratic—for one to choose any option if one rationally believes that that option will not maximize one's own happiness. But we can imagine an agent (let us call her Alice) who knows that a certain option will not maximize her happiness, but is still uncertain about whether or not to choose that option—perhaps because the option has some other feature that she is tempted to regard as highly important. Alice need not doubt that the fact that the option will not maximize her happiness is *some* reason for her not to choose it. But she may

---

[17] This instrumentalist version of the recognitional view must be distinguished from the decision-theoretic version of constructivism, since according to this instrumentalist view, the internal requirements of rational choice are explained by a more fundamental principle that defines when a choice counts as (externally) correct.

Choosing Rationally and Correctly / 213

still be uncertain whether to treat this fact as an *overriding* or *decisive* reason, as the egoistic view requires her to do. She might express her perplexity by asking, 'Why should I always choose options that maximize my own happiness? Why shouldn't I sometimes choose options that won't maximize my happiness instead?'

In asking this 'normative question', Alice seems to be seeking some compelling *further reason* not to choose any option that does not maximize her happiness. That is, she is looking for some consideration that could rationally *persuade* her not to choose any option that she believes not to maximize her happiness—even if she did not yet have the disposition to avoid choosing any options that she rationally believes not to maximize her happiness. But according to the egoistic version of the recognitional view, there are no such further reasons. The only way in which any considerations can rationally persuade one not to choose any option, according to this egoistic view, is by making it irrational for one to believe that the option maximizes one's own happiness. So according to this egoistic view, if someone lacked the disposition not to choose any option that it was not rational for her to believe to maximize her happiness, there would be no options that she could be rationally persuaded not to choose; such an agent would be beyond the power of rational persuasion altogether.

So, it seems, the egoistic version of the recognitional view must accept that if any agents lack the disposition to comply with this alleged rational requirement—the requirement that one should not choose any option that it is not rational for one to believe to maximize one's own happiness—there is no way of rationally persuading them to do so. In that sense, the egoistic view must regard this rational requirement as *basic*. If one is not already disposed to conform to this requirement, there is no way of rationally persuading one to do so, since rational persuasion precisely consists in exploiting a person's disposition to comply with this requirement.

There do seem to be some 'basic' rational requirements of this sort. For example, if someone is not already disposed to accept instances of the basic laws of logic, there will be no way of rationally persuading him to do so, since all arguments that one might employ in order rationally to persuade him will themselves involve instances of those very laws of logic. So why shouldn't the egoistic requirement also be a 'basic' rational requirement of this sort?

However, it does not seem plausible that this egoistic requirement is a basic requirement of this sort. If you violate a rational requirement—that is, if you make an irrational choice or form an irrational belief—this reflects a cognitive defect *in you*. (This is a fundamental difference between the internal notion of a rational choice and the external notion of a correct choice. There need be no defect in you at all if you make an incorrect choice, by choosing an option that is not in fact a good thing to do; it may be sheer bad luck that the stuff was petrol and not gin, so that your choice to mix the stuff with tonic and drink it was in fact an incorrect choice.) Since irrationality is always a defect in you, then, so long as you are being sufficiently sane and intelligent, you will tend to avoid such defects. At the very least, if it is a *basic* requirement of rationality that one should not form a set of beliefs or choices that has a certain feature, then if you *recognize* that a certain set of beliefs or choices has that feature, you will not remain uncertain about whether or not to form that set of beliefs and choices, unless you are being less than perfectly sane and intelligent. For example, suppose that it is a basic principle of rationality that it is irrational to believe any proposition that is logically self-contradictory. Then, if you recognize that a certain proposition is logically self-contradictory, you will not remain uncertain about whether or not to believe that proposition, unless you are being less than perfectly sane and intelligent.

Intuitively, however, it seems quite possible that Alice is being perfectly sane and intelligent, even if she recognizes that it is not rational for her to believe that the option in question will maximize her happiness, but still remains uncertain about whether to choose that option. Alice's uncertainty about whether or not to choose this option hardly seems in the same category as a failure to be convinced by instances of the elementary laws of logic. Indeed, her perplexity seems eminently intelligible. So it seems implausible to claim that it is a basic requirement of rationality that one should never choose any option that it is not rational for one to believe to maximize one's own happiness. But as we have seen, the egoistic version of the recognitional view entails that it is a basic requirement. So this seems to be a serious problem for the egoistic version of the recognitional view.

The same problem also arises for other substantive versions of the recognitional view. For example, according to the *instrumentalist* version of the recognitional view, a choice is rational if and only if it is rational for one to believe that the chosen option optimally satisfies the totality of one's present desires. So, according to this view, it is irrational (indeed akratic) for one to choose an option if one rationally believes that the option does not optimally satisfy the totality of one's present desires. But we can imagine an agent (call him George) who starts to regard the majority of his desires with suspicion; perhaps he becomes attracted to the ideal of detaching himself from all self-centred desires. George could be convinced that a certain option will not optimally satisfy the totality of his present desires, but still wonder whether or not to choose that option. He might ask himself, 'Why should I always choose options that optimally satisfy the totality of my present desires? Why shouldn't I sometimes choose options that don't optimally satisfy those desires instead?'

In asking this question, George appears to be seeking a compelling *further reason* not to choose any option that does not optimally satisfy the totality of his present desires. That is, he is seeking some consideration that could rationally persuade him not to choose any such option—even if he is not yet disposed to reject all options that it is not rational for him to regard as optimally satisfying the totality of his desires. But according to the instrumentalist view, there are no such further reasons. The only consider-ations that can rationally persuade one not to choose any option are considerations that make it irrational for one to believe that the option will optimally satisfy the totality of one's desires. So, unless George is already disposed not to choose any option that it is not rational for him to regard as optimally satisfying the totality of his desires, then there are simply no options that he could be rationally persuaded not to choose.

Thus, the instrumentalist must claim that it is simply a *basic* requirement of rationality that one should not choose any option that it is not rational for one to regard as optimally satisfying one's total set of desires. But it seems doubtful whether the instrumentalist requirement really can be a basic requirement of rationality. George could surely be perfectly sane and intelli-gent, even if he recognizes that it is not rational for him to regard a certain option as optimally satisfying his total set of desires, but still remains uncer-tain about whether to choose that option.

In general, this problem will arise for *all* substantive versions of the recognitional view. Whatever substantive concept of a 'good thing to do' the recognitional view takes as its central concept, it will have to take the requirement that one should not choose any option that it is not rational for one to believe to be, in this substantive sense, a 'good thing to do' as a basic requirement of rationality. But it seems doubtful whether there can be any basic requirement of rationality of this sort. For every such requirement, it seems that agents could be perfectly sane and intelligent, even if they recognize that it is not rational for them to believe a certain option to be (in this substantive sense) a 'good thing to do', and yet still feel uncertain about whether to choose the option. None of these alleged requirements

216 / Ralph Wedgwood

resembles the clear examples of basic requirements—such as the requirement that one should not believe logical contradictions. For every substantive concept of a 'good thing to do', one could always ask, without revealing any insanity or lack of intelligence, 'But why should I always choose options that are good things to do in that way? Why shouldn't I sometimes choose options that aren't in that way good things to do at all?' So the substantive versions of the recognitional view all seem to face a serious problem.

An Analogous Problem for Constructivist Views

As I shall argue, a closely analogous problem also arises for constructivist views of practical reason. As I mentioned in the first section, there are two main varieties of constructivism that have many proponents today: decision-theoretic constructivism and Kantian constructivism.

According to decision-theoretic constructivism, rational choices are choices that *cohere* in a certain way with each other and with one's preferences and beliefs. Specifically, one's preferences should be transitive, monotonic, independent, and so on; and it is rational to choose an option only if no alternative option is preferred. According to this view, one's choices 'should' (in the internal use of that term) satisfy these conditions of coherence. But now it seems that we can raise the 'normative question' again. *Why should* our choices satisfy these conditions of coherence? Why does it *matter* whether or not our choices are coherent in this way?

According to Kantian constructivism, rational choices are choices that are made by means of a *procedure* that satisfies certain formal conditions of *consistency* and *universality*. Specifically, one must make one's choice by following a general rule or 'maxim', which it must also at the same time be consistent for one to will to be a universal law. According to this view, one 'should' (in the internal sense of that term) always make one's choices by following a universalizable maxim of this kind. But the 'normative question' arises here too. *Why should* we always make our choices by following such universalizable maxims? Why does it *matter* whether or not we make our choices in this way?

According to the constructivists, the fact that one always 'should' make choices that meet these internal conditions of coherence or universalizability is not explained by the good external results to which such choices either will actually lead, or may rationally be expected to lead. But this seems to imply that it matters simply *in itself*, purely *for its own sake*, whether or not one's

Choosing Rationally and Correctly / 217

choices meet these internal conditions of coherence, or whether they are made by following a suitably universalizable maxim.[18]

On the face of it, however, this is a rather surprising idea. Why on earth should such a thing matter purely for its own sake? Perhaps choices that do not meet these internal conditions of coherence or universalizability are aesthetically unattractive in some way: they form a less pretty mental pattern than choices that do meet these conditions. But this hardly seems a sufficiently weighty consideration to explain why (in the internal use of the term) one 'should' *never* make choices that do not satisfy these internal conditions. It would defy belief to claim that it matters purely for its own sake whether or not one's choices meet these internal conditions in the relevant way, but absolutely no explanation can be given of why it matters. So constructivists must surely offer some further explanation of why it matters—that is, of why one's choices should meet these internal conditions of coherence or universalizability.[19]

Many constructivists try to offer such an explanation by arguing that it is 'constitutive' of having the capacity for choices at all that one's choices must tend to satisfy these internal conditions of coherence. For example, some of the decision-theoretic constructivists, such as David Lewis (1974), argue that we would not even be interpretable as having preferences at all unless our choices tended, by and large, to satisfy these conditions of coherence.[20]

But is this claim, that it is constitutive of having preferences at all that one's choices must tend, by and large, to satisfy these conditions of internal coherence, really enough all by itself to explain why it is *always irrational* to make choices that do not satisfy these conditions (that is, that one should never make choices that do not satisfy these conditions)?[21] Even if it is impossible to have preferences at all unless your choices tend, *by and large*, to

[18] This point is more or less explicit in Kant, who claims (Kant 1785, Ak. iv. 396–400) that the *good will*—i.e. the will that complies with the fundamental principle of rational choice, rejecting all non-universalizable maxims precisely *because* they are not universalizable in the relevant way—is valuable purely in itself, not merely because of its actual or expected results.

[19] Decision-theoretic constructivists often appeal to the so-called 'money pump' argument. For some criticism of the 'money pump' argument, see Broome 1999: 74–5 and Maher 1993: 36–8.

[20] Alternatively, this argument could be based on the idea that unless one conforms to these conditions of coherence, one will not count as a unified agent with a genuine will, as opposed to a bundle of disparate desires and needs; see Gauthier 1985.

[21] I need not claim that such constitutive claims are simply irrelevant to explaining why we should comply with the basic requirements of rationality. Indeed, I suggested that such constitutive claims provide part of the explanation in some of my earlier work (Wedgwood 1999, §4). All that I am claiming here is that these constitutive claims are not sufficient all by themselves to

218 / Ralph Wedgwood

satisfy these conditions, how can this explain why your choices should *always* satisfy these conditions? Perhaps it does not matter at all if you *sometimes* make choices that do not satisfy these conditions.

Anyway, it seems doubtful whether the claim that a disposition not to make such internally incoherent choices is constitutive of having preferences at all can be the *basic* explanation of why it is irrational to make such choices. If this claim were the basic explanation of why it is irrational to make such internally incoherent choices, then it would in effect be a basic principle of rationality that it is irrational for anyone to go against those dispositions that are constitutive of having preferences at all. But it is doubtful whether there can be any such basic principle of rationality.

As I argued in the previous section, if you make an irrational choice, this choice reflects a cognitive defect *in you*. Since irrationality is always a defect in you, then, so long as you are being sufficiently sane and intelligent, you will tend to avoid such defects. At the very least, if it is a *basic* principle of rationality that it is irrational for anyone to form a set of beliefs or choices that has a certain feature, then, if you recognize that a certain set of beliefs or choices has that feature, you will not remain uncertain about whether or not to form that set of beliefs and choices, unless you are being less than perfectly sane and intelligent. But it seems intuitively quite possible that a perfectly sane and intelligent agent might recognize that a certain choice would involve going against a disposition that is constitutive of having preferences at all, and still remain uncertain about whether or not to make that choice. Such a person might ask herself, 'I recognize that a disposition not to make choices of this kind is constitutive of having preferences at all, but why shouldn't I sometimes resist that disposition, and make a choice of this kind anyway?' So it seems doubtful whether the internal conditions of rational choice can be explained in this way.

The same problem also seems to arise for the Kantians' explanation of why we should never make any choices except by following their supreme principle of practical reason (see Kant 1785, Ak. iv. 446–7, and Korsgaard 1996*b*: 92–100). This Kantian explanation is based ultimately on the proposition that the will is *free*. Then the Kantians argue that it is 'constitutive' of having free will at all that one must have the capacity to follow a law that one gives to oneself. Finally, they argue that the only possible law of this kind is

provide such an explanation. In the case of the basic requirement that one should not believe logical contradictions, for example, it also seems crucial that it is rational for one to believe that one must conform to this requirement if one is to reach the *truth* about the question at issue.

their supreme principle of practical reason—the law that one ought always to make one's choices by following a general maxim that one can consistently at the same time will to be a universal law.

Now, the Kantians cannot argue that it is constitutive of having free will that one actually makes all one's choices by following this fundamental principle; then it would be impossible to violate this principle of rationality—in which case it would surely not be a genuine principle of rationality at all. So, instead, the Kantians typically argue only that it is constitutive of free will that one has the *capacity* to follow this law. But then the normative question arises yet again. A perfectly sane and intelligent person might ask himself: 'I recognize that having the capacity to follow this law is constitutive of having free will at all, but why should I always make my choices by exercising this capacity? Why shouldn't I sometimes make choices without exercising my capacity to follow this law?' So it seems most doubtful whether this approach can give a satisfactory explanation of why we should follow the Kantians' supreme principle of practical reason.

In general, it seems doubtful whether the constructivists can explain why we should comply with the internal requirements of rational choice, in a way that deals adequately with the 'normative question'. Indeed, it seems that constructivist views are just as vulnerable to this problem as the 'substantive' versions of the recognitional view.

The 'Formal' Version of the Recognitional View

So far as I can see, there is only one approach to practical reason that avoids this problem—namely, the version of the recognitional view that is based on a purely *formal* concept of a 'good thing for one to do'.[22] As I explained above, it is a conceptual truth, built into the nature of this formal concept of a 'good thing to do', that an option is a 'good thing to do' in this sense if and only if it is an option that it is 'correct' to choose. According to the 'formal' version of the recognitional view, a choice is rational if and only if it is rational for the agent to believe that the option chosen is, in this purely formal sense, a good thing to do.

Suppose that someone raises the normative question with respect to this notion of what is a 'good thing to do': 'Why should I always choose options

[22] One philosopher whom it may be correct to interpret as accepting this formal version of the recognitional view is Lawrence (1995).

220 / Ralph Wedgwood

that are good things to do? Why shouldn't I sometimes choose options that are not good things to do?' When the question is understood in this way, it is equivalent to the question 'Why shouldn't I sometimes choose options that it is not correct for me to choose?' But as I explained in the first section, to say that it is 'not correct' to choose an option is just to say that one 'shouldn't' choose it. So asking this question is also equivalent to asking: 'Why shouldn't I sometimes choose options that I shouldn't choose?' But that question will hardly perplex any sane and intelligent person! If you shouldn't choose it, you shouldn't choose it. That is an utterly trivial truth—not a truth that requires any further explanation. So it may well be a basic requirement of rationality that one should not choose any option that it is not rational for one to believe to be, in this formal sense, a good thing to do.

As I suggested in the second section, this formal concept of a 'good thing to do' may, more specifically, be a concept the very content of which is given by its special 'conceptual role' in practical reasoning. If so, then it is by definition a concept such that if one is rational, and judges that a certain option is in this sense not a good thing to do, then one cannot need any further reasons to persuade one not to choose that option. Any rational thinker who masters this concept will treat the judgement that an option is not in this sense a good thing to do as simply settling the practical question of whether to choose the option. In effect, it would be built into the very nature of this concept that it is a basic requirement of rationality that one should not choose options that one rationally believes not to be good things to do.

The objection that this view must face is not that it imposes substantive requirements that it cannot adequately explain, but rather that it is empty or trivial—an objection that has been pressed forcefully by Velleman (1996: 174–8).[23] When the term is used in this formal sense, to say that an option is a 'good thing to do' is just to say that it is correct to choose it. So the fundamental principle of the recognitional view—that it is correct to choose

---

[23] For Velleman (1996: 190), this 'emptiness charge' is just one stage in his argument for a conception of practical reason that seeks 'to avoid the twin pitfalls of internalism and externalism'. Specifically, Velleman attacks the recognitional view of practical reason because it appears to provide one way of defending 'externalism'—by which he means the view that there are some reasons for action that are entirely independent of the agent's contingent desires. Even if the recognitional view would provide one way of defending 'externalism', however, we should not assume without further discussion that the recognitional view is *committed* to 'externalism'. (Perhaps it is not rational to believe that an action is a good thing to do unless that action satisfies one of one's contingent desires.) At all events, I shall focus purely on Velleman's objection to the recognitional view, and ignore the other aspects of his arguments here.

an option if and only if the option is a good thing to do—amounts to nothing more than the trivial claim that it is correct to choose an option if and only if it is correct to choose it. So how can this principle explain anything at all?[24]

Proponents of the recognitional view could reply as follows. This specification of the fundamental principle, using this formal concept of a 'good thing to do', is indeed trivial. But perhaps the property of being in this formal sense a good thing to do can be also specified in other ways—not just by means of this purely formal concept. For example, perhaps this property is identical to the property of being a morally permissible option that, out of all such morally permissible options, best satisfies the agent's total set of desires. Then the fundamental principle could also be specified in a non-trivial way—as the principle that a choice is correct if and only if the option chosen is a morally permissible option that, out of all such morally permissible options, best satisfies the agent's desires.

However, the formal version of the recognitional view itself tells us nothing about which such non-trivial specifications are true. It just tells us to form rational beliefs, involving this purely formal concept, about which of the available options are good things to do and which are not, and then to choose accordingly. But all that it tells us about what it is for an option to be a good thing to do is simply that it is an option that it would be correct to choose. Velleman (1996: 175–6) objects that this 'would be . . . like asking [the agent] to hunt for something described only as "the quarry", or to play a game with an eye to something described only as "winning"'. According to this objection, the formal version of the recognitional view is too empty to tell us how to set about making rational choices about what to do. True, it tells us to form rational beliefs about which of the available options are good things to do and which are not. But according to this complaint, this view tells us so little about what it is for an option to be a good thing to do that it cannot tell us how to set about forming such rational beliefs.

In fact, it is not obvious that this objection is correct. It is true that the formal version of the recognitional view does not by itself give us any non-trivial specification of what it is for an option to be a good thing to do (although, as I have argued, it is quite compatible with the existence of true non-trivial specifications of this sort). Nonetheless, this view may tell

---

[24] As Velleman claims (Velleman 1996: 176–8), there cannot be any 'object of practical reasoning' unless there is some *substantive* specification of what achieving this object consists in. As he puts it: 'A game whose object was specifiable only as "winning" wouldn't have an object— that is, wouldn't have any object in particular' (176).

222 / Ralph Wedgwood

us enough about the nature of beliefs about what is and what is not in this formal sense a good thing to do, to explain how we are to set about forming such beliefs in a rational way. That is, this view of practical reasoning, together with other independently acceptable truths, may entail an informative *epistemology* for these beliefs.

As I explained in the first section, the recognitional view implies that beliefs about what is and what is not, in this formal sense, a good thing to do play a certain crucial role in practical reasoning. According to the recognitional view, if one is rational, and forms beliefs about which of the available options are good things to do and which are not, then one will choose an option that one believes to be a good thing to do, and not one of the options that one believes not to be a good thing to do. (Indeed, as I suggested in the second section, this may be precisely what determines the content of the formal concept of a 'good thing to do'.) So, for example, if one is rational and believes 'A is the only available option that is a good thing to do', then one will choose A.

In this sense, being rational and having a belief of this kind is sufficient to *motivate* one to make a choice. Nothing like that is true of most beliefs. For example, one might be perfectly rational, and believe 'A is the only available option that will lead to my winning this game of Scrabble', and yet not be motivated in any way to choose A (perhaps because one knows that one has compelling reason not to win this particular game of Scrabble). Thus, it is a quite special feature of beliefs about what is and what is not a good thing to do that they are sufficient to motivate choice in this way. But according to a plausible thesis, known as the 'Humean Theory of Motivation', all motivation of choice involves *desire*.[25] And according to another thesis, which Jay Wallace (1990: 370) has called the 'desire–out, desire–in' principle, 'processes of thought which give rise to a desire (as "output") can always be traced back to a further desire (as "input")'. Together, these two theses imply that no

---

[25] I have given a more careful statement of the argument for the conclusion that the Humean Theory of Motivation entails a broadly 'sentimentalist' epistemology for beliefs of this sort in other work (Wedgwood 2002c). But why should we accept the Humean Theory of Motivation? Very roughly, I suspect that the reason is that, as Dummett has often maintained (Dummett 1991: 287), there must be a sort of 'harmony' between the *grounds* for holding a certain belief, and what that belief *commits one to*. Beliefs about what is a 'good thing to do' have the very special feature that they commit one to making certain choices. So there must be something equally special about the grounds on the basis of which those beliefs are held; for example, perhaps these grounds must include *desires*—which are states that essentially involve a disposition to make the corresponding choices.

Choosing Rationally and Correctly / 223

belief can be sufficient to motivate choice in this way unless that belief was itself originally produced, at least in part, by some of one's desires. So, assuming these two theses about motivation, beliefs about what is a good thing to do must also be based, in some way, on some of one's desires. (This is not to say that these beliefs can be based on *any* of one's desires; it may be only certain *special* desires that can play this role as part of the ultimate rational basis for these beliefs.) Moreover, since one's practical reasoning must ultimately be based on ordinary empirical information about the available options and what their non-normative properties would be, the same must be true of these beliefs. Finally, the general principles of rational belief apply to these beliefs as much as to any others: one should try to keep these beliefs consistent, unified by relations of explanatory coherence, and so on.

Roughly, then, the epistemology of these beliefs is as follows. A belief about a particular option A, to the effect that A is, in the 'formal' sense, a 'good thing to do', must be based on (1) ordinary empirical beliefs about A, to the effect that A has such-and-such non-normative properties, and (2) some at least rough general principle to the effect that, at least typically and for the most part, options that have those non-normative properties are good things to do.[26] This rough general principle must in turn be based on a search for what John Rawls (1972: 46–53) has called 'reflective equilibrium'. This is a process that starts out by treating one's disposition to have a certain sort of desire for certain options as weak, prima facie evidence that those options are in the formal sense good things to do; this process then aims to form, on the basis of this evidence, a maximally coherent set of rough general principles about which options are (in this sense) good things to do.[27]

This is only a rough sketch of this epistemological account. Much more would have to be said to make it plausible that this is an adequate account of the epistemology of the relevant beliefs. My main point here is simply to argue

[26] Suppose that one of these 'rough general principles' is the principle that (at least typically and for the most part) no option that has property P is a good thing to do. Why can't someone raise the normative question again, 'Why should I (at least for the most part) avoid choosing options that have property P?' But this principle is not an internal requirement of *rationality*. It is an external fact about which options are good things to do. So even if it is just a basic principle that cannot be any further explained, there is no reason to expect that it must be convincing to all agents who are sufficiently 'sane and intelligent'.

[27] We should perhaps also require that it must be rational for one to expect that a process of further refining this rough general principle, and further empirical investigation of A and the other available options, would not finally defeat the conclusion that A is a good thing to do.

that it is far from obvious that no such account can be developed. Once such an account is developed, the formal version of the recognitional view will clearly be able to give an informative account of how rational practical reasoning proceeds: one first follows the rules and procedures that are specified in this epistemology to arrive at rational beliefs about what is and what is not a good thing to do; and then one chooses accordingly, by choosing an option that one rationally believes to be a good thing to do.

Instrumental Reasoning and Choosing in Uncertainty

The formal version of the recognitional view appears, then, to have the resources to deal both with Velleman's 'emptiness objection' and with the demand for explanation that is expressed by Korsgaard's 'normative question'. But can it really give a satisfactory account of practical rationality? In this final section I shall sketch a refined version of this recognitional view. I shall try to make it plausible that this refined recognitional view gives an adequate account of two crucial aspects of rational practical reasoning: the importance of *instrumental reasoning*, and the conditions for rational choice in *uncertainty*.

A great deal of practical reasoning is instrumental. One starts by considering an end that one intends to achieve, and then chooses which *means* to use in order to achieve that end. Indeed, such instrumental reasoning is involved in almost all cases when practical reasoning leads to action. (The only exception is the special case where the option that one judges to be a good thing to do and then chooses is what Arthur Danto (1965) has called a 'basic action'—that is, something that one can just do, without having to choose any further means in order to do it.) But how can the recognitional view account for the crucial role of such instrumental reasoning?

To account for instrumental reasoning, the recognitional view has to be refined, in two ways. First, the fundamental principle must be refined so that it applies not only to choices but also to *intentions*. (A choice is a conscious mental event involving the formation of an intention, while an intention is an enduring mental state that typically lasts until it either leads to action or is abandoned.) Secondly, this fundamental principle must be refined so that, for an intention to be correct, it is not enough that one's intended course of action should be a good thing to do; it must also be a course of action that *one will actually carry out* if one intends to do so. The underlying idea here is that an intention that one simply will not execute is pointless, and to that extent a

Choosing Rationally and Correctly / 225

mistaken or incorrect intention.[28] So I propose the following revised version of this fundamental principle: one's intentions about how to act in a certain situation are correct if and only if one will in fact execute those intentions and thereby do something that really is a good thing to do in that situation.[29]

The account of practical rationality must also be revised accordingly. I shall use the phrase 'the way in which one revises one's intentions' broadly. Thus, one 'way in which one may revise one's intentions' is to form a new intention; but another way is to abandon (or to reaffirm) an old intention; and a third way is not to form any intention at all. Then we can say that the way in which, on a given occasion, one revises one's intentions about how to act in a given situation is rational if and only if it is rational for one to believe that one will execute all one's intentions about how to act in that situation and thereby do something that is a good thing to do in that situation.

This account of rational intention revision can explain the role of instrumental reasoning. Suppose that you intend to achieve a certain end; but suppose that it is not rational for you to believe that you will execute this intention and successfully achieve this end, unless you also form an intention about which *means* you will use in order to achieve the end. According to this account, the way in which you revise your intentions about how to act in this situation will be rational only if it is rational for you to believe that you will execute all the intentions (if any) that you have about how to act in

---

[28] Objection: Sometimes, making a choice that one will not execute will have extremely good effects. For example, making a choice that one spectacularly fails to execute might shock one into mending one's ways, with the result that one does things in the future that are much better than one otherwise would have done. So why isn't the initial choice correct after all? Reply: It is true that in such cases, the higher-order choice to manipulate oneself into making a choice that one will fail to execute may itself be a correct choice. But this does *not* mean that the lower-order choice that one manipulates oneself into making is a correct choice after all. (Similarly, sometimes the choice to manipulate oneself into holding a false belief is a correct choice; this does not make the false belief a correct belief after all!)

[29] Ideally, this principle should also be refined so that it applies to such states of affairs as one's *failing* to hold an intention about how to act in a situation in which one will in fact find oneself. This could be done by revising the fundamental principle so that it reads as follows: one's holding of whatever intentions one holds (if any), about how to act in a certain situation, is correct if and only if (*a*) one will in fact execute all those intentions (if any), and (*b*) *if* one executes all those intentions (if any), one will do something that really is a good thing to do in that situation. This second clause can explain when failing to hold any intention at all is itself a mistake. (1) Not holding any intention about how to act in a given situation is itself a mistake if it is true that if one executes all one's intentions about how to act in that situation (i.e. no intentions at all), one will do something that is *not* a good thing to do (e.g. one will dither ineffectually while disaster strikes). (2) Often, however, there is nothing mistaken about not holding any intentions at all. If one will

226 / Ralph Wedgwood

this situation.[30] In this case, there are only two ways of revising your intentions that will meet this condition: you can *either* abandon your intention to achieve the end, *or* you can form an intention about which means you will use in order to achieve the end. For example, suppose that you intend to be in Montreal tomorrow; but suppose that, unless you form some intention now about how you will travel to Montreal—whether to fly or drive or take the train, for instance—it will not be rational for you to believe that you will actually be in Montreal tomorrow. Then, to be rational, you must *either* abandon your intention to be in Montreal tomorrow, *or* form an intention about how you will travel to Montreal.

In a case of this sort, which of these two ways of revising your intentions is rational—forming an intention to take the means, or abandoning your intention to achieve the end? The answer depends on which of the two it is rational for you to believe to be a good thing to do. For example, if it is rational for you to believe that abandoning the intention to achieve the end is a good thing to do, and *not* rational to believe that taking any of the available means to that end is a good thing to do, then the only rational response is to abandon your intention to achieve the end. On the other hand, if it is rational for you to believe both that abandoning your intention to achieve the end is a good thing to do, and that taking the means to that end is also a good thing to do, then the two ways of revising your intentions are equally rational.

Suppose that you do form an intention about which means to use to achieve your end. How is it rational to choose which means to use? Clearly, you must choose means that it is rational for you to regard as effective at achieving the end. But often there are many means that are equally effective at achieving the end, even though many of these means have grave drawbacks of other kinds (for example, some of these means might be excessively expensive, or boring, or painful, or morally impermissible). In these cases, the refined version of the recognitional view that we are currently considering implies that it is rational to choose a course of action as a means to your end only if it is rational for you to believe that course of action to be not only

do something that is a good thing to do in the situation in question even if one holds no intentions at all about how to act in that situation, then it is still true that if one executes all one's intentions about how to act in that situation (i.e. no intentions at all), one will do something that is a good thing to do.

[30] This point—that rationality requires that one revise one's intentions so that it is rational for one to believe that one will in fact execute one's intentions—explains the two demands that Bratman puts on intentions (Bratman 1987: 31): first, that one's intentions must be 'strongly consistent relative to one's beliefs'; and secondly, that they must be 'means–end coherent'.

Choosing Rationally and Correctly / 227

effective at achieving the relevant end, but also (in the purely formal sense) a 'good thing to do' overall.

Finally, how should one choose what to do if one simply does not have enough time or information for it to be rational for one to hold any outright belief about which of the available options is a good thing to do? How should one choose what to do if one cannot be rationally *certain* which of the available options are good things to do? I shall suppose here that even if it is not rational to have an outright belief in a proposition, it may still be rational to have a *partial* belief in that proposition; that is, one may put some credence in the proposition, but also put some credence in the proposition's negation. Specifically, I shall suppose that it is rational for one to proportion one's degree of belief in the proposition to the proposition's *probability* given one's evidence.

To take advantage of the fact that it is rational to have partial degrees of belief in some propositions, however, we must recognize that the goodness of options also comes in degrees. Some options are *better* (in a purely formal sense) than others. Just as the goodness of options comes in degrees, then, so too does the correctness of choices. The better the option that one chooses, the *closer* one's choice is to being correct. If one's choice is completely correct, the option chosen must be *optimal*—that is, there must be no available alternative that is better.

Moreover, options can not only be ranked according to which are better and which are worse. In some cases, an option might be only *slightly* less good than optimal, while in other cases, an option might be *much* less good than optimal. (For example, one might not know whether *A* or *B* is optimal, but know that if *A* is optimal, then *B* is much less good than *A*, while if *B* is optimal, *A* is only slightly less good than *B*.) At least to some extent, then, we can make sense of the notion of the *degree to which an option falls short of optimality*. Let us suppose that these 'degrees of shortfall from optimality' can, at least in principle, be measured by means of real numbers. (An option that is optimal can be regarded as falling short of optimality to degree 0—that is, not falling short of optimality at all.)

We can now define the notion of an option's 'expected shortfall from optimality' as follows. Consider a set of propositions each of which describes each of the available options as falling short of optimality to a certain degree. Let us call these propositions the 'relevant uncertain propositions'. One may not know for certain which of these relevant uncertain propositions is true.[31]

---

[31] This uncertainty may partly be due to uncertainty about what the causal effects of these options will be. But even if one is quite certain what all the causal effects of each of two options

228 / Ralph Wedgwood

But suppose that one does know for certain that *exactly one* of these propositions is true. Moreover, suppose that one is also rationally certain that these uncertain propositions are all beyond one's control; nothing that one can do can determine which one of these propositions is true. Finally, suppose that each of these relevant uncertain propositions has a certain *probability* given one's evidence. Then, we can say that an option's 'expected shortfall from optimality' is the sum of the degrees to which the option falls short of optimality according to each of these relevant uncertain propositions, weighted by the probability of that proposition's being true. I propose that it is rational to choose an option if and only if that option has *minimal expected shortfall from optimality*. (In effect, this proposal about how to make choices in uncertainty is directly modelled on *expected utility theory*, except that it uses an objective evaluative notion—'shortfall from optimality'—instead of the more familiar notion of a 'utility function'.[32])

This proposal—that one should always choose an option with minimal expected shortfall from optimality—is a plausible generalization of the simple version of the recognitional view that I considered above. This proposal entails that if there are any options such that it is rational for you to have the outright belief that those options are optimal, then it is rational to choose any of those options. If it is rational for you to have the outright belief that a certain option is optimal, then, given your evidence, the probability that that option is optimal is 1; so the expected shortfall from optimality of such an option will always be 0. On the other hand, this proposal seems a plausible extension of the simple version of the recognitional view to cases in which it is not rational to have any outright belief about which of the available options

will be, one may still be uncertain whether it is better for one to perform the first option, with all of its causal effects, or to perform the second option, with all of its causal effects. This is why we need to focus on uncertainty about *normative* or *evaluative* propositions of this sort.

[32] I have here followed so-called 'causal decision theory' (Joyce 1999: 115–18) in relying on the *unconditional* probability of the relevant uncertain propositions, rather than on their probability conditional on one's performing the option in question. (This is why I have also had to follow the causal decision theorists in assuming that the 'relevant uncertain propositions' are all 'beyond one's control'.) If the notion of an option's 'shortfall from optimality' according to a certain 'relevant uncertain proposition' is identified with the difference between its utility and the utility of the option that is optimal according to that proposition, then this account of rational choice will actually *coincide* with the 'causal' version of expected utility theory. It would be a worthwhile project to investigate what the consequences would be of revising this account by relying on *conditional* probabilities (instead of unconditional probabilities), and on other definitions of 'shortfall from optimality' as well. But unfortunately I cannot carry out this investigation here.

are optimal. In such cases, you cannot choose an option such that it is rational for you to have an outright belief in the proposition that that option is optimal, since *ex hypothesi* it is not rational for you to have any such outright belief. So it seems plausible that the best thing to do in this case is to choose an option with minimal *expected* degree of shortfall from optimality. If you cannot aim at what you firmly believe to be optimal, you can at least aim to *minimize your expectation* of *falling short* of optimality. In this way, then, the recognitional view may be able to give an adequate account of how it is rational to make choices if one is uncertain about which of the available options are good things to do and which are not.

Many more refinements may be necessary before the formal version of the recognitional view can give a fully satisfactory account of rational choice. But in this section I hope to have made it plausible that the view has the resources to provide such a satisfactory account. Given that this view also seems to have a plausible answer both to Korsgaard's 'normative question' and to Velleman's 'emptiness objection', it seems to me that this view is a uniquely promising approach to understanding practical reason.

9

Prudence and the Temporal Structure of Practical Reasons

Duncan MacIntosh

To be prudent is to choose which actions to do partly on the basis of desires one foresees having, but does not now have. It is widely thought that to fail to be prudent is to be guilty of practical irrationality on a par with weakness of the will, with failing to take steps one knows are necessary to attaining one's goals: other things equal, surely it is irrational not to arrange to be able to fulfil a desire you know you are going to have.

Thomas Nagel (in Nagel 1970) links this issue with two questions: What kinds of things can serve as reasons for a rational agent's actions? and Can the ultimate aims of her actions change? The standard answers are Hume's (1740/1978: 413–18, 455–9): one's reasons are one's desires: one has reason to do an act just if one desires an expectable outcome of doing it. Since our desires change, the ultimate aims of our acts can change, too. Notoriously, however, on the Humean account, it is not rationally obligatory to be prudent. Indeed, unless you happen now to have a desire to meet your foreseen desires, it

For general help, my thanks to David Braybrooke, Nathan Brett, Bob Bright, Richmond Campbell, Sue Campbell, Tori McGeer, Peter March, Bob Martin, Bill Matheson, Carl Matheson, Susan Sherwin, Howard Sobel, Heidi Tiedke, Mark Vorobej, Sheldon Wein, and Russ Weninger. Thanks also to my students at Dalhousie University, to colloquium audiences at the University of Manitoba and Dalhousie University, to the audience at the University Special Lectures Program at Auburn University, to the participants in the 2001 Montreal conference Weakness of Will and Varieties of Practical Irrationality, and to referees of various versions. Finally, my thanks to Sarah Stroud and Christine Tappolet for their judicious editing. My work was aided by a grant from the Social Sciences and Humanities Research Council of Canada.

Prudence and Practical Reasons / 231

would be irrational for you to be prudent, especially where this would require you to fail to advance your current desires for the sake of desires you do not now even possess.

But Nagel thinks this means that, on the Humean account, it can be rational for you now to act with the aim of fulfilling a desire you now hold, even if you know that soon you will have an opposing desire, one action on which will require you to try to undo the effects you now seek. That is, it would be rationally permissible for your acts now and later foreseeably to conflict in aims. And this Nagel finds absurd. He concludes that reasons cannot be desires, at least not directly. For desires are reasons only when held, and the desires one holds change; so even if one foresaw having a desire, if one did not now have it, one would have no reason in one's current desires to accommodate it.

Nagel thinks that, in order not to result in a rational agent's actions working against each other over time, whatever reasons are, they must be unchanging: a rational agent's ultimate reasons must always be the same. And yet the reasons must take account of her desires, current and foreseen; for, thinks Nagel, we have a categorical duty to our future selves to choose now in light of desires we foresee having, just as we have a categorical moral duty to consider the desires of other agents. So, for Nagel, a rational agent's reasons must be things timeless and impersonal, things which, nonetheless, take account of agents' foreseen desires. Nagel suggests that something can be a reason for a given agent at one time just if it could be a reason for any agent any time; and that there is reason to do an act just if doing it would likely bring about a state worth being brought about according to timeless, impersonal measures of worth.

I too shall use the issue of whether prudence is rationally obligatory as a way of exploring the temporal structure of reasons. But I say that, on any coherent account of what can be reasons for rational acts, reasons must be able to change. What, then, of the problem of inconsistency across an agent's acts over time? The solution lies in how a rational agent's future reasons would grow rationally out of her current reasons. Her current ones can dictate that her reasons change in new situations. And since the reasons appropriate later depend on those appropriate earlier, and don't become good reasons until later, one need not choose now using reasons one will not have until later (for one does not yet have reason to take them for one's reasons), nor using reasons one merely used to have (for one had good reason in one's old reasons to replace them). In some situations, one's reasons will justify one

232 / Duncan MacIntosh

in acquiring different reasons. Here it may be rational for one's acts to conflict in aims over time; but not when one's reasons justify their own retention.

One result is that there can be no general duty of prudence. Another is that there cannot be timeless reasons. For example, there cannot be good-making features of states of affairs such that necessarily we are always rationally obliged to desire, and to bring about, states with such features. Nor can there be deontological principles which necessarily we are always rationally obliged to have and to follow. The rational correctness of desires for kinds of states of affairs, and of actions which bring about such states, as well as the rational correctness of holding and following a given set of deontological principles, must be relative to agents and situations.

Some Theories of Reasons; Some Arguments for the Timelessness of Reasons

On Hume's theory of what things can be reasons, one's reasons or aims may well change. One's acts are made rational by their advancing one's current desires; for these represent what matters to one, what it is in one's rational self-interest to seek. One's reasons are one's ever-changing current desires. This parented the standard theory of rational choice: one must maximize one's expected utility; and one's expected utility is to be calculated by summing the products of the odds of the possible outcomes of one's acts and the utility of those outcomes according to one's *current* preference-function.[1] Derek Parfit calls this a Present-Aim Theory (P) (Parfit 1984: 117–20): one should now advance one's *present* aims. One need not consider one's future aims just because one will later have them, nor alter one's present aims on that account. In fact, unless one has a present aim to advance one's future aims, doing these things is irrational; only one's present aims can directly be one's reasons. Bernard Williams defends P (Williams 1976: 8).

The view that one should be prudent is what Parfit calls the Self-Interest Theory (S). A rational agent identifies with all of her temporal stages; since satisfying their desires is therefore part of her interest, she always tries to make her life go well all stages considered, to make choices reflecting all of their desires (Parfit 1984: 94–5). One's acts are made rational, on this view, by advancing a mix of all the desires one will ever have; since all of one's stages

---

[1] For a semi-technical statement of this view, see Gauthier 1986, ch. 11.

Prudence and Practical Reasons / 233

matter, their desires merit respect in one's choices now. Here, one's reasons are all the desires one will ever hold.

Nagel too enjoins prudence. For to be *imp*rudent is to fail to see oneself as a continuing being, resulting in one's stages being dissociated, denying each other's equal reality and value. And were it rational to choose only using the desires one has at the time of choice, if one now preferred a state one foresaw dispreferring, one would have reason now to begin causing a state one foresees having reason to prevent, one's rational acts at different times thus foreseeably conflicting in aims. Nagel thinks that, to avoid these things, which he believes to be absurdities, whatever things serve as the ultimate reasons for actions, they cannot be changeable. We will then always respect our future self's reasons in acting on our current ones, for our current reasons will always be the same as hers. And if our aims are always the same, we will never have reason to do an act conflicting in aim with acts we will have reason to do later. But then direct reasons for acts cannot be desires. For since desires exist only when held, they would rationalize acts only then, and only for their holder. So one would not be sure to have reason to respect one's foreseen reasons in one's current choices. So desires must not automatically be reasons, things by the mere having of which one is justified in causing their ends.

Instead, a rational agent has reason to cause the good: that an act of hers would cause the good is her reason for doing it. Now some states of affairs are made good by virtue of being desired. But the desires of all of one's temporal stages, past, present, and future, inform which states are good: for example, there may be certain things which are part of the good now, because you will desire them later. Thus the good is timeless, not time-relative. Other agents are as real and valuable as oneself, so their desires too inform the good. So the good is impersonal, not person-relative. Since the good is timeless and impersonal, so are one's reasons; they are the same always, for everyone. But since the desires of all of one's stages inform the good, and since the good is what one has reason to cause, one can have reason to act now against one's current desires, and for one's foreseen or even lapsed desires. This will occur when the good is a thing one will desire only later, or desired only earlier.

Nagel says that acts are made rational by causing states which are good by timeless, impersonal measures. What makes it rational to cause a state is not that one (pre-critically) desires it, but that it is desire-*worthy*. A related theory which denies that reasons are desires is Kant's view that what makes an act rational is its obeying principles one could will to be natural laws; otherwise

234 / Duncan MacIntosh

one is not choosing freely, let alone rationally, but just being ruled by one's animal nature. According to these views, one's reasons are, respectively, the goodness of the states which might result from acts, or deontic principles.

On the self-interest theory, one should choose not just by one's current desires, but also by old and foreseen ones. If I have sought x for years, I should not abandon x on a whim; I should keep pursuing x even if I do not now want x. And if I foresee desperately wanting y, I should now arrange to get y. So just because my desires will change need not mean my acts should seek different ends at different times. On Nagel's theory, reasons supposedly cannot change. What makes an act rational is that it would cause a good state; and what makes a state good is timeless and impersonal. (It could never happen, for example, that gratuitous harms are good for someone.) So all rational agents would always have the same reasons, namely, the factors always making states good. Kant's theory also seems to imply that all agents would always have the same reasons: an act is rational if, and only if, one could will its principle to guide everyone's acts always. And one supposes that Kant's and Nagel's theories are compatible; for surely one could will that all agents always act so as to bring about what is, by a permanent measure, the good.

So there are at least three ways in which reasons have been thought to be necessarily timeless and impersonal: (1) they depend on desires; but all persons' reasons should respect all the desires anyone will ever hold. So all of those desires are relevant to every choice at every time, not just the chooser's desires at the time of choice. (2) One has reason to cause a state of affairs just if it would be a good state of affairs; and the same factors always make states of affairs good. So everyone always has the same reasons, namely the factors making states of affairs good. (3) r is a reason now for me to do act a now just if r is a reason for any person to do act a at any time; so reasons must be able to be universal laws. If it is a reason for me to do something now that doing it would be keeping a promise I made, it must be a reason for anyone to do something at any time that doing it would be keeping a promise he made.

I now dispute the view that reasons must be timeless. I first show that while—according to the desire theory—reasons may change, and while this may yield inconsistency in an agent's actions over time, the kinds of conflict permitted are not rationally unacceptable, but, in fact, rationally required, on a proper understanding of the desire theory. Later, I show that the relation between desires which are suited to being reasons at different times holds generally between reasons over time, no matter what kinds of things reasons are.

The Desire Theory and the Temporal Structure of Practical Reasons

Nagel thought that if desires are reasons, since they can change, reasons can, too. So we might now have reason to do a thing we foresee having reason to undo (Nagel 1970: 40). Thus rational choices could be absurdly incoherent over time.[2]

He believed this was entailed by the thesis that reasons are desires because he thought a Humean-rational agent, one whose choices were rationalized by her desires—an agent obliged by those desires to choose means to their ends—would be *beset* by new desires over her life.[3] But this is false. In fact, her later desires would grow rationally out of her earlier ones.[4] For Humeanism implies rational constraints on acquiring desires given current desires. It says one rationally must take the means to one's ends: if you desire x and see that y's obtaining would conduce to x's, you should desire y. But say you desire state s, and your desiring s will make s likely because it will move you to cause s. Then your keeping that desire is the means to the end desired, so you should keep it. If you most want to get into law school, and will get in only if you study, and will study only if you keep desiring admission, you should keep desiring it.[5] So it is rationally obligatory to keep a desire so long as keeping it advances it.[6] You must also desire what you see is implicated by logic or

---

[2] Nagel gives other examples of incoherence: having reason to prepare to do a thing we foresee having reason not to do; failing to have reason to prepare to do what we foresee having reason to do.

[3] Nagel 1970: 40: 'suppose that I expect to be assailed by a desire in the future'.

[4] I am thinking of desires decision-theoretically as preference-functions, though I will sometimes speak of desires for short, and of specific preferences, desires, or values where this is more intuitive.

[5] For more on constraints on rational desiring in Humeanism, see MacIntosh 1992, 1993, 2001.

[6] Thus we criticize those who half-begin projects and then suddenly drop them as flighty, flaky. But my view is not completely conservative. (Thanks to Alison McIntyre and Veronica Ponce for the worry.) For as we will see, it finds permissible certain desire changes based on, for example, appetites, certain kinds of urges, and biological maturation. And it admits many standard pretexts for revising preferences, e.g. that (*a*) one realizes the thing now preferred lacks properties one thought it had in forming the preference for it; (*b*) one now realizes one hadn't reflected enough to know one preferred things to have those properties, and has decided one didn't really prefer this; (*c*) one hadn't known the costs of the means to the things preferred, so that, now knowing them, one does not all-in prefer those things; (*d*) one discovers a preference is unsatisfiable in the circumstances.

Pretexts (*a*)–(*c*) rationalize revising preferences because they amount to discoveries that one didn't really prefer, or shouldn't have preferred, the thing in question. Here, dropping the

236 / Duncan MacIntosh

identity in your desire's end: if you most want *a* and learn that *a* entails or is identical to *b*, you must want *b*, else you lack an attitude needed to make you advance the desire for *a*, a duty to do which you have by wanting *a*.

If your later desires are ones rationally so dictated, i.e. are the same as your earlier, or are for things conducive to, entailed by, or partly constitutive of, what you earlier desired, then your later desires will not make you do acts conflicting in ends with those of the acts your earlier desires made you do. Rather, your later desires will make you do acts which advance the ends of your earlier desires. Your acts will be coherent over time.

But Humeanism also entails that it is rational to supplant one's desires for an end *e* with desires for opposite ends, if this is the best means to *e*. Suppose you desire to minimize useless harms, and that they will be minimized only if your enemy will refrain from nuclear attack. Suppose he will refrain only if you credibly threaten retaliation. Suppose further that you can do this only by replacing your desire to minimize harms with a desire to retaliate with massive harms against those who would tend to have been deterred by the threat of retaliation. Then you should replace your desire. Here, your desires rationally oblige you to replace them with ones which may demand acts whose ends conflict with those of the acts your earlier desires demanded. Your earlier desires demanded the act of replacing those desires in service of the end of minimizing harm. Yet if your forming your new retaliatory desire fails to stop your enemy, that desire may make you retaliate in service of the end of acting on threats, thus making yet more harms.

So how is adopting the new desire rational? It makes other agents more likely to advance your first desires. True, your forming the retaliatory desire will, if it fails to stop your enemy, make you retaliate, causing more harms than had you kept the desire to minimize harms (which would ask you not to retaliate). But your forming the new desire also makes it less likely that your enemy will attack (and so unlikely that you shall have to retaliate), making the odds good that there will be *no* harms. It is rational to change because this

---

preferences is not anti-maximizing on one's real preferences, or not anti-maximizing on preferences one should have had, and so is rationally permissible—or even obligatory, if this would maximize on the preferences one really has, or should have had. Pretext (*d*) permits dropping the preference because, if the preference is unsatisfiable, no act could advance its satisfaction. So one does not fail to maximize on it in dropping it, because one is not dropping something which would have served as a motivation to do an act maximizing on the preference (since, by hypothesis, there is, now, no such act).

We may also have rational duties to revise our preferences so as to conform with morality. See MacIntosh 1998.

Prudence and Practical Reasons / 237

maximizes on your current desires; the probability-weighted benefits of changing exceed the probability-weighted costs.[7]

It may happen, then, that rationally you must do acts conflicting in ends with those of your earlier acts. But when a rational agent's old values ask her to form ones with opposite ends, and where the new values ask her to act against her old, the conflict is not rationally inappropriate. Any differences between her earlier and later values—and so any conflict between the ends of her earlier and later acts—will be rationally appropriate, given rational succession in her values. If her later rational acts undid an effect of her earlier acts, or if her earlier acts obstructed aims of her later acts, this would only be from her rationally changing her mind on what she wants. So the conflicts would not be absurd.

And the agent has no general duty of prudence.[8] Her later values are rationally dictated by her earlier—changing them was rational. Thus it is rational by the time of her new ones for her not to have the old. So in the future they have no claim on her conduct; she should then choose by her new ones. But for as long as she is rationally obliged or allowed to have her old values, her future ones are not yet rational to have; so they have no claim on her current conduct. For an agent rational in values, it is rational for her to choose just from the values she has when choosing. And that she will have new values later is no reason against her having her current ones, nor against her acting now just on them.

So rationally one may not change one's desires when this would make the achievement of their ends less likely. But conversely, one must form a desire

[7] For details, see MacIntosh 1991, 1992, 1993.

[8] Indeed, there could be no such general duty. For say I prefer A to B now and will prefer B to A later. If there were a duty of prudence, I should choose now using both rankings, i.e. on the basis of preferring A to B and B to A. But decision theory says this cannot form the basis of a rational choice. For as an incoherent ranking of states, it cannot give an unambiguous verdict on whether it is rational to bring about A over B. Not even the verdict that I should toss a coin. For there is no ranking by which I am indifferent between A and B, only *conflicting* rankings. But if it violates decision theory to say I should take both my current and future values as bases of current rational choice, I can have no such duty; for there is no such thing as making a rational choice from ill-ordered values, and so no such thing as a duty of prudence so conceived. The relation between values now and later, then, must either be as I say in the text, where one is to choose from the earlier ranking earlier, and the later one later, at least if the later is the earlier's rational successor. Or it must be as Nagel hoped: there is a timeless, objective, non-conflicted standard fixing which state is the best from among those on which my values now and later conflict; and prudence says to bring about that state. But there are problems with Nagel's account—see the later section 'The Temporal Structure of Reasons if Reasons are Based on the Goodness of States of Affairs'.

238 / Duncan MacIntosh

for things which are part of the obtaining of the end, *e*, of a current desire; for things which would make *e* more likely; and for things one's desiring of which would make *e* more likely. So one's current desires decide the rationality of one's acts while it is rational to keep them; and those desires decide the rationality of successor desires; and so on.

True, sometimes we *are* beset by values not justified by our prior ones. We fail to form values rationally demanded by our current ones, or form ones forbidden. But that we will later have *irrational* values is no reason not to be moved by our *current* ones while we have *them*, nor to choose now as if we had the later values. If the foreseen ones are crazy, we *should not* take them as bases of current choice. A soldier predicts being captured and brainwashed into traitorous values. Now, he would do anything for his comrades; later, he will want to betray them. On my reading of the Present-Aim Theory (P), P justifies him in trying to keep his current values, and says it would be irrational for him now to act as a traitor just because he will later have traitorous values. True, he should choose differently now in light of the fact that he may later have a value which it is irrational for him to acquire: for example, his current desire to help his comrades might justify him in suicide to prevent his being brainwashed into treachery. But he is not to choose *on the basis of* the future value, as if it were now a reason of his. Rather, he is to choose now, from his current values, as if dealing with a prospective force of nature, a psychological frailty around which he must now try to manoeuvre.[9]

True, his acts will be incoherent over time if he gets traitorous values. Earlier, he will seek to help his comrades, later, to hurt them. But this is not the Present-Aim Theory's fault; for he will be undergoing a desire change which P finds irrational. P asks him to act on his patriotic values so long as he has them; and to try to keep them. So P is saved from enjoining problematic incoherence in his acts over time by its asking him *not to form* traitorous values. (For they would make him betray the patriotic ends he *now* values.)

But if he did get such values, would P not ask him to act on them? For does it not say rational choice is from *present* values, whatever they are?[10] And is this not to give too much weight to present values? Surely the soldier should restore and/or act on his old, loyal value if he can. Rational choice is not always from current values. Sometimes it is choice from, or advancing, values one no longer holds, but should hold. But read right, P agrees; for it can criticize values.

---

[9] Thanks to David Schmidtz for help in phrasing this point.

[10] Thanks to a reader of an earlier version of this chapter for this issue.

Prudence and Practical Reasons / 239

Say another theory told our agent not to act on the new values, but to act as if he had the old, or to cause the good. This is idle advice unless he is not necessarily ruled by his new values. But then the Present-Aim Theory *would not* ask him to act on them either. For, assuming he will be value-ruled, so that if he gets the new ones they will make him defy his old, loyal ones, P forbids his changing values if he has a choice, since this is non-maximizing on the old values, the last ones it was rational for him to hold. He should not have changed them, because changing them was not maximizing on them. The general lesson here is that according to P, it is rational to do just what maximizes on values rational to have.

Now suppose that, even if the agent cannot but form new values, he *can* act as if he had the old. On *this* assumption, *that* is what P asks; for that is what would maximize on the value it is rational for him to hold, the loyal one.[11] So P demands that one form and be ruled only by *rational* values—ones maximizing to form given one's last values.[12] If the soldier became ruled by the new value, his acts would not be rational *tout court*, but only relative to a value irrational for him to hold. And if he had the power to reverse his new value, he should, for that returns him to, and maximizes on, the last value he had rationally.[13]

But imagine a value change sourced not externally, but in my natural urges or acquired addictions. I now want that tonight I not drink, so I lock up

[11] It might be objected that one cannot be rationally obliged to act on desires one does not now hold, especially not on my kind of account, a variant on the Present-Aim Theory. (Thanks to Daniel Laurier for this worry.) But that depends on what the link is between desires and action justifications—on what justifies acts—in instrumental practical rationality. It may be in the spirit of Hume to say that an agent ought to do the acts consistent with the desires for means to ends which she ought to have given her ends (or given her beliefs about what her ends are) and given her beliefs about the best means to her ends. If I desire to quench my thirst, believe drinking this water would quench my thirst, but then do not form the desire to drink, and so do not drink, arguably I fail to do an act I am rationally obliged to do, even though I have no desire to do it. For I *ought* to desire to do it, given my desires for ends. Likewise, if it would have been means to the ends of my prior desires to retain those desires, then I ought still to have those desires, and so ought to do the acts they would have recommended. So even on a Humean theory of means–ends rationality, we can criticize agents for failing to have certain desires, and for failing to do the acts the desires would justify doing. Thus even on Hume's account, it is not necessarily presently held desires that determine which acts are rational.

[12] I assume the first set of values one ever holds counts as rationally permissible by virtue of there being no values one held previously with reference to which one's acquiring the first set was anti-maximizing. Thereafter, any values are permissible just if forming them was not anti-maximizing on the values held just previously, and so on. See MacIntosh 1992.

[13] At least it is maximizing on that earlier value for him to return to holding it, provided his holding it generally makes it even more likely that he will do what would maximize on it.

240 / Duncan MacIntosh

the liquor. At night my desire reverses, and I get a crowbar. Next morning I throw it out. Does P not say I should act in the morning on my morning desire, in the evening, on my evening desire, thus advising incoherence over time? No. If the morning desire is rationally sound, whereas the evening desire is a genuine preference change, but one irrational given the morning desire, P treats the evening desire as it treated traitor values: one should not have acquired the evening desire, and one should not act on it.[14] Besides, maybe my evening 'desire' is not a change in my *values*. Maybe it is just an *urge*; and maybe I have no rational duty to urges, at least not when they oppose my values. In that case, *a fortiori* it is rational to try to meet my morning desire, not my evening urge.

But sometimes P criticizes values given urges. Say I want to work more, see eating as time-wasting, and so form the desire never to eat, this desire soon defeated by an urge. Here it is the fasting desire that is wrong. For desiring never to eat will not rid me of eating urges; and if I do not eat, I will soon be unable to work at all. So I would better meet the desire to work by forming a desire to get food for when I need to satisfy my hunger if I am to work more. Since my fasting desire is therefore an irrational one to have in dealing with eating urges, I have no duty to it.[15]

[14] What about cases in which, through simple biological maturation, e.g. from the hormones of puberty, one inevitably undergoes a change in preferences? The pubescent are not like the flake who too readily changes goals. For the desire changes of puberty are not irrational, but, at worst, non-rational; and it would be absurd to require that agents retain and/or act as if they had the old preferences. Perhaps, then, as I moot in MacIntosh 2001, while this change of preferences is not recommended, since it is anti-maximizing on one's prior preferences, neither is it forbidden, since that would violate the rule that, for it to be true that you (rationally) *ought* to do something, it must be true that you *can* do it. In puberty, you *can't* prevent the desire changes. So they are merely non-rational; and, once they happen, one rationally must advance one's then preferences, and so on.

The principle is this: if one *can* respond to maximization considerations, one should retain preferences so long as this maximizes on them. So if the flake had the option not to be a flake, he was irrational. But if one can't help but form new preferences, as in puberty, one is obliged only to maximize on the pre-revision preferences while one has them, and not, *per impossibile*, to retain them, nor to act as if one still had them.

[15] Or say I have an addiction I want to beat: should I form a desire never again to use? No. As twelve-step programmes tell us, one cannot beat addictions all at once; and the inevitable failure of trying to do that undermines resolutions to get clean. Instead, I should form a desire not to use *now*; and if I keep forming such desires when urges hit, the urges will abate. So if I formed a desire never to use, the desire would be irrational; I would have no duty to it. This may affect the drinking case: if my morning desire was irrational, given my foreseeable urges and my prior, rationally sound desires, we should treat it like the addiction case.

Prudence and Beliefs

We can now see that the temporal structure of desires is more like that of beliefs than one might have supposed. True, unlike desires, the rationality of beliefs is directly determined by evidence; and so, rationally, one should hold and act only on beliefs warranted by one's evidence. But just as appropriately acquired, currently held desires can be used to assess the rationality of acquiring new desires, so if my current beliefs are warranted, then I should use those beliefs to assess new evidence and prospective beliefs: if my current beliefs are warranted, my future beliefs should then be the same as my old, or be justifiable by them, or otherwise consistent with them. Alternatively, if the old ones embed a theory of evidence by which new evidence is seen as falsifying some subset of the old beliefs, then that subset of old beliefs should be dropped. Beliefs, then, can sometimes rationally demand their own revision, just as desires can.

Like desires, beliefs sometimes change by non- or irrational processes. But just as there is no rational duty of prudence for desires, neither is there a rational duty of prudence (as it were) for beliefs, no duty to choose now in light of a belief one foresees having just because one foresees having it. For suppose I foresee being made to get belief b by a non- or irrational process—hypnosis, say. That b was so acquired would hardly be reason to think it warranted. So my foreseeing having b does not make it rational for me to adopt b now, to have b inform current choice, nor to alter the content or strength of my current beliefs. True, sometimes foreseeing having a belief is evidence of its truth. Maybe you think you tend to form only true beliefs; or you trust the hypnotist to give you true ones. But here, it is the fact that you now have evidence that the belief you will have later is a true belief that makes it rational for you to proceed as if from that belief now, not the mere fact that you will hold this belief later.

So a rational agent's beliefs change just as required or allowed by new evidence, as construed by her current, warranted beliefs. So rationally she should proceed using just beliefs rational now to hold. She should not use ones once rational but since confuted by new evidence, nor ones foreseen but not now warranted. Thus there is no general duty of prudence for beliefs.

Yet some philosophers think *desires* foreseen to be non-rationally acquired should count now in the basis of current choice (if perhaps less weightily than

242 / Duncan MacIntosh

current desires).[16] Why do philosophers hold different views for beliefs and desires? Maybe they think this: beliefs can be rationally criticized; one should hold and act only on warranted ones. But desires, while they are the basis of rational choice, and while their satisfaction constitutes their holder's self-interest,[17] cannot be criticized. Since nothing makes any desires one will hold irrational, all of them should be seen as being part of one's basis for making choices, and one's interest consists in satisfying all of them. So foreseeing having one is reason now to seek its end.

But we can now reply to such thinking. For, as we saw, contrary to its premiss, there *is* a standard of rational desiring, namely, the values one now holds (provided one's forming them did not result from one's having formed values anti-maximizing on any values one held just previously in the sequence of changes leading to these values). It is irrational now to form or act on values whose acquisition would be anti-maximizing on current (appropriately arrived at) values. And contra Nagel, that one now has a value, v, can justify v's informing one's current acts and serving as a basis for evaluating prospective values. So, as with beliefs, just that one *will* hold a value is no reason to act differently now. Nor is satisfying just any later desire in one's interest: only desires one will acquire rationally, and only upon acquiring them.

Generalizing the Solution to the Coherence Problem

I gave a solution to the problem of the coherence of one's acts over time as it arises from conflict between one's current and foreseen values. A rational agent's values will change only as required or allowed by her current rational values; and it is rational for her to make just the choices that would serve them. So it is irrational for her to base her current choices on her future or past values. I shall now argue that reasons must be changeable no matter what kinds of things they are, whether desires, or cognizings of the goodness of possible states of affairs, or cognizings of the correctness of certain principles of action. Indeed, they must be changeable precisely because of the justificatory dependence of reasons at a later time on reasons earlier: reasons earlier can rationally demand that reasons be different later. But just as this was no

[16] See, for example, Parfit's discussion of such views in Parfit 1984, pts. 1 and 2, and the discussion of similar views in Savulescu 1998: 237–8.

[17] Or at any rate, her interests, not to presume egoism.

problem for the desire theory, because of the dependence of later desires on earlier ones, so, for reasons more generally, the justificatory dependence of later reasons on earlier will prevent unacceptable inconsistency in the aims of rational action over time.

The Temporal Structure of Reasons if Reasons are Based on the Goodness of States of Affairs

Nagel thinks that what makes acts rational is that they would cause states of affairs that would count as good states by an impersonal, timeless standard of goodness; so, he thought, my reasons now and later would always be the same. To be sure, the acts they rationalize would vary depending on the varying possible effects of my acts in my varying situations. I may be in a position to bring about one part of the good now, a different part later; and so I should now aim to bring about the first part, later, the second. Thus my immediate aims would change. But my acts would always have the same ultimate aim: causing things that are part of the overall good, whatever that calls for at each time.

In a moment I shall raise a difficulty for this view, arguing that reasons cannot be timeless. My argument will depend on the following claim: no matter the psychological or metaphysical kind of the reasons which fix an act's rationality, they must be like preference-functions in two ways. First, they must afford an *evaluation* of the rationality of acts. This means the reasons *must be commensurate and summable so as to be unambiguous on which acts are rational*: they must coherently rank all possible states of affairs that could result from doing each act, so as to be a function from beliefs about the effects of each act onto the rationality of the act, rational acts being those expected to yield as outcomes the states ranked highest.[18] Secondly, *reasons must be executive*—able to motivate acts, and so to explain acts where they are rational. Otherwise, the fact that the reasons would make it rational for an agent to do a certain act cannot be what makes her do the act. It could not be because a choice was rational that she made it; and so her choice could not count as reason-guided.

---

[18] I do not mean to stipulate that rationality is consequentialist; perhaps there are acts which are rational regardless of consequences. But we can represent this by treating it as a state that a certain act was done; and a ranking of states might then make an act rationally obligatory by requiring one to bring about the state in which the act was done, which one could do by doing that act, this yielding the required state.

244 / Duncan MacIntosh

So any agent able to make a choice because it is rational must be motivated by whatever things are reasons. They must be reflected in her preferences *qua* things able to move her. She must prefer to act on the reasons that fix which acts are rational, or her reasons must *be* her preferences.

Maybe Hume was wrong to think that only desires could both decide the rationality of acts and induce their performance. Maybe *beliefs* can do this; or perceptions of states as calling for acts. These cognizings might take as objects universal standards of rational choice, or situation-specific facts to the effect that a certain act is rational, or facts making it so (as in moral particularism). But even on a cognitivist moral psychology, where the reasons determining and inducing rational acts are, say, our beliefs about the good, these must rank states by goodness and be executive. So they amount to preferences.

Now the difficulty I shall pose for Nagel arises out of the fact that one's having a reason to bring about a state involves two things. First, believing that the state would have a certain property if it existed (e.g. that of being a state whose existence would be good); and secondly, being inclined to bring about states one believes to have the former property. It is this second feature of reasons that will prevent their being timeless.

One might think reasons could lack temporal order, if they are not things like—or based on—agents' desires, but are instead based on the independent goodness of possible states. Some such states are good, others bad; rationally we should cause the good, prevent the bad.[19] Indeed, we can imagine the evaluative aspect of reasons to consist in timeless conditionals[20] of the following sort: if it would be good to bring about x now (or if one believes this), then one should bring about x; if it would be bad for y to exist now, then one should act so as to prevent the occurrence of y.

But recall that, whatever reasons are, in order to be able to fix the rationality of an act—to make it that an act would count as a rational act—they must be like preference-functions, ranking acts for rationality. And in order to induce one's acts, and so make it that the acts one performs are the rational acts, the function must be internalized in one's psychology. Now recall that sometimes it advances a desire, d, to supplant it with one for ends opposite d's. So consider this scenario. Say x is timelessly good, and one believes this, and so one should internalize something like a preference-function which ranks procuring x as the aim of highest priority, and which ranks acts more likely to procure x as more rational than acts less likely to

[19] So says Jonathan Dancy (Dancy 1993, chs. 1–4).

[20] Thanks to Michael Smith for help with this phrasing.

Prudence and Practical Reasons / 245

procure x. Say one has internalized the function: that is, one has, in effect, come to prefer x. Under some conditions, in order to advance the good, x, one must become a seeker of the bad, $-x$. Under these conditions, one is then obliged by the rational duty to advance x, and so by one's preference to procure x, to adopt $-x$ as one's end instead.

Here is a case in point, a case which varies the deterrence scenario I explored in the earlier section 'The Desire Theory and the Temporal Structure of Practical Reasons' to reveal that desires can sometimes rationally require their own renunciation. Suppose it is good that harm be minimized; so I must deter nuclear attack; so I must form the goal of retaliating if attacked. Say I form this goal. If my deterrent threat fails to stop my enemy, my new goal will make me do an act causing more harms than would have ensued had I not formed the goal. (Assume my retaliating will not deter any future harms; its only effect will be to cause massive harms.) Yet arguably my act would be rational, because dictated by a goal I rationally had to form. But if this is right, then the ultimate ends of early and later rational acts may conflict. The end of my act of adopting a preference for the good conflicts with that of my later act, which is to retaliate if attacked. And so the reasons of rational agents are not necessarily timeless.

But Nagel would object that this is not a case of reasons for rational acts having changed. It is not that rational acts started out being those that cause good states, and then reasons for rational acts changed so that, for example, acts aimed at bringing about the bad state of pointless retaliation now count as rational. Rather, this is a case of my having had reason to become *irrational*, to acquire the crazy motives of someone favouring useless retaliation. And an *irrational* agent's motives are not reasons of a rational agent. Thus my case is no counter-example to his theory.

So the issue is now this: when I become a seeker of the bad in order to advance the good, do I become irrational, exhibit rationally motivated irrationality? Or do the changes in me preserve rationality, so that my new aims and the actions they induce count as rational? I say it must be the latter. For to hold the former is to say that I am rational if and only if I have the rationally right value, v, namely a preference for the good (else I have irrational values—my motives are not good reasons), and I act on v (else I act irrationally). And it is to say that the rationally right value is a constant: it is always a preference for the good, and the good is constant.

But this standard of rationality is incoherent. For it asks me to do the act of renouncing v, since that advances v, but also not to do that act, since that act

246 / Duncan MacIntosh

will make me lack *v*. And so this standard of rationality cannot reflect a true theory of reasons. For it violates decision theory's monotonicity condition on reasons, the bases of rational choice. This condition says that, on pain of generating conflicting verdicts on the rationality of acts, one's acts must be evaluated for rationality by *one* ranking only, namely, one's coherent ranking of the possible outcomes of one's acts. But the theory I am criticizing has conflicting rankings: it says acts are rational if, and only if, they would cause good states, and if, and only if, they would leave one preferring good states; and these two requirements conflict for the case where the only way to cause good states is to do an action that would result in one ceasing to prefer good states.

To make the theory consistent we must drop part of it. The theory has the following parts: (1) (*a*) the rationally right value is constant, because, (*b*) the right value is always for the good, and (*c*) the good is constant; (2) one must always have the right value; (3) one must always do what would advance the right value. Let us see whether we can produce a consistent theory of our rational obligations by dropping one of these parts.

Were (3) false, I would not be obliged to do whatever actions would advance the right value, *v*, and so would not be obliged to do the *v*-advancing act of replacing *v* with values the theory calls irrational. But it cannot be that only (3) is false, i.e. that I am obliged always to have value *v*, but am not necessarily obliged to act on *v* by doing the act which would advance *v* (here, the act of replacing *v*). For to have a preference, e.g. *v*, is to have a disposition to do the acts that would advance the preference. And so this fix would be incoherent, saying that I both should and should not be disposed to act as per *v*.

Were (2) false, I would not be rationally obliged always to have the right value; and so when, to advance the right value, I had to replace it with a wrong value, I would not be violating a duty. But it cannot be that only (2) is false, i.e. that I can be obliged to do the actions that would advance value *v*, but also not be obliged to have *v*. For if I do not have *v*, then even if I behaved in ways that made more likely the existence of the states of which *v* is a positive valuing, my behaviours would fail to count as the *actions* I am obliged to do. This is because a behaviour of mine can count as an *action* of mine to bring about *v*'s end only if it is done for the reason of—i.e. with the aim of— bringing about *v*'s end. And a behaviour of mine is an action done with the aim of bringing about *v*'s end only if I value that end when I so behave, i.e. only if I then have value v. (Otherwise, it is *mere* behaviour, not action.) So this fix too would make the theory incoherent, asking that I act to advance a value which I do not have, and so which cannot serve as a reason for acting for me, and yet which I must have in order for any of my behaviours to count as the acts I am rationally obliged to do.

The only option left is to deny (1), that the rationally right preference is a constant. Thus either (1*b*) or (1*c*) is false. If the former, the right preference is not always for the good. When, in order to advance a preference for the good, I must come to prefer the bad, the right (rationality-defining, rationally required, reason-constituting) preference for me is one for the bad.[21] Alternatively, while the right preference is always for the good, goodness is not constant. When, in order to advance a preference for the good, I must form one for the bad, the formerly good now counts, for me, as bad, and the formerly bad as good.[22] Either way, the reasons of a rational agent—the preference-functions by which she should rank states, and which fix which acts are rational for her—may change; they are relative to the agent's situation.

This argument is a *reductio* of the idea that there are things we are always rationally obliged to desire and to cause.[23] It also shows that there can be failures of coherence in the aims of a rational agent's actions over time even if the reasons for rational actions are (at least initially) based on the goodness of states of affairs. The solution to the coherence problem as it then arises parallels the solution offered on the supposition that reasons are agents' desires: the ends of rational choices may vary with time and may have to conflict, depending on events.

---

[21] I argue for this more fully in MacIntosh 2001.

[22] I defended this possibility in MacIntosh 2002.

[23] And of analysing rationally motivated irrationality as one's having good reason to arrange to fail these expectations. I discuss what *would* count as such irrationality in MacIntosh 2001, pt. II, esp. n. 38. Here, I shall only say that, while agents could get into situations where it is rational to become irrational, a theory of rationality cannot both have it that it can be rational (because maximizing) to form certain preferences given prior preferences, which prior preferences the theory calls rationally correct, and also have it that the new preferences are irrational. For that gives conflicting standards of rationality: it says that it is rationally obligatory to do what maximizes on preferences, and obligatory not to have certain preferences, and so not to have formed certain preferences. And these standards conflict when, in order to maximize on obligatory preferences, one must form supposedly forbidden ones. (Thanks to Ralph Wedgwood for discussion.)

248 / Duncan MacIntosh

The Temporal Structure of Reasons if Reasons are Deontic Principles

What of the view that one has a reason to do an action if and only if the action could issue from a principle able to be a universal law of nature? If reasons were such deontic principles, what then would be their temporal structure? Wouldn't they be timeless by virtue of being universalizable, things one can coherently will to govern all people's behaviours at all times?

I say the principles able to be willed will necessarily vary over agents' situations; so they will be relative, not timeless. Consider this argument from Philip Pettit (2000: 180–4): suppose that one has reason to keep promises just if one could will that everyone keep them. And suppose that if one could will this, so could anyone, so everyone would have reason to keep promises. Thus one has reason to keep promises only if everyone has reason to do so. Then if one thinks one has reason to keep promises, one has reason to think everyone should keep them. Now if one has a reason to keep promises, one has a reason to prefer to keep them; and if one has a reason to think everyone should keep them, then one has a reason to prefer that everyone keep them. But say you become a public figure who made a big promise; and suppose that your breaking this promise would cause a national debate on promise-keeping's value, resulting in more people keeping promises than would do so if you kept your promise. Then you have reason to prefer to break it, and so to break it.[24] Pettit concluded that the non-consequentialist view that acts are made right (he could have said rational) by conforming to principles contradicts the view that reasons must universalize—the view that something can be a reason for one person now just if it can be a reason for all persons always. For the principles one will have reason to follow will be relative to persons and situations.

I would go further than Pettit: I say his argument refutes the view that genuine reasons must timelessly universalize, i.e. must hold for all persons *always*. For it shows that a thing which could timelessly universalize if anything could cannot so universalize: namely, the notion that I should keep this promise, which should be able to universalize into the principle that all people should always keep their promises. This suggests that *no* reasons can be so universalized; so *nothing* is a reason if a thing must timelessly universalize

---

[24] Perhaps you still have reason to prefer to keep your promise as well, and so to keep it; you have become conflicted in your duty. But you still have *a* reason to break your promise.

Prudence and Practical Reasons / 249

in order to be one. I suggest then that even on the theory that reasons are deontic principles, reasons need not be the same for all rational agents always. Instead, the theory's reasons can self-efface. In Pettit's scenario, before you became a public figure, you were justified in keeping promises—you had reason to keep them. But because you had reason to keep promises, you now have reason to try to maximize the total amount of promise-keeping in the world. However, that means that in a new situation, one in which you have become a public figure who made a big promise, you are justified in breaking a promise—you have reason to break a promise.

This yields a new coherence problem. Even if reasons are deontic principles, one's reasons will change; so should one choose now using the current reason? the future one? or, somehow, both? Which reasons should regulate now?

The solution lies in the fact that, even if reasons are deontic principles, they can justify their own revision, and so fall under my treatment. Let me illustrate this with a case simpler than Pettit's. For *reductio*, suppose the motive principle, p, of an act, a, would be a reason to do a if, and only if, p could be a natural law, a reason for everyone always. For *reductio*, suppose 'always keep promises' is such a principle, so that one has reason to keep promises; and suppose one has internalized that principle: one most prefers to keep promises, and prefers acts likely to yield keeping them.

Now: you promised your doctor to diet. But a demon will tempt you with irresistible food, making you overeat now, unless you so revise your values that you most prefer to overeat—thus breaking your promise—in the unlikely event that the king visits, and otherwise to diet. Since you have reason to keep your promise, you have reason to form the conditional preference to break it, lest you be led to break it now. Better to lower the odds of lapsing by placating the demon, that is, by forming the preference to overeat in the unlikely event of a royal visit. So you alter your values. Alas, the king visits; driven by your new goal, you overeat. Yet you do so with good reason, since your act is dictated by a goal you rationally had to form. You have gone from having reason to keep promises to having reason to break one.

Nor is this rationally motivated irrationality. For that would imply a standard of rationality according to which there is a principle which agents must always have and act upon. But this case shows that for any principle x, there can be a situation where the act which x requires is that of renouncing x. So the standard which requires both always having, and always acting on, x is incoherent. Agents whose right principles ask them to change principles are like agents whose right attitudes to good states ask them to change attitudes. And just as no state can consistently be said to be one which we rationally must always desire and cause, no principle can be one which we rationally must always have and act upon. The principles we have good reason to have and to act upon change when, in order to make it more likely that we will now do what our current right principles ask, we must give ourselves new principles for later—whence *they* become our right principles. So when it advances acting on current right reasons to form *new* ones, *they* become right. This is the logic relativizing reasons to situations. Reasons can self-efface.

Conclusion

The solution to the coherence problem lies in how reasons rationally evolve themselves. Whatever reasons are, a *rational* agent is not arbitrarily beset by reason changes; nor are her choices now based on both her current and her foreseen future reasons. If her reasons are her interests *qua* values, her interests now are not all the values of all her stages; instead, they change as rationally dictated by her earlier interests and her beliefs about how to get her ends. Her rational duty now is to choose from reasons she now has; there is no general duty of prudence. The rational kinematics of values—the theory of how values rationally change—favours a Present-Aim Theory. And the kinematics of reasons more generally favours a time-relative theory of reasons. However, it does not license acts wrongly incoherent over time. Sometimes our later acts will fit with our old reasons, because the new reasons rationalized by the old will justify only acts conciliant with the old. Other times, our acts will not be conciliant. But this will occur only when, and only because, the old reasons demanded their own replacement, in which case there is no duty now to act conciliantly with them. Here, incoherence between early and later acts is appropriate.

10

Practical Irrationality and the Structure of Decision Theory

Joseph Heath

There is a clear sense in which an individual can be said to act rationally, despite being in some respects misinformed or misguided. We may grant that it was rational for Pierre to bring his umbrella to work, given that he thought it was going to rain, even though the weather forecast lent no credence to this view. Similarly, we can say that it was rational for Pierre to go to work, given that he wants a promotion, even though we may consider this ambition ill-considered. Thus any theory of practical rationality, or irrationality, imposes a division of labour between, on the one hand, an account of the agent's intentional states and how these are formed, and on the other hand, an account of how these intentional states get applied in particular circumstances in order to recommend a particular course of action.

Standard decision theory imposes such a division of labour by treating beliefs as subjective probabilities, and desires as subjective preferences. Both are then taken to be determined exogenously.[1] The theory of practical rationality deals only with how intentional states of these two types get hooked together at the point of decision. Thus the theory implicitly distinguishes between epistemic rationality, which governs the production of beliefs, volitional rationality, which governs the production of desires, and then practical rationality strictly construed.[2] It is the latter part of the theory

---

[1] For the classic statement, see Savage 1972 and Jeffrey 1983.

[2] There are of course many who deny that there is such a thing as volitional rationality. This denial is most often associated with Humean theories of action. More often, such theories contain

252 / **Joseph Heath**

that provides the well-known conception of practical rationality as utility-maximization.

Unfortunately, much of the discussion of practical irrationality does not achieve this level of clarity. Questions that seem clearly to concern the *content* of the agent's beliefs and desires are still routinely lumped together with questions that deal with the way the agent chooses *in the light of* these beliefs and desires. This generates an enormous number of pseudo-problems.

Sadly, it is not possible to clean up the conceptual terrain simply by looking to decision theory—or some other adequately specified formal model of practical rationality—for a way of dividing up the issues. This is because the house of decision theory is in much less than perfect order. In particular, there is no general consensus on which parts of that theory belong in the theory of preference formation, and which parts belong in the theory of practical rationality. To take just one example: owing to the influence of certain economic modes of thought, there is a tendency in standard treatments to suppose that preferences provide only an ordinal ranking of states of affairs. A cardinal ranking is achieved by imposing a set of axiomatic constraints on the agent's choice behaviour.[3] Thus principles like transitivity wind up getting treated as a dimension of practical rationality, rather than of coherent desire.

This is highly artificial, and needlessly confusing. It is much easier to start out with the assumption that just as beliefs come with confidence levels, desires come with intensity levels (and thus cardinality). The latter assumption is no more problematic than the former, and can be justified with the usual sort of Bayesian arguments. But, of course, even if we grant some weight to our intuitive conception of what is 'artificial' and what is 'natural', we may still feel the need for some more rigorous way of deciding how decision theory should be organized.

One way of stating the problem is in terms of how much *structure* the theory of practical rationality should have. We can have a very minimal theory of practical rationality, along with a very substantial theory of belief and desire formation, or the opposite, or something in between. Generally speaking, the way we decide these questions will determine the extent to which we regard

instrumental theories of volitional rationality—claiming, for example, that 'unmotivated' desires get combined with beliefs in order to generate 'motivated' desires. For an overview, see Wallace 1990.

[3] For the classic treatment in this style, see Luce and Raiffa 1957.

The Structure of Decision Theory / 253

agents as victims of practical irrationality, as opposed to simply unfortunate desires or questionable beliefs.

Thus we have two questions: What criteria should we apply in order to decide how much structure our theory of practical rationality should have?; and then, What sort of structure should it have? I would like to propose an answer to each question. First, I will argue that our approach to formulating decision theory should be governed by a norm of 'expressive adequacy'. Its goal, I will argue, is not to represent what is *really* going on when agents make decisions. Its goal is to provide a perspicuous articulation of the system of intentions implicit in social interaction. The second stage of my argument concerns the structure that the theory should have. Here I would like to argue that the theory should have a bit more structure than it is given in standard treatments. In particular, I will try to show that injecting a bit more structure allows us to explain the rationality of two classic 'anomalies' in traditional theories of practical rationality, namely, temptation and rule-following.

The Structure of Decision

Decision theory is normally understood to be a conceptual structure used to explain an agent's action in terms of two underlying intentional states: belief and desire. This is reflected in the usual treatments, such as those of Leonard Savage or Richard Jeffrey, where the distinction is introduced between three classes of events: actions, states, and outcomes. Deliberation is a process through which the agent's set of desires over possible outcomes gets hooked up with a set of beliefs about the possible states, in order to generate a ranking of actions. The beliefs allow the agent to 'project' a set of preferences over outcomes onto the set of available actions, and thus to determine which action is most preferred.

It is important to recognize just how conventional this explanatory structure is. Why two intentional states, and not three, or one? For example, there is no reason why we could not develop a decision theory that explained each action, a, in terms of a single intentional state, namely, a preference for a. Such a theory would be neither interesting nor informative, but there can be no objection to it in principle. It is always open to us to supplement this theory with an account of preference formation, which would explain how the agent came to prefer a. Such a story could even include reference to

254 / Joseph Heath

some sub-preferential components, like beliefs and desires, although it need not do so.

It is also quite open to us to go in the opposite direction, and include more elements than just the standard belief–desire pair. In particular, it is quite common for economists and game theorists to introduce a unique type of higher-order preference into the characterization of the agent's deliberation, namely, a time preference. This idea is based on the observation that, for any given desire, agents seem to have a preference for seeing that desire satisfied sooner rather than later. Some of this attitude seems to involve concerns about risk, but another dimension seems to be a pure time preference.

To see how such a preference gets represented, take a very concrete example. Imagine an individual checking into the hospital, who is asked to select a meal plan. Three meals are offered: p, q, and r. Suppose that the agent's preferences rank them in that order: $p \succ q \succ r$. The standard procedure for determining the agent's utility function is to assign p a value of 1, r a value of 0, then determine the intensity of the agent's desire for q by constructing a set of lotteries over p and r, and finding the lottery that renders her indifferent between q and that lottery. So if the agent is indifferent between q and a lottery that gives her a 60 per cent chance of getting p, we would assign q a utility of 0.6.

Things get a little bit more complicated when we introduce a temporal dimension into the choice. Suppose that, upon check-in, she is asked to select the meals that she will be served over the course of three days. At this point, there are different modelling strategies that we might pursue. The more minimalist versions of decision theory make no special accommodation for time. Take, for instance, the form of decision theory often referred to as 'world Bayesianism'. According to this view, 'rational actions maximize probability-weighted averages of values of total consequences—"worlds" that are complete at least with respect to all things of relevance in the theory' (Sobel 1994: 177). In other words, what counts as the outcome in this view is the entire possible world that is brought about through performance of the action. The agent's preferences represent a ranking of the full set of possible worlds confronting her (or some partitioning thereof) from best to worst, and a cardinal utility function can be derived by offering the agent a set of lotteries over these possible worlds.

So in this example each permutation of meal plans amounts to a different possible world, with an associated utility level (representing the intensity of the agent's desire to see that world come about). If we run through all the

The Structure of Decision Theory / 255

TABLE 10.1 *Utility of twenty-seven possible worlds*

World	Utility
p,p,p	1
p,p,q	0.942857142857143
p,p,r	0.857142857142857
p,q,p	0.885714285714286
p,q,q	0.828571428571429
p,q,r	0.742857142857143
p,r,p	0.714285714285714
p,r,q	0.657142857142857
p,r,r	0.571428571428571
q,p,p	0.771428571428571
q,p,q	0.714285714285714
q,p,r	0.628571428571429
q,q,p	0.657142857142857
q,q,q	0.6
q,q,r	0.514285714285714
q,r,p	0.485714285714286
q,r,q	0.428571428571429
q,r,r	0.342857142857143
r,p,p	0.428571428571429
r,p,q	0.371428571428571
r,p,r	0.285714285714286
r,q,p	0.314285714285714
r,q,q	0.257142857142857
r,q,r	0.171428571428571
r,r,p	0.142857142857143
r,r,q	0.085714285714285
r,r,r	0

options, we may come up with a utility function that looks like the one shown in Table 10.1.

256 / Joseph Heath

Following Jeffrey, the 'desirability' of an action can be inferred by multiplying the utility associated with each possible world by the probability that the action will result in that world coming to be, then adding these all up:

$$(1) \quad d(a) = \sum_w p(w\,|\,a) \cdot u(w).$$

(In the meal plan example, if we assume that the individual is certain to receive the meals that she selects, then determining the 'desirability' of each action is trivial.)

Incidentally, an abnormally attentive reader will have noticed some peculiarities in the utility function shown in Table 10.1. The table was constructed under the assumption that the agent prefers p to q to r. Thus, for instance, she prefers $[p,p,p]$ to $[q,q,q]$ to $[r,r,r]$. But the agent also prefers $[p,q,r]$ to $[q,q,p]$. This is peculiar, since the latter seems to give the agent more of what she likes than the former. Furthermore, we can note that the agent prefers $[p,q,q]$ to $[p,q,r]$. Thus the agent's preferences seem inconsistent. What is going on here?

This example reveals one of the weaknesses of the more minimalist versions of decision theory. The utility function shown in Table 10.1 was in fact constructed by taking the preference ordering of meals as originally introduced, then simply adding the assumption that the agent is impatient. In other words, she cares more about the meal that she is to receive *tonight* than the meal that she is going to receive *tomorrow* or the next day. So even though the agent prefers p to q to r, she prefers $[p,q,r]$ to $[q,q,p]$ because she would rather get her favourite meal right away than wait two days, even if it entails having to eat a meal that is somewhat worse further down the line. She may regret that decision on the third day, but she would make the same choice again, given the same *ex ante* circumstances.

The standard way of representing these differences in temporal perspective is to say that the agent *discounts* future satisfaction. A discount rate (ρ) can be defined as the extra fraction of a pay-off needed to make an agent indifferent between satisfying some desire now and satisfying it in one period. (The analogy here is to interest rates—which represent the amount that an agent must be paid in order to defer consumption.) From the discount rate, one can define a discount factor $\delta = 1/(1+\rho)$ as the value in present pay-offs of one unit of pay-offs to be received one period in the future. It indicates, in other words, the present value of future satisfaction (see Rasmusen 1989: 108). So if I am willing to save \$1,000 once annual interest rates go as high as 10 per cent, that means I need to be paid an extra \$100 in order to compensate me for the hardship of deferring that much consumption for a year. Thus the present

The Structure of Decision Theory / 257

value to me of having $1,000 in a year's time is only $909 (which, when added to the *present* value of the $100 interest payment, comes to $1,000).

The same analysis can be generalized to cover future time periods. Having $1,000 two years from now will be worth $909 in one year, and therefore is worth $826 in the present. Thus if $u_k(a)$ represents the expected pay-off at time k from some action a, the value of some stream of future pay-offs is worth the following to me in the present (where n is the total number of time periods):

$$(2) \quad d(a) = u_1(a) + \delta u_2(a) + \delta^2 u_3(a) \ldots + \delta^{n-1} u_n(a),$$

which can also be written as:

$$(3) \quad d(a) = \sum_{k=1}^{n} (\delta)^{k-1} u_k(a).$$

This of course assumes that the agent's preferences are relatively stable across time. So, to return to our example of the patient in a hospital choosing a meal plan, we would assume that the agent has relatively stable preferences for different types of food. If we can ascertain the agent's discount rate, we can then calculate the *present* value of each meal on each day. Table 10.2 shows the outcome of such a calculation for our agent, given a discount rate of 0.5.

Using a table like this, the expected utility of any meal plan can be calculated just by adding up the three values, so, for example, $[p,q,r]$ would be worth $(1 + 0.5 + 0.25)$, or 1.75. One can see by inspection that the utility function shown in Table 10.1 is identical to the one that could be generated by looking up each permutation in Table 10.2, then normalizing. The two utility functions are simply notational variants of one another.

Because of this, there is no way to say that one of these representations is either correct or incorrect. However, it is perhaps worth noting that Table 10.1 can be derived from Table 10.2 quite easily, whereas one would be

TABLE 10.2. *Discounted value of three meals*

Meal	Time		
	t_1	t_2	t_3
p	1.0	0.5	0.25
q	0.6	0.3	0.15
r	0.0	0.0	0.00

258 / Joseph Heath

hard-pressed to go the other way. Of course, it would be very easy to supplement the 'world Bayesian' view with a theory of preference formation that explains how the ranking of possible worlds comes about. Here one might specify that each 'world' w is actually a set of temporally ordered possible worlds, w_1, w_2, w_3, etc. One might then claim that:

$$(4) \quad u(w) = u(w_1) + \delta u(w_2) + \delta^2 u(w_3) \ldots + \delta^{n-1} u(w_n).$$

Thus the whole discounting issue would be shifted out of the theory of practical rationality and into the theory of preference formation. The two versions, though, seem to come down to pretty much the same thing. So does it matter which one we choose?

Another Example

Before answering this question, I would like to run through one more example of a debate over how much 'structure' the theory of decision should have. As is well known, experimental game theory has generated a series of consistently anomalous results (see Cemerer and Thaler 1995; Güth and Tietz 1990). Actual human behaviour deviates from the recommendations of 'ideal rationality' in a number of extremely predictable ways. Some of this clearly reflects cognitive biases, limited information, or inadequate computational ability. Some of it also reflects systematically flawed probabilistic reasoning. But some of it seems to involve genuinely counter-preferential choice. In other words, agents sometimes seem consciously to choose their own lesser good.

The best-known examples of this involve people's behaviour in 'public goods' games and 'ultimatum' games. In the former, individuals are given a choice between investing in a high-interest 'public' savings account, the proceeds of which will be split evenly among all participants, or else 'free-riding' by investing in a lower-yield private account, whose benefits accrue directly to them as individuals. In this game, a typical North American will split his or her investments about 50-50 between the two accounts. In the ultimatum game, two individuals are given a sum of money, on the condition that they can agree upon a mutually acceptable division. The mechanism for securing this agreement, however, is that the first player makes a single, take-it-or-leave-it offer to the second. If the second accepts, the money is divided; if the second refuses, neither gets anything. Here, the typical North American

The Structure of Decision Theory / 259

makes an offer close to 50 per cent of the sum. Furthermore, offers much below that are often rejected.

These experiments are all painstakingly designed in order to isolate the outcome of the game from any long-term social consequences. The interactions are one-shot, anonymous, and often involve no direct communication between the parties. Given this experimental design, it might be tempting to dismiss the behaviour as simple irrationality. The problem, however, is that agents are generally able to provide an explanation for their conduct that has, at the very least, all of the structural features of a rational account. They do so by appealing to social norms that either prescribe or proscribe particular actions in such interactions.

Agents generally classify the interaction according to a 'cultural template', which in turn gives them guidance on how they should behave. Thus in cross-cultural studies of such games, the kind of templates available in the culture have an important influence on the behaviour patterns that can be observed (see Henrich *et al.* 2001). North Americans, for instance, tend to classify the ultimatum game as a 'cutting-the-cake'-style division problem, and so apply a norm of fairness. As a result, offers and acceptances tend to cluster around the 50-50 division (Marwell and Ames 1981: 308). In many parts of New Guinea, on the other hand, the interaction tends to be classified as gift-giving, and so offers of more than 50 per cent are common, along with refusals of such offers (Henrich *et al.* 2001).

How are we to provide a formal representation of the sort of reasoning that generates such differences? The problem for traditional models of rational choice is that the relevant set of considerations has an overtly deontological structure. The norm of politeness, for instance, which specifies that gifts must be refused, regardless of their value, prescribes an action directly. Standard interpretations of rational choice theory, however, assume that practical deliberation has a consequentialist structure. Actions are thought to be valued only for the sake of their consequences, having no intrinsic value of their own. From such a perspective, the results of experimental game theory constitute a very significant anomaly.

Of course, none of this is a problem if one adopts a more minimalist conception of decision theory. The world Bayesian approach, outlined above, has so little structure that it is actually neutral with respect to the consequentialism–deontology debate. There is a lot of confusion on this subject, since decision theory is usually assumed to represent an instrumental conception of practical rationality. However, world Bayesian decision theories

260 / Joseph Heath

define the outcome as the complete possible world that results from the performance of an action. This implies that the action itself will be one of its own outcomes. One can see this clearly in (1) above. If possible worlds are interpreted as sets of true sentences, then *a* is going to be one of the sentences that is true in *w*. Such a theory of decision is therefore not consequentialist, since it defines consequences so broadly as to include anything that an agent could possibly care about, including the action itself.

Consider what this means in the ultimatum game. Imagine a player presented with an offer of $40 out of $100. Our ordinary intuition is that if the agent accepts, the outcome will be that he receives $40, and if he refuses, that he gets $0. But in the world Bayesian reading, the choice is between two conjuncts: 'I accept & I receive $40' or 'I refuse & I receive $0'. Thus any feelings that the agent happens to have towards either action will automatically be factored into the utility function.

Adopting a minimalist theory of this type is one quick way to make any experimental anomalies disappear. If 60 per cent of subjects cooperate in a public goods game, one can easily explain this as a consequence of a preference for cooperating in the provision of public goods. This amounts to saying that the interactions were not in fact a public goods game.[4] Of course, such a response displaces most of the interesting questions into the theory of preference formation. But there is no problem with doing so in principle. We simply need to supplement the theory with an account of social norms that explains how agents come to have a preference for certain types of actions on the basis of cultural context, socialization, or what have you. The way that these preferences over actions get weighted against the desire for various consequences will also get explained as part of this theory. Thus, for example, an agent who is offended by an unfair offer in the ultimatum game, but would nevertheless like to get some of the money, is not faced with a problem of practical deliberation strictly construed. What she needs to decide is simply which state of the world is more desirable: one in which she accepts and gets the money, or one in which she refuses and gets nothing.

Nevertheless, one might like to see a bit more structure in the theory of practical rationality. After all, the distinction between consequential considerations and deontic constraints is one that has enormous salience at the point of decision. We often find ourselves attracted to certain outcomes, but hesitant about the means that we must employ to achieve them. Thus a

---

[4] For an argument of this type, see Binmore 1994: 28.

number of game theorists have developed more complicated utility functions, which include multiple sources of utility, such as a 'material pay-off' and a 'fairness function' (see Rabin 1993 and Bolton 1991). Unfortunately, these proposals generally fail to capture the deontological flavour of the agent's choice. In order to remedy this, I have proposed a way of representing the agent's utility function that takes the agent's evaluation of the outcomes, and adds to it a representation of the preferences that the agent has for the various actions at her disposal (Heath 2001). We might call this a *value function*, in order to distinguish it from the consequence-based utility function u, and the world Bayesian desirability function d.

With such a value function, the intensity of the agent's preferences over actions can be ascertained using the standard device of hypothetical lotteries over the extremes. One can then introduce something akin to the discount factor, reflecting how the agent trades off consequences against actions. I call this the agent's 'fundamental choice disposition', represented γ. Putting all this together, where $c(a)$ represents the agent's direct preferences over actions, and $u_t(a)$ represents the agent's expected utility at time t from action a, we can express the agent's value function as:

$$(5) \quad v(a) = \gamma c(a) + \sum_{k=1}^{n} (\delta)^{k-1} u_k(a).$$

The primary advantage of this formulation is that it allows us to represent more clearly what is going on in certain cases where individual behaviour appears to violate the expected-utility-maximization hypothesis. In the public goods game experiments, the most natural way of analysing the observed outcome is simply to suppose that, despite wanting the money, individuals are also somewhat averse to engaging in selfish or uncooperative behaviour. It is not that they like the money any less; it is that they are not indifferent to the means through which the money is acquired. Thus their reasoning incorporates a non-consequentialist element—a direct preference for a kind of action. A value function, constructed along the lines shown above, allows us to represent quite clearly how these different considerations get factored into the agent's deliberations. And it situates the agent's weighing of the action and the consequence within the theory of practical rationality. But of course this representation is equivalent to the more minimal theory, which pushes all this into the theory of preference formation. So again, how do we choose between the two?

262 / Joseph Heath

An Expressive Conception

Perhaps the first temptation when approaching the question of how best to model decision problems is to formulate the issue in terms of some underlying psychological reality. According to such a view, the agent undergoes a process of deliberation when deciding what to do, and the job of a decision theory is simply to represent the relevant psychological factors, along with how they come together at the point of decision. Thus the question of whether actions should be represented separately from outcomes, for instance, should be decided by determining whether the agent actually balances these two considerations at the point of decision, or whether the agent approaches the problem with these deontic constraints already factored into the evaluation of the consequences.

In my view, this line of reasoning is one that should be resisted. There are very good reasons why decision theorists should want to avoid committing themselves to the claim that the theory has psychological reality. The primary reason is that even comparatively simple decision problems impose computation demands that easily exceed the capacities of the average person. It is equally obvious that even sophisticated decision-makers do not normally associate explicit probabilities with events, much less rank all possible states of the world. It is also not clear that the agent is motivated by some unitary psychological state like a 'desire', rather than a set of completely heterogeneous emotions and urges. Thus anyone who wants to claim that the theory corresponds to some underlying psychological process is likely to find himself quickly buried under an avalanche of objections.

Faced with the psychological implausibility of the theory, others are tempted to defend rational choice theory on the grounds that it is purely 'normative'. Unfortunately, the conception of normativity in use is subject to several different understandings. Normative theory is sometimes understood as a theory 'constructed in order to tell people what they should do'. In this respect, decision theory is a very poor normative theory, since following its precepts often leaves actors with sub-optimal outcomes. But in any case, this sort of normative characterization does not allow us to decide how much structure the theory should have. Since all of the different versions wind up generating the same practical recommendations, there seems to be nothing at stake in the issue of how the deliberative process gets represented.

A far more interesting conception of what it means for rational choice theory to be 'normative' is suggested in the work of Robert Brandom (1994).

The Structure of Decision Theory / 263

Brandom argues that the intentional states posited in standard decision theory must themselves be understood as a set of *normative statuses*. More specifically, he argues that the content of our beliefs and desires is given by their inferential role, and that this inferential role amounts to a set of practical entitlements and commitments. Thus an agent who believes that it is going to rain, for instance, is thereby also committed to believing that the sidewalks will be wet, that various picnics will be ruined, and so forth. The agent's understanding of the meaning of the assertion 'it is going to rain' consists in a grasp of these epistemic relations.

Making an assertion, on this view, amounts to making a move in what Brandom calls, following Wilfrid Sellars, 'the game of giving and asking for reasons' (see Brandom 1994: 89; Sellars 1963). The assertion entitles the agent to other assertions, but also commits her to providing reasons for the assertion upon demand. In the same way that 'being on second base' means occupying a certain status in the game of baseball—determined by a structure of entitlements and obligations—saying 'it is going to rain' means taking on a certain status in the game of giving and asking for reasons. The agent's beliefs, according to this view, are essentially the set of statuses that the agent occupies in this game.

This is why, according to Brandom, we cannot give the vocabulary of intentional states a straightforwardly psychological interpretation. By virtue of having a certain belief, for example, the agent will always be committed to some set of further beliefs. Thus if the agent believes x, and believes y, then the agent also believes 'x and y', even though the agent may never have explicitly drawn this conclusion, or entertained the logically complex proposition 'x and y'. What we are claiming, when we say that the agent believes 'x and y', is that the commitment to x and the commitment to y entail the commitment to 'x and y', and thus that the latter counts among the agent's commitments whether he realizes it or not. Belief vocabulary is unfortunately ambiguous between the external 'score-keeping' perspective and the agent's own perspective. This is one of the reasons why there is often no underlying psychological state for a given ascription of belief.

Brandom's thesis is not limited to beliefs, but includes desires as well. To say that one desires x is to commit oneself not just to further assertoric utterances, but to certain actions as well. An agent who says he 'wants to go for a walk' thereby adopts a commitment to act in certain ways, and to desire other things (e.g. to go outdoors, to get some exercise, etc.). It is in fact this structure of accompanying commitments, and the relationship between

264 / Joseph Heath

them and the particular desires, which provides these latter with their content. In a certain sense, having the desire to go for a walk is nothing more than the commitment to do the various things needed in order to realize this objective. Failure to do so suggests that one does not really have the relevant desire.

This normative conception of the agent's intentional states provides a very attractive way of understanding the 'normative' character of decision theory. What decision theory does, in effect, is work out the implications of the commitments that are implicitly taken on by an agent who occupies a certain position in the game of giving and asking for reasons. Thus an agent who wants to get some exercise, doesn't want to get wet, but thinks that it may rain, is committed to performing a certain sort of calculation. In the same way, someone who accepts all of the axioms of Euclidean geometry is committed to a certain set of conclusions. Neither individual may have any idea precisely what the further commitments are. But there is, nevertheless, a correct account of these commitments. A theory that works them out is one that, in Brandom's vocabulary, renders explicit what is implicit in the original set of commitments. Decision theory is one such theory.

According to this view, decision theory is not directly accountable to an underlying psychological reality, but neither is it purely conventional. The theory is accountable to the underlying practice of giving and asking for reasons. The goal of the theory is to render explicit what is implicit in the practice. Thus it needs to satisfy a standard of expressive adequacy. It needs to supply a more perspicuous articulation, in order to help us better grasp what it is that we are doing when we engage in practical deliberation. In the same way that logical vocabulary allows us to state what we are doing when we make inferences, decision theory allows us to state what we are doing when we make decisions.

This is why a 'monistic' decision theory—one that explains every action a in terms of a direct preference for a—is inadequate. It conceals more than it reveals. It also glosses over some of the important distinctions that are made in our everyday score-keeping practices, such as the distinct role of belief and desire in motivating the agent's conduct. The question of whether decision theory should explicitly represent the agent's discount rate, or the agent's fundamental choice disposition, can be decided in the same way.

The fact that the theory is held accountable to an underlying score-keeping *practice* is significant. It is precisely when modelling social interactions that the expressive power of the theory becomes most important. For example, we have seen that when it comes to modelling a single, non-social decision problem, it does not matter very much whether the agent is regarded as discounting the future, or simply having 'global' preferences over a sequence of events. The score-keeping consequences are approximately the same. But consider the case of two agents involved in a repeated game, e.g. a ten-stage prisoner's dilemma, with perfect information. This can be thought of as a game with two strategies per player, and four possible outcomes, played ten times. A discount rate can then be introduced in order to show how players relate outcomes in one stage to outcomes in another. But it is also possible to model this interaction as a 'supergame' with 1,024 strategies per player, and 1,048,576 possible outcomes. There is no need to introduce discounting in this model, since each agent can be represented as having a global preference ordering over the complete set of outcomes.

However, for the players to find a solution to the interaction, each must ascribe to the other a set of beliefs and strategies that is in equilibrium. It is quite certain that in such a case the formulation that includes the discount rate gives a better representation of the kind of intentional states that the players are likely to ascribe to one another. This cannot be dismissed as merely an empirical detail, because it is this mutual ascription of intentional statuses that provides the basis for the resolution of the choice problem. There is a model of intentional states implicit in strategic deliberation, to which the theory of decision must remain faithful if it is to provide an expressively adequate account of rational deliberation. The model is still normative, and so the expressive theory should not include the limitations that we find in 'bounded' or 'psychologically realistic' conceptions of rationality. But it should reflect the way that agents partition a larger choice problem into a series of more restricted ones, since there is no tension between this and the normativity of the theory.

The same reasoning also suggests that the distinction between actions and outcomes be kept explicit in the representation of the agent's utility function, as it is in (5). It is worth noting that agents themselves often implicitly represent one another as being governed by both principles—associated directly with actions—and desires for outcomes. But there is also the fact that in many social interactions, strategic reasoning alone does not generate a single recommended course of action. This is the well-known problem of multiple equilibria in games. Under such circumstances, agents are unable to develop the beliefs necessary in order to translate their preference over outcomes into preferences over actions. But it is important to recognize

266 / Joseph Heath

that, in many cases, this does not leave the agent entirely without reasons for acting. If the agent has a preference for a particular action as well, then not all of the agent's motive is caught up in the regress of strategic expectations. In other words, the agent may still have reason to act in one way or another, even if she is unable to determine what the other is likely to do.

Elsewhere I have argued that knowledge of such preferences over actions can provide agents with the resources needed to solve interaction problems that traditional game theory has been at a loss to explain (Heath 2001). For instance, in many coordination problems, a simple preference for one action over another can provide an agent with precisely the motive needed to break the deadlock between the various equilibria. Such a theory provides an attractive alternative to the older 'focal point' account.

Thus a more highly structured decision theory, which explicitly represents the agent as having separate preference orderings over a sequence of possible events—both actions and outcomes—provides a much more expressively adequate articulation of the logic that governs practical deliberation in social contexts. It also provides us with the conceptual resources needed to achieve greater clarity when dealing with many of the traditional problems of practical irrationality. Or so I will attempt to show.

Temptation

In order to see the advantages associated with the introduction of more structure into the theory of decision, consider the problem of temptation (perhaps the oldest chestnut in the literature on practical irrationality and akrasia). Clearly, in order to discuss the issue within a more structured theory of decision, it will be necessary to have some concept of how the agent is discounting. Economists introduced the standard discounting function (δ^t), as mentioned, on the basis of an analogy with interest rates, not on the basis of psychological studies. One of the characteristics of these 'exponential' functions is that they guarantee intertemporal consistency. In other words, if option a is better than option b at time t^1, then it will also be better at time t^{1-x}, for all values of x, positive or negative. Such a perspective makes it clear why agents might sometimes favour their short-term over their long-term interests. It even explains why agents might later come to regret their decisions. It offers no explanation, however, of why agents might change their decisions from one moment to the next.

However, there is a lot of empirical evidence to suggest that individuals do not actually discount the future in the way that standard 'economic' models suggest. George Ainslie has illustrated this in a variety of very simple studies (Ainslie 1992). For example, given a choice between a cheque for $100 that can be cashed right away, and a cheque for $200 that can be cashed in two years, many people will choose the former. But many of these same people, when given a choice between a $100 cheque that can be cashed in six years, and a $200 cheque that can be cashed in eight years, will take the $200 (Ainslie 1992: 78). What we see here is a temporal inversion of preferences. The $200 seems better than the $100 while both are far away, but the $100 becomes increasingly attractive in the near term—enough to outweigh its inferior monetary value.

One way of explaining these temporal inversions is to assume that agents discount satisfaction quite sharply in the very near term. Ainslie refers to this a 'hyperbolic' discounting. Suppose, for the sake of argument, that the agent discounts the future in the following way:

$$(6) \quad \sum_{k=1}^{n} \frac{u_k(a)}{k}.$$

Such a discount rate will generate temporal preference inversion. This is illustrated in Figure 10.1. Both charts show the utility that the agent assigns to two events: p, which is worth ten, and q, worth seven, at different time periods. The twist in the story is that q is scheduled to occur one period

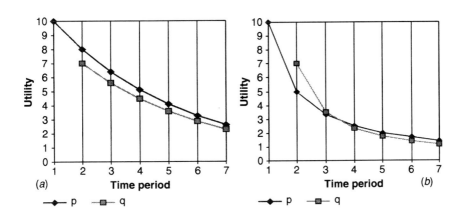

Fig. 10.1 (a) Exponential discounting and (b) hyperbolic discounting

268 / Joseph Heath

sooner than p. Each series shows the value of the two events at seven periods removed, at six periods removed, etc. The fact that q will occur sooner is reflected in the fact that, for instance, at $t = 3$, q is discounted only once, while p is twice discounted. With the exponential discount rate, p is always preferred to q. With the hyperbolic discount rate, on the other hand, p is preferred to q when the two events are far away, but as the time approaches, q begins to look more attractive—not because it is 'intrinsically' more desirable, but simply because it occurs sooner.

Here we can recognize a very common feature of human psychology, which we often identify as the effect of temptation. We can decide 'in advance' that p is better than q, but then find that when the time comes to choose between the two, we prefer q. The interesting feature of Ainslie's analysis is that it goes a long way towards dispelling the aura of irrationality that surrounds this sort of temptation. *Given* the agent's discount rate, and the agent's preferences, it is perfectly rational for the agent to choose the 'lesser good' in this example. It is also perfectly rational for the agent, at the point in time where the events are still a long way off, to take actions aimed at preventing herself from making this choice when the time comes. Again, there is no practical irrationality involved here.

However, the popularity of more unstructured forms of decision theory in philosophical discussions has helped to obscure many of these issues. In a world Bayesian view, an agent who undergoes temporal preference inversion is likely to appear as simply someone with highly unstable desires, or, worse, as someone who acts contrary to his or her 'true' interests. The more structured formulation allows us to see more clearly that neither of these two interpretations is necessary.

What is going on in the standard discussions of practical irrationality, in effect, is that theorists are taking issue with the discount rate that many agents have. Philosophers and economists alike have tended to prefer exponential to hyperbolic discount rates. Some have even argued that any time preference is irrational—after we have factored in risk, we should be completely neutral with respect to present and future satisfaction.[5] None of these arguments is conclusive, in my view. For example, the mere fact that hyperbolic discount rates generate dynamic inconsistency is neither here nor there. People change their more substantive preferences all the time, without thereby standing convicted of irrationality. In any case, this is a potentially interesting discus-

---

[5] For economists, see Pigou 1920: 25. For a philosophical discussion, see Broome 1994.

sion, but it should really be partitioned off from the discussion of practical rationality, and treated under the separate heading of 'optimal discounting', or words to that effect. Such a repartitioning of the conceptual terrain would reveal many formulations of the problem of temptation to be pseudo-problems.

Rule-Following

Much the same can be said of the various examples of norm-conformative behaviour that generate such systematic deviations from the 'ideal' of rationality in experimental game theory. Take the ultimatum game. In the typical North American trial, offers are observed to be consistent with utility maximization *given* the pattern of rejections. In other words, the individual making the offer usually tries to keep as much of the money as possible, but knows that 'low-ball' offers are likely to be rejected. Thus the most common strategy for this player seems to be to make an offer that is low, but not *too* low. This is often felt to be an especially anomalous result, given the peculiar combination of maximizing behaviour (on the part of the player making the offer) and non-maximizing behaviour (on the part of the player deciding whether to accept) (Cemerer and Thaler 1995: 212). However, separating out the deontic from the consequential features of the decision problem helps to dissolve this air of paradox.

First, consider the situation of the individual faced with the choice of how much money to offer his opponent. He wants to keep as much of it as possible. Yet he knows that the norm of fairness applies to this situation, and thus that the cooperative solution is to split the money 50-50. He also believes that his opponent takes this norm to apply, and so will have some propensity to punish anyone who violates it. But he also believes that his opponent wants the money just as much as he.

How should all this be represented? The type of structured value function presented in (5) suggests that we should find a way of representing how each agent feels about the money, and how each feels about the fairness norm, keeping the two separate. Let us suppose, for the sake of simplicity, that for both agents utility is linear with money. Then we can set the utility of $100 at 1, and $50 at 0.5, etc. This much is pretty standard. Now consider how the players' attitudes towards the norm should be represented. Suppose that for the first player, perfect conformity with the norm gives the action a value of 1,

270 / Joseph Heath

while complete violation of the norm is worth 0. Suppose further that offers are considered better the closer they are to the ideal of even division, so that 'more fair' is better than 'less fair' in a linear fashion. Thus an offer of $50 will be worth 1, an offer of $30 worth 0.6, and offer of $10 worth 0.2, and so on. (Offers above $50, along with any possible 'supererogatory' valuation, will be set aside here.)

For the second player, we can imagine a perfectly symmetric scale, except that it will be the action of *rejecting* unfair offers that is positively valued. Thus rejecting an offer of $0 will be worth 1, rejecting an offer of $10 will be worth 0.8, rejecting an offer of $40 will be worth 0.2, and so on again. Finally, we can assign each player a fundamental choice disposition γ, which we will assume to be common knowledge. Suppose that it is 0.4, so that both agents consider the normative dimension of the situation be a fair bit less important than the monetary stake.

If we grant that this model provides a relatively adequate representation of the interaction, it is now easy to see why individuals select the actions that have been observed. Under these circumstances, the player making the offer suffers from some loss of value in making unfair offers, but this is easily outweighed by the monetary advantage. As a result, we can expect this player's actions to conform to the utility maximization hypothesis (i.e. he will offer the other player as little as possible). However, the second player is in a different situation. For the person making the offer, the more unfair the offer, the more lucrative it is. But for the second player, the more unfair the offer, the less lucrative it is. As a result, while the second player has a financial incentive to accept offers that are only somewhat unfair, there will be a point where the desire to accept will be outweighed by the desire to punish the other for making a low-ball offer. In other words, the opportunity cost of punishing unfair offers decreases as the offers become more unfair.

The value of player 2's options is shown in Figure 10.2. Rejecting overtakes accepting at around $22. Thus player 1, anticipating this, will try to maximize his own value by making an offer just high enough that player 2 will not reject it.

This analysis of the problem clearly explains the asymmetry between the two players' behaviour—the fact that one appears to be maximizing pay-offs while the other is not. It is revealed to be a structural feature of the interaction, not a consequence of any asymmetry in their orientation towards either the social norm or the money. Thus we can expect the two players to behave identically when their situations are reversed.

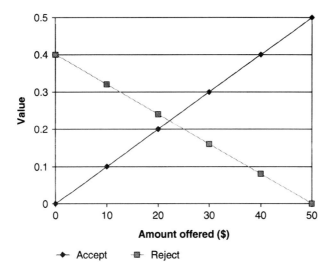

Fig. 10.2 The value of rejection

Of course, in the actual experiments, the mean offer is much higher (around $44). This can be attributed to a number of factors. First, some individuals making offers feel strongly enough about the fairness norm that they immediately select the 50-50 split, without making any calculations about what their opponent is likely to do. There is also considerable uncertainty in the actual experiments, so fundamental choice dispositions are not common knowledge. Since 'playing it safe' in this game means making a higher offer, we can expect to see a mean in actual trials that is much higher than would obtain under perfect information.

Conclusion

Formal models of rational choice have an enormous amount to contribute to our discussions of practical rationality and irrationality. The two examples given above are designed to show that a structured theory is able, not only to represent more clearly all of the factors that weigh in a complex choice problem, but even to shed light upon the nature of the problem. They help us to understand the decision better than we did before. The more general advantage of such theories arises when an agent makes a choice that seems problematic or ill-advised. A formal model allows us to state with

272 / Joseph Heath

much greater precision exactly which aspect of the decision we are taking issue with.

For example, philosophers quite routinely characterize the individual who stays up late at night, or drinks one too many at a party, despite the morning-after consequences, as suffering from some type of irrationality—especially if that individual is aware of these consequences at the point of decision. However, more careful attention to the phenomenon of discounting shows that the mere fact that agents later regret their decisions, or even anticipate at the point of decision that they *will* regret their decisions, is not necessarily a sign of irrationality. Such phenomena are a straightforward consequence of even well-behaved exponential discount rates. Agents with hyperbolic discount rates will exhibit even more extreme inconsistencies, such as temporal inversions of their preference ordering. But again, it is not at all obvious that this is a form of irrationality. What does it mean to say that one time preference is 'more rational' than some other?

If we take seriously the idea that discounting reflects a pure time preference, then what we really want to be saying, when we present this sort of criticism, is that agents *should* discount their future satisfaction in some other way, or at some other rate. This is not the same thing as saying that the individual is irrational. First of all, such a criticism is vulnerable to the old *de gustibus non disputandum est* response in a way that accusations of irrationality are not. Classifying the debate as one over what sort of preference the agent should have also opens up a range of argumentation strategies that have been inadequately explored in the literature. It is naturally amenable, for instance, to purely consequentialist arguments.

Thus there is a strong case to be made for decision theories that offer a more perspicuous articulation of the way that temporal perspective affects our deliberations. The same can be said for theories that highlight the role of deontic constraints. Consider, for example, the well-known story of the Roman general Marcus Atilius Regulus. Captured by the Carthaginians, he was sent to Rome to negotiate peace with the Senate, on the condition that he would return if the negotiations failed. When the Senate decided to continue the war, Regulus promptly returned to his captors in Carthage, where he was tortured to death. Many people throughout history have regarded this is as a praiseworthy but essentially crazy course of action. The obvious thing for Regulus to have done, once released, would have been to defect from the agreement under which he was released.

The Structure of Decision Theory / 273

The question is whether Regulus' somewhat unusual choice reflected irrationality on his part, or simply the assignment of somewhat excessive value to the principle of promise-keeping. There is an important school of thought that suggests that rational agents must always reoptimize as events unfold, and that adhering to a promise is therefore inherently irrational. According to this view, a sort of 'that was then, this is now' reasoning is imposed by the structure of practical rationality. If, however, the agent is seen as acting on the basis of both consequentialist and deontological considerations, it is no longer obvious that rationality is what is at issue in this case. We may feel that Regulus suffers from a type of hyperconformism—in this case, a somewhat overweening sense of personal honour—which led him to a rather imprudent disregard for the consequences of his actions. But this is a substantive debate, not one that will be resolved by one or another stipulative definition of practical rationality.

In any case, it is my hope that these examples show how formal theories of decision can contribute to our understanding of practical rationality. Traditionally, though, these theories have served more as a source of confusion. This is because decision theorists have been remarkably evasive about the philosophical commitments underlying their views—and have chosen to offer successively weaker, less structured versions of the theory in response to criticism. I have argued that a standard of expressive adequacy should be applied to these theories, both to counteract this tendency, and to bring the philosophical motivation for these views closer to the surface. Only then may they begin to serve as a help, rather than a hindrance, in the broader philosophical discussion.

11

Paradoxical Emotion: On *Sui Generis* Emotional Irrationality

Ronald de Sousa

Dante pourquoi dis-tu qu'il n'est pire misère
Qu'un souvenir heureux dans un jour de malheur?

(Alfred de Musset)

Pourquoi indeed?

(R. de Sousa)

Competing Frameworks of Rationality

Weakness of will has sometimes been construed as a moral failing; but at least since Davidson 1970*a* it has been viewed as a pathology of agency. As such it infringes strategic rationality, which aims at maximizing the likelihood of success of a given course of action. On an alternative, Socratic view, it is an epistemic failing, violating the sort of rationality that aims to maximize the propensity for arriving at truth afforded by a given method of settling on a belief. Strategic and epistemic rationality are distinct. Each provides a familiar framework within which questions of rationality and irrationality are discussed; but where both seem applicable there is no obvious way to decide which of the two is the correct framework of evaluation.

On *Sui Generis* Emotional Irrationality / 275

This would pose no special problem, if the two frameworks could never clash. We are used to finding paradoxes and antinomies within each framework of rationality. Jon Elster's Ulysses problem and the Prisoner's Dilemma are notorious examples that arise within the framework of strategic rationality.[1] The liar paradox with its innumerable epigones is the classic example in the epistemic framework. These problems have given rise to a large literature. But less often considered is the question of what we should say when a conflict arises between the two standard frameworks. Ultimatum games and Newcomb's paradox are two much discussed classes of examples that involve issues *both* of strategy and of belief, but they do not involve *competition* between the two frameworks.[2] If a genuine conflict is possible, the question arises whether one framework can subsume the other, or whether there might be a third, more general point of view in terms of which the conflict might be arbitrated. If, as I shall argue, such a third framework exists, might it not, in turn, yield its own paradoxes and antinomies?

If one framework is to subsume the other, the claim of the strategic may seem immediately preponderant. Settling on a belief may be regarded as a type of action, and we can devise strategies for discovering truth. More pertinently, the notion of correctness or truth itself can fall under the aegis of a pragmatic criterion, as urged by a long tradition in philosophy, running from Protagoras to Richard Rorty through Blaise Pascal and William James, for whom the point of seeking truth, or more radically the very *test* of truth, lies in the goal of making people fare better. Similarly, when Freud contrasts the 'reality principle' with the 'pleasure principle', the former is merely a means to satisfying the latter in the long run: truth is ancillary to the search for satisfaction, and its claims must presumably remain subservient to the larger goal.

Conversely, however, as Socrates pointed out to Protagoras in the *Theaetetus*, an exclusive focus on pragmatic success cannot avoid the epistemic burden of

[1] Ulysses predicted his own inability to resist the Sirens' call, and had himself tied to the mast lest he respond to it. The Prisoner's Dilemma is the name given to a large class of two-person or multi-person decision problems in which if each agent chooses the act with the preferable outcome regardless of the other's choice, all agents end up worse off than they would be if all had chosen the dominated option. On both, see Elster 1979.

[2] On ultimatum games, see Thaler 1992. Newcomb's problem (Nozick 1986) might be seen as an exception. It does present a clash between the two frameworks, if one insists that the dominance principle that requires taking both boxes is a strictly strategic principle, while the expected-utility calculation preferred by the one-box party depends crucially on epistemic principles. I will not dip my toes into that quicksand on the present occasion, though the view developed in this chapter might find here an application worth exploring.

276 / Ronald de Sousa

correctly predicting the consequences of a course of action. Epistemic rationality, a champion might claim, subsumes the strategic, in that in all strategic reasoning the real work is done by principles of epistemic inference that happen to be applied to conditional predictions. That premises and results may allude to practice is a mere accident of subject matter, not a reflection of the existence of a different sort of rationality. In every case of practical inference, it must be *true* that some goal is sought, that some means are appropriate and available, and so forth. Moreover, even if we regard the principles of epistemic rationality as simply designed to foster the beliefs most likely to underwrite successful action, the epistemic need not concede anything to the strategic. Epistemic norms are like those of gastronomy: there would be none were it not for the imperatives of nourishment; yet nourishment does not wholly determine the norms of gastronomy. Similarly, pragmatic considerations may be thought to underlie our interest in truth; yet practical concerns are insufficient to account for the norms of rational belief.

Each framework, then, can make a case for swallowing up the other. Yet unless just one of these claims is spurious, it seems the two may indeed conflict when a belief is both more likely to lead to good consequences and less likely to be true. In such cases our commitment to the truth and our allegiance to the good part company. Pascal urged us to believe in God even if the probability of his existence is as close to zero as you like (provided it is not actually zero). For if God exists, and our faith earns a heaven of infinite worth, the expected gain remains infinite even when multiplied by that tiny probability. Conversely, if disbelief incurs eternal damnation, the expected loss is infinite, and outweighs all earthly gains. If Pascal's options were exhaustive, the reasoning would be strategically sound.

But would it be *right?* Certainly it is epistemically worthless. And one might claim that no transcendent point of view is required, for the epistemic rationality Pascal recommends flouting and the strategic rationality he advocates are not really focused on the same object.[3] Pascal, like James (1896/1979), recommends strategies of self-improvement that explicitly require cultivating self-deception. But the intrinsic aim or point of belief is truth: that is not a normative principle, but a definitional one. So recommending self-deception is inherently irrational, regardless of the desirability of the goal it is intended to serve. By even speaking of belief—if only to subvert it—the Pascalian move

---

[3] The importance of this point was stressed to me in conversation by Sergio Tenenbaum, who deplores my continued refusal to give it due weight.

On *Sui Generis* Emotional Irrationality / 277

implicitly commits itself to the norms of belief and so must recognize the irrationality of flouting them. But what is the force of this 'must'? Surely it is not the 'must' of logical necessity. For if it were, then the views of Pascal and James would be not just irrational, but impossible. If it is the 'must' of epistemic necessity, then the point has already been granted, and is irrelevant to my dilemma as I try to decide, simply, *what to believe*. Is the 'must' then to be taken as a *moral* 'must'? The claim that it is might be grounded in the observation that we don't just classify self-deception as irrational, but commonly condemn it even when it may have solid strategic justification.[4] The propensity for each side to claim moral high ground is attested by the title of William Clifford's famous article on the '*ethics* of belief' (Clifford 1866) no less than by the tone of James's rejoinder (James 1896/1979). The dispute is easy to describe in terms of self-righteous rhetoric: Should one not care more about truth than advantage? says one side (and your practical rationality be damned). Should one not care about real consequences and not abstract truth? says the other (and your epistemic scruples be damned).

To each of these accusations, I shall argue, the best reply is to ask, quite literally, *Why should I care?* Taking that question literally involves recognizing that *reasons to care* are powerless to move us unless they are grounded in what we actually do care about. The normative claims made on us by either of the two standard frameworks of rationality—the epistemic and the strategic— will work on us *only if we care*.

Emotions and Norms

I have suggested that neither strategic nor epistemic rationality can arbitrate between Pascal and Clifford, because each is antecedently committed to one framework or the other. If adjudication between them is to be achieved, therefore, it must be in virtue of a third kind of rationality. The hypothesis I shall advance is that there is indeed such a third framework of rationality, governing emotions capable of delivering objective *axiological* verdicts. Such emotions constitute *perceptions of value*. Only an emotional attitude towards the two distinct sorts of appropriateness defined by the frameworks of strategic and epistemic rationality can arbitrate between them. In this sense, emotions

---

[4] There is also a vigorous literature that stresses the benefits of self-deception. Examples are to be found among the essays in Lockard and Paulhus 1988.

278 / Ronald de Sousa

are capable not only of functioning as arbiters of appropriateness, but more particularly of adjudicating *appropriateness of kinds of appropriateness*.

Much needs to be done to make this plausible, but my central concern here will not be to build a defence of the thesis that some emotions constitute perceptions of value.[5] Rather, it will be to explore the landscape that might be revealed if we could assume such a defence had been successful. And in that spirit my central claim is a strongly naturalizing one. It is that in the ultimate analysis the *facts* of emotion are all that can be appealed to by way of justification of the *normative* claims of rationality.

Emotional Irrationality: Close but No Cigar

The easiest way to grasp the nature of a framework of rationality is to look at examples of cases that fail of it. I shall therefore offer a sampling of the ways in which our attitudes and emotions might be deplored as systematically paradoxical or irrational. (One needs to add: *systematically*, for we are not concerned with the fact that a rational being can be irrational on this or that particular occasion.) But rather than plunge straight into that list, I first want to offer, for the sake of contrast, some examples that illustrate less interesting forms of disorders. These are cases that may involve emotions, but can be accounted for without going outside the bounds of the standard norms.

My first two cases are inspired by Jon Elster.

1. Emotions are typically possessed both of motivating power and of intrinsic positive or negative valence (Elster 1999: 329). Sometimes, states with intrinsic positive valence induce us to act in such a way as to land us in states of negative valence. In a state of euphoria, induced by coffee or other benign drugs, I may find everyone I meet delightful and judge them to be wholly trustworthy. This pleasant condition, however, is one I may live to regret. What's more, I may know it at the time, but repress the thought as mean.

2. Conversely, I may prefer the emotion with negative valence, for the sake of some other gain. Elster cites Robert Solomon's nice case of the woman who 'continues to patronize a shop which she knows has cheated her [because] her small losses are more than compensated for by the self-righteous satisfaction

---

[5] For a defence of the view, see Tappolet 2000.

On *Sui Generis* Emotional Irrationality / 279

of her continuing indignation' (quoted from Solomon 1993 at Elster 1999: 310).

3. If my irascible disposition induces my lover's disaffection, and I am moved to anger by that very disaffection, my anger is clearly counter-productive.

4. 'A rolling stone gathers no moss'. Here is an anthropological fact.[6] Ask a European to explicate this proverb, and she will be most likely to interpret the moss as representing culture and accomplishments, and the proverb as recommending that one settle down. For most Americans, on the contrary, the proverb is in praise of roving: being a rolling stone is a good thing, avoiding parasitic growths and encumbrances. For Europeans, it seems, positive emotional valence attaches to the thought of moss; for Americans, the emotional valence of moss is negative.

Cases (1)–(4) are essentially prudential cases. They illustrate straightforward economic choices based on calculations of gains and losses. In the first two, I am merely being squeezed between desires for outcomes that happen to be incompatible in practice. In the third case, there is nothing paradoxical about my emotion considered in itself. It is just bad luck that my emotional propensities haven't been fine-tuned well enough to avoid such counter-productive displays. As for the fourth, perhaps it merely exploits a disagreement about values. These examples may present a certain paradoxical flavour, but they involve no antinomies, nor do they signal any unavoidable irrationality.

The next example introduces a crucial element of additional complexity, in that it involves second-order attitudes adjudicating potential conflicts between first-order and second-order attitudes. But it is not yet a case of the kind I am looking for.

5. As Jonathan Schell pointed out, the logic of deterrence

commits us in certain circumstances to do what we must never do in any circumstances.... Deterrence theory is indeed a marvel of circularity and contradiction. To obtain the benefit of the policy, we must threaten to perform an insane action. But the benefit we seek is precisely *not* to perform that action. We thus seek to avoid performing an act by threatening to perform it...

(Schell 1984: 64)

---

[6] For which I flatter myself I can claim credit as an original discovery, if a somewhat anecdotally grounded one.

280 / Ronald de Sousa

Each side must reason thus: I must assume you are rational in your willingness to be deterred. Otherwise there would be no point in my threat, since only a rational calculation can lead an agent to be deterred. But inasmuch as I am willing to be deterred, I must also assume you are irrational, indeed 'insane' in your willingness to carry out your threat. For since retaliation guarantees an agent's own destruction, retaliating can never be rational. The equilibrium of deterrence is a symmetrical one, with both sides figuring as X in the deterring role and as Y in the role of the one deterred. X must believe Y to be rational as deterred but irrational as deterring. For X must believe he has convinced Y that he, X himself, is insane enough to carry out his threat, yet sane in his ability to be deterred by Y's threat of the same insane behaviour. Robert Frank (1988) presents a consequence of this situation, adverting to the case where, in a personal confrontation, it is rational to give free rein to the most irrational emotions in order to convince my opponent that I am capable of ignoring my own interests for the sake of harming him. Otherwise, he might think me ready to compromise when rational calculation shows that pursuing the case will cost me more than dropping it.

This last example is, I believe, a genuinely paradoxical result. Moreover, in Frank's version and perhaps in Schell's original version too, it clearly involves emotions. For deterrence will work only if it arouses fear, and it will arouse fear only if my opponent is persuaded that my emotions will overcome my concern for my own interests. Yet the paradox arises purely from the structure of a certain game-theoretical situation, and so it is not clear that it involves emotions essentially, in any sense in which emotion might not be simply reducible to *preference*.

In the cases I am looking for, the paradox or antinomy is even more intimately tied to the nature of the emotion itself. The following cases might do, in that they are not obviously describable in terms of the standard modes of rationality. They share two features: first, in one way or another they involve temporality; secondly (and partly as a consequence), they represent essentially contestable evaluations and can themselves be adjudicated only in terms of their holistic ties to one another. They will also help to make plain the powerful and yet curiously exposed and *arbitrary* position of axiological evaluations.

Questionable Attitudes and Emotional Antinomies: A Sampling

1. *Remembering happiness in sorrow.* My epigraph from Alfred de Musset alludes to Dante, *Inferno* V. 121–2:

> Nessun maggior dolore
> che ricordarsi del tempo felice
> ne la miseria.[7]

Musset continues:

> Quel chagrin t'a dicté cette parole amère,
> Cette offense au malheur?[8]
>
> (Musset 1908: 79)

Both attitudes are intelligible and neither seems to rest on a persuasive argument that could topple the other. The two judgements constitute an *emotional antinomy*, which can't be translated out of the domain of emotion into some more familiar strategic or epistemic terrain. It clearly isn't the case that Dante and Musset have some strategic disagreement about how best to pursue some goal in view. Nor are they disagreeing about truth or about the validity of inference rules.

2. *Does it matter, now, that now won't matter when I'm dead?* Thomas Nagel has advanced an argument about the incoherence of the thought that life is absurd because nothing we do now will matter in a million years. It goes like this: if it matters *now* that our lives will seem insignificant in a million years, then what is a million years away can matter. But if what is a million years away can matter, why can our present lives not matter in a million years? Conversely, if being a million years away makes an event meaningless, then not mattering in a million years can't matter now, and therefore cannot make our present lives absurd (Nagel 1971: 11).

This argument can form the basis of an *anti-Epicurean* argument concerning death. Epicurus' well-known argument to show that it is irrational to fear

---

[7] 'No greater suffering than to remember happiness in times of sorrow.'

[8] 'What misery inspired such bitter words, such an insult to sorrow?' The epigraph at the head of this chapter quotes the immediately preceding words: 'Dante, why do you say there is no greater misery | Than happy memories in times of sorrow?'

282 / Ronald de Sousa

death seems irrefutable: *When I am, death isn't; when death is, I am not there to care.*
What could be plainer? Rather than attempting to refute it, one may well
wonder why such an irrefutable argument leaves so many people unmoved.
Nagel's argument can be extended to attack it more directly. It would go
something like this:

> If Epicurus can console me now with the thought that I will feel nothing
> at future time d, then something matters to me now about a future time.
> So why shouldn't I be distressed now by that very same thought?
> Epicurus can't bring up his old argument to show that such an attitude
> would be irrational, for against the present objection his old argument
> merely begs the question.

Nagel's original argument is open to an objection from the asymmetry of
time. Perhaps the future matters but the past doesn't. So it might be
reasonable to mind what the distant future will think or fail to think of us,
while it might also be reasonable for the denizens of that distant future to
think we don't matter. The present argument about death, however, doesn't
suffer from that defect, since both considerations face the same way, towards
my future death. Nor is it liable to appraisal in terms of standard norms. The
Epicurean argument comes as close as anything to an argument that it is
epistemically sound; but, as we have just seen, it begs the question. And
from the strategic point of view, to be sure, given the fear of death's negative
valence, we might be better off without it. But that doesn't suffice to make
it inappropriate. What would suffice? We need a standard capable of
adjudicating the claims of emotional attitudes, as well as arbitrating between
the types of appropriateness dictated by the epistemic and the strategic
standards.

3. *Dessert Last, and related principles.* Some people leave the best until last.
Foolish, say others, for by the time the last is due you may be dead, or the best
have spoiled. My 3-year-old daughter has offered this version of Dessert Last.
Teachers at day care take shifts, and Teresa, her 'favourite teacher', comes
either in the morning shift or for the afternoon. She sees her van in the
parking lot as we arrive at day care. Often this has caused her to utter cries of
delight, but today she is terribly disappointed.

'Oh, I'm so disappointed, Teresa is here.'
'But aren't you glad that she's here?'
'No, if she's here this morning, she won't be here in the afternoon.'

On *Sui Generis* Emotional Irrationality / 283

4. *Violations of the Philebus principle:*[9] In the *Philebus* Plato defends the thesis that there are 'false pleasures'. From his discussion we may distil the following principle:

> (PP) A *pleasure of anticipation* should be proportional in intensity to the *anticipated pleasure* which it represents.

Taking great pleasure in the anticipation of something from which one expects none when it comes seems (to Plato and to me, at least) intuitively irrational. The principle does not say anything about what to believe about the future pleasure. It is not, therefore, captured by or reducible to an epistemic principle. Nor, for two reasons, does it seem to be reducible to strategic canons. First, one might think it great good fortune to be able to squeeze some pleasure in advance out of what isn't going to provide any when it actually occurs. That is surely the attitude enjoined by strategic considerations (such as *maximize pleasant moments*). Secondly, the principle doesn't say anything about choices, or desires, but only about the pleasure or emotion itself. One might offer a justification of the PP on epistemic or on pragmatic grounds. Epistemically, one might note that the sheer quality of a pleasure of anticipation might afford *information* about the quality of the future pleasure. Strategically, one might appeal to the likelihood that the *motivational* aspect of disproportionate pleasures of anticipation might disrupt the course of practical planning. But neither of these considerations suffices to account for the PP, which in itself is about the quality and intensity of *experience* in pleasures of anticipation, not about their informational or motivating functions.

5. *Aspectual mismatch.* Aristotle associates happiness with *activity* rather than with being in a certain *state* or having completed some *achievement*. Now a desire, it seems, can envisage a future event under one or another of different temporal aspects, in the sense of that word that corresponds to the grammatical sense of 'aspect'. Thus desire can focus on a future event *under the description* of the achievement of a certain goal, or on the activity that leads to its achievement. And in certain cases it seems plausible to claim that the focus is irrational or even *mistaken*, because the objectively desirable aspect of the event is its enduring quality, not its achievement. My stock examples here are tourism, art, and sex: if the hurried tourist cares only about having completed a visit to some beautiful site, her attention is likely to be diverted from the experience of its contemplation; if the concert-goer or impatient lover is

---

[9] I have discussed this item and the next elsewhere, most fully in de Sousa 2000.

284 / Ronald de Sousa

focused on the approach of a symphony's last chord, or on orgasm, they may be missing out on the more valuable experience of the music or the sexual caress.

It is intriguing to wonder about the relation of the requirement of aspectual match to the next phenomenon, which might seem to lend comfort to the hurried lover's preoccupation with endings.

6. The *peak–end rule*. Daniel Kahneman has offered evidence to show that one's assessment of a series of episodes is governed not by the total or the average of its hedonic intensity and duration, but largely by the measure of representative moments at the peak and at the end. The paradoxical consequence follows that by judiciously adjusting the pattern of intensity, you can make the subject rate as *less aversive* a sequence of pain episodes by actually making the pain last longer.

Consider the series 2-5-8 and 2-5-8-4, where the numbers refer to reports of pain provided on a 10-point scale every five minutes (10 was worst, 1 was least painful). Although it may seem obvious that the addition of five extra minutes of pain can only *increase* total discomfort, the mean subjective ratings were in fact *lower* for the longer sequence. The sequence 2-5-8 was rated 64 for total unpleasantness, but 2-5-8-4 was rated only 53 (Kahneman 2000: 696–7). In this case, then, people rated *more pain* as significantly *less unpleasant*.

This finding reveals a surprising discounting of the value of duration in the past. I return to it in a moment, after some remarks concerning discounting of the future.

7. *Future discounting and weakness of will*. In his fascinating book *Picoeconomics* (Ainslie 1992), Ainslie gives a long list of pathological or irrational behaviours which can, he claims, be explained in terms of our propensity to discount the future at a hyperbolic rate.[10] All involve the propensity to *preference reversal* which results from the hyperbolic pattern of discounting. Prospects at unequal temporal distances, like buildings unequally far away, will reverse the order of their apparent sizes as one approaches. Thus when walking towards a small building which stands in front of a large one, you first see clearly that the more distant one is larger. But as you get nearer, while the actual distance from both diminishes in a linear way, the ratio between the distance to the small building and the distance to the large building changes, and as it does so the smaller building comes to occlude the taller. So it goes

---

[10] These include the various patterns of resistance or surrender to temptations and addictions; obsessive behaviour; procrastination; sexual exhibitionism; anorexia nervosa; Don Juanism; gambling; and many others. For more discussion, see de Sousa 1997.

On *Sui Generis* Emotional Irrationality / 285

too, with the future prospects that we value: a preference for a lucid morning tomorrow over a bibulous evening tonight may be clear by the early light of this morning, but as the evening approaches the 'temptation' of the now looming bottle occludes the picture of tomorrow's hangover.

Temporal Attitudes

My sample cases all involve comparisons or changes across time, or ways of envisaging temporal events. In addition they all illustrate a certain *arbitrariness* of our attitudes, particularly where they are subject to change, or where they affect our temporal perspectives. This is not surprising when we recall that the temporal domain is one on which classical utilitarian calculation is generally silent. Recent moral philosophy affords a number of discussions of the morality of increasing the number of sentient beings in order to increase the total amount of hedons in the world,[11] but contains very little about the weight that should be assigned to the *duration* of experiences. Most of us, unlike Achilles, take it for granted that a long life is to be preferred to a short one, but apart from that prejudice we tend to ignore the question altogether.[12]

On the question of rationality through time, self-evident principles are hard to come by. Any reasonably stable emotional dispositions with regard to such evaluation may therefore have a prima facie claim to being deemed criterial, if only by default. From the biological point of view, one might expect that evaluations of the future and evaluations of the past might obey rather different rules (it seems reasonable, for example, to prefer *having suffered* some unpleasant episode to *being about to suffer* it). One might also expect that a number of principles will govern rational attitudes to temporal characteristics of experience. When such principles turn out to be violated in practice—as in the case of the 'peak–end' phenomenon, which contradicts the plausible idea that a shorter period of suffering will always be ranked as more desirable than a longer one—we might infer that human beings are systematically

[11] See Parfit 1984, pt. 3, and the literature it has spawned.

[12] One notable exception is found in discussions of animal welfare, where this issue comes up in two ways. One is that animal liberationists such as Singer are ready to acknowledge a greater value to the continuation of a life that admits of development, such as a typical human life, than to one that merely consists in prolonging a constant state, such as we plausibly attribute to other animals (see Singer 1993). The second pertains to the trade-off between animal populations that would not exist if we didn't raise them for food, against the disutility of being killed and eaten.

286 / Ronald de Sousa

irrational. Alternatively we might think we have misinterpreted the principles actually at work, and assume that once we identify them correctly no general systematic irrationality will be found. Those are, crudely put, the two sides involved in the 'rationality debate' pitting Kahneman, Slovic, and Tversky (1982) against Gigerenzer, Todd, and ABC Research Group (1999).

Part of what is at issue in the rationality debate is whether the question itself is an empirical one. From a methodological point of view, therefore, the issue is very difficult to settle, since either side can dispose of many stratagems of conceptual gerrymandering which will neutralize the empirical facts adduced by the other (Stein 1996). My aim in this chapter is to exploit this stand-off, in both a negative and a positive sense. The negative stage consists in pointing out that a stand-off is to be expected, because there is no higher and impartial court before which principles of temporal rationality can be assessed. Inevitably, if we try to *justify* such standards, we will travel in a circle. In the positive stage, the contention is that, in the final analysis, *the facts of emotional attitudes* are all that can be appealed to, both by way of justification of the normative claims of rationality, and by way of adjudication between such normative claims when they conflict. I believe that both the negative and the positive stages of this project are essentially part of Hume's legacy, in a way that I now briefly digress to explain.

Hume's Legacy

In relation to epistemic rationality, the view that the normative is rooted in the facts of entrenched practice is far from novel. Still, it is hard to swallow. Surely, we want to say, there is a difference between the factual question of what we do and the normative question of what we ought to do. Yet the justification of basic normative principles seems doomed to circularity. Hume showed this for the justification of induction. Nelson Goodman (1983) and Susan Haack (1976) have extended this respectively to our choice of projectible predicates and to deduction: there too, the question of justification can't be answered without begging the question.

The portion of the Humean argument which I shall attempt to extend to axiology goes something like this.

Take seriously for a moment the choice between induction and anti-induction. It might be suggested that induction doesn't need to be grounded in any deeper principle, because it is *self-justifying*. But anti-induction is self-justifying too: since inferring that the future will be different from the past has not worked in the past, anti-induction predicts that anti-induction will work next time, just as induction predicts that induction will work next time. So there is no difference there.

It might seem, however, that an asymmetry can be made out at the second-order level, in the following way. When we do expect that anti-induction will work—my gas tank has been non-empty for several hundred miles now, so it's bound to run out soon—we do so on *inductive* grounds. By contrast, it is not the case that when we are confident that induction will work, our confidence rests on *anti-inductive* grounds. So is there not here, at least, an irreducible asymmetry? Actually that appearance is illusory. It is akin to the illusion that there is an asymmetry between the predicates *blue-green* and Goodman's alternative *grue-bleen* (Goodman 1983): while the first pair is projectible and the second is not, that is not because the first enjoys any logical advantage. The only advantage that projectible predicates have is that they are 'entrenched', that is, actually projected (Goodman 1983: 94). Similarly, our impression that induction is asymmetrically related to anti-induction may be due to the entrenchment of our intuitions about what constitute reliable inferences from the past to the future. If those very intuitions are what is being called into question, therefore, they cannot be appealed to in their own defence without begging the question.

Hume's essential message is *Don't ask why we do it, ask what we do*. The asymmetry just discussed supports the answer: *What we do is make inductions*. That doesn't in itself support the claim that making inductions is what we *should* be doing: that is precisely Hume's 'problem' of induction. But Hume's *answer* to the problem is that our practices are all the justification we will ever get. When extending the problem to the 'new riddle' and deduction, this is a point which Nelson Goodman makes very explicit: 'Principles of deductive inference are justified by their conformity to accepted deductive practice' (Goodman 1983: 63). We may invoke increasingly deep and general principles, but in the end the same holds for the ultimate principles of rationality, no less than for our knowledge of the ultimate causes acting in the physical universe: 'The most perfect philosophy of the natural kind only staves off our ignorance a little longer' (Hume 1777/1975: 19).

Applying this to the principles of rationality may cast light on the current 'rationality debate'. To see how, consider this passage from Richard Thaler: '[Rubinstein 1982: 97] explicitly distinguishes [the question of what will happen...if both parties behave rationally] from two others, namely

288 / Ronald de Sousa

"(i) the positive question—what is the agreement reached in practice; (ii) the normative question—what is the just agreement" ' (Thaler 1992: 21).

By 'the normative question' Rubinstein and Thaler apparently mean the *moral* question. Let us leave that aside for the moment. In a sufficiently strong sense, the first question is already a normative one, since 'what would happen if the parties behave rationally' presupposes that there is an answer to what the parties *should* do (according to the canons of rationality). But while on a particular occasion it may seem obvious that this question is to be answered differently from 'the positive question', it is far from clear that the questions can be kept apart all the way down.

Let me try to make this plausible for some of the cases sketched above. As we shall see, some can be accounted for without appealing to the sort of paradoxical emotions I have in mind; but others, as far as I can see, cannot. (Those I leave out from further discussion are left as a challenge to the reader.)

Extending the Humean Moral to *Sui Generis* Emotional Rationality

In the Dessert Last cases, one might find cultural as well as individual variation in the attitude that people take to ordering one's future pleasures. This blunts the paradoxical force of the competing attitudes. A similar cultural dependency is suggested by the contrast of interpretations of 'A rolling stone gathers no moss'. In addition, the discrepancy noted between American and European interpretations of the proverb doesn't amount to an emotional antinomy, because the two evaluations are based on different mappings of the elements of the proverb. For the European, 'moss' symbolizes culture and 'rolling stones' are referred to persons who never focus on a stable project; for the American, 'moss' symbolizes undesirable attachments and rolling stones are those who keep up the search for fresh experience.

The conflicting intuitions of Dante and Musset, on the other hand, might well pertain to *the very same* memory of happiness in times of sorrow. A dissenter might argue that the difference can be traced to the fact that each attends to a different aspect of the situation. Dante focuses on the present suffering afforded by the contrast of past happiness, whereas Musset attends to the past happiness itself. If each were to switch his focus of attention, he might concede the other's point. Perhaps: but then each might insist that the other's focus of attention was somehow perverse, inappropriate to the situation as a whole. And in the face of that persisting disagreement, what is called for is again some criterion capable of arbitrating not merely between two attitudes associated with different points of view, but also between the two standards of appropriateness favouring the contrasting points of view.

Much the same seems to be true of attitudes to death. We must, I argued, concede that the Epicurean consolation is question-begging. If so, to prefer it over the despair so well expressed in Philip Larkin's *Aubade*[13] is also question-begging in assuming that a strategic value placed on comfort should outweigh the value of an adequate emotional response. But what is an 'adequate emotional response' to death? *Where there's death, there's hope*, my friend Malcolm Deas is fond of saying. To me, that sometimes seems a very touchstone of rationality.

In my own previous discussions of the Philebus and aspectual matching principles I have argued that both are irreducible to standard norms: both represent *sui generis* principles of rationality. In the context of the present argument I would further stress that while one can find things to say in their favour, we are unlikely to find any knock-down proof of their validity. In fact, one will not find any stronger justification for them than an appeal to one's reasoned feelings about what kind of life is better. In the light of my remarks on Hume's legacy, that places them in just the same position as the standard norms themselves.

Is this claim excessively pusillanimous? To be sure, some have been more sanguine about the prospects for appraising emotional rationality. We can find stronger claims, explicitly or implicitly, both in Kahneman's discussion of 'evaluation by moments' and in Ainslie's discussion of temporal discounting.

Kahneman elaborates as follows on the 'heuristic of moments': 'as a good first approximation, the affective value of the representative moment is a simple average of the most extreme affect experienced during the episode (Peak) and of the affect experienced near its end . . . . The affective value of that representative moment, in turn, determines the global evaluation of the

---

[13]   . . . And specious stuff that says no rational being
　　　Can fear a thing it cannot feel, not seeing
　　　That this is what we fear—no sight, no sound,
　　　No touch or taste or smell, nothing to think with,
　　　Nothing to love or link with,
　　　The anaesthetic from which none come round.

290 / Ronald de Sousa

entire episode' (Kahneman 2000: 697). He concludes that this heuristic of evaluation by moments 'leads to violations of logic, because the temporal dimension of experience is not directly included in the representations that are evaluated' (Kahneman 2000: 707).

But where, actually, is the violation of logic? I see only a discrepancy between points of view: when you propose to inflict on me a continuous series of painful episodes, I might well prefer 2–5–8 to 2–5–8–4. That choice isn't *contradicted* by the fact that I may reverse my ranking of their desirability in retrospect. Since the temporal perspectives are as different as the future is from the past, there are no stable grounds even for accusing people of inconsistency when they insist that they would always prefer a shorter episode of pain to a longer one, and later choose the longer. But that may just show that they evaluate the past and the future differently: and why should they not?

Temporal reversals brought about by hyperbolic discounting often look very much like standard cases of weakness of will. Yet as described, such a reversal doesn't necessarily constitute or involve akrasia. The reason is this. On the usual view, whether an act (say, of drinking) involves akrasia depends on whether I continue, even when reaching for the bottle, to affirm sincerely that, all considered, I prefer not to drink now. But if I deny this and declare instead that I have changed my preference, and experience no concurrent conflict, I cannot automatically be convicted of akrasia. This observation may leave us uneasy, for we might like to leave room for the possibility that my sincerity in such a case simply indicates that I have successfully masked my akratic conflict with self-deception. The problem here is that what I have called 'the usual view' assumes that an agent always has access to her own real preferences. But that assumption is surely gratuitous, for self-deception may indeed cover my tracks in the way just suggested. If we give up the assumption, then some cases of akrasia might be held to be only apparently irrational, on the ground that the agent's articulated overall preferences don't really reflect her real preferences. The point has been forcefully made by Alison McIntyre (1990), who points out that if akrasia is defined as a conflict between one's avowed best reasons and the reason on the basis of which one acts, akrasia is not necessarily irrational, for one may be mistaken in one's belief that one's avowed best reasons reflect one's deepest commitments.

McIntyre applies this to the well-known Huck Finn example first discussed by Jonathan Bennett (1974). McIntyre claims that Bennett sees Huck as irrational because he characterizes the latter's dilemma 'as one in which

On *Sui Generis* Emotional Irrationality / 291

general moral principles and reasons conflict with "unreasoned emotional pulls" ' (McIntyre 1990: 381, quoting Bennett 1974: 127). Instead she suggests that in at least some similar cases one is not irrational in being akratic, because there is no inconsistency between one's actual values and one's act, even though there might be an inconsistency between what one *believes* to be one's values and one's acts:

> agents might not see what reasons they have for acting in a certain way. If one accepts this, then ... the practical judgments that she arrives at will express what she *believes* that she has most reason to do, but they might fail to express what she actually has reason to do or what it would be most rational for her to do.
>
> (McIntyre 1990: 386)

McIntyre's thesis isn't merely that some objective reasons might exist to justify the akratic action. It is rather that the so-called akratic action might be better from the point of view of the authentic preference ranking of the agent herself. Rationality in action, she contends, is 'evaluative consistency', and evaluative consistency might exist, for example, in view of the fact that if the agent had had more time to reflect, she would have changed her explicit opinion about what would be best to do. Thus she would have been saved from akrasia not by changing her behaviour but by changing her evaluation of it.

But what is the ground on which one might ascribe to an agent a system of values different from the one avowed by the agent herself? McIntyre's point evinces a certain kind of *epistemic opportunism* in the defence of an akratic agent: luckily for the agent, she has mistaken her own preferences. This is opportunism, because it wouldn't occur to us to make such an ascription, prying apart avowed from true preferences, unless one were antecedently convinced (as in the case of Huck Finn) that the agent had *done the right thing*. For what other motive, in the face of the agent's explicit avowal, could there be for thus rehabilitating the akratic act? Such a reassessment is itself not without cost, since it still entails ascribing *some* form of irrationality, namely the inability to bring one's beliefs about one's own preferences into line with those actual preferences themselves.

The point can be clarified by considering the converse case: suppose you are always *enkratic:* you do always (and infuriatingly) just what your avowed preferences warrant. Armed with McIntyre's insight, I can impugn your every act. The very smoothness of that surface betrays you: no one could have such constant harmony between their values and their every choice! *Your whole life is inauthentic!* Why not? Well, because the issue of akrasia only arises

292 / Ronald de Sousa

if there is a disturbing factor, an apparent discrepancy. It arises, as in the case of Huck Finn, because there is an issue about the morality, that is about the overall value, of his act. But that involves an axiological judgement, typically embodied in an emotional reaction.

A similar message of rehabilitation is conveyed by Luc Bovens (1999), elaborating on a charming 'cure for akrasia' proposed by Roy Sorensen (1997). Sorensen's idea was this. First, send me $1,000 in trust. Whenever you are about to commit an akratic act, let me know and I will refund your $1,000. The act will then be rescued from akrasia, providing the value of *the act plus $1,000* is greater than the value of the alternative act. (If it is likely not to, then you had better invest more at the first stage.) The moral that Bovens draws is that we seem to have a second-order attitude which favours resistance to weak will, inasmuch as we tend to seek, whenever we feel conflicted, ways of struggling against 'temptation'. But why not instead take 'temptations' as indications of our true natural preferences, and use them to transform our second-level preferences? Is this not, Bovens asks, just a sort of puritanical prejudice? In assessing what is and what isn't akratic, we need to assess the contrary values to which the agent is apparently committed by the act on the one hand and its repudiation on the other. What are at stake here are not just opposed desires, but *attitudes*. And while the criteria for contrariety of desires are already somewhat murky (cf. de Sousa 1974), the criteria for contrariety of attitudes or emotions are even more obscure. So much emerged from the antinomies that arise from the divergent attitudes about death, past happiness, postponement of satisfaction, and future-discounting.

These examples have been offered in the hope of making clear what exactly might be meant by the claim that emotions are sometimes paradoxical in a *sui generis* sense. Just as the epistemic and strategic can move to swallow one another up, however, one might attempt to show that the axiological can also be swallowed up by one or the other of the standard norms. Fully to deploy the reasons for rejecting this suggestion would take us too far afield. But before turning to the somewhat pessimistic considerations that will form my conclusion, I want rather dogmatically to sketch the main reasons for thinking that the attempt to reduce the axiological either to strategic or to epistemic rationality must fail.

For anyone who sympathizes with the view that emotions have a biological aspect and arise from functional capacities, there is an obvious temptation to think an emotion justified just in case it is practically useful. Frank's conception of deterrence cited above illustrates this nicely: the very irrationality of emotions of rage and indignation is the source of their utility as deterrents, and we might therefore say that *precisely by virtue of their irrationality* they are strategically rational. But the reason this is not persuasive as a reduction is that it is simply irrelevant to the question of their *axiological* appropriateness. In this respect appropriateness is just like truth: sometimes it may be pragmatically counter-productive, but that only establishes that it is strategically irrational, not that such strategic irrationality suffices to convict it of inappropriateness in its own terms.

Precisely because of this parallel with truth, the claim of the epistemic might seem stronger. If emotions are indeed (as I have assumed but not here attempted to argue) *perceptions of value* (Tappolet 2000), are they not simply true or false, as other perceptions are, according to whether or not they represent those values correctly? In one sense, this is unobjectionable. But it is also trivial, in the sense that while it can be agreed that emotions are true if they correctly apprehend evaluative facts, this says nothing about whether the 'facts' in question are significantly different from other sorts of 'facts'. In my own ongoing attempt to make sense of emotional truth, I have argued that the sort of truth applicable to emotions—the sort of 'facts' to which they relate—is indeed significantly different from the sort of truth typically ascribed to propositional or 'factual' beliefs (de Sousa 2002). The main reason is that each emotion provides its own conditions of appropriateness, or 'formal object', in terms of which its success or failure must be assessed. This is, in all cases, different from the criterion of truth as *semantic satisfaction* which constitutes the formal object, or condition of epistemic success, for ordinary propositional beliefs. In this more interesting sense, then, in which the notion of emotional truth is not trivial, it is also quite distinct from the notion of truth ordinarily dealt with in epistemology. The present chapter is intended to exemplify more concretely some of the ways emotions can give rise to paradoxes and antinomies that are not reducible to those with which traditional epistemology is accustomed to dealing.

Paradoxical Emotions: Some Biological Sources of Disharmony

In the past I have suggested three candidates for what I called 'basic tragedies of life', which I defined as involving 'a necessary condition of a fundamental good, where that condition itself conflicts directly with the enjoyment or the

294 / Ronald de Sousa

perpetuation of that good' (de Sousa 1987: 328–31). The three are *death*, *solidarity*, and *biography*. Death brings life, and therefore meaningful life, to an end, yet death is the very condition of the meaningfulness of life. Our inescapable solidarity with the social context in which we live is what makes it possible for each person to develop genuine individuality; yet it also makes possible and perhaps even necessary the existence of conflict between society and the individual. Finally, the values we espouse typically aspire to universality and objectivity; yet the psychological possibility of their acquisition depends on the specific details of our upbringing. The necessary force of the categorical imperative, if you subscribe to it, is but a contingent consequence of your biography.

In all three cases, my claim was that the status of the paradox was *ontological*, in the sense of arising not from some internal characteristic of the emotional disposition, nor from some remediable malfunction or maladaptation of the disposition to its context, but from some deeper necessary fact about the human situation.

That claim might well be overblown. I might now prefer to reconstrue this alleged metaphysical necessity in terms of constraints pertaining to our psychological dispositions and their biological origins. For example, the fact of death constitutes a 'tragedy' in my sense only on the assumption that one has a certain attitude to it. Suppose I espouse a purely Epicurean attitude: then I effectively cease to care one way or another about death. Death ceases to give meaning to life, and it ceases to take it away. I might then claim that fear of death is a kind of *perversion*: a sentiment which is perhaps explicable in terms of certain mechanisms, but not one for which any supportable rationale can be constructed (de Sousa forthcoming). Conceding that fear of death exists regardless, one might explain it in terms of its stimulating effect on organisms threatened with perishing before they had a chance to reproduce. Manifestly such an explanation would fall short of a justification; yet it might be sufficient to block an objectivist claim about the uniquely *appropriate* attitude to death.

The alleged tragedies of solidarity and of biography could be dismissed in a similar spirit. The very whiff of paradox that attends my attitude to society, or my attitude to the objectivity and to the origin of my moral values, should be sufficient to motivate me to stop worrying about either. Why not espouse wholeheartedly my embeddedness in society? (When communitarians urge me to do this, is not the frisson of repulsion this injunction arouses in me merely a manifestation of my own irrationality?) And as for the objectivity

On *Sui Generis* Emotional Irrationality / 295

of my values, the attitudinally correct stance here is surely that of *irony* in Rorty's sense (R. Rorty 1979): These are my values, and I stand by them—but I might be wrong, and what's more I might be *shown* to be wrong, in a way that might carry conviction not merely with others but with myself as well.

These observations have the apparent effect of casting doubt on the suggestion that we have any access to objective standards of emoting and therefore of apprehending value through emotion. This scepticism might seem vindicated in the light of a number of biological factors that seem calculated to promote disharmony in our emotional life.

First, organ design, including the design of brain functions, is constrained by the nature of adaptation by natural selection, which of necessity is a kind of 'tinkering'.[14] Our emotions have been cobbled together at different times in response to different selective pressures. As a result, our most basic emotional capacities are very likely to be relatively independent modules, often driven by unrelated biological needs (Cosmides and Tooby 2000; Ledoux 2000; Panksepp 1998). There is no reason to think that they will work harmoniously together, any more than we can hope that the need to flee an enemy will never interfere with a peaceful digestion.

Secondly, most biologists have tended to agree that group selection can be assigned only a minimal role in the explanation of our emotional dispositions. This entails that selfish motives will frequently conflict with group interests (defined either as the sum of the interests of other members of the group, or in some other way that might appeal to emergent group interests). That, in turn, entails that the dispositions fostered by biology are likely to conflict with those nurtured (historically if not genetically) by the constraints of group interaction.

Thirdly, constraints present in the environment of evolutionary adaptation do not necessarily correspond to those that affect contemporary life. Vestigial emotions, analogues of our vestigial appendix, might conflict with more currently functional ones.

Fourthly, some of our dispositions may have their origins in the peculiar features of 'Baldwinian selection'. This has recently given rise to a variety of interpretations.[15] The Baldwin effect was originally conceived as a way to explain certain Lamarckian appearances in strictly Darwinian terms. In its

---

[14] This useful term was first coined by François Jacob (Jacob 1976).

[15] See Baldwin 1896, Richards 1987, and for a recent account Dennett 1991: 184–7. The most compelling interpretation of Baldwinian selection is in Deacon 1997: 322–34. The remarks in the text are inspired by this last account.

most general form it consists in a feedback loop that begins with non-instinctive behaviour, bringing about a change in environment, which change, in turn, leads to new selective pressures that favour genetic dispositions for certain types of behaviour. When the behaviour at the end of this loop is of the same type as the behaviour at the beginning, we may have something that looks rather like an episode of Lamarckian evolution, since it will actually be the case that a particular (group of) organisms' *choosing* a certain mode of behaviour can ultimately lead to a predisposition for that type of behaviour to be coded in the genes. *Sexual selection*, which involves a positive feedback loop in which the hypertrophy of a certain trait results from the (random or functional) mate's preference for the trait, can be seen as a special case of Baldwinian evolution. It favours the survival value of the trait, by favouring the predisposition to choose it on the part of the mate. In its full generality, the Baldwin effect merely records the fact that *behaviour can influence genes by affecting the environment in which selection takes place.* The indirect character of the influence will usually guarantee that the results will be entirely unpredictable, so that what the Baldwin effect actually does is take the evolution of behaving organisms on a novel course which may for a time look as if it has a direction. Notoriously, that 'direction' may be maladaptive: sexual selection need not result in any trait that is in the ordinary sense adaptive, and that is generally true of other forms of Baldwinian evolution. For my purposes here, the interest of the Baldwin effect lies in the fact that at the level of species evolution it presents a particularly vivid example of the extreme *contingency* and unpredictability of biological change. Yet from the point of view of a given organism in specific circumstances, the constraints stemming from Baldwinian selection are just as rigid as any other strictly compulsory hereditary trait or any ineluctable environmental constraint. The result is that Baldwinian evolution could have saddled us with disparate emotional propensities unlikely to be easily harmonized. These could easily exacerbate the arbitrariness and disparity between our different emotional predispositions.

Pessimistic Concluding Remarks

The puzzling cases I have adduced as examples of putative axiological irrationality share three features. First, they all concern emotions and *attitudes*, rather than simple preferences or desires. Secondly, they are specifically concerned with evaluating experience in and through time. Thirdly, they do not appear to be susceptible of being accounted for in terms of a recognizably coherent *authoritative point of view*. On the contrary, as I have illustrated in the last section, our emotional capabilities constitute an anarchic, disparate, and potentially conflicted amalgam of dispositions. Despite the obvious drawbacks of this situation, I have contended that the search for equilibrium—or more modestly accommodation—between the components of this anarchic amalgam is the only game in town. The Humean perspective I have argued for implies that no privileged pragmatic or epistemic vantage point can claim to stand in judgement on the attitudes in question, any more than they are able to arbitrate between themselves. Despite the incoherence apparently built into our emotional capabilities, only they can constitute the ultimate arbiters of our axiological judgements. Emotions remain the last court of appeal in the judgement of the appropriateness of other emotions. At the same time, they are also the last court of appeal in the conflicts between different modes of rationality, strategic and epistemic. The paradoxes and antinomies that characterize our emotions must therefore infect the whole field of our 'ultimate' values.

The view presented here has an important (though hardly novel) political consequence. This is that an education into rationality—and equally, and for similar reasons, an education into the capacity to lead a moral life—must rest, as Aristotle well knew, on an education of the emotions. Needless to say, this view of rationality and morality will condone short cuts, much in the way that Mill points out that one can hardly be expected to calculate the pertinent entry of the Nautical Almanac at every turn of the tiller. But despite the intrinsic incoherence of our fundamental emotional attitudes, the best hope of emotional rationality lies in the broadest possible assessment of our emotions, *by our emotions themselves*, in the light of a comprehensive educated emotional range. The heart of both rationality and morality lies in a holistic assessment of one's emotional dispositions, constantly tested against one another. It therefore becomes crucial that those dispositions be rooted in as comprehensive a set of experiences as possible. The word *partiality* incorporates an inspired pun; for *partiality*, the failure of *impartiality*, has its roots in the inevitably *partial* (that is, piecemeal and incomplete) character of emotional experience. However desirable the ideal of impartiality or comprehensiveness, the biological considerations I have raised make it unlikely that such an ideal can ever be realized. That is no reason not to pursue it.

REFERENCES

ADAMS, ROBERT M. 1985. 'Involuntary Sins'. *Philosophical Review*, 94: 3–31.

AINSLIE, GEORGE. 1992. *Picoeconomics: The Strategic Interaction of Successive Motivational States within the Person*. Cambridge: Cambridge University Press.

—— 2001. *Breakdown of Will*. Cambridge: Cambridge University Press.

ALBRITTON, ROGERS. 1985. 'Freedom of Will and Freedom of Action'. *Proceedings and Addresses of the American Philosophical Association*, 59: 239–51.

ALLISON, HENRY. 1990. *Kant's Theory of Freedom*. New York: Cambridge University Press.

AMERICAN PSYCHIATRIC ASSOCIATION. 2000. *DSM-IV-TR*. <www.psychologynet.org/dsm.html>.

ANSCOMBE, G. E. M. 1963. *Intention* (2nd edn.). Ithaca, NY: Cornell University Press.

—— 1965. 'Thought and Action in Aristotle', in R. Bambrough (ed.), *New Essays on Plato and Aristotle*. London: Routledge & Kegan Paul, 143–58.

ARISTOTLE. 1985. *Nicomachean Ethics*, trans. Terence Irwin. Indianapolis: Hackett.

—— 2002. *Nicomachean Ethics*, trans. (with historical introd.) by Christopher Rowe, philosophical introd. and comm. by Sarah Broadie. Oxford: Oxford University Press.

ARKONOVICH, STEVEN. forthcoming. 'Goals, Wishes, and Reasons for Action', in Tenenbaum forthcoming *b*.

ARPALY, NOMY. 2000. 'On Acting Rationally against One's Best Judgement'. *Ethics*, 110: 488–513.

AUDI, ROBERT. 1979. 'Weakness of Will and Practical Judgement'. *Noûs*, 13: 173–96.

—— 1990. 'Weakness of Will and Rational Action'. *Australasian Journal of Philosophy*, 68: 270–81.

AUSTIN, JOHN. 1869. *Lectures on Jurisprudence; or, The Philosophy of Positive Law*. London.

BACH, KENT. 1995. 'Review of George Ainslie's *Picoeconomics*'. *Philosophy and Phenomenological Research*, 55: 981–3.

BALDWIN, JAMES MARK. 1896. 'Consciousness and Evolution'. *Psychological Review*, 3: 300–8.

BANDURA, ALBERT. 1992. 'Exercise of Personal Agency through the Self-Efficacy Mechanism', in R. Schwarzer (ed.), *Self-Efficacy*. Bristol, PA: Taylor & Francis, 3–38.

BARGH, JOHN A., and CHARTRAND, TANYA L. 1999. 'The Unbearable Automaticity of Being'. *American Psychologist*, 54: 462–79.

References / 299

BAUMEISTER, R., HEATHERTON, T., and TICE, D. 1994. *Losing Control*. San Diego: Academic Press.

—— BRATSLAVSKY, E., MURAVEN, M., and TICE, D. 1998. 'Ego-Depletion: Is the Active Self a Limited Resource?' *Journal of Personality and Social Psychology*, 74: 1252–65.

BENNETT, JONATHAN. 1974. 'The Conscience of Huckleberry Finn'. *Philosophy*, 49: 123–34.

BINMORE, KEN. 1994. *Game Theory and the Social Contract*. Cambridge, MA: MIT Press.

BLACKBURN, SIMON. 2001. 'Group Minds and Expressive Harm'. *Maryland Law Review*, 60: 467–91.

BLOCK, NED. 1981. 'Psychologism and Behaviorism'. *Philosophical Review*, 90: 5–43.

BOLTON, GARY E. 1991. 'A Comparative Model of Bargaining: Theory and Evidence'. *American Economic Review*, 81: 1096–1136.

BOVENS, LUC. 1999. 'The Two Faces of Akratics Anonymous'. *Analysis*, 59: 230–6.

BRADDON-MITCHELL, DAVID, and JACKSON, FRANK. 1996. *The Philosophy of Mind and Cognition*. Oxford: Basil Blackwell.

BRANDOM, ROBERT B. 1994. *Making it Explicit: Reasoning, Representing, and Discursive Commitment*. Cambridge, MA: Harvard University Press.

—— 2000. *Articulating Reasons: An Introduction to Inferentialism*. Cambridge, MA: Harvard University Press.

BRATMAN, MICHAEL. 1979. 'Practical Reasoning and Weakness of the Will'. *Noûs*, 13: 153–71.

—— 1987. *Intentions, Plans, and Practical Reason*. Cambridge, MA: Harvard University Press.

—— 1992. 'Practical Reasoning and Acceptance in a Context', in Bratman 1999: 15–34.

—— 1995. 'Planning and Temptation', in Bratman 1999: 35–57.

—— 1996. 'Identification, Decision, and Treating as a Reason', in Bratman 1999: 185–206.

—— 1998. 'Toxin, Temptation and the Stability of Intention', in Bratman 1999: 58–90.

—— 1999. *Faces of Intention: Selected Essays on Intention and Agency*. Cambridge: Cambridge University Press.

BRENNAN, GEOFFREY. 2001. 'Collective Coherence?' *International Review of Law and Economics*, 21: 197–211.

BRENTANO, FRANZ. 1889/1969. *The Origin of our Knowledge of Right and Wrong*, trans. Roderick M. Chisholm and Elisabeth H. Schneewind. London: Routledge & Kegan Paul.

BRINK, DAVID O. 1997. 'Moral Motivation'. *Ethics*, 108: 4–32.

BROAD, C. D. 1954. 'Emotion and Sentiment', in *Broad's Critical Essays in Moral Philosophy*, ed. David R. Cheney. London: Allen & Unwin, 1971, 283–301.

300 / References

BROOME, JOHN. 1991. *Weighing Goods*. Oxford: Basil Blackwell.

—— 1994. 'Discounting the Future'. *Philosophy and Public Affairs*, 23: 128–56.

—— 1999. *Ethics out of Economics*. Cambridge: Cambridge University Press.

—— 2001. 'Are Intentions Reasons? And How should we Cope with Incommensurable Values?', in C. Morris and A. Ripstein (eds.), *Practical Rationality and Preference: Essays for David Gauthier*. Cambridge: Cambridge University Press, 98–120.

BUSS, SARAH. 1997. 'Weakness of Will'. *Pacific Philosophical Quarterly*, 78: 13–44.

—— 1999. 'What Practical Reasoning must be if we Act for our Own Reasons'. *Australasian Journal of Philosophy*, 77: 399–421.

—— and OVERTON, LEE (eds.). 2002. *Contours of Agency: Essays on Themes from Harry Frankfurt*. Cambridge, MA: MIT Press.

CARROLL, LEWIS. 1895. 'What the Tortoise Said to Achilles'. *Mind*, 4: 278–80.

CARVER, CHARLES S., and SCHEIER, MICHAEL F. 1998. *On the Self-Regulation of Behaviour*. Cambridge: Cambridge University Press.

CEMERER, COLIN, and THALER, RICHARD. 1995. 'Ultimatums, Dictators and Manners'. *Journal of Economic Perspectives*, 9: 209–19.

CHAPMAN, BRUCE. 1998. 'Law, Incommensurability, and Conceptually Sequenced Argument'. *University of Pennsylvania Law Review*, 146: 1487–1582.

CHARLTON, WILLIAM. 1988. *Weakness of Will*. Oxford: Basil Blackwell.

CLIFFORD, WILLIAM KINGDON. 1866. 'The Ethics of Belief', in *Lectures and Essays by William Kingdon Clifford*, ed. Leslie Stephen and Frederick Pollock. 2 vols. London: Macmillan, 1879: ii. 177–211.

CODE, LORRAINE. 1987. *Epistemic Responsibility*. Hanover: University Press of New England.

COHEN, L. JONATHAN. 1989. 'Belief and Acceptance'. *Mind*, 98: 367–89.

COPP, DAVID. 1997. 'Belief, Reason, and Motivation: Michael Smith's *The Moral Problem*'. *Ethics*, 108: 33–54.

COSMIDES, LEDA, and TOOBY, JOHN. 2000. 'Evolutionary Psychology and the Emotions', in Lewis and Haviland-Jones 2000: 91–115.

CULLITY, GARRETT, and GAUT, BERYS (eds.). 1997a. *Ethics and Practical Reason*. Oxford: Clarendon Press.

—— —— 1997b. 'Introduction', in Cullity and Gaut 1997a: 1–27.

DALGLEISH, T., and POWER, M. (eds.). 1999. *Handbook of Cognition and Emotion*. Chichester: John Wiley.

DAMASIO, A. R. 1994. *Descartes' Error*. New York: Avon Books.

DANCY, JONATHAN. 1993. *Moral Reasons*. Oxford: Basil Blackwell.

—— 1995. 'Arguments from Illusion'. *Philosophical Quarterly*, 45: 421–38.

—— 2000a. 'The Particularist's Progress', in Brad Hooker and Margaret Little (eds.), *Moral Particularism*. Oxford: Clarendon Press, 130–56.

—— 2000b. *Practical Reality*. Oxford: Oxford University Press.

References / 301

Danto, Arthur. 1965. 'Basic Actions', in A. White (ed.), *The Philosophy of Action*. Oxford: Oxford University Press, 1968, 43–58.

D'Arms, Justin, and Jacobson, Daniel. 2000a. 'The Moralistic Fallacy: On the "Appropriateness" of Emotions'. *Philosophy and Phenomenological Research*, 61: 65–90.

—— —— 2000b. 'Sentiment and Value'. *Ethics*, 110: 722–48.

Darwall, Stephen. 1995. *The British Moralists and the Internal 'Ought': 1640–1740*. Cambridge: Cambridge University Press.

Davidson, Donald. 1963. 'Actions, Reasons, and Causes', in Davidson 1980: 3–19.

—— 1970a. 'How is Weakness of the Will Possible?', in Davidson 1980: 21–42.

—— 1970b. 'Mental Events', in Davidson 1980: 207–27.

—— 1978. 'Intending', in Davidson 1980: 83–102.

—— 1980. *Essays on Actions and Events*. Oxford: Oxford University Press.

—— 1982. 'Paradoxes of Irrationality', in Richard Wollheim and James Hopkins (eds.), *Philosophical Essays on Freud*. Cambridge: Cambridge University Press, 289–305.

Deacon, Terrence W. 1997. *The Symbolic Species: The Coevolution of Language and the Brain*. New York: W. W. Norton.

DeHelian, Laura, and McClennen, Edward. 1993. 'Planning and the Stability of Intention: A Comment'. *Minds and Machines*, 3: 319–33.

Dennett, Daniel C. 1984. 'Cognitive Wheels: The Frame Problem of AI', in Christopher Hookway (ed.), *Minds, Machines and Evolution: Philosophical Studies*. Cambridge: Cambridge University Press, 129–51.

—— 1987. *The Intentional Stance*. Cambridge, MA: MIT Press.

—— 1991. *Consciousness Explained*. Boston: Little, Brown.

Descartes, René. 1641a/1967. 'Arguments Demonstrating the Existence of God and the Distinction between Soul and Body, drawn up in Geometrical Fashion', in *The Philosophical Works of Descartes*, trans. Elizabeth S. Haldane and G. R. T. Ross. 2 vols. London: Cambridge University Press, ii. 52–9.

—— 1641b/1984. 'Author's Replies to the Sixth Set of Objections', in Descartes 1984: ii. 285–301.

—— 1641c/1984. *Meditations on First Philosophy*, in Descartes 1984: ii. 1–62.

—— 1649/1984. *The Passions of the Soul*, in Descartes 1984: i. 325–404.

—— 1984. *The Philosophical Writings of Descartes*, trans. John Cottingham, Robert Stoothoff, and Dugald Murdoch. 3 vols. Cambridge: Cambridge University Press.

de Sousa, Ronald. 1974. 'The Good and the True'. *Mind*, 83: 534–51.

—— 1987. *The Rationality of Emotion*. Cambridge, MA: MIT Press.

—— 1997. 'What Can't we Do with Economics? Some Comments on George Ainslie's Picoeconomics'. *Journal of Philosophical Research*, 22: 197–209.

—— 2000. 'Deux Maximes de rationalité émotive', in E. Angehrn and B. Baertschi (eds.), *Emotion und Vernunft; Émotion et Rationalité*, Studia Philosophica, 59. Bern: Paul Haupt, 15–32.

302 / References

DE SOUSA, RONALD. 2002. 'Emotional Truth'. *Proceedings of the Aristotelian Society*, suppl. vol. 76: 247–63.

—— forthcoming. 'Perversion and Death'. *The Monist*.

DREIER, JAMES. 1994. 'Perspectives on the Normativity of Ethics'. *Noûs*, 28: 514–25.

—— 1997. 'Humean Doubts about the Practical Justification of Morality', in Cullity and Gaut 1997a: 81–99.

—— 2000. 'Dispositions and Fetishes: Externalist Models of Moral Motivation'. *Philosophy and Phenomenological Research*, 61: 619–38.

DUMMETT, MICHAEL. 1991. *The Logical Basis of Metaphysics*. Cambridge, MA: Harvard University Press.

ELSTER, JON. 1979. *Ulysses and the Sirens: Studies in Rationality and Irrationality*. Cambridge: Cambridge University Press; Paris: Éditions de la Maison des Sciences de l'Homme.

—— 1983. *Sour Grapes*. Cambridge: Cambridge University Press.

—— 1999. *Alchemies of the Mind: Rationality and the Emotions*. Cambridge: Cambridge University Press.

EVANS, GARETH. 1982. *The Varieties of Reference*, ed. John, McDowell. Oxford: Oxford University Press.

FAUCHER, LUC, and TAPPOLET, CHRISTINE. 2002. 'Fear and the Focus of Attention'. *Consciousness and Emotion*, 3: 105–44.

FISCHER, JOHN MARTIN, and RAVIZZA, MARK. 1998. *Responsibility and Control: A Theory of Moral Responsibility*. Cambridge: Cambridge University Press.

FODOR, JERRY. 1983. *The Modularity of Mind*. Cambridge, MA: MIT Press.

FOOT, PHILIPPA. 1995. 'Does Moral Subjectivism Rest on a Mistake?' *Oxford Journal of Legal Studies*, 15: 1–14.

—— 2001. *Natural Goodness*. Oxford: Clarendon Press.

FRANK, ROBERT H. 1988. *Passion within Reason*. New York: W. W. Norton.

FRANKFURT, HARRY. 1969. 'Alternate Possibilities and Moral Responsibility', in Frankfurt 1988: 1–10.

—— 1987. 'Identification and Wholeheartedness', in Frankfurt 1988: 159–76.

—— 1988. *The Importance of What we Care About*. Cambridge: Cambridge University Press.

FUMERTON, RICHARD. 1995. *Metaepistemology and Skepticism*. Lanham, MD: Rowman & Littlefield.

GAUTHIER, DAVID. 1985. 'The Unity of Reason: A Subversive Reinterpretation of Kant'. *Ethics*, 96: 74–88.

—— 1986. *Morals by Agreement*. Oxford: Clarendon Press.

—— 1994. 'Assure and Threaten'. *Ethics*, 104: 690–721.

—— 1997. 'Resolute Choice and Rational Deliberation: A Critique and a Defense'. *Noûs*, 31: 1–25.

GEACH, P. T. 1956. 'Good and Evil'. *Analysis*, 17: 33–42.

References / 303

GIGERENZER, GERD, TODD, PETER M., and ABC RESEARCH GROUP. 1999. *Simple Heuristics that Make us Smart*. New York: Oxford University Press.

GILBERT, MARGARET. 1989. *On Social Facts*. Princeton: Princeton University Press.

GOLDIE, PETER. 2000. *The Emotions: A Philosophical Explanation*. Oxford: Oxford University Press.

GOLLWITZER, PETER M. 1996. 'The Volitional Benefits of Planning', in Gollwitzer and Bargh 1996: 287–312.

——— and BARGH, JOHN A. (eds.). 1996. *The Psychology of Action*. New York: Guilford Press.

GOODMAN, NELSON. 1983. *Fact, Fiction, and Forecast* (4th edn.). Cambridge, MA: Harvard University Press.

GREENSPAN, PATRICIA S. 1988. *Emotions and Reasons: An Inquiry into Emotional Justification*. New York: Routledge.

GRIFFITHS, PAUL E. 1997. *What Emotions Really Are*. Chicago: University of Chicago Press.

GÜTH, WERNER, and TIETZ, REINHARD. 1990. 'Ultimatum Bargaining Behavior: A Survey and Comparison of Experimental Results'. *Journal of Economic Psychology*, 11: 417–49.

HAACK, SUSAN. 1976. 'The Justification of Deduction'. *Mind*, 85: 112–19.

HARE, R. M. 1952. *The Language of Morals*. Oxford: Clarendon Press.

——— 1963. *Freedom and Reason*. Oxford: Clarendon Press.

——— 1992. 'Weakness of Will', in L. Baker (ed.), *Encyclopedia of Ethics*. New York: Garland, 1304–7.

HEATH, JOSEPH. 2001. 'Rational Choice with Deontic Constraints'. *Canadian Journal of Philosophy*, 31: 361–88.

HEIL, JOHN. 1983. 'Doxastic Agency'. *Philosophical Studies*, 43: 355–64.

HENRICH, JOSEPH, BOYD, ROBERT, BOWLES, SAMUEL, CAMERER, COLIN, FEHR, ERNST, GINTIS, HERBERT, and McELREATH, RICHARD. 2001. 'In Search of Homo Economicus: Behavioral Experiments in 15 Small-Scale Societies'. *American Economic Review*, 91/2: 73–8.

HERMAN, BARBARA. 2002. 'Bootstrapping', in Buss and Overton 2002: 253–74.

HOFFMAN, DONALD. 1998. *Visual Intelligence*. New York: W. W. Norton.

HOLTON, RICHARD. 1999. 'Intention and Weakness of Will'. *Journal of Philosophy*, 96: 241–62.

HORNSBY, JENNIFER. 1998. *Simple-Mindedness*. Cambridge, MA: Harvard University Press.

HUME, DAVID. 1740/1978. *A Treatise of Human Nature*, ed. L. A. Selby-Bigge (2nd edn.). Oxford: Oxford University Press.

——— 1777/1975. *Enquiry Concerning Human Understanding; A Letter from a Gentleman to his Friend in Edinburgh*, ed. Eric Steinberg. Indianapolis: Hackett.

HURLEY, SUSAN. 1989. *Natural Reasons*. New York: Oxford University Press.

HUTCHESON, FRANCIS. 1738/1971. *An Inquiry into the Original of our Ideas of Beauty and Virtue*. Hildesheim: Georg Olms.

304 / References

IGNATIUS of LOYOLA. 1996. *Spiritual Exercises*, in *Personal Writings*, trans. with introds. and notes by Joseph A. Munitiz and Philip Endean. London: Penguin, 283–358.

IRWIN, TERENCE H. 1992. 'Who Discovered the Will?' *Philosophical Perspectives*, 6: 453–73.

JACKSON, FRANK. 1984. 'Weakness of Will'. *Mind*, 93: 1–18.

JACOB, FRANÇOIS. 1976. *The Logic of Life: A History of Heredity*, trans. Betty Spillman. New York: Vintage.

JAHANSHAHI, M., and FRITH, C. 1998. 'Willed Action and its Impairments'. *Cognitive Neuropsychology*, 15: 483–533.

JAMES, WILLIAM. 1896/1979. 'The Will to Believe', in his *The Will to Believe and Other Essays in Popular Philosophy*, ed. Frederick H. Burkhardt, Fredson Bowers, and Ignas K. Skrupskelis. Cambridge, MA: Harvard University Press, 13–33.

JEFFREY, RICHARD C. 1983. *The Logic of Decision* (2nd edn.). Chicago: University of Chicago Press.

JOHNSTON, MARK. 1993. 'Objectivity Refigured: Pragmatism without Verificationism', in John Haldane and Crispin Wright (eds.), *Reality, Representation and Projection*. Oxford: Oxford University Press, 85–130.

—— 2001. 'The Authority of Affect'. *Philosophy and Phenomenological Research*, 63: 181–214.

JONES, KAREN. forthcoming. 'Emotion, Weakness of Will, and the Normative Conception of Agency', in A. Hatzimoysis (ed.), *Philosophy and the Emotions*. Cambridge: Cambridge University Press.

JOYCE, JAMES M. 1999. *Foundations of Causal Decision Theory*. Cambridge: Cambridge University Press.

KAHN, CHARLES. 1985. 'Discovering the Will: From Aristotle to Augustine', in J. M. Dillon and A. A. Long (eds.), *The Question of 'Eclecticism'*. Berkeley: University of California Press, 234–59.

KAHNEMAN, DANIEL. 2000. *Evaluation by Moments: Past and Future*, in Daniel Kahneman and Amos Tversky (eds.), *Choices, Values, and Frames*. Cambridge: Cambridge University Press; New York: Russell Sage Foundation, 693–708.

—— SLOVIC, PAUL, and TVERSKY, AMOS (eds.). 1982. *Judgment under Uncertainty: Heuristics and Biases*. Cambridge: Cambridge University Press.

KANE, ROBERT. 1996. *The Significance of Free Will*. New York: Oxford University Press.

KANT, IMMANUEL. 1785. *Grundlegung zur Metaphysik der Sitten*. Riga: Hartknoch.

—— 1785/1996. *Groundwork of the Metaphysics of Morals*, in Kant 1996: 37–108.

—— 1788. *Kritik der praktischen Vernunft*. Riga: Hartknoch.

—— 1788/1956. *Critique of Practical Reason*, trans. Lewis White Beck. New York: Macmillan.

—— 1788/1996. *Critique of Practical Reason*, in Kant 1996: 133–271.

—— 1797/1991. *The Metaphysics of Morals*, trans. Mary Gregor. New York: Cambridge University Press.

—— 1797/1996. *The Metaphysics of Morals*, in Kant 1996: 353–603.

—— 1996. *Practical Philosophy*, trans. and ed. Mary Gregor. Cambridge: Cambridge University Press.

KARNIOL, R., and MILLER, D. 1983. 'Why not Wait? A Cognitive Model of Self-Imposed Delay Termination'. *Journal of Personality and Social Psychology*, 45: 935–42.

KAVKA, GREGORY. 1983. 'The Toxin Puzzle'. *Analysis*, 43: 33–6.

KENNETT, JEANETTE. 2001. *Agency and Responsibility: A Common-Sense Moral Psychology*. Oxford: Clarendon Press.

—— and SMITH, MICHAEL. 1994. 'Philosophy and Commonsense: The Case of Weakness of Will', in Michaelis Michael and John O'Leary-Hawthorne (eds.), *Philosophy in Mind: The Place of Philosophy in the Study of Mind*. Dordrecht: Kluwer Academic Publishers, 141–57.

—— —— 1996. 'Frog and Toad Lose Control'. *Analysis*, 56: 63–73.

KORNHAUSER, LEWIS A. 1992a. 'Modelling Collegial Courts. I. Path-Dependence'. *International Review of Law and Economics*, 12: 169–85.

—— 1992b. 'Modelling Collegial Courts. II. Legal Doctrine'. *Journal of Law, Economics and Organization*, 8: 441–70.

—— and SAGER, LAWRENCE G. 1986. 'Unpacking the Court'. *Yale Law Journal*, 96: 82–118.

—— —— 1993. 'The One and the Many: Adjudication in Collegial Courts'. *California Law Review*, 81: 1–59.

KORSGAARD, CHRISTINE M. 1983. 'Two Distinctions of Goodness', in Korsgaard 1996a: 249–74.

—— 1986a. 'Kant's Formula of Humanity', in Korsgaard 1996a: 106–32.

—— 1986b. 'Skepticism about Practical Reason', in Korsgaard 1996a: 311–34.

—— 1989. 'Kant's Analysis of Obligation: The Argument of *Groundwork I*', in Korsgaard 1996a: 43–76.

—— 1996a. *Creating the Kingdom of Ends*. Cambridge: Cambridge University Press.

—— 1996b. *The Sources of Normativity*. Cambridge: Cambridge University Press.

—— 1997. 'The Normativity of Instrumental Reason', in Cullity and Gaut 1997a: 215–54.

—— 1999. 'Self-Constitution in the Ethics of Plato and Kant'. *Journal of Ethics*, 3: 1–29.

LAWRENCE, GAVIN. 1995. 'The Rationality of Morality', in Rosalind Hursthouse, Gavin Lawrence, and Warren Quinn (eds.), *Virtues and Reasons: Philippa Foot and Moral Theory: Essays in Honour of Philippa Foot*. Oxford: Clarendon Press, 89–147.

LAZAR, ARIELA. 1999. 'Akrasia and the Principle of Continence, or What the Tortoise would Say to Achilles', in Lewis Edwin Hahn (ed.), *The Philosophy of Donald Davidson*, Library of Living Philosophers, 27. Chicago: Open Court, 381–401.

LEDOUX, JOSEPH E. 2000. 'Emotional Circuits in the Brain'. *Annual Review of Neuroscience*, 23: 155–84.

306 / References

LeDoux, Joseph E., and Phelps, Elizabeth A. 2000. 'Emotional Networks in the Brain', in Lewis and Haviland-Jones 2000: 157–72.

Lewis, David. 1969. *Convention.* Cambridge, MA: Harvard University Press.

—— 1974. 'Radical Interpretation'. *Synthese,* 23: 331–44.

—— 1979. 'Counterfactual Dependence and Time's Arrow', in Lewis 1986: 32–66.

—— 1981. 'Are we Free to Break the Laws?', in Lewis 1986: 291–8.

—— 1986. *Philosophical Papers Volume II.* Oxford: Oxford University Press.

—— 1997. 'Finkish Dispositions'. *Philosophical Quarterly,* 47: 143–58.

Lewis, Michael, and Haviland-Jones, Jeannette M. (eds.). 2000. *Handbook of Emotions* (2nd edn.). New York: Guilford Press.

List, Christian, and Pettit, Philip. forthcoming. 'Aggregating Sets of Judgments: Two Impossibility Results Compared'. *Synthese.*

——————2002. 'The Aggregation of Sets of Judgments: An Impossibility Result'. *Economics and Philosophy,* 18: 89–110.

Lockard, Joan S., and Paulhus, Delroy L. (eds.). 1988. *Self-Deception: An Adaptive Mechanism?* Englewood Cliffs, NJ: Prentice Hall.

Locke, John. 1690/1975. *An Essay Concerning Human Understanding,* ed. P. H. Nidditch. Oxford: Clarendon Press.

Luce, R. Duncan, and Raiffa, Howard. 1957. *Games and Decisions.* New York: Dover Publications.

McCabe, Mary Margaret. 1994. *Plato's Individuals.* Princeton: Princeton University Press.

McCann, Hugh. 1974. 'Volition and Basic Action', in McCann 1998: 75–93.

—— 1986. 'Intrinsic Intentionality', in McCann 1998: 127–46.

—— 1998. *The Works of Agency: On Human Action, Will, and Freedom.* Ithaca, NY: Cornell University Press.

McClennen, Edward F. 1990. *Rationality and Dynamic Choice.* Cambridge: Cambridge University Press.

McDowell, John. 1979. 'Virtue and Reason', in McDowell 1998b: 50–73.

—— 1985a. 'Functionalism and Anomalous Monism', in McDowell 1998b: 325–40.

—— 1985b. 'Values and Secondary Qualities', in T. Honderich (ed.), *Morality and Objectivity: A Tribute to John Mackie.* London: Routledge & Kegan Paul, 110–29.

—— 1995. 'Might there be External Reasons?', in McDowell 1998b: 95–111.

—— 1998a. 'Having the World in View'. *Journal of Philosophy,* 95: 431–50.

—— 1998b. *Mind, Value, and Reality.* Cambridge, MA: Harvard University Press.

McGeer, Victoria, and Pettit, Philip. 2002. 'The Self-Regulating Mind'. *Language and Communication,* 22: 281–99.

MacIntosh, Duncan. 1991. 'Preference's Progress: Rational Self-Alteration and the Rationality of Morality'. *Dialogue: Canadian Philosophical Review,* 30: 3–32.

—— 1992. 'Preference-Revision and the Paradoxes of Instrumental Rationality'. *Canadian Journal of Philosophy*, 22: 503–30.

—— 1993. 'Persons and the Satisfaction of Preferences: Problems in the Rational Kinematics of Values'. *Journal of Philosophy*, 90: 163–80.

—— 1998. 'Categorically Rational Preferences and the Structure of Morality', in Peter Danielson (ed.), *Modeling Rationality, Morality and Evolution*, Vancouver Studies in Cognitive Science, 7. New York: Oxford University Press, 282–301.

—— 2001. 'Prudence and the Reasons of Rational Persons'. *Australasian Journal of Philosophy*, 79: 346–65.

—— 2002. 'Moral Paradox and the Mutability of the Good', unpub. paper.

MCINTYRE, ALISON. 1990. 'Is Akratic Action Always Irrational?', in Owen Flanagan and Amélie Rorty (eds.), *Identity, Character, and Morality: Essays in Moral Psychology*. Cambridge, MA: MIT Press, 379–400.

MAGILL, KEVIN. 1997. *Freedom and Experience*. Houndmills, Basingstoke: Macmillan Press.

MAHER, PATRICK. 1993. *Betting on Theories*. Cambridge: Cambridge University Press.

MARTIN, C. B. 1994. 'Dispositions and Conditionals'. *Philosophical Quarterly*, 44: 1–8.

MARWELL, GERALD, and AMES, RUTH E. 1981. 'Economists Free Ride, Does Anyone Else?' *Journal of Public Economics*, 15: 295–310.

MATTHEWS, G., and WELLS, A. 1999. 'The Cognitive Science of Attention and Emotion', in Dalgleish and Power 1999: 171–92.

MEIJERS, ANTHONIE. 1994. *Speech Acts, Communication and Collective Intentionality: Beyond Searle's Individualism*. Utrecht: de Jonge.

MEINONG, ALEXIUS. 1917/1972. *On Emotional Presentation*, trans. with introd. by Marie-Luise Schubert Kalsi. Evanston, IL.: Northwestern University Press.

MELE, ALFRED R. 1987. *Irrationality: An Essay on Akrasia, Self-Deception and Self-Control*. Oxford: Oxford University Press.

—— 1995. *Autonomous Agents: From Self-Control to Autonomy*. New York: Oxford University Press.

—— 1996. 'Addiction and Self-Control'. *Behavior and Philosophy*, 24: 99–117.

—— 2000. 'Deciding to Act'. *Philosophical Studies*, 100: 81–108.

—— 2002. 'Akratics and Addicts'. *American Philosophical Quarterly*, 39: 153–68.

MILLER, SEUMAS. 2001. *Social Action: A Teleological Account*. Cambridge: Cambridge University Press.

MISCHEL, WALTER. 1996. 'From Good Intentions to Willpower', in Gollwitzer and Bargh 1996: 197–218.

MOGG, K., and BRADLEY, B. P. 1999. 'Selective Attention and Anxiety: A Cognitive-Motivational Perspective', in Dalgleish and Power 1999: 145–70.

MOORE, G. E. 1903. *Principia Ethica*. Cambridge: Cambridge University Press.

MORAN, RICHARD. 2000. *Authority and Estrangement*. Princeton: Princeton University Press.

308 / References

MULLIGAN, KEVIN. 1998. 'From Appropriate Emotions to Values'. *The Monist*, 81: 161–88.

MURAVEN, M., and BAUMEISTER, R. 2000. 'Self-Regulation and Depletion of Limited Resources: Does Self-Control Resemble a Muscle?' *Psychological Bulletin*, 126: 247–59.

——— and TICE, D. 1999. 'Longitudinal Improvement of Self-Regulation through Practice: Building Self-Control Strength through Repeated Exercise'. *Journal of Social Psychology*, 139: 446–57.

——— TICE, D., and BAUMEISTER, R. 1998. 'Self-Control as a Limited Resource: Regulatory Depletion Patterns'. *Journal of Personality and Social Psychology*, 74: 774–89.

MURPHY, DOMINIC, and STICH, STEPHEN. 2000. 'Darwin in the Madhouse: Evolutionary Psychology and the Classification of Mental Disorders', in Peter Carruthers and Andrew Chamberlain (eds.), *Evolution and the Human Mind: Modularity, Language and Meta-Cognition*. Cambridge: Cambridge University Press, 62–92.

MUSSET, ALFRED DE. 1908. *Les Chefs-d'Œuvres lyriques d'Alfred de Musset: Choix et notice d'Auguste Dorchain*. Paris: Perche.

NAGEL, THOMAS. 1970. *The Possibility of Altruism*. Oxford: Clarendon Press.

——— 1971. 'The Absurd', in his *Mortal Questions*. Cambridge: Cambridge University Press, 1979, 11–23.

NORMORE, CALVIN. 1998. 'Picking and Choosing: Anselm and Ockham on Choice'. *Vivarium*, 36: 23–39.

NOZICK, ROBERT. 1986. 'Newcomb's Problem and Two Principles of Choice', in Nicholas Rescher (ed.), *Essays in Honor of Carl G. Hempel*. Dordrecht: Reidel, 114–46.

——— 1993. *The Nature of Rationality*. Princeton: Princeton University Press.

OGIEN, RUWEN. 2002. 'La Faiblesse de la volonté est-elle toujours irrationnelle?', in Philippe Saltel (ed.), *La Volonté*. Paris: Ellipses, 273–83.

O'SHAUGHNESSY, BRIAN. 1980. *The Will: A Dual Aspect Theory*. 2 vols. Cambridge: Cambridge University Press.

OWENS, DAVID. 2000. *Reason without Freedom*. London: Routledge.

PANKSEPP, JAAK. 1998. *Affective Neuroscience: The Foundations of Human and Animal Emotions*. New York: Oxford University Press.

PARFIT, DEREK. 1984. *Reasons and Persons*. Oxford: Clarendon Press.

PEACOCKE, CHRISTOPHER. 1985. 'Intention and Akrasia', in B. Vermazen and M. B. Hintikka (eds.), *Essays on Davidson, Actions and Events*. Oxford: Clarendon Press, 51–73.

PEARS, DAVID. 1982. 'Motivated Irrationality'. *Proceedings of the Aristotelian Society*, 56: 156–78.

PETTIT, PHILIP. 1993. *The Common Mind: An Essay on Psychology, Society and Politics*. New York: Oxford University Press.

——— 1999. 'A Theory of Normal and Ideal Conditions'. *Philosophical Studies*, 96: 21–44.

—— 2000. 'Non-Consequentialism and Universalizability'. *Philosophical Quarterly*, 50: 175–90.

—— 2001a. *A Theory of Freedom: From the Psychology to the Politics of Agency*. Cambridge: Polity Press; New York: Oxford University Press.

—— 2001b. 'Two Sources of Morality'. *Social Philosophy and Policy*, 18/2: 102–28.

—— 2002. 'Groups with Minds of their Own', in F. Schmitt (ed.), *Socializing Metaphysics*. New York: Rowman & Littlefield.

—— and SMITH, MICHAEL. 1990. 'Backgrounding Desire'. *Philosophical Review*, 99: 565–92.

—— —— 1993. 'Practical Unreason'. *Mind*, 102: 53–80.

—— —— 1996. 'Freedom in Belief and Desire'. *Journal of Philosophy*, 93: 429–49.

PIGOU, A. C. 1920. *The Economics of Welfare*. London: Macmillan.

PINK, THOMAS. 1996. *The Psychology of Freedom*. Cambridge: Cambridge University Press.

PLATO. 1961. *Protagoras*, trans. W. K. C. Guthrie, in *The Collected Dialogues of Plato*, ed. Edith Hamilton and Huntington Cairns. Princeton: Princeton University Press, 308–52.

PUGMIRE, DAVID. 1982. 'Motivated Irrationality'. *Proceedings of the Aristotelian Society*, 56: 179–96.

QUINN, WARREN. 1993. 'Putting Rationality in its Place', in his *Morality and Action*, ed. Philippa Foot. Cambridge: Cambridge University Press, 1994, 228–55.

QUINTON, ANTHONY. 1975. 'Social Objects'. *Proceedings of the Aristotelian Society*, 76: 1–27.

RABIN, MATTHEW. 1993. 'Incorporating Fairness into Game Theory and Economics'. *American Economic Review*, 83: 1281–1302.

RACHLIN, H. 2000. *The Science of Self-Control*. Cambridge, MA: Harvard University Press.

RAILTON, PETER. 1992. 'Some Questions about the Justification of Morality'. *Philosophical Perspectives*, 6: 27–53.

RASMUSEN, ERIC. 1989. *Games and Information* (2nd edn.). Oxford: Basil Blackwell.

RAWLS, JOHN. 1972. *A Theory of Justice*. Cambridge, MA: Harvard University Press.

RAZ, JOSEPH. 1996. 'On the Moral Point of View', in J. B. Schneewind (ed.), *Reason, Ethics, and Society*. Chicago: Open Court, 58–83.

—— 1999. 'When we are Ourselves: The Active and the Passive', in his *Engaging Reason: On the Theory of Value and Action*. New York: Oxford University Press, 5–21.

RICHARDS, ROBERT J. 1987. *Darwin and the Emergence of Evolutionary Theories of Mind and Behavior*. Chicago: University of Chicago Press.

ROBERTS, ROBERT. 1984. 'Willpower and the Virtues'. *Philosophical Review*, 93: 227–47.

RORTY, AMÉLIE O. 1980a. *Explaining Emotions*. Berkeley: University of California Press.

—— 1980b. 'Where does the Akratic Break Take Place?' *Australasian Journal of Philosophy*, 58: 333–46.

RORTY, RICHARD. 1979. *Contingency, Irony, and Solidarity*. Cambridge: Cambridge University Press.

310 / References

ROVANE, CAROL. 1997. *The Bounds of Agency: An Essay in Revisionary Metaphysics*. Princeton: Princeton University Press.

RUBINSTEIN, ARIEL. 1982. 'Perfect Equilibrium in a Bargaining Model'. *Econometrica*, 50: 97–109.

SAVAGE, LEONARD. 1972. *The Foundations of Statistics*. New York: Dover Publications.

SAVULESCU, JULIAN. 1998. 'The Present-Aim Theory: A Submaximizing Theory of Reasons'. *Australasian Journal of Philosophy*, 76: 229–43.

SCANLON, T. M. 1998. *What we Owe to Each Other*. Cambridge, MA: Belknap Press of Harvard University Press.

—— 2002. 'Reasons and Passions', in Buss and Overton 2002: 165–83.

SCHELER, MAX. 1913–16/1973. *Formalism in Ethics and Non-Formal Ethics of Value*, trans. Manfred S. Frings and Roger L. Funk (5th rev. edn.). Evanston, IL.: Northwestern University Press.

SCHELL, JONATHAN. 1984. *The Abolition*. New York: Knopf.

SCHUELER, G. F. 1995. *Desire*. Cambridge, MA: MIT Press.

SEARLE, JOHN R. 1995. *The Construction of Social Reality*. New York: Free Press.

SELLARS, WILFRID. 1963. 'Some Reflections on Language Games', in his *Science, Perception and Reality*. London: Routledge & Kegan Paul, 321–58.

SHAFTESBURY, ANTHONY ASHLEY COOPER, THIRD EARL OF. 1711/1964. *An Inquiry Concerning Virtue or Merit*, in his *Characteristics of Men, Manners, Opinions, Times*, ed. John M. Robertson (2nd edn.). New York: Bobbs-Merrill, 235–338.

SINGER, PETER, 1993. *Practical Ethics* (2nd edn.). Cambridge: Cambridge University Press.

SKYRMS, BRIAN. 1996. *Evolution and the Social Contract*. Cambridge: Cambridge University Press.

SMITH, MICHAEL. 1994. *The Moral Problem*. Oxford: Basil Blackwell.

—— 1997a. 'In Defense of *The Moral Problem*: A Reply to Brink, Copp and Sayre-McCord'. *Ethics*, 108: 84–119.

—— 1997b. 'A Theory of Freedom and Responsibility', in Cullity and Gaut 1997a: 293–319.

—— 2001. 'The Incoherence Argument: Reply to Schafer-Landau'. *Analysis*, 61: 254–66.

—— forthcoming. 'Humean Rationality', in Alfred Mele and Piers Rawling (eds.), *Handbook of Rationality*. Oxford: Oxford University Press.

SOBEL, HOWARD. 1994. *Taking Chances: Essays on Rational Choice*. Cambridge: Cambridge University Press.

SOLOMON, ROBERT. 1993. *The Passions*. Indianapolis: Hackett.

SORENSEN, ROY. 1997. 'Advertisement for a Cure for Incontinence'. *Mind*, 106: 743.

STAMPE, DENNIS. 1987. 'The Authority of Desire'. *Philosophical Review*, 96: 335–81.

References / 311

STEIN, EDWARD. 1996. *Without Good Reason: The Rationality Debate in Philosophy and Cognitive Science*. Oxford: Clarendon Press.

STOCKER, MICHAEL. 1979. 'Desiring the Bad: An Essay in Moral Psychology'. *Journal of Philosophy*, 76: 738–53.

SUNSTEIN, CASS. 2002. 'The Law of Group Polarization'. *Journal of Political Philosophy*, 10: 175–95.

TAPPOLET, CHRISTINE. 1995. 'Les Émotions et les concepts axiologiques'. *Raisons Pratiques*, 4 (special issue, *La Couleur des pensées*, ed. Patricia Paperman and Ruwen Ogien), 237–57.

——— 2000. *Émotions et valeurs*. Paris: Presses Universitaires de France.

TENENBAUM, SERGIO. 1999. 'The Judgement of a Weak Will'. *Philosophy and Phenomenological Research*, 49: 875–911.

——— forthcoming *a*. 'Desire and the Good', in Tenenbaum forthcoming *b*.

——— (ed.). forthcoming *b*. *New Perspectives in Philosophy: Moral Psychology*. Amsterdam: Rodopi.

THALER, RICHARD H. 1992. *The Winner's Curse: Paradoxes and Anomalies of Economic Life*. New York: Free Press.

THOMSON, JUDITH J. 2001. *Goodness and Advice*. Princeton: Princeton University Press.

TUOMELA, RAIMO. 1995. *The Importance of Us*. Stanford, CA: Stanford University Press.

ULEMAN, J., and BARGH, J. (eds.). 1989. *Unintended Thought*. New York: Guilford Press.

VAN INWAGEN, PETER. 1983. *An Essay on Free Will*. Oxford: Clarendon Press.

VELLEMAN, J. DAVID. 1992. 'The Guise of the Good', in Velleman 2000: 99–122.

——— 1996. 'The Possibility of Practical Reason', in Velleman 2000: 170–99.

——— 2000. *The Possibility of Practical Reason*. Oxford: Clarendon Press.

VOHS, K., and HEATHERTON, T. 2000. 'Self-Regulatory Failure: A Resource-Depletion Approach'. *Psychological Science*, 11: 249–54.

WALKER, ARTHUR F. 1989. 'The Problem of Weakness of Will'. *Noûs*, 23: 653–76.

WALLACE, R. JAY. 1990. 'How to Argue about Practical Reason'. *Mind*, 99: 355–85.

——— 1994. *Responsibility and the Moral Sentiments*. Cambridge, MA: Harvard University Press.

——— 1999*a*. 'Addiction as Defect of the Will: Some Philosophical Reflections'. *Law and Philosophy*, 18: 621–54.

——— 1999*b*. 'Three Conceptions of Rational Agency'. *Ethical Theory and Moral Practice*, 2: 217–42.

——— 2001. 'Normativity, Commitment, and Instrumental Reason'. *Philosophers' Imprint*, <www.philosophersimprint.org>, 1/3.

WATSON, GARY. 1975. 'Free Action'. *Journal of Philosophy*, 57: 205–20.

——— 1977. 'Skepticism about Weakness of Will'. *Philosophical Review*, 86: 316–39.

——— 2001. 'Reasons and Responsibility'. *Ethics*, 111: 374–94.

312 / References

WAUGH, EVELYN. 1945/1967. *Brideshead Revisited*. New York: Dell.

WEDGWOOD, RALPH N. 1995. 'Theories of Content and Theories of Motivation'. *European Journal of Philosophy*, 3: 273–88.

—— 1998. 'The Fundamental Principle of Practical Reasoning'. *International Journal of Philosophical Studies*, 6: 189–209.

—— 1999. 'The A Priori Rules of Rationality'. *Philosophy and Phenomenological Research*, 59: 113–31.

—— 2001*a*. 'Conceptual Role Semantics for Moral Terms'. *Philosophical Review*, 110: 1–30.

—— 2001*b*. 'Sensing Values?' *Philosophy and Phenomenological Research*, 63: 215–28.

—— 2002*a*. 'The Aim of Belief'. *Philosophical Perspectives*, 16: 267–97.

—— 2002*b*. 'Internalism Explained'. *Philosophy and Phenomenological Research*, 65: 349–69.

—— 2002*c*. 'Practical Reason and Desire'. *Australasian Journal of Philosophy*, 80: 345–58.

—— 2002*d*. 'Practical Reasoning as Figuring Out what is Best: Against Constructivism'. *Topoi*, 21: 139–52.

WEGNER, DANIEL. 1989. *White Bears and Other Unwanted Thoughts*. New York: Viking Press.

—— 1994. 'Ironic Processes of Mental Control'. *Psychological Review*, 101: 34–52.

WELLS, A., and MATTHEWS, G. 1994. *Attention and Emotion: A Clinical Perspective*. Hove: Lawrence Erlbaum Associates.

WIGGINS, DAVID. 1980. 'Weakness of Will, Commensurability, and the Objects of Deliberation and Desire', in Wiggins 1987: 239–67.

—— 1987. *Needs, Values, Truth*. Oxford: Basil Blackwell.

WILLIAMS, BERNARD. 1976. 'Persons, Character and Morality', in Williams 1981: 1–19.

—— 1978. *Descartes: The Project of Pure Inquiry*. London: Penguin Books.

—— 1980. 'Internal and External Reasons', in Williams 1981: 101–13.

—— 1981. *Moral Luck*. Cambridge: Cambridge University Press.

WOLF, SUSAN. 1990. *Freedom within Reason*. New York: Oxford University Press.

WOOD, ALLEN W. 1999. *Kant's Ethical Thought*. Cambridge: Cambridge University Press.

WRIGHT, LARRY. 1995. 'Argument and Deliberation: A Plea for Understanding'. *Journal of Philosophy*, 92: 565–85.

YAFFE, GIDEON. 2000. *Liberty Worth the Name: Locke on Free Agency*. Princeton: Princeton University Press.

YOUPA, ANDREW. 2002. 'Descartes and Spinoza on Freedom and Virtue'. Ph.D. diss., University of California, Irvine.

ZAGZEBSKI, LINDA. 1996. *Virtues of the Mind*. New York: Cambridge University Press.

—— 2001. 'Must Knowers be Agents?', in A. Fairweather and L. Zagzebski (eds.), *Virtue Epistemology: Essays on Epistemic Virtue and Responsibility*. New York: Oxford University Press, 142–57.

INDEX

accidie 12–13, 147, 149, 153–6, 160, 163, 167–71

action
  akratic 5–7, 99–102
  basic 224
  emotional 110–20
  intentional 3, 4, 40, 100, 114, 154
  group 69–89
  Humean or belief-desire account of 10, 40, 43–9, 55, 60
  weak-willed vs. akratic *see* akrasia

Adams, R. M. 93

agency 7, 73
  cognitive or doxastic 178, 186–96
  collective 78–95
  counter-normative 179–81, 183, 185, 192, 195, 196
  internalist vs. externalist conceptions of 177–81

agent
  accidic *see* accidie
  akratic *see* akrasia
  enkratic 291

Ainslie, George 44, 45, 267–8, 284, 289

akrasia
  as distinct from weakness of will 10, 39
  as rational 6, 115–17, 205, 291
  distinguished from compulsion 5–6, 17, 32–8, 114
  emotional 11–12, 102–5, 115–18

global 12, 141–3
group 10–11, 69, 81–7
theoretical 94–5, 192

Albritton, Rogers 178, 180

Allison, Henry 200

Anscombe, G. E. M. 144, 150–1, 152, 153, 196–7

Aristotle 57, 97–8, 177, 179, 191, 196–7, 207, 283, 297

Arpaly, Nomy 114, 116

attitudes
  emotional 286
  intentional 73, 292, 296

Audi, Robert 5, 6

Bayesianism, world 254, 258–61, 268

Block, Ned 28–9

Bovens, Luc 292

Brandom, Robert 127, 144, 262–4

Bratman, Michael 5, 41, 48, 50, 62–3, 65, 66, 71, 105, 107, 126, 182, 192, 193, 226

Buss, Sarah 178

capacities, rational 10, 19
  and 'could' claims 19–38

Carroll, Lewis 132–3

Clifford, W. K. 193, 277

compulsion *see* akrasia

conditioning, relation of 160–71
  strong and weak conditionality 164

314 / Index

consequentialism 248–9
continence, Davidson's principle of 4, 101, 103, 128, 134
Cullity, Garrett 203

Damasio, Antonio 104, 110
Dancy, Jonathan 138, 141, 143, 244
Davidson, Donald 2–5, 8, 98, 99–102, 106, 107, 112, 119, 125, 128, 134, 139, 140, 151–3, 274
decision theory 251–73
    and deontic constraints 259–62
deliberation, practical 175–7, 183–5, 187, 253–4
Descartes, René 149, 186, 197–9
de Sousa, Ronald 8, 98, 101–6, 120
determinism, causal 21
deterrence 236, 245, 279–80
dilemma, discursive 74–6, 82–7
discounting, temporal 44, 256–8, 266–9, 284–5, 290
dispositions 19, 24–5
Dreier, James 135, 136

Elster, Jon 103, 275, 278–9
emotions 278, 280, 296–7
    as perceptions of values 11, 98–9, 108–12, 277–8, 293
    impact on attention 8, 104–5, 107–8, 110
    role in akratic action 11, 98–99, 101–6, 108, 111–2, 115–6
    see also action; akrasia; rationality
Epicurus 281–2, 294
Evans, Gareth 157
expected utility theory 251–73
explanation 30–1, 35–7, 122, 123, 125, 127, 129–30
    intentional 151–3
    rational 138–40

externalism, Humean 12, 126–35, 140–1, 143–6
    see also internalism

Fischer, John Martin 19
Frank, Robert 108, 280, 292–3
Frankfurt, Harry 19, 23, 172, 182
free will 21, 218–9

game theory 15, 71
    multiple equilibria, problem of 265–6
    public goods games 258–9, 261
    ultimatum games 258–9, 269–71, 275
Gaut, Berys 203
Gauthier, David 65, 209, 217, 232
Geach, P. T. 142
Goldie, Peter 98
good, the
    formal vs. substantial conceptions of 154
    general conception of, one's 158–60
Goodman, Nelson 286–7
groups
    capable of akrasia 78–80
    collections 69–70
    cooperatives 69, 71–6
    unified cooperatives 69, 76–8

Hare, R. M. 2–3, 97
Heil, John 189, 191
Herman, Barbara 178, 200
Holton, Richard 99, 173, 181
Hume, David 32, 89, 230, 232, 286–7, 289

Ignatius of Loyola 52–3
imperatives, categorical and hypothetical 184–5
induction 286–7
instrumentalism
    basic instrumentalist principle 134

see also practical reason, recognitional view of; present-aim theory; reasoning

intentionality 100–1, 114–5
  see also action

intentions
  as distinct from beliefs and desires 40, 48, 60
  group or shared 71–2
  rational revision of 226–7

internalism 2–3, 7, 182, 201–9
  Descartes on 197–9
  Kant on 199–200
  vs. externalism 12–14, 126–35, 195–6

irrationality 1–2, 5, 15–16, 136, 153
  see also accidie; akrasia; rationality

Irwin, Terence 197

Jackson, Frank 89, 98
James, William 192–3, 275–7
Jeffrey, Richard 208, 256
Johnston, Mark 24–5, 110
Jones, Karen 110, 116–17
judgements
  group 71
  practical 122–32, 136–46
  relational vs. unconditional 3–5, 100–1, 107, 125, 128

Kahneman, Daniel 284, 289–90
Kane, Robert 178, 180
Kant, Immanuel 13, 136, 148, 160–1, 163–6, 169, 182, 184–5, 199–200, 208, 217, 218, 233–4
Kavka, Gregory 64–6
Kennett, Jeanette 129, 136, 137
Korsgaard, Christine 69, 87, 93, 136, 164, 178, 203, 208, 209, 212, 218, 224, 229

Lawrence, Gavin 219
Lewis, David 22, 72, 217
liar paradox 275
Locke, John 198–9
Luce, R. Duncan 252

McCann, Hugh 187, 191
McDowell, John 149, 152, 159, 175, 185
McIntyre, Alison 6, 115, 290–1
Mele, Alfred 5, 8, 95, 105, 106, 130, 175, 187
Mill, John Stuart 297
mind, modular theory of 90–1
Mischel, Walter 53–5
Moore, G. E. 164
Moore's Paradox 179–80, 193
Moran, Richard 175, 179, 185
motivation
  'hydraulic' conception of 159
  Humean theory of 48, 222–3

Nagel, Thomas 14, 122, 139, 149, 151, 230–1, 233–5, 237, 242–5, 245–7, 281–2
Newcomb's problem 275
non-cognitivism 125–6
'normative question', the 212–13, 216, 219, 224, 229, 288

O'Shaughnessy, Brian 9, 172, 173, 174, 180, 184, 187–8, 198
Owens, David 176, 182, 183, 186, 189, 192, 194

Parfit, Derek 211–12, 232, 242, 285
Pascal, Blaise 275–7
Peacocke, Christopher 105, 119
Pears, David 5
Pettit, Philip 150, 248–9
Pink, Thomas 173, 182, 186, 188

316 / Index

Plato 68, 69, 93, 97, 275, 283

possible worlds 10, 21–9, 31, 33, 254, 260

practical reason 175–7
  constructivist view of 207–9, 216–19, 251–3
  Humean conception of 40, 43–50, 55, 60, 67
  Kantian conception of 218–19
  procedural requirements on 207
  recognitional view of 14, 203–7, 209
    egoist version of 212–14
    formal version of 210–11, 219–44
    instrumentalist version of 214–15
    substantive versions of 211–16
    'scholastic' conceptions of 12–13, 147–71

preferences 243, 244, 252, 284

present-aim theory, instrumental version of 212, 214–15, 232, 238–40, 250

Prisoner's Dilemma 265, 275

pro-attitudes 112–13

prohairesis 196–7

prudence 230–50

Quinn, Warren 112, 165

Quinton, Anthony 70–1

Raiffa, Howard 252

rationality
  collective 83–5
  emotional 278–96
  pragmatic approach to 62–6
  strategic vs. epistemic 274–7
  theoretical vs. practical 62
  see also present-aim theory; self-interest theory

Ravizza, Mark 19

Rawls, John 184, 223

Raz, Joseph 193

reasoning 132–5
  instrumental 224–9

recklessness 17, 29–32, 38

resolutions
  as a special kind of intention 41–2
  as distinct from desires 48
  reconsideration, rehearsal, revision of 49–53, 63–7

responsibility 194–5

Roberts, Robert 173

Rorty, Richard 275, 295

Rovane, Carol 79

Scanlon, T. M. 7, 122, 123, 132, 138, 139, 149, 176, 192

Schell, Jonathan 279–80

Schueler, G. F. 149

self-control 19, 55–6, 80, 85–7

self-deception 276

self-interest theory of rationality 211–14, 232–4

Singer, Peter 285

Smith, Michael 7, 128, 134, 149, 150

Sobel, Howard 254

Socrates 2, 274

Sorensen, Roy 292

Stampe, Dennis 157

Stocker, Michael 7, 113, 147, 154, 168

strength of will *see* will

temptation 253, 266, 284–5, 292

Tappolet, Christine 278, 293

Thaler, Richard 275, 287–8

Thomson, Judith 210

timelessness of reasons 230–4

Tortoise, Achilles and the 132–5

van Inwagen, Peter 21

Velleman, J. David 7, 176, 180, 205–6, 210, 220, 221, 224, 229

voluntarism 192–3

Wallace, R. Jay 19, 173, 178, 179–180, 181, 183, 184, 186, 188–9, 196, 222, 252
Watson, Gary 5–6, 9, 13, 17–18, 20, 29, 159
Wedgwood, Ralph 145
will, the 9, 172–5, 181–3
    distinguished from judgement 192
    doxastic 173, 190–3
    executive function of 181–3
    strength of 10, 39, 42–67

will-power
    faculty of 19, 40, 49, 53–9
    motivation to employ 58–61
    reasonableness of using 61–7
    will-power account of intentional action 40–1
Williams, Bernard 6, 14, 33, 188, 199, 201, 208, 232
Wright, Larry 174

Zagzebski, Linda 193, 194